D1452583

The Lost Wine

seven centuries of french into english lyrical poetry

by

John Theobald

Perdu ce vin, ivres les ondes !···
J'ai vu bondir dans l'air amer
Les figures les plus profondes···
Le Vin Perdu: Paul Valéry

the green tiger press

ISBN 0 914676 36 9

For the eyes severe and friendly
and in tribute, wheresome'er he is,
to Ezra Pound

ERRATA
The Lost Wine

Page ix, six lines from the end: for *j'etois* read *j'étois*

Page x, 1. 14: for *Ode a* read *Ode à*

Page xiii: for *crepuscule du matin* read *crépuscule du matin*

Page xiv and passim: For Stephane *read* Stéphane

Page xv, six lines from the end: for *premiéres* read *premières*

Page xxi, 12, 528, 597, 611, 612: for Schéhade *read* Schehadé

Page xxii, last line but one: for *a l'aube* read *à l'aube*

Page 22, line 4: *For* disparties *read* disparities

Page 23, 1. 12: for *Faun* read *Faune*

Page 23, last line but one: *For* five *read* six

Page 112, Fourth line of Malherbe's quoted stanza: *For* lasson-nous *read* lassons-nous

Page 127, first line of last stanza: *For* Lord, 'tis thou, 'tis thou, who-coming nigher *read* 'Tis thou, Lord, yes, once more 'tis thou, who-coming nigher

Page 183, seven lines from end: *For* second line of the sixth stanza *read* second stanza of the sixth section

Page 193, line 5: *For* saluting *read* recruiting

Page 213: *eliminate the arabesque*

Page 260, line 1: *For* bientot *read* bientôt

Page 294, line 3: *For* anticipates *read* anticipate

Page 390, line 1 and p. 603 1. 18: for *Des* read *Dès*

Page 450, line 13: *For* deroule *read* déroule

Page 451, line 13: *For* Yet *read* And

Page 567, sixth line from the end: *For* hippopotemus *read* hippopotamus

Page 590, under "Desnos, Robert," last line: *For* Coutrée *read* Contrée

Page 595, under "Nerval, Gérard de," last line: *For* Pleiade *read* Pléiade

Page 602, six lines from the end: for *c'etait* read c'était

Page 604, right column 1. 10: insert *Fitzgerald, Robert, 22, 23*

Page 604, right column: for *Fowlie, Wallace, 447* read *Fowlie, Wallace, 291, 447*

Page 607, right column, 1. 11: for *s'eveille* read *s'éveille*

Page 608, right column, 1. 20: for *'N'egraine* read *'N'égraine*

Page 610, left column, eleven lines from the end: for *Cheniér* (!) read *Chénier*

Page 613, left column, thirteen lines from the end: insert *Wilbur, Richard, 22, 23*

CONTENTS

(Certain unfamiliar spellings, with absent accents, belong to an early period)

Contents

IV. The Future Drags Its Feet: *Nineteenth Century*

Stephane Mallarmé

Contents

Preface

Only a limited materialism fails to see that the energy of poetry should be of greater concern than the energy derived from oil; and this book may be viewed as a large glyph, to advance a truth going back to Pharaonic Egypt: that form precedes being.

Then seven centuries of poetry not our own, as they demonstrate movement of the forms through well recorded time, will naturally issue in questions concerning the direction of poetry now and hereafter. Such projections may be no more calculable than the future condition of individuals, whose voice, by the way, changes significantly less than their appearance. Yet we see how the future state of a person is subsumed in what he now is in essentially the same way as how the thing he is stems from what he was; and so it must be with the arts, whose leaps forward are bound to be waste motion unless their apparent discontinuities of form are proved to be at a deeper level deceptive.

For this direction finding a strange language may work as an advantage and, provided that the craving for novelty does not deafen us to the true line of descent in the melody and harmony of poetry, may actually sharpen hearing. There's really only one way to find out where we are going, and that is to listen to what we have been, sometimes at its best a lost sound, even if we know the language, and all the more so, of course, if we don't. Thus, though the book is both for those who know French and those who don't, it is more for the latter and must fail to the extent that the distillation in English lyrics is for them not there. They may already have been thrown by the prevailing doldrums in lyrical translation: a slump which has occasioned some scolding here about the present condition of poetry. My wider hope has been, without futile notion of setting the clock back, to further some restoration of the lyric itself, as well as of its translation, an affair in which only partial success could still stir thirst for the source in these perennially elusive poems.

There is no one to blame but myself for all these lines of English verse, nor for these commentaries—which is not to be ungrateful for the sanctions and reservations from acute and learned friends and colleagues. These include Ernest Marchand and George Sanderlin for their passing grade on the Bibliography and initial Introduction, respectively, and John Monteverde for his ruthless scrutiny of the latter. As for the poetry, the discerning enthusiasm of W.R. Johnson of Cornell and the University of California has been with the whole book. Most helpful too has been my friend Herbert Kelly, whilst Françoise Baker and Janice Glasgow, both bilingual, were consulted for certain fine points of the language, and the former proof-read all the French. Let not my long suffering typesetters be forgotten, Laurence McGilvery and Cheryl Ritter, not to speak of the steady faith of Harold Darling, the publisher of The Green Tiger Press, and the dependable judgment of his crack editors, Dixie Richards and Curt Bouterse. Above all always was my wife, Mary Lee, who whenever presented with five or fifty options, frowned or confirmed the best. Some of these friends or closer must certainly have grown sick of me, but not one admitted it, and now it is too late.

"The realm of the Final Inch! The work has been almost completed, the goal almost attained, everything seems completely right and the difficulties overcome. But the quality of the thing is not *quite* right. Finishing touches are needed. In that moment of fatigue and self-satisfaction it is especially tempting to leave the work without having attained the apex of quality. Work in the area of the Final Inch is very, very complex and also especially valuable, because it is executed by perfected means. In fact the rule of the Final Inch consists in this: not to shirk this crucial work. . .And not to mind the time spent on it, knowing that one's purpose lies not in completing things faster but in the attainment of perfection."

> Aleksandr I. Solzhenitsyn
> *The First Circle*

"Rubin was not a poet. He had never enough skill in polishing rhymes and working out rhythms."
                                                                    Ibid.

". . .the power to convey universal truth being in fact proportional to formal strictness as regards the means of expression. . ."

> Marco Pallis
> *The Way and the Mountain*

It could be that you did all this to suit
Some critic with a taste for paraphrase,
Or, even if this be not what you praise,
That for the actual sense we should not root.
Now if your poetry is to yield some fruit,
Surely it should be clear without a gloss;
And if your muse would hide from all pursuit,
You could resolve on silence without loss.

> *After* Jacques Pelletier
> "To a Poet Writing Obscurely"

Introduction

Although it may have lapsed in time and passion, we had better not try to dodge the function of poetry as song. If we confine ourselves to the poetry of one language, it is easy to be, as I think we are, ". . .per una silva oscura,/che la diretta via era smarrita," in a dark wood, the straight way lost. How can they choose their path who only one path know? How hear their own poetry if deaf to all other? If we look away and listen to the songs from another part of the forest, we stand some chance of finding our way. Verse translations should resemble arrangements, easy for our voices, of strange airs heard at a distance, giving hope that, by taking bearings on those unfamiliar sounds, we may trace a path out of our mazes to the future poetry.

Every good poem wants to be translated; and although not all of them can be, it is the point of this book that many, and of a wide variety, can. Now if this is so, it is clearly of the first importance that poets should continue to try their hand at this mocking challenge for as long as there continues to be a single great poem untranslated. What? We need yet more translations of Baudelaire, Rimbaud, Mallarmé, when of the attempts upon their lives there has already been no end? Yet another pianist to record the preludes and fugues, the "Hammerklavier," the polonaises? Must other Siegfrieds rise? Were not Klemperer and Von Karajan enough? Yes, they must; and no, they were not.

There are substantial advantages for the translating poet himself in this activity, which may be the finest discipline available to him; and if the justification for poetry resides at all in the writing of it,[1] as distinct from the reading, then translating poetry as a means of writing it better is not a consideration to be ignored. But this fringe benefit to the poet is out-weighed by another: immeasurable gain to the state of poetry, deriving from cross-fertilization of the muse, a collateral which accrues gainfully from the French classics today, when our own liberties with form have become so total as to create the need for some sort of massive reversal (see the third epigraph of this book).

Several devoted studies have sought to cultivate the idea that to combine poetry, accuracy, and a degree of formal resemblance is simply impossible in translating poetry. It is true that the improbabilities of such a result compound, mostly in proportion to the translator's deficiencies as

1

poet or linguist; or to his inability or unwillingness to go to the laborious delight of working out the problem, as Stefan George did for Shakespeare's sonnets, Nerval for Goethe, Rilke for Valéry (and *mutatis mutandis*), Larbaud for Coleridge, Binyon for Dante, Roy Campbell and Frank Sturm for many successes with Baudelaire, and Pound, notwithstanding his preemptive individuality, for a wide variety of poets of different languages, of which he seems to have known only Italian really well.

Much comfort derives from the disclosure of a translator (or translating supervisor) of Homer, D.S. Carne-Ross.[2] This scholar had been assigned the task of presenting the Iliad to the British public on the "Third Program" of the B.B.C. Having made a cut version of the epic and distributed it among twelve chosen translators, he found his results proving that the most successful translations were by poets who knew no Greek and had to rely on a "pony." Far from suggesting that a direct knowledge of the nuances of the language would have been useless to these translators, I am sure that the forced reliance on seeing-eye guides must often have been a pretty drastic handicap. Still, the point is good that even knowledge of the language is less of the essence than is a sense for the poetry and a knack of doing something about such matters as tone, mood, speed, stress, grace, fire, cadence, and harmony; the ideal situation being, obviously, where the translator makes, in his own language, a twin poem, having the freedom born of a kindred impulse.

Every poem wants to be translated. Most can be. Some few can't. Given an understanding of the requirements of lyric poetry, what stands in the way?

Pound's bequest to the translation of poetry ought to have been, at its best, decisively influential and, with a very few followers, was so. Having confessed concerning Cavalcanti that he first intended "to print only his poems and an unrhymed gloze," Pound goes on to say: "This has not been practicable. I cannot trust the reader to read the Italian for the music after he had read the English for the sense."[3] In his French translations, his Arnaut Daniel is so much more successful than his Rimbaud, for example, because his way of rendering Daniel's effect is the one magical way: having strenuously steeped himself in the provenance of Provençal, to refine its gold with a new-old music; whereas Rimbaud is close enough in time and spirit to solicit a more stringent fidelity in both melody and meaning, or rather, the harmony of the two: an affair calling less for "invention," let alone intervention, than for simple and complex attention.[4]

2

Few have understood as well as Pound that, in poetry sound and sense must be given simultaneously, or they are not given at all. Hence it is that ninety-five percent of what passes as translation of poetry is nothing but, in Pound's words, "unrhymed gloze." The translation, for example, of the poems which Mallarmé named "Airs" into versions that renounce pretence to any "tune" has an effect essentially no different from out-of-tune "melodies" in music, except that the un-poetry can sound as painfully, but more laughably, "off" than the un-music. We could illustrate at length this failure to be poetry in all those literal translations, stripped of form; only to do so might spoil the reader's temper before we got off the ground. For either his ear might be offended by such anti-poetry; or, conversely, he might belong to those who say, "But what's wrong with free verse?" (the answer, of course, being, "Nothing, so long as verse it truly is, and it is free verse that is being translated")[5] Then he would be disquieted for precisely the opposite reason.

The *a priori* despair of any adequate translation, particularly of French poetry, has been advanced by W.H. Auden, in his introduction to Valéry's *Analects*.[6] Auden begins with the assertion that "no two languages could be more different"—a hyperbole made scarcely less arresting by the obvious respects in which it is untrue, as that the common basis of half English and almost all French words is Latin, and that many words in English and French are identical, not to speak of the rich heritage the Norman Conquest brought. But I felt the sharpness of the statement when I recently had to translate simultaneously Rilke and Valéry, who translated each other; for the former breeds naturally with English verse, whilst the latter, at best (it can be a good best) cross-breeds, as sylphs having intercourse with salamanders should produce neither, but an elf, beautiful maybe, but not quite all there.

Auden was thinking especially of the indurated longevity of that supreme restrictive opportunity, until recently considered the *sine qua non* of French verse—the alexandrine,[7] the sound of which in English he has fun comparing to "The Assyrian came down like a wolf on the fold." It was he too, I think, who suggested that if someone had for the first time surfaced with the alexandrine in a world in which verse had hitherto always been "free," he would have passed for crazier than Dada, and instantly there would have formed behind him a revoluntionary cult! But behind this archness is Auden's serious conviction that no English-speaking person can learn to hear French poetry properly, which, even if again less true than false, would at least be a strong argument for presenting the benighted with ways to get as close to it as possible.

3

It is unfortunate that the translation of poetry is such a war-torn country, the translators themselves being the contending warlords. (See "Other Voices," the addendum of this introduction.) An inveterate condition of warfare is a certain repetitiousness; but the particular stage of infatuation with formlessness that we have reached in this perennially ravaged territory suggests that we could do worse, even at the risk of the banal, than go back to school about the optimum requirements and besetting hazards of verse translation. As John Aherne is made to say, "When the candle is burnt out an honest man does not pretend that grease is flame."[8]

In any translation of a poem, the sense of loss is prone to be so heavy, that, if the reader has a love and knowledge of the original, his attention will be distracted from all but that loss. Meanwhile, the translator himself, feeling the loss even more keenly, rivets his attention with exaggerated pride on what he feels has been saved and manages to draw a discreet curtain on the loss, thus rendering himself increasingly vulnerable; for his readers, even if they have not themselves tried their hand at translating the same poem, may require no more than a glance at this latest upstart to be deeply disturbed by those things which have been done and those left undone.

Small wonder that the poem, as a poem, in its wholeness still withholds. The race is not for the faint-hearted, for the hurdles are at least a seven-barred gate: precision of sense and image; naturalness of expression; truth to the feeling; unobtrusive control of the rhyme; ductile deployment of that favorite English metre, the iambic pentameter; wholeness of effect; and finally, lyricism as an English poem. To surmount all seven without lowering any of them is a thrill and a headache, requiring a cultivated and constantly renewed misery about the details of solutions which have previously pleased the translator himself. (Note this book's first epigraph from Solzhenitsyn.)

The fundamental fallacy of all literal translations of poetry, as Pound signifies, is the assumption that the form has an accidental, rather than essential, relationship with the poem's meaning; that the melody of the poem is something distinct from the poem itself, like a striking necktie. The only difference between the meaning of the poem and that of the sonata is that the latter integrates only sounds into the meaning, whereas the poem integrates sounds, ideas, and pictures. Nevertheless, if you take away from the poem any of these elements, you take away the poem. It could be that the obliviousness to what was once this truism is more than half responsible for the creeping paralysis of poetry.

4

Here is the most thorough and conscientious literal translation that I know of a complete poem by Mallarmé. The poem may be the most difficult and beautiful for its length in the language—also, perhaps, the most profound, if only for that stunning "glancing reflection" of the Absolute Subject of Consciousness in the individual subject. This translation, modestly described as "slavish" by R.G. Cohn, appears in his book *Toward the Poems of Mallarmé* (University of California, 1965). He was generous in giving me permission to use it.

Quelconque une solitude
Sans le cygne ni le quai
Mire sa désuétude
Au regard que j'abdiquai
 Ici de la gloriole
Haute à ne la pas toucher
Dont maint ciel se bariole
Avec les ors de coucher
 Mais langoureusement longe
Comme de blanc linge ôté
Tel fugace oiseau si plonge
Exultatrice à côté
 Dans l'onde toi devenue
Ta jubilation nue

Some indifferent solitary place
Without the swan or the quay
Reflects its disuse
In the glance I removed
 Here from the vainglory
Too high to touch
In which many a sky daubs itself
With the golds of sunset
 But languorously runs along
Like white linen doffed
Some fleeting bird if [you] plunge
Exulting beside [me]
 In the water you [having] become
Your naked jubilation

No English version could hope to recover the marvelous sound effects of this poem—the *longe, linge, plonge;* the luxurious *langoureusement,*

5

exultatrice; the play of sounds for cutting through the air and splashing into the water; the *jubilation nue,* that conveys both the wave and the naked woman. . .much of which and more has come to Mr. Cohn's *critical* attention. But how thickly a literal translation can fog the clear sense, as he must know!

I now leave it to the reader to decide whether this literal translation or the late great art critic Roger Fry's unrhymed poem[9] is further from the original:

> Just a solitude
> Without the swan and quay
> Mirrors its loneliness
> In the look which I turned
>   Here from the glitter
> Too high to touch
> In which the sky's streaked
> With sunset golds
>   But languidly coasts
> Like white linen doffed
> Some shy bird if plunges
> Exulting beside
>   In the billow become you
> Your nude jubilation

This *sounds* a little better, but unfortunately, here too, the syntax, far from being transcended, as by Mallarmé, simply sinks; whilst the *meaning,* the exultant process of the vision's descent from showy sunsets to the simple girl splashing about in the lake, together with so much that this descent implies, has somehow, whether or not in the interests of a closer approximation to poetry, been "doffed."[10]

Admitting that the ideal of matching forms with the original has the discouraging built-in flaw that the rhythm of a pentameter can never precisely correspond with that of an alexandrine, will it not therefore be just that much more important to preserve any other elements of form which are not placed under similar duress in translation? Now probably the most important single element that can remain to a degree unaffected by translation is the rhyme; and it is partly for this reason, but also because the best French poetry, until a few years ago, is all rhymed, that the translations in this particular book are almost all of rhyme in rhyme—the more live the rhyme, of course, the better.

Since the name of the game here has to be anything but originality, this may be the time for that "refresher course," maddeningly redundant for some, in the rationale of rhyme, about what is rhyme, why rhyme, and why preserve this embarrassing anachronism, let alone labor it. To confine ourselves in these remarks to the questions of rhyme and rhythm is not to prejudice the multifarious other facets of sound in the translation of poetry, such as are suggested by the intricate analyses of an approach like that of Katherine M. Wilson in her *Sound and Meaning in Poetry*, London: Jonathan Cape, 1930. This is clearly not the place for any such exhaustive, and to tell truth rather exhausting study. The hope here is that by thus narrowing our focus, we may pin-point certain considerations more crucial to the reading of the following translations.

The dazzling Valadimir Nabokov, apropos of his translation of Pushkin's *Eugene Onegin*, clowning from his exalted cloud, makes use of the surprising expression, "the slime of rhyme."[11] What would Pushkin have thought of this barb, or of the massive earthworks constructed around the English transplant of his rhymed masterpiece? Everything is there, in these laborious transcriptions, except "the poem itself."[12] Yet Nabokov is the only poet I know of who, if he chose to take the time to employ his magic properly, could have given us, with finality, a living English version of the greatest Russian poem.

Rhyme is not slime, it is chime; or that is how we may think of the return of a word close in sound. We scarcely need to be reminded that the practise has been standard for just about every known language since poetry began. We can easily test its power by listening to the result when the rhyme has been subtracted from any English poem that lives by it, from Chaucer to "Tiger, tiger, burning bright." The same damage would be sustained by a similar interference with a French lyric:

> Quand vous serez bien vieille, à la chandelle, au soir,
> Dévidant et filant, assise auprès du feu,
> Direz, chantant mes vers, en vous emerveillant:
> Ronsard me célébrait du temps que j'étais belle. . .

But this is no more lamed than to translate it without the rhyme:

> When you are old, by candlelight, at nightfall,
> Crouching close to the fire, winding and spinning,
> You will say with wonder as you sing my verses,
> Ronsard honored me so when I was fair.[13]

For if rhyme belongs to the pulse and flow of the poem translated, as it is especially prone to do if the poem is in French, then for the translator to defy this coercion must always be a defection.

There can be no question as to what has been consistently the attitude of French poets and critics towards the claims of rhyme. Theodore de Banville (1823-1891) spoke for many of them when he wrote, "In French versification, when Rhyme is what it should be, everything flourishes and prospers; when Rhyme grows feeble, everything shrinks and atrophies.' This is the key to all else.'' Mallarmé speaks of "the primacy in the enchantment that is given by rhyme. . .the hereditary instrument.'' An illuminating analysis of the functional presence of rhyme has been made by Joseph Ciari,[14] who, writing of Mallarmé's Parnassian respect for rhyme, insists that he followed Banville in extending "the influence of rhyme from the very first syllable of the line,'' and continues: "Rhyme is to the line what determinism is to liberty—a necessary foundation; at the same time rhyme creates an unfavorable climate for the birth of the *isolated* beautiful line'' (italics mine).

Nor will it do to say that these are considerations that we have left behind, as D.H. Lawrence does, proclaiming in a letter to Edward Marsh in 1913, "Skilled verse is dead in fifty years''—a stirring spasm of Laurentian impenitence, somewhat weakened by the durability of his own rhymed poems, as well as by the precarious survival of rhyme in a brilliant, if dwindling, company. Let their herald be Louis Aragon, who, confronting "the disgust with rhyme among modern poets,'' admits that the resources of rhyme are more susceptible of exhaustion in the French language than in others, but goes on to insist that rhyme is "le propre'' (natural province) of poets, reminds us of how Apollinaire was able to revitalize rhyme, and concludes that the real difficulty is not that rhyme is "usée'' (used up), but that the heart of poets has become "lâche'' (slovenly) in surrendering to the idea that there is "no new metal under the sun. . .no new rhymes in a world that is new.''[15]

The one least ambiguous on the subject is Baudelaire, who, in a letter to Armand Fraisse, says of the sonnet, "Because the form is restrictive, the idea projects with more vigor. . . The sonnet is hospitable to all sorts of matter: buffoonery, gentle wooing, passion, reverie, philosophical reflection.'' Here this powerful poet gives heavy weight to the suspicion that if we don't manage the sonnet form of the French without our rhymes protruding, there can never be a representative selection of their lyrics in anything of an English counterpart, because too many of the best French lyrics are sonnets. Furthermore, he seems determined not to have such prescriptions unprovided with a firm pedestal in poetics; for in the second of his three "Drafts of a Preface,'' he complains of the "indolence weighing twenty atmospheres upon me when faced by the appalling uselessness of explaining anything whatever to anyone"; but this he does stoop to explain, and rather pointedly: *"Rhythm and rhyme* answer the immortal need in man for Monotony, Symmetry, and Surprise."

It should be clear by now that Pound's haughty, "I have no special interest in rhyme" is not an indifference shared by most of his sources, certainly not his French sources. Pound himself has a genius for rhyme, ignored by his sycophants; but to read, at this date, such brusque disclaimers, side by side with such statements as these by Banville, Baudelaire, and Mallarmé (the latter with his formative impact on later poetry), is to realize the transmogrification of our views, or non-views, on certain aspects of verse in the intervening century, and to what end?

Two concerns akin to rhyme and vital to translation are the narrower one of word-play, and (a kinship that must be defined) the wider one of rhythm. Maybe the most serious loss resulting from untransferable word play, especially when combined with very great frequency of the same rhyme, befalls the wonderful ballades, rondeaux, and chansons of Villon and d'Orleans. Villon may never be done into English *poems* that resemble him and become air-borne. Who would thank us for trying to warm over what danced on the griddle, as no words, not even Skelton's, have ever danced before or since?

A classic example of word-play, nearer to us in time, for which nothing could correspond in English is the following much anthologized poem of Verlaine's:

> Il pleure dans mon coeur
> Comme il pleut sur la Ville,
> Quelle est celle langueur
> Qui pénètre mon cœur?
>   O bruit doux de la pluie
> Par terre et sur les toits!
>   Il pleure sans raison
> Dans ce cœur qui s'écoeure.
> Quoi! Nulle trahison?
> Ce deuil est sans raison.
>   C'est bien la pire peine
> De ne savoir pourquoi,
> Sans amour et sans haine,
> Mon cœur a tant de peine.

The untranslatability of this "ariette oubliée" reverts finally to the insuperable obstacle that not only does the five times repeated "cœur" set up "pleure" as an internal rhyme, but "il pleure" (it is raining) puns with "il pleut" (it is weeping). These simultaneous meanings and sounds are the special desolation of the poem, peculiarly for those fond of Verlaine; whilst in English, unlike the original, one is forced to choose *between* "it is weeping in the town" (and my heart), on the one hand, and "it is raining in my heart" (and the town), on the other. A similar difficulty in the second line of the third stanza might be half met by writing "In this disheartened heart." But no, it is too disheartening. One feels for the difficulty that Miss Muriel Kittel experienced with it.[16] There comes the time when the better part of valor is retreat.

When the book is written entitled, *Why Rhyme?*, it will be shown that somewhere near the root of rhyme, which is the "patterned expectancy" and return of sound, lies the justification of rhythm, which is likewise that of movement. Both rhyme and rhythm are incantatory spells, having profound affinities with such biological factors as the systole and diastole of the blood; such kinetic ones as the pendulum; astronomical, as the wheeling of the planets; mathematical (and sexual) as pairs; metaphysical, as thesis and antithesis, yin and yang. As for the physical, a most instructive archetype of this universal polarity has been uncovered by the new physics, a prime feature of which declares force to be coterminous with pattern—a pattern of synaptic balance. According to these formulations, the sub-atomic particles are not so much subordinated to a "gestalt" as they are themselves that gestalt.

Rhythm is the rhyme of motion; poetic rhythm is the verbal department of balanced motion; and disturbance of that balance, through changes of velocity, hidden shifts of stress, or whatever, if not the proof that it is balance which is being disturbed, merely proves the resultant pseudo-balance at best a dazzled hope and at worst a dazzling fake. *Vers libre?* Whether English, French, or prosodic grandparent Hebrew, it lives less by trope than by cadence, singing counterpart of the simultaneous oneness and manyness of Primal Being, without which *vers libre* is neurasthenia masquerading as novelty, besides having faintish breath.

Neither rhyme nor rhythm is subject to a servile duplication in a foreign tongue. For French and English poetry, we have already observed the rhythmic independence to be grounded in the accentual character of the Anglo-Saxon and Germanic languages, and the contrary with those of Latin roots, where we have to match as best we can. And we can. There is also a divergence affecting rhyme, one that is easier on us—with a condition. The practice of rhyme in English admits of more freedom than in French, as witnessed by the comparative disuse of slant-rhymes in French poetry. For that matter, in English poetry too, the awareness has come comparatively late that a slant-rhyme is capable of serving rhyme's inward impulse to chime, better than a full rhyme would. Emily Dickinson was perhaps the first poet in English to resort constantly to slant-rhyme; and Wilfred Owen, who died in 1918, the first to make systematic use of slant-rhyme. Late as these liberties came in English, however, they are more at home with the boundless, misty English muse than with the more confined and sunlit French, where not until Corbière and Laforgue are rhymes allowed to fall in a manner at all random, and not until such poets as Jammes and Apollinaire is a poet willing to employ such remote rhyming as *semaines, reviennent, Seine,* as Apollinaire does in the beautiful but unfortunately unworkable (by me) "Le pont Mirabeau."[17]

If my own rhymes in these translations had invariably been fully as strict as their originals, it must be admitted that many of the poems here would not have got translated at all; for, to put it bleakly, the stiffness which must result from reducing a choice of, say, twenty words, with slant-rhymes, to, say, five, with strict rhymes only, would have lowered the level of English "inevitability" hopelessly below the passing point, thus threatening to bring too many of these two hundred fifty poems to the unviable condition of those *five* that forced surrender for every *one* that could be carried off to any satisfaction.

In fact, every poem here imposed its own peace terms, with the desired agreement having to be wrestled for by a) closeness to the sense, b) closeness to the sound, and c) closeness to the condition of an original English poem. It is as though you really were Klemperer, trying for a certain accent fifty times, saying to yourself, "It must have been easier to compose it," and finally settling for the best effect available. But always there were the untamable ones.

To pass from difficulties intrinsic to translating these poems, especially as regards the relentless primacy of rhyme, to options attending the selection and ordering of them, the following should be considered.

The chief principle governing selection was rank favoritism. That is to say, the number and distribution of the poems selected were to this extent controllable: they would have to be poems to which the translator could respond properly; and he would have to be satisfied that he could make English poetry out of them without forsaking either the sense, the form, or the lyric élan—these conditions together being alone enough to make for quite a self-limiting ordinance. Doubtless much could be learned concerning taste and the limitations of translation and translator, especially the latter, by an anthology of poems rejected. But taste can't be exercised in total disregard of the historical context. Baudelaire may never have published a grade-B poem, and Parny and Prudhomme seldom if ever a grade-A one; but however heavy a preponderance this disparity gives to Baudelaire's representation, a poem each of the other two helps to fix a reach in the tides of poetry.

As to ordering of the poems, at one point the scholiasts' "schools" of poetry oppressed with such a heavy incubus that I adopted a simpler, perhaps simplistic, arrangement that would be chronological within thematic,[18] and was surprised by how little forced was the poems' cooperation with the six prevailing themes into which it was resolved that they should fall. Not that many of the poems might not have been assigned to more than one of these six thematic units; but in the great majority of instances, the poem would seem to choose its unit unerringly, according to its primary preoccupation. Overall considerations, notably of convenience, countervailed this format, and space lacks to provide in toto what was thus obtained; but here, for the light it throws on prevailing orientations in French poetry, is a sketch of the scheme:

CRAFT: Nineteen poems, more or less directly related to thought of the creative artist's inspiration, and most of them poems on the making of poems—this theme especially absorbing to French poets and able to elicit some of their best poems (e.g., Baudelaire's "The Jinx," Mallarmé's "Gift of the Poem," Emmanuel's "Thimble Song: No. 4").

LANDSCAPES: Thirty-two poems, many of which witness to the distinction between the "hard-edge" language of scenes from nature in French poetry, and the brooding "communion with nature" of the English and German—distinction developed in the introduction to the section entitled "A New Sound" (Leconte de Lisle's "Noon," Rimbaud's "Mutation of the Word").

LOVE: Seventy-five poems (living up to France's popular fame in this haunt and region), a plurality that sings of the love of the sexes. Although we have seven centuries of love poetry spread before us, it all sounds, in a strange way, French love, and in many poems what might be called "love in reverse," as will be explained. (How exemplify? Almost any Ronsard, Baudelaire, Eluard.)

DISTANCES: Thirty-two poems, roughly definable (or undefinable) as concerning the far away and long ago. They could be specifically dream poems (Verlaine's "Recurrent Dream," Schéhade's "In Sleep Sometimes," Joyce Mansour's "Pericoloso Sporghesi"); or poems inspired by the yearning to take flight (Mallarmé's "Sea Breeze," Baudelaire's "The Voyage," La Tour du Pin's "Children of September"); or poems of backward looking nostalgia (Valéry's "Helen," both Francis Jammes' poems), as well as other expressions of looking far away.

DEATH: Forty-four poems. Someone has said that all poetry is about death, a useful hyperbole; for if a poem rejoices in the passing moment, the emotion is prone to be tinged with the sense that it *is* passing (Villon's "Ballade"; Chénier's "Iambes," Bonnefoy's "Douve" poems).

DIVINITY: Forty poems that dwell on eternity, as distinct from time, or that swell the revolt against theological preposessions, or that, without speculating, are adoring (Margaret of Navarre's "Epistle," Claude Hopil's "Divine Dungeon," Madame Guyon's "Faith Without Assurance," Rimbaud's "First Communions," Marc Alyn's "It is a Face"). It is only human to look beyond. The French have not, however, shown a notable passion or genius for metaphysical poetry in either sense shortly to be defined. This allocation may require more critical attention than the other five.

We are not going to be deluded into supposing that lasting poems address themselves to *subjects,* such as Love, Death, or Landscapes. Less wide of the mark would be the suggestion that all poetry is about death, or all about love. Poetry does not embellish subjects. One might say that it transmutes objects and emotions to make them new: itself, I admit, a slightly short-changed prescription, which should, however, appeal to W.C. Williams' "things"-oriented school (see f.n. 2 of the introduction to *Whither Poetry*). But poetry's aversion to packaging would not deprive of value the six-unit arrangement here tentatively advanced, which could be viewed as a sort of atlas, sparse and modest, the first five continents belonging to maps with a horizontal orientation, and the last to one with a vertical; or as a less pedantic and unnatural way than most to straddle the ages, without getting quite so bogged down by the standard occupational hazards of the anthologist: amnesia, imperious eclecticism subject to stylistic whims and phobias, or just blurred vision. At the same time, within and across these shifting thematic frontiers, we shall be led to ask, "What is most French about French poetry?"

Leonard Forster concludes the introduction to his collection of German verse by quoting the "ecstatic cry" of Clemens Brentano, which Leonard Forster suggests as a condensation of the main themes of German poetry:

O Stern und Blume, Geist und Kleid,
Lieb, Leid und Zeit und Ewigkeit!

O star and flower, spirit and garment,
Love, sorrow, and time and eternity![19]

Very good—particularly if it is understood that *Lieb* is not quite the
same thing as *l'amour,* which would be responsive to somewhat different specifications. Thus, for example, paralleling what we shall find
to be true of "religion in reverse," there is, as already said, the special
French intensity of "love in reverse," as witnessed supremely in *Les
Fleurs du Mal:* poems wrung from the poet in sharp cries by *her,* "âme
cruelle et sourde," (mind cruel and deaf) and reaching a sort of
desperate definition in "I adore you like the vault of night. . .," (p.
250)—not to speak of the coarser torments of Laforgue's unresolved turmoil "For the Book of Love," (p. 378); "Aesthetic," (p. 380).

Love is love; but is it that love in German seems both less physical and
less tormented than in French? Or, if such squirmings do not appeal,
one may call it less masochistic. In any case, the German is more
swollen with the wind of *romance,* object of Rimbaud's laughter in the
poem titled accordingly (p. 322: the title could be a mild French pun,
the primary meaning of "Roman" being "Novel," of course): a little
further, perhaps, from the actual battle and bliss? If Catherine Pozzi's
"Ave" and "Vale" (pp. 422 and 424) are in a totally different key, we
may attribute this, partly to Catherine Pozzi herself, partly to an
enhancement of that selflessness which has been ascribed as in special
measure belonging to her sex, thus serving to bring into sharper relief
the plunging possessive violence of Baudelaire and his fellow poets. One
should insist, however, that love poems like those of Eluard (pp. 500,
502) are less to be read as exalting the sexual thrill of women than as
tuning the relationship with a single woman to a high pitch, in lines
charged with a plausible rhythm—one that is all too apt, I may add, to
sound a good deal less plausible in English.

I am not sure that I care for this phrase, "love in reverse." However it
is named, it may be seen as responsible for peaks of French poetry, or
those same peaks as fissures. A parallel option is open to much of the
poetry of Divinity. If eternity is the "Ewigkeit" of Brentano, this might
well be less a "peak" than a "fissure" for the French. Here we have to
be careful of what is a peculiarity of the English language, rather than a
special usage on my part. The word "metaphysical," as we know, has
two meanings, quite diverse, even divergent. The philosopher naturally

associates the word with what is outside the physical: the special preserve of the Platonist, from whose "ideal forms" the manifold of sense suffers an irremediable alienation. This, or something like it, I think, is "Ewigkeit," as Brentano means it; and it is this isolated, autonomous transcendence (semantic difficulties notwithstanding) which is metaphysical, not only for the philosopher, but also for some of the greatest poets: Dante, Rumi, Milton, Blake, Coleridge, one side of Wordsworth, Silesius, Hölderlin—to name but a few.

I can think of no poets quite corresponding to these in French poetry. Nor do I forget that France has been the home of certain illuminated sectarians, such as Madame Guyon and François Fénelon; or (going to their counter culture) of Louis Claude de St. Martin, who said, "We are nearer to that which is not than to that which is,"[20] and, "The universe is a great fire, lighted since the beginning of things for the purification of all corrupted beings."[21] Or, for that matter, of Pascal, who was certainly something more than a sectarian when he said, in words not to be estranged by translation this time, "Le silence éternel de ces espaces infinis m'effraie." These are not, except loosely, poets—even if Madame Guyon did write verses.

But the "metaphysical" domain which is more special to poetry witnesses, not a separation, but a unique *fusion* of the One and the Manifold, "a green thought in a green shade": Andrew Marvell's image so apt for our purpose—he, with Donne and Vaughan, being a leading representative of the school of poets in England who have been called "metaphysical," who had little or no interest in Plato, and who would have been quite baffled by Kant, Coleridge, or Emerson.

When we come to this second order of the "metaphysical," French poetry undoubtedly fares better. In fact, as we shall see, there is a fleeting conception of timeless immersion, of an order akin to Donne's, in Rimbaud's poem, "Eternity" (p. 350)—enough, together with his "Memory," (p. 346) to arouse speculation, at least, as to what might have developed from his "Illuminations" if he had not deserted poetry so early.

Nevertheless, I would question whether the sort of passion which inspired Donne's "Extacie" and certain of his Holy Sonnets ever quite *arrives* in French poetry either, though there are intimations of it in Reverdy, Bonnefoy, and Jaccottet. Glimpses of the second significance of "metaphysical" in these poets would lead to further exploration of it in a study more closely searching of the moderns; for there are intriguing hints of it also in the conversation of a poet like Guillevic (b. 1907), as reported by Serge Gavronsky;[22] and the poem, "It Is a Face," by Marc Alyn (b. 1937), is infused with it.

15

When the word for "God" does appear in French poetry, it is most often with overtones essentially parochial: that is to say, either rooted in an essentially sectarian devotion ("Let God Speak" by Emmanuel, p. 552; Verlaine's "Parsifal," p. 364); or defiant of such devotion (Baudelaire's "The Rebel" and "Peter's Denial," p. 278; Noaille's "If You Spoke, Lord," p. 418; above all, again, Rimbaud's "First Communions," p. 336). Once more, considered as poetic achievement, this subjection and this rebellion may plunge as "fissures" or soar as "peaks," according to how they are estimated. The first of the above-named poems, Emmanuel's, although without the Mariolatry so kind to poetry, does resemble in its feeling numerous intensely devout Catholic poems by such poets as Claudel, Péguy, Jammes, and Jouve: poems frequently affecting, which are addressed to a sectarian deity, rather than possessed of a direct, original vision of a divine order of being, unconfined to planet earth. For the most numinous of sects are still sects. Their prepossessions are unlikely to be shared on a planet circling Sirius, although it is noteworthy that Mr. James Irwin, the former astronaut, like the priests of the Conquistadors, if by methods less robust, has in all sincerity extended the dominion of his own sect to our satellite. It was the sectarian Christ of whom Rimbaud wrote, "J'étais bien jeune, et Christ a souillé mes haleines" (I was still young when Christ tainted my breath," see p. 344). This is the Christ that St. Augustine worshipped, Nietzsche denounced. It is a focus of the higher parochialism, or what one might name "slanted mysticism."

A proviso: no one is saying that to make a doctrinal commitment, or, better still, to belong to a certain spiritual tradition must therefore expect to be denied the impartial mysticism which belongs to direct and intrinsic illumination. Bach, Dante, Fra Angelico, Jalal-ud-Din Rumi, whatever may have been the actual, deeper, unrecognized sources of their inspiration, were not exactly benighted! It is just that, on the one hand, the enlightenment traced to its universal springs, and, on the other, the historically contingent "faith," have the faintest real mutual dependence, and would even seem capable of exerting some reciprocal discouragement. For the idiosyncrasies of access to "the Supreme Mystery," as Claude Hopil called it (p. 126), may be more various than culture itself; but it is to the undifferentiated light bathing these particularities that we owe the radiance which reaches us, and the depth of penetration is likely to be in rather direct proportion to the surrender of exclusive proprietary rights to the ultimate truth. "The One remains, the many change and pass;"—one of the more cliché-ridden of the mightier truths.

In the great French *non*-sectarian poets themselves, however, the matter is further complicated by what is seen as an apathy, even antipathy, towards worlds *beyond*, if inclusive of, this world: an attitude confirmed and conveyed by the very character of their veracity. Such an assertion will always be subject to exceptions: but in France, these exceptions will be even rarer, I think, than in most other lands: an occasional Claude Hopil, or Saint-Pol-Roux, or, more recently, fleeting suggestions from a Pierre Oster, in the footsteps of Perse, or a Marc Alyn, in no one's steps but his own. It is a little more seldom even than usual that the remoter constellations impart their secrets to French poets, who tend to be too surely, too passionately at home in this world to enjoy flights that spurn it.

To pursue this further into conceptual qualifications would be certain to debouch upon apologetics too far beyond our immediate province, which is poetry. But it should not be forgotten that there are poets for whom "Aesthetic" itself has been raised to a mystique, even if it be one whose claim to "Divinity" would be passionately denied by a dogmatic polemicist like Claudel, whose ambitious epodes speak for one of the more eminent omissions from this book. Yet it is by this door of the aesthetic, hard for relentless catechists to open, that we should look to see the poets of France enter the temple. In Baudelaire, Rimbaud, Mallarmé, Pozzi, Valéry, and, of Belgium, Verhaeren, we may frequently feel ourselves circling near another world, a world outside the scope of analytical philosophy, one alien to prepossessed apologetics of any persuasion whatever, a world of which Baudelaire, seeming to become this time unshyly "unlike himself" about such matters, maintained that it was a poet's principal task to make us aware, even bring into being.

So much for Divinity in French poetry, not a small subject. The alternative, thematic arrangement of poems was found to be at least as descriptive of the areas into which the poems naturally fell as Brentano's effusion would work for German poetry. The intent thus formed to meditate on the provinces hospitable to the French lyric and those alien to it soon began to crystallize perceptions, beyond the original concern, of style special to that poetry through the ages: the dense and monumental character of the French lyrical line, whether of Ronsard or Baudelaire, as constrasted with the swift, airy movement of the English, whether of Shakespeare or Shelley. And finally, for this anthologist at least, this arrangement became something of a divining rod for the levels at which the French genius is richest, or where it tends to dry up; and especially, after we have made all exceptions and provisions, how, in the domain of the divine, it remains true that the vitality of most of the best French poetry, with its restlessness and pain, gets in the way of "le silence éternel," and could always be stigmatized as suffering some sort of alienation from "Dieu." But then the question would be: of whom might this not be said, if only to a less degree?

As we come closer to our own time, and in other realms than poetry, the metaphysical achievements of a Bergson find fascinating counterparts in all those spiritual explorers of the Orient who have come from France or French Switzerland. One thinks of René Guénon, Hubert Benoit, E. Bréhier, Alexandra David-Neel, A.J. Festugiére, Frithjof Schuon, Lizelle Reymond, and others: individuals whose thought, fervor, and travels have contributed so much to the conciliation and embrace of ancient and modern, Eastern and Western points of view. Such minds may have their raptures, but more characteristically, theirs is an unecstatic, X-ray vision, which is intensely French. The poetry to which these kinds of enquiry may eventually give rise remains to be seen. It is Madame Lizelle Reymond who, speaking of the plunge into the self, and of the consequent deceptively apparent loss of creative force, says, "This force will reappear, but where and when?"[23] I would expect its reapperance as *poetry*,[24] "substance of things hoped for," in a further sense than *faith:* poetry, which solicits coalescence of waking and dream, embrace of earth and sky. And whenever that poetry is French, however high it climbs, it may be expected to be lucid, terrestrial, and brilliant.

For if we are content to forget what French poetry does not abound in and to look at the positive prerogatives and achievements special to it, then what a shining country unfolds before our eyes! what verve and dash and splendor! what quintessence of the city! what air-to-air targeting of thought and mood, not to speak of passion! above all, what an irremediably human voice, and no less so when one such voice—of a Rimbaud, of a Mallarmé—will undertake to speak for the angels! But then too the mortal sting inflicted by that voice derives from a superhuman humanity; and if, even at best, it does not converse with angels so intimately as Dante, Blake, or Rilke, the sourest Francophobe could never call this poetry dull.

"Bénédiction," "Mémoire," "Quand l'ombre menaça. . ."—such poems work as charms, spells, amulets, to recover the lost wine; and as we circle back compulsively to the misty signs of landfall, we thrill with a surmise more unerring, less prescriptive than maps or charts. We gaze, marvel, and adjust our bearings. Thus, like pilots who prevail by occult instincts while propitiating the perfect course, these starry adepts dispense with the solemn rituals of mechanical survey.

To effect a transfusion of so precarious an essence into English poetry might offer some hope for the revival of *that* poetry. Reconnaissance, hypnosis, incantation, propitiation, navigation, intoxication, veneration (and venenation!), transfusion, cross-fertilization. I see our figures have proliferated. Well, here is yet one more metaphor to mix: like Baudelaire in "Le Guignon" (see Epilogue), think of it as diamond mining. The miners do not have to delve here and now; but someone, sometime, somewhere, should surely enter "the dark, unfathomed caves" for these gems, that they may be set in English verse, lest we grow so enured to drab uniforms—automatic writing, "poetry of sleep," mutiny against music, cult of scrambled coherence, angelology of the bizarre, and every other regiment of insurgent group-grope—that it will be for us as if neither natural wings nor the famed cut diamonds had ever been known.

1. Compare the following statement by Valéry: "My poems have always been to me, above all, exercises. Logical calculation, design, regular versification, are all exercises of the first order for the spirit." I translate from Lefèvre's *Conversations with Paul Valéry,* Chamontin, 1926.

2. See his "Translation and Transposition" in *The Craft and Context of Translation,* Arrowsmith and Shattuck, University of Texas, 1961.

3. *Ezra Pound's Translations,* New Directions, p. 24.

4. A single example of E.P.'s difficulty with Rimbaud might be his version of the exquisite "Lice Pickers," (ibid., p. 332), where he loads some lines superfluously, allows the problem of accommodating the "harmonica" to send us to the dictionary in vain for the baffling word "squiffer," which is an accordion, and slips into such outright gaucheries as the pleonastic: *"Neath* their electric and so soft fingers death assails/The little lice *beneath* their regal nails" (italics mine). To be startling was always easiest for Pound, whose fastidious taste could usually be trusted to stand in the way. He knew Rimbaud couldn't be dull. Why go about to prevent it?

5. To go into the old squabble of when and why verse without measure (dance without steps) can be lyrical would be worthwhile here only if the course of poetry in France had shown any interest until recently in *vers libre.* It is only with the rise of surrealism that it has done so, and it is in this connection that we shall give it later attention. At present we need only say that the inward situation, as it affected the behavior of lyrical poetry, remained thereafter unaltered in essence: that is to say, the immemorial principles of emotional unity, directness, and intensity still had to be served; and if nowadays they more often falter, a crucial disability is the lack of help from structures and strategies intrinsic to song.

6. Princeton University Press, Bollingen Series XLV, vol. 14, 1971.

7. The temptation to which Millay and Dillon yielded (*Flowers of Evil,* Harper, 1936) to turn the alexandrine into English hexameters should be resisted as long as that meter is as ill-at-ease in English as the pentameter in French. Here "doing what comes naturally" means flexing the supple capacities of the iambic pentameter, with which Chaucer, Shakespeare, Milton, Wordsworth, etc., felt so much at home. (Pound once

Introduction

declared to me that he had spotted a pentameter in Shakespeare with seventeen syllables but remained uncommunicative about where! I didn't disbelieve him.)

8. *A Vision,* W.B. Yeats, Macmillan, 1956.

9. *Poems,* Roger Fry, Chatto and Windus, 1936.

10. My own attempt is among the poems of Mallarmé in the section entitled "The Future Drags its Feet."

11. "The Art of Translation," *New Republic,* August 4, 1941. See also "Reply to my Critics," *Encounter Magazine,* February, 1966 (reprinted in *Nabakov's Congeries,* Viking, 1968).

12. This phrase forms the title of a book by Stanley Burnshaw (Holt, 1960), where he farms out poems to a stable of eminent translators, not to translate them, but to perform autopsies upon their every phrase, a procedure from which the poem itself never rises from the dead.

13. The sonnet as written, together with my translation, appears in the section entitled "Gracious Springtime."

14. *Symbolism from Poe to Mallarmé: The Growth of a Myth,* Gordon Press, New York, 1970.

15. *Le Créve-cœur,* 1940.

16. This difficulty manifests itself on page 92 of *An Anthology of French Poetry from Nerval to Valéry,* ed. by Angel Flores, Doubleday Anchor, 1958.

17. One cannot help admiring W.S. Merwin's shot at it, which is not without merit as an English poem.

18. The priority of poetry's timeless order obtains an eloquent advocate in Arnold Toynbee, who, speaking of "any two poems of different date, side by side," says, "The Time-relation between them is irrelevant. . .; for a later poem cannot be brought into a relation with an earlier one in which it will abrogate the earlier poem or be abrogated by it. . . The explanation of this relation of mutual independence between one poem and another seems to be that each poem springs separately from a common source, and that this common source of all poems is timeless." *An Historian's Approach to Religion,* Oxford, p. 125.

19. Penguin Books, 1957.

20. "Œuvres Posthumes," included in *The Unknown Philosopher,* A.E. Waite, Rudolf Steiner Publications, 1970, Part i, p. 17.

21. "Tableau Naturel," ibid., Part ii, p. 127.

22. *Poems & Texts,* October House, 1969. Especially apposite is Guillevic's remark: "I try to circumscribe a poetic thought, not the philosophic thought which lies behind this thing with which I have come in contact. . ."

23. *To Live Within,* Penguin Metaphysical Library, 1973.

24. It would have to be conceded that the *ultimate* realization has a certain intrinsic inaccessibility, even to the sublimest poetry; as the Rigveda puts it (Deussen's translation): "The poets give many names to that which is one only." But this would not alter the

fact that the *Paradiso, B minor Mass,* certain passages in Shakespeare, Shelley, Blake, are the best way given to man to reflect awareness of this inexpressible radiance.

OTHER VOICES

The poetry-translating business has become quite complicated, not to say confused. For prod and need of this work, herewith, as promised, is a summary sampling of the field, starting with the acknowledgment, understated, that translators are seldom happy with other translators, a discontent often provoked by our own shortcomings; but also that, if an existing translation looked fine, the resultant esteem would entail grateful avoiding action.

By far, and rightly, the French poet most Englished is Baudelaire. I jotted down twelve publications devoted to translating him, of which the most recent by a single translator is Joanna Richardson's selection (Penguin, 1975). This sustains a conscientious level, with many excellent lines that help to resolve the translations' tendency to stiffness and to quicken the poetry. What a difference between her "Le Crépuscule du Matin" (which starts out bravely to tackle the rhyme and falters there but keeps up her struggle with those fearful mini-dramas of Paris at night) and the version by the once prestigious Arthur Symons, prominent Yellow Book poet of the *fin de siècle!* Symons commences his assault on this magnificent, somber poem with the extraordinary Ogden Nashism,

> The awakening sang in the courts of all the barracks,
> And the morning winds breathed on the lanterns like their arracks. . .

(I looked up "arracks" in the dictionary, to find that it was a species of oriental toddy) and thereafter "respires," to use his word, from weak to worse, collapsing at intervals on couplets such as:

> Where the soul, under the weight of the body peevish,
> Fights with the lamp and the daylight, these being thievish (!)

No doubt it was this sort of thing that brought upon rhymed translations Nabakov's "slime of rhyme"; for it is not long since it must have been what was expected of verse translations. To this day, as far as I know, the only access that the non-French speaking public has to the poems of Gautier is in the old edition of the collected works, edited by the late Professor de Sumichrast of the Harvard French Department, where *Enamels and Cameos* (1906) are translated into would-be corresponding verse form by a Mrs. Agnes Lee, who sets forth with "To a Rose Dress":

> How I love you in the robes
> That disrobe so well your charms!
> Your dear breasts, twin ivory globes,
> And your bare sweet pagan arms.

And yet this turns out to be one of the less embarrassing stanzas.

The Symons-Baudelaire fiasco appeared in company with Verlaine, translated by Gertrude Bell (who is in the Agnes Lee league), and Rimbaud, by Norman Cameron, in a volume edited by Joseph Bernstein, and considered to be of sufficient value to be reissued in 1947. Cameron is mostly fine and excelled only in completeness by the largely unrhymed, but otherwise admirable Paul Schmidt (*Rimbaud,* Harper Row, 1967), who alas! like the others, omits the originals. Yet Mr. Bernstein shows no awareness of the drastic difference of quality between these translations.

The juxtaposition of these disturbing disparties continues as a familiar abuse. Take the two editions of *The Flowers of Evil,* brought out by New Directions, in 1955 and 1963, respectively, and both edited by Marthiel and Jackson Mathews. The earlier of these two volumes represented, according to the editors, the fifty-three poems "most successfully rendered in English." One third of that half of Baudelaire's total poetic output which has been salvaged here gives some pleasure to be read in English, especially most of the poems translated by Roy Campbell, some few of those by David Paul (though neither his "Morning Twilight" nor his "Benediction") Aldous Huxley's "Lesbians," Richard Wilbur's "Invitation to the Voyage," and all those recovered from the forgotten and now practically unobtainable F.P. Sturm, an admired friend of Yeats, a good poet, and an exceptionally close, as well as tuneful translator. It is especially unfortunate that Robert Fitzgerald, *primus inter pares,* has done so little French poetry and is here conspicuous by his absence.

The second and more comprehensive New Directions edition is by no means entirely the advance upon the first that it aspired to be. Whilst holding the door open to future translations of Baudelaire, it stakes out this volume as definitive, claiming that it consists of all the best translations of Baudelaire that have been made to date. Frederick Morgan happily appears again. The newly imported translators who stand out are Anthony Hecht, Naomi Lewis, and (for one poem) Stanley Kunitz. Most of the misfires from the earlier edition remain, and not all the other new additions are an improvement. The reversal of the policy followed by the format of the earlier volume, where the French and English appeared on facing pages, could have been a frustrated gesture of defiance, promoted by protests against distortions thus made manifest. The editors now deplore what they call the "criss-cross testing of the translation that keeps it from ever being read as a poem in its integrity." But there was nothing in the earlier policy (and our own) to prevent the reader from confining his attention to one language at a time, whilst there is everything to encourage unwarranted liberties of form, imagery, and sense in this kenneling of Baudelaire himself in the rear of the volume, another practise now commonly followed.

It is when we come to the volumes devoted to an entire period by a group of translators that the uneven performance concentrates attention on the employment of such variously gifted delegates between the same covers. I think of three of these books that solicit detailed review, such as would here be out of place. The first in time is the British *A Mirror for French Poetry: 1840-1940,* selected and edited by Cecily Mackworth, George Routledge, 1947. This book consists of sixty-eight poems by thirty-four poets, with thirty-nine translators! The English poetry may be sustained at the highest level of the three volumes in question, thanks to a contingent of modern poets, at or near the level of Flecker, A. Huxley, Watkins and Macneice. The editor herself translates four of the poets and would be equal to the job if her nerve had not presumably faltered before rhyme. The poetry she seems most to kindle to is that singed by the fire of revolt, as her eloquent preface testifies. If she had forgotten about the paler neo-symbolists, like Régnier, Salmon, and Viélé-Griffin, and stuck to the firebrands she loves, like Fargue and Tzara, and done them all herself, we might have had a book balanced, as it were, in imbalance, instead of one where first-rate poets and translators mix on equal terms with second-rate ones, to impel on us a talent-scout syndrome. But the talent does come out on top—most of the time.

The second is the much more spottily valuable *Anthology of French Poetry from Ner-*

val to Valéry, edited by Angel Flores, Doubleday Anchor, 1958. This again is a winnowing which would make us more grateful if it were itself ruthlessly winnowed. It comprises two hundred poems by nine eminent poets of the nineteenth and twentieth centuries, poems that have been assigned to a mixed squadron of thirty-four recruited translators, some of whom, and they the ones most resorted to, do not quite have what it takes to carry over French poets alive into English, and only a quarter of whom, at best, would be capable of adequately handling more than two or three of the poets represented, even if they had the inclination, time, and persistence. Hence it is not surprising that the results are so unequal. Only a few of these translators, and they the stars, acknowledge much if any obligation of formal equivalence. These are: Wilbur and Fitzgerald, of course; Watkins again; Kunitz—alas! offering only one; W.J. Smith, with several of Laforgue's; Frederick Morgan, who is splendid with "L'Après Midi d'un Faun," except that it could have been left, as by Cecily Mackworth, to the surprising Aldous Huxley, even better. The rest are often allowed to waddle on deck with lamed versions of the elusive bird; and "waddle" is not to include that contrived lurch of the verse which might be solicited by the poet's subject and treatment (as in the opening lines, for instance, of Baudelaire's "The Albatross"), but refers only to translations totally unwinged for *flight.*

When we come to the translation of contemporary poetry, we see much of it dropping rapidly from sight—or is it the poetry itself which is soon forgotten? An impressive group, whose fine intentions deserved less neglect, were recruited to make *Contemporary French Poetry: Fourteen Witnesses of Man's Fate,* edited by Alexander Aspel and Donald Justice, University of Michigan Press, 1965. Here the translators are almost twice as numerous as the poets, and one short poem commonly requires three collaborating translators, besides the Iowa University Writers' Workshop and a variety of outside experts drawn into consultation, we are told, on every word. Of the ninety-four poems upgathered in this volatile, somewhat amorphous, and necessarily eclectic levy, some few are beautiful in both languages and about half in just one, the original.

So has it been wont to happen with the translation of contemporary poetry and, except that they did not *have* to court every defeat, not always by fault of the translators, who do, however, sometimes tend to lack historical perspective and a presiding poetic, capable of supervising strategies to command interest beyond the moment. It is almost inevitable that the gift of a Bonnefoy or a Jaccottet should be blurred, tossed as they are into an impartial hopper with poets whose tribal insignia are not immediately apparent, whose rich obscurity is partly obscurantism, as with André de Bouchet or André de Mandiargues, and then the original obscurity thickened by the translations of eager jobbers, muscling in on the more durable craftsmen, to co-opt their prey into a tribal counterpart of affiliated English free verse.

Of the later arrivals, we are left with one venture which proves somewhat less unresponsive to joint translators, one which in most academic circles, for a while anyway, will be considered as making a bold and special claim. This is *Modern French Poetry: A Bilingual Anthology,* edited and translated by Patricia Terry and Serge Gavronsky, Columbia University Press, 1975. Here we have seventy-seven poems by only thirteen poets of startlingly uneven stature in relation to coverage (Michaux equaling in number of pages Baudelaire and Rimbaud combined), thus imparting an outré, amphictyonic effect, which is rather hard on all those fine poets made conspicuous by absence, and which might be better served by skipping the giants entirely. Once again the poems are beautifully laid out *en face.* The bibliography and critical apparatus, within their self-confining limits, are meticulous. There is much emphasis on the machinery of scansion; yet five of the poets are given "prose poems"—Baudelaire, Rimbaud, Lautréamont, Jean Faillan, Francis Ponge, and Henri Michaux: a preponderance which would be more

23

persuasive if fulfilling the following minimum conditions: the poets themselves would have established a really corresponding claim for such "prose poems"; the editors' ascription of lyricism to these fascinating inventions would have been grounded in a clearer, or more clearly defined, conception of the lyric; and more of their "lyrics" in translation, whether or not in verse, would be recognizable as lyrics. This last condition is saved only by about half of "P.T." 's Verlaine and Laforgue, two each of which sing both impulsively and conformably enough to sound thoroughly at home with the original—in itself not a bad score for this game.

There is one group enterprise that strives to be more comprehensive and, for its modest scope, has good proportion. This is *Poems from France,* edited by William Jay Smith, 1967—one of the respectworthy multilingual series published by Thos. Crowell. Like Mackworth's book, it confers the blessing of the original poems on facing pages, and of these last four it may well be the one which focuses least randomly the question of the unities solicited by an anthology. It contains ninety-five poems, mostly short, by forty-seven poets and fifty-two translators. The introduction demonstrates a measure of presiding insight into the special character of French poetry. Once more, the most successful translators are the best poets, past and present, who have also taken the trouble to assume the responsibilities of form, however baffling: that is to say, Wilbur and Fitzgerald again; the two Smiths, i.e., A.J.M., and the editor himself, the latter with now wider success; Flecker and Watkins again; then, from the past, Edmund Spenser; both Swinburne and Francis Thompson to signalize Hugo; an extraordinary tour de force by Santayana for Gautier's untranslatable (I had thought) "L'Art"; but a disconcerting miscarriage by Pound, though of a medieval poem; finally, two poets unknown to me: Louis Coxe, for Apollinaire's "Les Sapins" (why not give him Apollinaire's others there?) and Brian Hill, for a poem each, both unusually well turned, of Nerval and Gautier. Say twelve prizes out of fifty-two? But that would be a good average in this league. The book as a whole might get best marks to date and would be more indispensable if, once more, both original poets and translator poets, were given representation corresponding with their importance.

The frustration facing us in all these group translations, however, is probably intrinsic to the plan, which requires us to leap, not only from poet to poet, and period to period, but also from one to another interpreting "voice." This is when the cumulative life of the book can become indigestible. If also, in the exercise of the translator's individual gift, we see displayed a varying license to distort either form or meaning or both, the result is likely to be that not the best editorial discrimination may be able to save a harmonious book from discord, or the transparency required of all true translation from polychrome distraction. There could hardly be such scattered battening on the Ionian lyrists or the Palatine Anthology, for example, probably because the cumulative light of those stars is instinctively recognized as immune to the praise for ideosyncrasy, endemic to our times.

Are there, then, no inclusive representations, by a single translator, of entire fields of French poetry? I know of only two such. One is the recent *French Poems in English Verse,* 1850-1970, by Dorothy Brown Aspinwall, Scarecrow Press, 1973, which contains forty-one slight poems by twenty-eight poets. Here pride of place belongs easily to Henry Régnier, with four times as many poems as Baudelaire! This translator provides the originals, does all her own work, and, with the rhymed poems, only in emergency abandons the rhyme. If the English verse does not often fall flat, neither could it truthfully be said that it observes the third criterion of Alexander Tytler, in his 'Essay on the Principles of Translation," as quoted by this translator herself: ". . .the translation should have the ease of original composition. . ."—admittedly no easy provision.

The other is the only known publication which essays a comprehensive representation of the entire field of French poetry by a single translator, *French Lyrics into English Verse,* by William Frederic Giese, University of Wisconsin Press, 1946. To the extent that it preserves, with some consistency, a reasonable facsimile of the original form, including the rhyme, this book is an encouraging endeavor. The poems in French are not included, perhaps advisedly, for the meaning in English is often distant, whilst the poetry sustains, at best, a middle flight of faltering strength and prevailing prettiness. To take a typical example of what happens here: as is well known, Baudelaire spent an inordinate amount of his time translating Poe and improving him in the process; but even in those rare moments when Baudelaire allowed his own poetry to be tainted by the tawdriness of most of Poe's verse, he would never degenerate to anything remotely like the following rendering of the magnificent "L'Invitation au Voyage," since done properly by Richard Wilbur:

> My loved one, my sweeting,
> Oh heed my entreating,
> Hand in hand let us wander away. . .

this for:

> Mon enfant, ma sœur,
> Songe à la douceur
> D'aller là-bas vivre ensemble.

It is, in fact, only with the greatest difficulty that one can imagine Baudelaire "wandering hand in hand" with anyone at any time. Fortunately, all fiercer or more complex poems are avoided by this volume. (Maybe "là-bas vivre ensemble;" was a trifle too fierce). Rimbaud is totally absent! Mallarmé escapes with only one poem, his "'Apparition,'" one of the three near-juvenile, *soi distant* "Premiers Poèmes," where, however, the lines:

> Et dans le soir, tu m'es en riant apparue
> Et j'ai cru voir la fée au chapeau de clarté. . .

become:

> So wreathed in happy smiles you seemed to be,
> That old-time fairy floating in the air. . .(?)

And so forth. The late Professor Giese was clearly a most attractive, old-time gentleman. Unfortunately, not all French poets were even particularly attractive men.

It would be awkward if it turned out that we'd be better advised, after all, to stick to a single poet, like Paul Schmidt to Rimbaud, Cecil Day Lewis to Valéry, or prevailingly, Dudley Fitts to Apollinaire. Obviously there are elective affinities that draw us to certain poets. Dudley Fitts, for example, wins a clear right to try his luck with Apollinaire. At his best, Fitts is one of the best in the business, but he can make it difficult to decide when to lift one's hat and when to look the other way. In the unflinching tour de force of his attempted translation of Apollinaire's long hurtling poem, "La Chanson du Mal-Aimé," there is no questioning the courage of his random-rhymed experiment in the subjection of both formal melody and close sense to vigor and flavor; but he gets into some difficulties. Thus it belongs integrally to Apollinaire's magical fusion of sound and sense to be able to dispense with punctuation without bewildering us. But his is a license which Mr. Fitts, whose vestigial rhyming allows little or no connection with the original rhyme scheme, is less able to bear in his translation. For example, the strangely lucid lines,

> Tu est à moi en n'étant rien
> O mon ombre en dueil de moi-même. . .

which, to inflict on ourselves a literal translation, would have to be twisted into something like: "You are what you are to me in being nothing, O my shade in mourning for me," are by Fitts split asunder and telescoped into the cryptic, syntactically opaque:

> You are mine for ever nothing you
> My ghost wears mourning for myself. . .

We come next to such outright mistranslations as in the crucially climactic last stanza but one. Here the nostalgic hurdy-gurdy is loosely but brilliantly rendered by Mr. Fitts:

> Les cafés gonglés de fumée
> Crient tout l'amour de leurs tziganes
> De tous leurs siphons enrhumés
> De leurs garçons vêtus d'un pagne. . .

> Paunchy with smoke the cafés grunt
> Love love love from the gypsy dance
> Love from siphons sniffly-nosed
> Love from the apron'd waiter-boys. . .

But then, quite unaccountably,

> . . .l'amour. . .
> De leurs garçons vêtus d'un pagne
> *Vers* toi toi que j'ai tant aimé.

becomes:

> Love from the apron'd waiter-boys
> Love *from* you whom I loved. (Italics mine)

But surely it is here the focal paradox that this low-life love goes out so easily and acceptably *towards,* or *for,* her whom the speaker has loved with passion. Admittedly, this is a pretty drastic instance, but if these things be done in the green tree (i.e., Fitts), what shall be done in the dry—all those "also-rans" whom it pleases to dress these vagaries as "imitations." Nothing is extenuated by calling translations this, or even "versions": a vogue to which we must return, and shall in the addendum to the introduction of "A New Sound," with a closer examination of a prominent operator in this kind.

A more strident variant of this vogue enters with the slang problem. It is hard enough and usually impossible to match existing foreign slang, without gratuitously resorting to

English or American slang for those passages which, in the original, are a well of French undefiled. But this is what occurs in some of Mr. Fitts' attempts to find matching movements for Apollinaire's darting speed afoot by uncalled-for embellishments with the Yank vernacular: ". . .That's all right by me" for "Je suis content. . ."; or ". . . worse news than Barabbas" for ". . .plus criminel que Barrabas. . ." etc. Apollinaire was lord of the moderns and liege lord of the epoch-separating blood-bath of World War I, whose great retinue in England included Owen, Grenfell, Brooke, Sorley, Rosenberg, Nichols, Thomas, Graves, and Sassoon. None of these stood as tall as Apollinaire, who deserves all the modernity he can get, and Fitts is one who can mostly get away with such leaping liberties as the above. It is when modernism infiltrates what makes no effort to be modern that a translator's effects can become most anomalous, and it is regrettable that Mr. Fitts' type of brillance has set a vogue among sorcerors' apprentices with a more fallible taste. What has made us think to enhance a nineteenth-century voice with a twentieth-century microphone? For (to shift the metaphor) the inner lights of century-old jewels do not shine more luminously by plastering them with a sparkling film of modernity, or by trying to steal their own light with a rival but ersatz glitter.

We may take leave of these particular danger signals with the rather dim conclusion that, notwithstanding his scattered Pyrrhic victories in translating this poem, it might have been better for himself and for the poem if this exciting Greek scholar had left it alone.

But how often have I wished that some Yves Bonnefoy, say, had been standing by me with advice concerning which poets and poems to stay away from! It's a safe bet that, when this book is out, there will be no lack of such advice as is here offered for "other voices." And another grave consideration: just because so many of these French poems are frittered away in English by confused aims and mistaken company does not mean that a wondrous love did not often sustain the effort to perpetuate them, whereby so many of them cling to life in their strange surroundings. So by all means let us cleanse the stables, but *requiescant in pace,* Arthur Symons, Frederic Giese, and Agnes Lee!

As for Dudley Fitts, (d. 1968) I knew him, Horatio, and no faint unintended implication could be less true than that his pursuit of Apollinaire had anything in common with the proprietary narcissism of certain modern critics.

Gracious Springtime

from *Tres Riches Heures of Jean, Duke of Berry*

Gracious Springtime
Thirteenth through Sixteenth Centuries

To one scrupulous about origins, to begin with fourteenth-century motets would make "springtime" a misplaced metaphor, if only because medieval French poetry had been going for at least five centuries previous to the thirteenth. The *chansons de geste* reached their apogee in the *Chanson de Roland,* written early in the eleventh century about an event of the eighth. The first romances appeared in the middle of the twelfth, which in Provence saw the actual springtime of the lyric. But Provençal is not really French, is it, and the Provençal lyric can be left to others.

The first stirrings of this book belong to the courtly *vita nuova,* to that birth of romantic love. Then, almost immediately, we have the extraordinary music, savage and civilized, of François Villon, who strikes me (and I long to be proved wrong) as untranslatable into any corresponding song. What makes his poems so inaccessible to translation is the combined impetuosity of movement and insistence of rhyme. The same difficulty applies in some measure to all the earliest poems in this section; for whilst the thronging rhymes are integral to their music, to match them in English presents an almost insuperable barrier to the impulsive effect which belongs to them in French.

It is a happy circumstance for the section and for the book that the very first poem is an *aube,* or dawn poem. *Aubes* have been placed variously as belonging to the thirteenth century and earlier. In fact, although the speaker in this one, as is often the case, is a woman, some scholars have tentatively ascribed it to a celebrated *trouvère* named Gace Brulé, a knight, possibly a crusader, born in the first half of the twelfth century. The subject of *aubes* is traditional enough. It is lovers' partings at daybreak, like that of Romeo and Juliet.

The motets also proceed from the same suprapersonal sanctuary of longing, joined so indissolubly to the sound that I should think they might almost be felt as intelligible to one ignorant of the language. True, "Je sui joliete" is a part-song addressed to a specific occasion: a girl got with child and packed off to a convent. But here likewise it is the unrest of imprisoned puberty that so immediately communicates itself, where even the "*maus,*" or pangs, are felt as "*dous,*" sweet. Thus, if the joy exacted its penalties from the vernal frolic, the song could be a very spirited protest against all more bloodless consequences. Hence, the tone of this lyric is more exasperated than despondent.

Like our English and Scottish lyrics, medieval and Elizabethan, these thirteenth- and fourteenth-century motets, rondeaux and ballades never allow us to forget that the music came first; and that they were composed to be sung to existing tunes by voices—seldom more numerous than four. Again, as with the ballads of Percy's "Reliques," which first reached print in the eighteenth century, the *chanson populaire* ("Ma belle, si tu voulais. . .") had a long, untraceable life by word of mouth, whose ancient tune, which we still have, makes the poem belong here, though I found it, in an esteemed anthology, jostling Voltaire. Perhaps this was because the six couplets here, which by good chance can also be lyrical in English, were made part of a later narrative ballad of less intensity.[1]

No one will deny that these lyrics, by their *joliveté,* come honestly by the thought of spring. If the period felt scruples about indulgence of joy, they are not heard here. It is almost as if, in the words of our *aube,* they were "mindless of wrong." Recurrent themes are May Day joys, broken joy of lovers' partings, joyous reunions of lovers, killjoy of unions blighted by age disparities, (as in Clément Marot's rondeau), surreptitious joys betrayed by a careless look of intimacy ("Trop me regardez..."), or simply joy.

None of these songs depend on thought, as understood by Voltaire or ourselves. They are driven by pulsating emotions that transcend the strictures of rhyme in a totally unburdensome fashion. Certainly most of this poetry is love poems, but the same dominance of emotion over thought is found where we might less expect to find it, in the religious poetry. There is very little thought to complicate the rush of devotional ardor, for example, in the "Epistle" of the Queen of Navarre.

The unmannered freshness of the women poets was early made manifest. Observe that, of the first twenty poets here, ostensibly half are women, of which there might be three who are anonymous, and one who is a queen. Let the anonymity of the motets speak for the modesty, and their moving sincerity speak for itself. It is when we read Christine de Pisan's "Ballade" that we are brought to believe, if not understand, how vitality and exuberance can carry the day over the technical obstacles with which the tradition confronted itself. It is true that the strong hold on poetry asserted by this lady of the court, by Mary of France, and, more famously, by Marguerite of Navarre, never equaled in monopolistic mastery the ladies surrounding Lady Murasaki Shikabu in the imperial court of the Heian Age in Japan; nevertheless, those "Ladies Whose Bright Eyes" illumined Versailles were sufficiently *bien*

32

aisées with their ballades and motets that for them to surmount their own rhymes with agility and grace was an accepted and expected feature of the charm which transmits its fragrance across six centuries. When we come to the sixteenth century and the *Pléiade,* this charm certainly does not falter. Pernette du Guillet, who unfortunately died in her twenties in 1545, makes us think in some of her *rimes* that we are eavesdropping on actual snatches of conversation of a woman speaking from her heart to her lover, very openly, but without hurt to her pride, the ostensible submissiveness being only a shade too subtle, on occasion, for the irony to be readily detectable! We may trust, at least, that Maurice Scève was equal to that irony, for it was he who, whilst supposedly being her mentor in poetry, addressed most of his poems to her, including, we may infer, those in this section. Perhaps the most magically funny poem in this volume is Du Guillet's beautifully balanced "Combien de foy. . .," where her master and lover is revealed in solitude, stalking beside his fountain, intoxicated by the exuberance of his own verbosity, as he bathes in his own verses, and she in the nude sneaks up on him to accompany his performance on the lute, splashing him in the face, while he tries to move in on her: high jinks with copious female detail, nimble as air, and completely unconscious of being witty, sly, or attractive. However far the translation may lag as an English poem, Du Guillet leads us across all frontiers to favor both English poetry and English humor.

In an equally human voice, within the intricate sonnet, Gabrielle de Coignard of Toulouse, who died in 1594, writes with deep feeling about her farm—the flocks, the thick-foliaged trees, the silence into which the birds dropped their notes, to match the "linked sweetness" of her lines.

But it is in Louise Labé that we are made most oblivious to the skill of the verse by the passion behind it. We are lucky in the number of her sonnets preserved, but less lucky as to their succesful translatability, a resistance owing now to the reverse of any elevated artifice, Malherbe having yet to cast his iron shade. She is the poet, perhaps more than any other, whose *intensity,* strictly dressed, might well baffle the translator who hopes to retain any of that freshness, along with indispensable infusions from the age. Let us suppose that he takes the sonnet commencing, "Claire Venus, qui erres par les cieux" ("Bright Venus, wandering through the sky"), and that, with the assist of a twist, he roughly matches the direct cry of the climactic lines:

> J'endure mal tant que le soleil luit:
> Et quand je suis quasi toute cassée,

Et que me suis mise en mon lit lassée
Crier me faut mon mal toute la nuit.

by something like:

While the sun shines I bear my suffering ill:
And when exhausted on my bed I lie,
Near broken by the load, I have to cry
All through the night with pangs that rend me still.

But finding ten more rhymes for these torments, even by cutting corners with similar liberties, would affect us as a trifle unseemly, whereas, without all these rhymes, once more, it would travel on four flat tires, of course. Still, as long as there are translators, this intensity will continue to lure and ambush new attempts.

It may be nothing but an ancient conspiracy of neglect that prevents the discovery of more women of genius belonging to this period. "For man to man so oft unjust," as Byron said, "is always so to women." Imagine the *Oxford Book of French Verse* including, out of one hundred seven poets, only six who were women! As things stand, however, there do not appear to have been so many gifted women again in one period until the twentieth century, in which it may turn out that there will have been as many first class poets that were women as men.

In an ideal world, the refreshing directness of these women poets could have thrown up a couple of them whose genius might have presided over the Renaissance, but of course this didn't happen. There were two such towering men in France, by whom, as by their counterparts in Italy and England, we can best estimate the greatness and shortcomings of the age. They are Du Bellay and Ronsard. In England, the parallel liberation was by the elite of court associated entirely with the lyrical poetry of such poets as Sidney, Spenser, and the Shakespeare of the sonnets. The enormous enlargement of that rapture, effected by the blank verse of the plays, may seem to us a more palpable emolument, but actually the literary repercussions of the drama were more gradual.

The liberation was primarily linguistic and originated, as we know, in Italy, especially, of course, with Petrarch. The rediscovery of Greek and Latin poetry was the infusion which set loose, in all these lands, that flood of wonderfully beautiful sonnets—thousands and thousands of singing sonnets. Yes, the courts of the Medici and the Pope were exhilarating, whether evil or benign; and yes, their ships "held the glorious East in fee"; and yes, Marie, Hélène, Barbara ("hair done in

Italian style," as Ronsard says in "Fay refraischer mon vin. . .") possessed endowments, no doubt, to inspire venturesome verse. But
beyond the more obvious glitter of these enticements was the effect
upon Ronsard, as he emerged from his inner chamber, of having been
immersed for three days there with the *Iliad.* It was a new style that was
"determined, dared, and done."

To the extent that Ronsard eludes us, the problem may well lie, in
part, with a wide shift of thought since then, which threatens to put our
understanding at a distance from their priorities. Previous to the seventeenth century, the three prevailing, one might almost say pre-emptive,
subjects of poetry were love, war, and religion, all settling down, certainly for French poetry, and I think one could say for Chaucer and
Spenser too, into what would lend itself to that pat dichotomy of sacred
and profane.

Our slow alienation from those inflexible acceptances, whether
French or English, of what is sacred, arises in part from the excessively
anthropomorphic theology which sat easier on our fathers than on us. As
for the profane, this was chiefly absorbed by the love poetry, a domain
more circumscribed than love in modern poetry, since for these early
poets it had been so long confined within a set of ground rules for the
expression of the passion—rules which, like the passion they were to
govern, were distinctly masochistic, not yet wholly dissociated from the
"Tournaments of Love," and still within the frontiers of "Chivalry."
The lover himself insisted on being victimized, at a properly respectful
distance, by "the cruel fair," resorting to the sighs of dreamy affliction
best known in the sonnets of Pierre de Ronsard. It is a beauty which can
and does prevail by sheer grace, hence presenting even sharper
discouragements than usual to that victimized adorer, the translator. Indeed, in the sonnet commencing, "That evening when Love brought
you down to the hall," we are made witness to an actual audio-visual
minuet or quadrille—the "steps" in sonnet form.

In England, as we know, in the sonnets of Sidney, Spenser, and
Shakespeare, the influence of Petrarch made itself felt decisively
somewhat later than upon Ronsard and, let us not forget, Du Bellay, who if
with less learning than Ronsard, perhaps, and only less elegance, may
be said to have been the first to consummate the familiar, conversational
note in poetry which is in the best sense poetry. Sometimes we may have
been tempted to think, concerning all those thousands of sonnets, that
graceful movement and melodious sound were enough. But there is
something over and above music and dexterity, experienced supremely
in Ronsard and Shakespeare. It is a fragrance. Throughout the countless

sonnets of Ronsard, as in so many of Shakespeare's we are seldom beyond the reach of the smell of roses. One is reminded of Laertes' words in *Hamlet,* though these were of violets: ". . .forward, not permanent, sweet, not lasting, /The perfume and suppliance of a minute." Both Ronsard and Shakespeare, however, had a way of making this perfume last beyond the grave. Ronsard seldom intrudes the hot breath of passion; and I can imagine one with no love for this sort of poetry complaining, again with *Hamlet,* "Thought and affliction, passion, hell itself, /He turns to favour and to prettiness." If this is prettiness, who would wish to fall out of favor with it?

We are speaking still of lyrical poetry. Rabelais and Molière were clearly, by both nature and performance, very great poets, who were also, in different ways, free spirits when writing of love between the sexes. But for lyricists, France would have to wait for Baudelaire, two centuries later, to break up that cult of sedate and worshipful suffering. It was a cult which, in England, was aired out much earlier by Donne and Marvell, both deeply religious, of course, and one passionately so; yet neither of them interested in attempting to separate the power exerted by women, or the worship of them, from practically every shade of sexuality.

But this period has shown us too much intensity—in those sonnets of Louise Labé, in Du Bellay and Ronsard themselves, when they speak of the exile's longing for home, or of the shadow of death—for us to identify the *Pléiade* with varieties of graceful play. The incandescence of Labé, for example, should not dull us to the impact of other passions than love in the all too few poets among the immediate successors of Ronsard who, as the period dies and the intensity begins to cool, still show themselves capable of transmitting heat and light. Take, for example, the passion of disgust in Jean de Sponde, as he brings what he most despises in the court beneath his lash, stationing himself, like Swift, under the foreshortening shadow of the grave, "ubi saeva indignatio cor ulterius lacerare nequit" ("where wild wrath can no longer tear the heart").

The "cooling" was slow. What forms it took is a subject that belongs to the next section, entitled, "Lyrical decline."

1. Old spelling is a grey area. The earlier the poem, the harder it is to dissociate from the Old French orthography, at best casual, the lyricism we wish to preserve. To me that spelling (anyway, through Jean de Sponde) belongs with the bouquet. I may add that a happy hunting ground for these words for music is the volume, *Poètes et Romanciers du Moyen Age,* ed. by A. Pauphilet, Bibl. de la Pléiade, 1952, from which a selection appears in the first volume of *The Penguin Book of French Verse,* ed. by Brian Woledge, 1961. To this I am indebted for certain selections.

Anonymous

Aube

Entre moi et mon ami,
En un bois qu'est lès Betune,
Alames jouant mardi,
Toute la nuit à la lune,
  Tant qu'il ajourna
Et que l'aloue chanta
Qui dit: "Amis, alons ent."
Et il respont doucement:
   "Il n'est mie jours,
  Saverouse au cors gent;
   Si m'aït amours,
  L'alouette nous ment."

Adonc se trait près de mi,
Et je ne fui pas enfrune;
Bien trois fois me baisa il,
Ainsi fis je lui plus d'une,
  Qu'ainz ne m'enoia.
Adonc vousissions nous là
Que celle nuit durast cent,
Mais que plus n'alast disant:
   "Il n'est mie jours,
  Saverouse au cors gent;
   Si m'aït amours,
  L'alouette nous ment."

Anonymous

Aube

THERE were two, my love and I,
In a wood beside Bethune,
Of a Tuesday late did lie
All night long beneath the moon,
      Till the morning sprang,
And the lark in heaven sang,
"Dear one, let us now arise."
Softly then my love replies:
      "It is not yet day;
    Nay, my sweet, no sun doth rise,
      So to Love I pray
That the lark was telling lies."

Closer then he drew and I
Not unwillingly to him;
Kisses given multiply
Thrice and more, mine joining them,
      Mindless of a wrong.
Could we but the night prolong
For a hundred nights of these,
So he never say with sighs:
      "It is not yet day;
    Nay, my sweet, no sun doth rise,
      So to Love I pray
That the lark was telling lies."

Anonymous

Motet

Beaus douz amis, or ne vous enuit mie
Se d'estre ensemble faisons tel demouree,
Car on dit: "Qui bien aime à tart oublie."
Pour ce n'ert ja nostre amour desevree,
Ne n'ai aillors ne desir ne pensee
Fors seulement qu'ensemble estre puissomes.
Hé! beau cuers douz, je vous aim sur tous homes:
Aiez pitié de vo loial amie,
Et si pensez que par tens i soiomes,
Pour mener joie, com amans à celee.
                    Dieus! car nous herberjomes.

Anonymous

Motet

My fair sweet love, now may it not thee fret
If we must tarry long to be close joined;
They say, "Who loves well does not soon forget."
Therefore our love will not so early end,
And I have no desire or thought to spend
Save only to be with you once again.
Oh! fair sweet heart, I love you most of men.
Have pity on the one who loves you yet
And find a place to be together soon,
That our twin joys secluded may be met.
                    Dear God, just we alone!

Anonymous

Motet

AMIS, dont est engendree
En vo cuer tel volentez
Qu'estre cuidiez refusez,
Pour ce que vous ai monstree
Chiere autre que ne voulez?

Mais se bien saviez
Comment on doit retenir
Amant qu'on crient departir,
Entendre porriez
Que le fis par tel desir
Qu'enaigrir
Vous feïsse en moi amer.
Fins cuers, ne veuilliez cesser,
Car aillours que vous chierir
Ne puis penser.

Anonymous

Rondeau

TROP me regardez, amie, souvent;
Vostre doux regart trahissent la gent.
Cuers qui veut amer jolietement
— Trop me regardez, amie, souvent —
Ne se doit vanter pardevant la gent,
Ainz se doit garder pour les mesdisant.
Trop me regardez, amie, souvent;
Vostre douz regart trahissent la gent.

Anonymous

Motet

My love, what notion made
Your foolish heart reflect
That I would you reject
Or give of what I had
Less than you might expect?

But if you only knew
By what arts we constrain
The one whose love we'd gain,
Then you would see into
My hope, by what I've done,
To sharpen pain
Of love for me anew.
Then cease not loving when
The one thought in my brain
Is loving you.

Anonymous

Rondeau

You look at me too often, dear;
With gentle looks folk interfere.
Hearts that would love without a fear
—You look at me too often, dear—
Should make the evidence less clear
And guard lest rumors come too near.
You look at me too often, dear;
With gentle looks folk interfere.

Anonymous

Motet

JE sui joliete,
Sadete, plaisans,
Jeune pucelete;
    N'ai pas quinze ans;
    Point mamelete
    Selonc le tans;
    Si deüsse aprendre
    D'amors, et entendre
    Les semblans
    Deduisans.
Mais je sui mise en prison.
De Dieu ait maleïçon
        Qui m'i mist!
    Mal et vilanie
        Et pechié fist
    De tel pucelete
    Rendre en abiete.
Trop i mesfist, par ma foi;
En religion vif en grant anoi,
    Dieus! car trop sui jonete.
Je sens les dous maus desous ma ceinturete:
Honis soit de Dieu qui me fist nonnete.

Anonymous

Motet

I AM a comely one,
Frolicsome of mien,
Springing fair anon,
    Come not all fifteen,
    Breasties risen soon
    In the time between,
Featly to be learning
Love and such concerning,
        Every sign
        Making mine.
But I'm cast in jail.
May God send to hell
        Him who put me there!
    Knavery, despair,
        Sin it is to snare
    Such a girl as me
    In a nunnery.
Too much, by my faith, to irk;
For this wicked convent work,
    Dear gods, I am far too young.
Sweet pangs beneath my girdle have begun:
    May God curse him who made of me a nun.

Anonymous

Ma belle, si tu voulais...

MA belle, si tu voulais,
    nous dormirions ensemble,

Dans un grand lit carré,
    couvert de taies blanches;

Aux quatre coins du lit,
    un bouquet de pervenches.

Dans le mitan du lit,
    la rivière est profonde;

Tous les chevaux du roi
    pourraient y boire ensemble.

Et là, nous dormirions
    jusqu'à la fin du monde.

Anonymous

My fair one, if it is your will...

My fair one, if it is your will,
    we two would sleep together yet,

Together in a great square bed,
    supplied with pillow-slips of white;

And at the base and at the head,
    a sprig of periwinkle set.

Lo, in the middle of the bed,
    a mighty river floweth deep,

That all the horses of the king
    together there might drink of it,

And there, until the world shall end,
    we two together yet might sleep.

Jehannot de Lescurel

1290? - 1350?

Rondeau

DOUCE dame, je vous pri,
Faites de moi vostre ami.

Belle, aiés de moi merci.
Douce dame, je vous pri

Qu'il soit ainsi com je di.
De cuer amoureus joli,
Douce dame, je vous pri
Faites de moi vostre ami.

Jehannot de Lescurel

1290? - 1350?

Rondeau

GENTLE lady, pray thee send
Leave I be thy dearest friend.

Fair one, in thy mercy bend.
Gentle lady, pray thee send

That it be as I commend.
Fond of heart, well-favored, and
Gentle lady, pray thee send
Leave I be thy dearest friend.

Christine de Pisan

1365 - 1431?

Ballade

Tu soies le tres bien venu,
M'amour! Or m'embrace et me baise.
Et comment t'es tu maintenu
Puis ton depart? Sain et bien aise
As tu esté toujours? Ça vien,
Coste moi te sié et me conte
Comment t'a esté, mal ou bien;
Car de ce vueil savoir le compte.

— Ma dame, à qui je suis tenu
Plus qu'autre, (à nul n'en desplaise!)
Sachez que desir m'a tenu
Si court qu'onques n'oz tel mesaise,
Ne plaisir ne prenoie en rien
Loin de vous: Amour, qui cuers dompte,
Me disoit: "Loyauté me tien,
Car de ce vueil savoir le compte."

— Dont m'as tu ton serment tenu;
Bon gré t'en sai, par saint Nicaise.
Et puis que sain es revenu,
Joie avrons assez; or t'apaise
Et me dis se ses de combien
Le mal qu'en as eu à plus monte
Que cil qu'a souffert le cuer mien;
Car de ce vueil savoir le compte.

— Plus mal que vous, si com retien,
Ai eu; mais dites sans mescompte
Quans baisiers en avrai je bien?
Car de ce vueil savoir le compte.

Christine de Pisan

1365 - 1431?

Ballade

"DARLING, thou art the welcome one!
Hold me and kiss, as was our way.
How hast thou been since thou wast gone?
In health and gladness every day?
Come sit thee down beside me here
And tell me how thy days were spent;
The well and ill I fain would hear,
For I must know the full account.

"My Lady, best loved for my own,
(Not that with other loves I play)
My longing held me with a rein
So short I never lived less gay;
From thee removed, naught gave me cheer.
Love, that the stoutest heart will daunt,
Adjured me, 'Hold thy credit dear,
For I must know the full account.'

"Thou kept thy word with fair renown!
By Saint Nicasius, I say,
Since thou art safely home, let crown
Our joy together sans delay.
Peace unto thee! But, for arrears,
Tell me how far thy languishment
Surpassed the tally of my tears,
For I must know the full account.

"More grief than thou had I to bear:
How much, then, is the true amount
Of kisses owed, to render fair?
For I must know the full account."

Charles d'Orléans

1394 - 1465

Rondeau

Les en voulez vous garder,
Ces rivieres, de courir,
Et grues prendre et tenir
Quant haut les veez voler?

A telles choses muser
Voit on fols souvent servir:
Les en voulez vous garder,
Ces rivieres, de courir?

Laissez le temps tel passer
Que Fortune veut souffrir,
Et les choses avenir
Que l'on ne set destourber.
Les en voulez vous garder?

Charles d'Orléans

1394 - 1465

Rondeau

WOULD you stay what flies away,
All those rivers as they flow?
Catch and keep the cranes below
When you see them on their way?

Such a dream is idle play,
Only fools would have it so:
Would you stay what flies away?
All those rivers as they flow?

Let the time pass with the day,
Just as Fortune would bestow,
And the future have its say,
Since to that no man says no.
Would you stay what flies away?

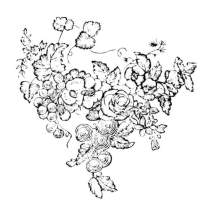

Ballade

Bien moustrez, printemps gracieux,
De quel mestier savez servir,
Car hiver fait cuers ennuieux
Et vous les faites resjouir;
Si tost comme il vous voit venir,
Lui et sa meschant retenue
Sont contrains et prestz de fuir
A vostre joyeuse venue.

Hiver fait champs et arbres vieux,
Leurs barbes de neige blanchir,
Et est so froit, ort et pluieux
Qu'emprés le feu couvient croupir.
On ne peut hors des huis issir,
Comme un oiseau qui est en mue;
Mais vous faites tout rajeunir
A vostre joyeuse venue.

Hiver fait le soleil, es cieux,
Du manteau des nues couvrir;
Or maintenant, loué soit Dieux,
Vous estes venue esclercir
Toutes choses et embellir;
Hiver a sa peine perdue,
Car l'an nouveau l'a fait bannir
A vostre joyeuse venue.

Ballade

GRACIOUS Springtime, well you know
How your handicraft to ply:
Winter maketh hearts beat slow
You are swift to gratify;
When he sees you coming by,
He and his fell retinue
Soon in haste are forced to fly
From your joyous rendezvous.

Winter ageth all with snow,
Bearded trees and fields comply;
Cold as rain and mud is, so
Close the fire we huddle nigh.
Less than moulting birds can fly
Mankind out of doors may go.
All that's young you glorify
At your joyous rendezvous.

Winter hides the sun below
Mantle of a cloudy sky,
Yet may God be praised! for lo,
You come shining from on high,
Every grace to multiply.
Lost is all the Winter's woe
Since the new year made him die
For your joyous rendezvous.

François Villon

1431 - 1465?

Ballade (L'épitaphe Villon)

FRERES humains, qui apres nous vivez,
N'ayez les cuers contre nous endurcis,
Car, se pitié de nous povres avez,
Dieu en aura plus tost de vous mercis.
Vous nous voiez cy atachez cinq sis,
Quant de la chair, que trop avons nourrie,
Elle est pieça devorée et pourrie,
Et nous, les os, devenons cendre et pouldre.
De nostre mal personne ne s'en rie,
Mais priez Dieu que tous nous vueille absouldre!

Se vous clamons freres, pas n'en devez
Avoir desdaing, quoy que fusmes occis
Par justice. Toutesfois, vous sçavez
Que tous hommes n'ont pas bon sens assis;
Excusez nous puis que sommes transsis,
Envers le filz de la Vierge Marie,
Que sa grace ne soit pour nous tarie,
Nous preservant de l'infernale fouldre.
Nous sommes mors, ame ne nous harie;
Mais priez Dieu que tous nous vueille absouldre!

La pluye nous a debuez et lavez,
Et le soleil dessechié et noircis;
Pies, corbeaulx, nous ont les yeux cavez,
Et arrachié la barbe et les sourcis.
Jamais nul temps nous ne sommes rassis;
Puis ça, puis là, comme le vent varie,
A son plaisir sans cesser nous charie,
Plus becquetez d'oiseaulx que dez à couldre.
Ne soiez donc de nostre confrairie,
Mais priez Dieu que tous nous vueille absouldre!

François Villon

1431 - 1465?

Villon's epitaph (The ballade of the hanged)

My brother men who after us live on,
Let not your hearts be hard to us; forbear!
The sooner for us wretches pity is shown,
The sooner therefore God for you will care.
You see some five or six of us hang here;
As to the flesh, in life we did not spare
To fatten that to rot for birds to tear,
Till we, these bones, to dust and ashes fall.
Let no one laugh at what we had to bear,
But pray to God that He forgive us all.

If now we call you brothers, don't take on,
Although we came to dangle in the air,
For after all, you know not every man
Is blessed with such good judgment as you were.
Now that we're gone, just offer up a prayer
Of intercession to the Virgin's son,
That of His grace our souls may not despair,
But He may shield us from the storms of hell.
For we are dead; your vain molesting spare,
But pray to God that He forgive us all.

The rain has washed and scoured us, and the sun
Has made what's left of us all black and sere;
Magpies and crows our eyes have feasted on
And plucked our beards and even eyebrows bare.
Never a respite from some scavenger;
With every changing wind blown here and there,
The birds have pecked at us till we are more
Pitted than thimbles in the interval.
That you may never join us, then, take care;
But pray to God that He forgive us all.

Prince Jhesus, qui sur tous a maistrie,
Garde qu'Enfer n'ait de nous seigneurie:
A luy n'ayons que faire ne que souldre.
Hommes, icy n'a point de mocquerie,
Mais priez Dieu que tous nous vueille absouldre.

May Jesus Prince, who ruleth everywhere,
Avert the fate hell's kingdom doth prepare
That we may enter no infernal deal.
Here is no cause, men, for a mocking air;
But pray to God that He forgive us all.

Marguerite de Navarre

1492 - 1549

Epître

Si Dieu m'a Christ pour chef donné,
Fault il que je suive aultre maistre?
S'il m'a le pain vif ordonné,
Fault il du pain de mort repaistre?
S'il me veult saulver par sa dextre,
Fault il en mon bras me fier?
S'il est mon salut et mon estre,
Point n'en fault d'aultre édifier.
S'il est mon seul et sûr espoir,
Fault il avoir autre esperance?
S'il est ma force et mon pouvoir,
Fault il prandre ailleurs assurance;
Et s'il est ma perseverance,
Fault il louer ma fermeté,
Et pour une belle apparence,
Fault il laisser la sureté?
Si ma vie est en Jésus-Christ,
La fault il croire en ceste cendre?
S'il m'a donné son saint escript,
Fault il aultre doctrine prendre?
Si tel maistre me daigne apprendre,
Fault il à aultre escolle aller?
S'il me faict son vouloir entendre,
Fault il par craincte le celer?
Si Dieu me donne son enfant,
Fault il craindre à l'appeler Père?
Si le monde le me défend,
Fault il qu'à son mal j'obtempere?
Si son esprit en moy opere
Fault il son ouvraige estimer?
Non, mais Dieu, qui partout impere,
Fault en tout veoir, craindre et aymer.

Marguerite de Navarre

1492 - 1549

Epistle

If God has given me Christ for chief,
Shall I some other master need?
If He ordained the bread of life,
Must I choose bread of death for meed?
If He would save me by His strength,
Shall I in my weak arm put trust?
If He is all my being and health,
I need no other, He is best.
He being my only certain hope,
What need of other confidence?
For if to Him I may look up,
No other stay may make pretence.
If He provides my perseverance,
Why praise this fortitude as mine,
Or make a beautiful appearance,
Neglecting what alone can win?
If all my life is Jesus Christ,
Why place my faith in this poor dust?
If He has given His holy word,
What doctrine else should I hold fast?
If such a master has concurred
To teach me, why some other school?
And if He makes His wishes heard,
Should we in fear conceal them all?
If God has given me His son,
Why falter Father Him to call?
And if the world defends its sin,
Must I for this obey its will,
Or, if its spirit in me dwell,
Compound to wish its dealings well?
Not so, but God, who rules above,
In all things we must see, fear, love.

Clément Marot
1497 - 1544

De la jeune dame qui a vieil mary

Eⁿ languissant, et en grefve tristesse
Vit mon las cueur, jadis plein de liesse,
Puis que lon m'a donné Mary vieillard.
Helas pourquoy? rien ne sçait du vieil art
Qu'apprend Venus, l'amoureuse Deesse.

    Par un desir de monstrer ma prouesse
Souvent l'assaulx: mais il demande: où est ce?
Ou dort, peult estre, et mon cueur veille à part
    En languissant.

    Puis quand je veulx luy jouer de finesse,
Honte me dict: Cesse, ma fille, Cesse!
Garde t'en bien, à honneur prens esgard!
Lors je respons: Honte, allez à l'escart:
Je ne veulx pas perdre ainsi ma jeunesse
    En languissant.

Clément Marot

1497 - 1544

Of the young lady who has an old husband

LANGUISHING and weighed with heavy sadness
Lives now my heart, that once was full of gladness
Since they have given me an ancient consort.
Ah, why? He knows naught of the ancient art
Instilled by Venus, love's most sovereign goddess.
    Desiring to reveal to him my prowess,
I often scale him, but he asks: "Why this?"
Or sleeps, perchance, while wakeful is my heart,
        Languishing.
    Then when I would deceive him with some slyness,
Shame chides me with a "Cease, my girl, deny this!
Bethink thee well and take thine honor's part!"
But then again I answer, "Shame, depart!
I do not wish my wasting youth to die thus,
        Languishing."

Maurice Scève

1501? - c.1563

Dizain CCCLXXVIII
(de *Delie*)

La blanche Aurore à peine finyssoit
D'orner son chef d'or luisant et de roses,
Quand mon Esprit, qui du tout perissoit
Au fons confus de tant diverses choses,
Revint à moi soubz les Custodes closes
Pour plus me rendre envers Mort invincible.
    Mais toy qui as — toy seule — le possible
De donner heur à ma fatalité,
Tu me seras la Myrrhe incorruptible
Contre les vers de ma mortalité.

Dizain CLXI
(de *Delie*)

Seul avec moy, elle avec sa partie:
Moy en ma peine, elle en sa molle couche.
Couvert d'ennuy je me voultre en l'Ortie,
Et elle nue entre ses bras se couche.
    Hà — luy indigne — il la tient, il la touche:
Elle le souffre: et, comme moins robuste,
Viole amour par ce lyen injuste
Que droict humain, et non divin, a faict.
    O saincte loy à tous, fors à moi, juste,
Tu me punys pour elle avoir meffaict!

64

Maurice Scève

1501? - c. 1563

Dizain CCCLXXVIII
(from *Delie*)

WHITE dawn had scarcely decked her head
With gleaming gold and roses when
My spirit, which before was dead,
Confounded by the ways of men,
Returned beneath the curtains drawn,
Its life the more inviolate.
    But you alone, who on my fate
Possess the power to lavish joy,
Will be for me the myrrh too sweet
For worms to blemish or destroy.

Dizain CLXI
(from *Delie*)

I ALL alone, she sleeping with her mate,
I painfully, she pleasantly bestead:
Covered with stings, I wallow profligate
In nettles, she naked with him lies wed.
    Not fit to touch her he, less hold in bed:
Thus suffering him and being the weaker, she
Violates love, by wrong bonds made unfree:
A human right, perhaps—no way divine.
    O holy law, most just to all but me,
You punish me in payment for her sin!

Dizain XLI
(de *Delie*)

Le veoir, l'ouyr, le parler, le toucher
Finoient le but de mon contentement,
Tant que le bien, qu'Amantz ont sur tout cher,
N'eust oncques lieu en nostre accointement.
    Que m'a valu d'aymer honnestement
En saincte amour chastement esperdu?
Puis que m'en est le mal pour bien rendu,
Et qu'on me peult pour vice reprocher
Qu'en bien aymant j'ay promptement perdu
La veoir, l'ouyr, luy parler, la toucher.

Dizain CCCLXVII
(de *Delie*)

Asses plus long, qu'un Siecle Platonique
Me fut le moys, que sans toy suis esté:
Mais quand ton front je revy pacifique,
Sejour treshault de toute honnesteté,
Où l'empire est du conseil arresté,
Mes songes lors je creus estre devins,
    Car en mon corps, mon Ame, tu revins,
Sentant ses mains, mains celestement blanches,
Avec leurs bras mortellement divins
L'un coronner mon col, l'aultre mes hanches.

Dizain XLI
(from *Delie*)

ONLY to see, to hear, to speak, to touch:
No other consummation fed my flame;
So that for me the bliss was never such
As lovers always make their vaunted aim.
　　How does it profit to forego such claim
Or purchase chastity at such a cost,
Since for this good I'm offered ill at most,
And it can be imputed as so much
Folly that, loving thus, I promptly lost
The right to see, hear, speak to her, and touch.

Dizain CCCLXVII
(from *Delie*)

THE month I've been without you stretched between
With time to fill a whole Platonic Year;
But when I saw again your brow serene,
High dwelling place of all that's most sincere,
Where sovereignty is held in wisdom's care,
I thought my dreams had truthfully divined.
　　For to my body you, my Soul, returned,
Feeling her hands, as white as from the skies,
And then her arms divine, of mortals spawned,
One garlanding my neck and one my thighs.

Dizain CCCCXLII
(de *Delie*)

POURROIT donc bien — non que je le demande —
Un Dieu causer ce vivre tant amer?
Tant de travaulx en une erreur si grande,
Où nous vivons librement pour aymer?
     O ce seroit grandement blasphemer
Contre les Dieux, pur intellect des Cieulx!
Amour si sainct, et non point vicieux,
Du temps nous poulse à eternité telle,
Que de la Terre au Ciel delicieux
Nous oste à Mort pour la vie immortelle.

Dizain CCCCXLII
(from *Delie*)

COULD it have been—not that I would insist—
A God who caused such bitterness in life?
So much despair from one mistake so vast,
That we might love in freedom, hence with strife?
　　Oh, what vast blasphemy were this belief
Against the Gods, pure intellect of Heaven!
A love so pure, to vice so little driven,
From time projects us to eternity,
That we, lent here on earth what gods are given,
Make haste to die for immortality.

Pernette du Guillet
1520 - 1545

Dizain
(de *Rymes*)

Je te promis au soir, que pour ce jour
Je m'en irois à ton instance grande
Faire chés toy quelque peu de sejour:
Mais je ne puis... Parquoy me recommande,
Te promectant m'acquicter pour l'amande,
Non d'un seul jour, mais de toute ma vie,
Ayant tousjours de te complaire envie.
Donc te supply accepter le vouloir
De qui tu as la pensee ravie
Par tes vertus, ta grace, et ton sçavoir.

Dizain
(de *Rymes*)

A qui plus est un Amant obligé:
Ou à Amour, ou vrayement à sa Dame?
Car son service est par eulx redigé
Au ranc de ceulx qui ayment los, et fame.
        A luy il doibt le cueur, à elle l'Ame:
Qui est autant comme à tous deux la vie:
L'un à l'honneur, l'autre à bien le convie:
Et toutesfois voicy un tresgrand poinct,
Lequel me rend ma pensee assouvie:
C'est que sans Dame Amour ne seroit point.

Pernette du Guillet

1520 - 1545

Dizain
(from *Rymes*)

YESTERDAY evening I said that I would stay
A little while, at your request, with you,
And promised we would make it be today:
And now I can't; but if you should pursue
That hope, I could arrange to make it true,
Not for a single day but for my life,
Since to ensure your peace is all my strife.
I pray you, then, accept this willingness
From one whose ravished thought of you is rife
With your wide lore, your virtues, and your grace.

Dizain
(from *Rymes*)

WHAT is it that a lover should put first?
Is it his love or she who lit the flame?
For those that ask would have us all coerced
To join the ranks who worship praise and fame.
　　To love he owes his heart, soul to his dame,
Which means he owes to both of them his life:
For honor one, and one for joy made safe.
Yet there is one point never hard to prove,
Which sets my doubt at rest about this strife:
Without the Lady there would be no Love.

71

Qui dira ma robe fourrée…

Qui dira ma robe fourrée
De la belle pluye dorée
Qui Daphnes enclose esbranla:
Je ne sçay rien moins, que celà.
　　Qui dira qu'à plusieurs je tens
Pour en avoir mon passetemps,
Prenant mon plaisir çà et là:
Je ne sçay rien moins que celà.
　　Qui dira que t'ay revelé
Le feu long temps en moy celé
Pour en toy veoir si force il a:
Je ne sçay rien moins, que celà.
　　Qui dira que, d'ardeur commune
Qui les Jeunes gentz importune,
De toy je veulx… et puis holà!
Je ne sçay rien moins que celà,
　　　　Mais qui dira, que la Vertu,
Dont tu es richement vestu,
En ton amour m'estincellà:
Je ne sçay rien mieulx, que celà.
　　　　Mais qui dira que d'amour saincte
Chastement au cueur suis attaincte,
Qui mon honneur onc ne foulà:
Je ne sçay rien mieulx, que celà.

If they say my dress is lined...

Iғ they say my dress is lined
With the gold rained down to find
Captive Danaë* below
Nothing of all that I know.

If they say I share my leisure
With the ones who give me pleasure
Anywhere the fun may flow,
That is what I wouldn't know.

If they say I have revealed
Want for you so long concealed,
Trying if it worked for you,
None of this they ever knew.

If they say all youth must burn
With the passion that I yearn
You will share... Ah! let it go!
This I never ask to know.

But if now they say the good
Wherewith you are richly clad
Lit a spark in me also,
Nothing better would I know.

Then if they can find no stain
On my honor for the pain
Suffered when love struck me low,
That's the best thing I could know.

*Pernette had the right idea, wrong girl.

73

Combien de foy ai je en moy souhaicté...

COMBIEN de foy ai je en moy souhaicté
Me rencontrer sur la chaleur d'esté
Tout au plus pres de la clere fontaine,
Où mon desir avec cil se pourmaine
Qui exercite en sa philosophie
Son gent esprit, duquel tant je me fie,
Que ne craindrois, sans aucune maignie,
De me trouver seule en sa compaignie:
Que dy je: seule? ains bien accompaignee
D'honnesteté, que Vertu a gaignee
A Apollo, Muses et Nymphes maintes,
Ne s'adonnantz qu'à toutes œuvres sainctes.
    Là quand j'aurois bien au long veu son cours,
Je le lairrois faire appart ses discours:
Puis peu à peu de luy m'escarterois,
Et toute nue en l'eau me gecterois:
Mais je vouldrois lors quant, et quant avoir
Mon petit Luth accordé au debvoir,
Duquel ayant congneu, et pris le son,
J'entonnerois sur luy une chanson
Pour un peu veoir quelz gestes il tiendroit:
Mais si vers moy il s'en venoit tout droict,
Je le lairrois hardyment approcher:
Et, s'il vouloit, tant soit peu, me toucher,
Lui gecterois — pour le moins — ma main pleine
De la pure eau de la clere fontaine,
Lui gectant droict aux yeulx ou à la face.
    O qu'alors eust l'onde telle efficace
De le pouvoir en Acteon muer,
Non toutesfois pour le faire tuer,
Et devorer à ses chiens, comme Cerf:
Mais que de moy se sentist estre serf,
Et serviteur transformé tellement
Qu'ainsi cuydast en son entendement,
Tant que Dyane en eust sur moy envie,
De luy avoir sa puissance ravie.

How often have I nourished...

How often have I nourished in my heart
The thought of meeting in a place apart,
Beside a fountain, some warm summer day,
The one with whom my fancy's wont to stray.
There to philosophizing he's inclined,
This gallant spirit, who inspires my mind
With perfect trust, such that I'd never fear
To be alone with him, no servant near.
Why say "alone", so well accompanied
By probity, a virtue credited
To god Apollo, Muses, nymphs galore,
All dedicated to the sacred lore.
 There as I watch him, hidden from his sight,
I let him spout the verses he would write:
Little by little, having drawn aside,
Into the water naked would I glide,
Then gradually contrive to make my lute
Accompany my discourse, note for note,
And having tuned the music to belong,
Pour out on him an unexpected song,
Intent to see what he would do exactly;
For if perchance he came toward me directly,
I would allow him boldly to approach
And even (if so minded) slightly touch.
Though I would throw a handful, at the least,
Of water from the fountain till he ceased,
Squirting it straight into his eyes or face.
 What if the water reenact the case
Of poor Actaeon, moulting all his skin,
Without, of course, the power to finish him,
Or have him, like a stag, devoured by hounds?
No, but with his lordly mind fast bound,
I'd cause that he would feel to be my serf—
At least that he should be transformed enough
To turn Diana's disposition sour,
Finding me steal the secret of her power.

Combien heureuse, et grande me dirois!
Certes Deesse estre me cuyderois.
Mais, pour me veoir contente à mon desir,
Vouldrois je bien faire un tel deplaisir
A Apollo, et aussi à ses Muses,
De les laisser privees, et confuses
D'un, qui les peult toutes servir à gré,
Et faire honneur à leur hault chœur sacré?
Ostez, ostez, mes souhaitz, si hault poinct
D'avecques vous: il ne m'appartient point.
Laissez le aller, les neuf Muses servir,
Sans le vouloir dessoubz moy asservir,
Soubz moy, qui suis sans grace, et sans merite.
Laissez le aller, qu'Apollo je ne irrite,
Le remplissant de Deité profonde,
Pour contre moy susciter tout le Monde,
Lequel un jour par ses escriptz s'attend
D'estre avec moy et heureux, et content.

Huitain

Non que je vueille oster la liberté
A qui est né pour estre sur moy maistre:
Non que je vueille abuser de fierté,
Qui à luy humble et à tous devrois estre:
Non que je vueille à dextre, et à senestre
Le gouverner, et faire à mon plaisir:
Mais je vouldrois, pour noz deux cueurs repaistre,
Que son vouloir fust joinst à mon desir.

How grandly, how exultantly I speak,
To dream myself a goddess for his sake!
But would I, just to satisfy a mood,
Incur the deep displeasure of a god?
And not alone Apollo, but each Muse
Deprive of such a neophyte, confuse
One who so ministers to their desire
As to win honor for their sacred choir?

Cease, then, my wishes, to aspire above
Ambitions that your humble state behove!
Let him go serve the sacred Muses nine,
Without one thought to make his service mine,
Who lack all merit and have lapsed in grace.

Yes, let him go! Why make Apollo's face
Frown on me with Olympian majesty,
And raise against me the indignant cry
Of all posterity, that waits to dote
On me that I inspired the poems he wrote?

Huitain

Not that I ever want to crowd
His freedom, born for mastery:
Not that I want to be too proud,
Who should be humble and agree:
Not that I want, because of me,
That he should turn to left or right:
But I want both our hearts to be
Glad that his want was my delight.

Huitain
(de *Rymes*)

Là n'est besoing que plus je me soucie
Si le jour fault, ou que vienne la nuict,
Nuict hyvernale, et sans Lune obscurcie:
Car tout celà certes riens ne me nuit,
Puis que mon Jour par clarté adoulcie
M'esclaire toute, et tant, qu'à la mynuict
En mon esprit me faict appercevoir
Ce que mes yeulx ne sceurent oncques veoir.

Huitain
(from *Rymes*)

THERE is no longer need for me to care
If the day close, or when the night may fall,
A night of winter with the moon obscure.
Nothing of that can hurt me now at all,
Since my Day shone with total light and pure,
All radiance in one flashing interval
That made my soul perceive for evermore
Something my eyes had never known before.

Joachim du Bellay

1522 - 1560

Sonnet

(de *Les Regrets*)

HEUREUX qui, comme Ulysse, a fait un beau voyage,
Ou comme cestuy-là qui conquit la toison,
Et puis est retourné, plein d'usage et raison,
Vivre entre ses parents le reste de son aage!
Quand revoiray-je, helas, de mon petit village
Fumer la cheminee: et en quelle saison
Revoiray-je le clos de ma pauvre maison,
Qui m'est une province, et beaucoup d'avantage?
Plus me plaist le sejour qu'ont basty mes ayeux,
Que des palais Romains le front audacieux:
Plus que le marbre dur me plaist l'ardoise fine,
Plus mon Loyre Gaulois, que le Tybre Latin,
Plus mon petit Lyré, que le mont Palatin,
Et plus que l'air marin la doulceur Angevine.

Sonnet

(de *Les Regrets*)

MARCHER d'un grave pas, et d'un grave sourci,
Et d'un grave soubriz à chascun faire feste,
Balancer tous ses mots, respondre de la teste,
Avec un *Messer non,* ou bien un *Messer si;*
Entremesler souvent un petit *Et cosi,*
Et d'un *son Servitor* contrefaire l'honneste,
Et comme si lon eust sa part en la conqueste,
Discourir sur Florence, et sur Naples aussi:
Seigneuriser chascun d'un baisement de main,
Et suivant la façon du courtisan Romain,
Cacher sa pauvreté d'une brave apparence:
Voila de ceste Court la plus grande vertu,
Dont souvent, mal monté, mal sain, et mal vestu,
Sans barbe et sans argent, on s'en retourne en France.

Joachim du Bellay

1522 - 1560

Sonnet
(from *Les Regrets*)

HAPPY the man of Ulyssean voyage,
Or finder of a golden fleece, like Jason,
Who turns back home, with ripened skill and reason,
To live beside his parents till old age.

When shall I see again my little village,
Smoke rising from its chimneys, in what season
My humble house, surrounded with a garden,
More than a throne to me, this heritage?

More to my mind, the house of my forebears,
Than Roman villa with a front that glares;
More pleasing than hard marble, slate will do,

My Gallic Loire the Tiber will outshine,
My little Liré top the Palatine,
And softer than sea air the mild Anjou.

Sonnet
(from *Les Regrets*)

To walk sedate, raise eyebrows to impress,
And smile sedate for greetings left unsaid,
Weigh every word, incline a courteous head,
With *Ah no, Sir,* or else, *Why, yes, Sir, Yes;*

Oft with a *cosi* manage to digress,
Or a *son Servitor* appear well-bred,
And, if no siege of Naples you have led,
Discourse as if you have and they'll not guess;

To dub all ranks Milord, while kissing hands,
And, in the style of Roman courtezans,
Hide one's privation with a daring glance:

Then, from this court, the utmost gain of wealth
Would be, ill-clad, ill-mounted, ill in health,
Beardless and penniless, to regain France.

Sonnet
(de *Les Regrets*)

Tu ne me vois jamais (Pierre) que tu ne die
Que j'estudie trop, que je face l'amour,
Et que d'avoir tousjours ces livres à l'entour
Rend les yeux esblouïs et la teste eslourdie.

Mais tu ne l'entens pas ! car ceste maladie
Ne me vient du trop lire ou du trop long sejour,
Ains de voir le bureau, qui se tient chascun jour:
C'est, Pierre mon amy, le livre ou j'estudie.

Ne m'en parle donc plus, autant que tu as cher
De me donner plaisir et de ne me fascher:
Mais bien en ce pendant que d'une main habile

Tu me laves la barbe et me tonds les cheveulx,
Pour me desennuyer, conte moy, si tu veulx,
Des nouvelles du Pape et du bruit de la ville.

Sonnet
(from *Les Regrets*)

You never see me Peter,* but you're harping still
On how I read instead of making love,
How worming in these books makes victims of
My heavy head and eyes that grow more dull.

But you don't understand. This pitiful
Disorder's not from books, nor does it prove
I rust indoors, dear Peter; nay, I move
Much among folk—a book I read too well.

So don't keep on about this matter; since
You wish to please me and not give offence,
Just do what suits you best to cheer me up:

Like, while you trim my hair and wash my beard,
To chat the way you like of what you've heard,
Talk of the town and ailments of the Pope.

*Putative name of the poet's Roman barber.

Sonnet
(de *Les Regrets*)

Las où est maintenant ce mespris de Fortune?
Où est ce cœur vainqueur de toute adversité,
Cest honneste desir de l'immortalité,
Et ceste honneste flamme au peuple non commune?
    Où sont ces doulx plaisirs, qu'au soir soubs la nuict brune
Les Muses me donnoient, alors qu'en liberté
Dessus le verd tapy d'un rivage esquarté
Je les menois danser aux rayons de la Lune?
    Maintenant la Fortune est maistresse de moy,
Et mon cœur qui souloit estre maistre de soy,
Est serf de mille maux et regrets qui m'ennuyent.
    De la posterité je n'ay plus de souci,
Ceste divine ardeur, je ne l'ay plus aussi,
Et les Muses de moy, comme estranges, s'enfuyent.

Sonnet
(de *L'Olive*)

Si nostre vie est moins qu'une journée
En l'eternel, si l'an qui faict le tour
Chasse noz jours sans espoir de retour,
Si perissable est toute chose née,
        Que songes-tu, mon ame emprisonnée?
Pourquoy te plaist l'obscur de nostre jour,
Si, pour voler en un plus cler sejour,
Tu as au dos l'aele bien empanée?
        Là, est le bien que tout esprit desire,
Là, le repos où tout le monde aspire,
Là, est l'amour, là, le plaisir encore.
        Là, ō mon ame, au plus hault ciel guidée,
Tu y pouras recongnoistre l'Idée
De la beauté qu'en ce monde j'adore.

Sonnet
(from *Les Regrets*)

ALAS! where now is that contempt of Fate?
That heart which conquers all adversity,
The seemly love of immortality,
And that true flame for which the people wait?
　　Where those sweet joys beneath the shade of night
The Muses gave me when, with fancy free,
On a green sward secluded near the sea,
I led their dances by the pale moonlight?
　　Now Fate has gained the mastery of me,
Until my heart, that would her master be,
Must serve a thousand pangs and qualms a day.
　　For my posterity I do not care,
Of sacred rage no longer I'm aware:
Like strangers now the Muses fly away.

Sonnet
(from *L'Olive*)

IF life on earth for us is less than a day
In the eternal, and the revolving year
Bears off our days never to reappear,
If nothing that is born can ever stay,
　　Why drowse, imprisoned soul, in this delay?
Why does the darkness of our atmosphere
Please you if there are wings provided here
And fastened on your back to fly away?
　　Yonder the joy that spirits all desire,
Yonder repose to which all men aspire,
Pleasure is yonder, love you thought had flown;
　　Led yonder to highest heaven, O my soul,
You will attain to know the pure Ideal
Of beauty which in this world I enthrone.

D'un vanneur de blé, aux vents
(du latin de Naugérius)

O vous, trope légère,
Qui d'aile passagère
Par le monde volez,
Et d'un sifflant murmure
L'ombrageuse verdure
Doucement ébranlez,

    J'offre ces violettes,
Ces lis et ces fleurettes,
Et ces roses ici,
Ces vermeillettes roses,
Tout fraîchement écloses,
Et ces oeillets aussi.

    De votre douce haleine
Eventez cette plaine,
Eventez ce séjour:
Ce pendant que j'ahanne
A mon blé, que je vanne
A la chaleur du jour.

From a winnower of corn to the winds
(from the Latin of Naugerius)

To you, airy array,
Who pass winging your way,
Over the world below,
And with a rustling noise,
Whisper among the boughs
And stir them where you blow,

I offer these violets,
Lilies and flowerets,
And roses here for you,
Roses pink to crimson,
Fresh blossoms in profusion,
And these carnations too.

With soft breath fan this plain,
And let your breath sustain
This farmstead where we stay,
I toiling at my corn
To winnow it since morn,
All through the heat of day.

Pierre de Ronsard

1524 - 1585

Amours de Marie (VI)

Douce, belle, amoureuse et bien-fleurante Rose,
Que tu es à bon droit aux amours consacrée!
Ta delicate odeur hommes et Dieux recrée,
Et bref, Rose, tu es belle sur toute chose.

Marie pour son chef un beau bouquet compose
De ta fueille, et tousjours sa teste en est parée;
Tousjours ceste Angevine, unique Cytherée,
Du parfum de ton eau sa jeune face arrose.

Hà Dieu! que je suis aise alors que je te voy
Esclore au poinct du jour sur l'espine à requoy,
Aux jardins de Bourgueil, pres d'une eau solitaire!

De toy les Nymphes ont les coudes et le sein,
De toy l'Aurore emprunte et sa joüe et sa main,
Et son teint la beauté qu'on adore en Cythere.

Continuation des amours

Je vous envoye un bouquet, que ma main
Vient de tirer de ces fleurs épanies;
Qui ne les eust à ce vespre cueillies,
Cheutes à terre elles fussent demain.

Cela vous soit un exemple certain,
Que vos beautez, bien qu'elles soient fleuries,
En peu de tems cherront toutes fletries,
Et, comme fleurs, periront tout soudain.

Le tems s'en va, le tems s'en va, ma Dame,
Las! le tems non, mais nous nous en allons,
Et tost serons estendus sous la lame,

Et des amours, desquelles nous parlons,
Quand serons morts, n'en sera plus nouvelle:
Pource aimez moy, cependant qu'estes belle.

Pierre de Ronsard

1524 - 1585

Loves of Mary (VI)

SOFT, fair, and amorous, sweet-smelling rose,
How right it is that you belong to love!
Your scent restores men here and gods above;
In short, you are the fairest thing that grows.

Let Mary for her head a crown compose
Of rose leaves, that her fair hair interwove,
This Cytherean Angevin to lave
With perfumed water, sprinkled where she goes.

Dear God, the joy to me when you are born
At break of day, hidden behind a thorn,
Within a Borgueil garden by still water!

From you the nymphs obtain their elbows and
Their breast, from you the Dawn her cheek, her hand,
And skin of that high Cytherean daughter.

Continuation of loves

I SEND you a bouquet which, if my hand
Had not this evening gathered it fullblown,
Tomorrow would be petals fallen down,
To lie there withering upon the ground.

And therein may a lesson sure be found
To prove your beauties, lovely as they've grown,
Must in a little while lose their renown
And, like the flowers, reach a sudden end.

The time goes by, the time will soon be gone:
Alas! 'tis not the time, for it is we,
My Lady, soon will lie beneath the stone,

And loves we tell about so willingly
When we are dead will be no news at all:
Give me your love, then, while still beautiful.

Sonnets pour Helene (XLII)

Ces longues nuicts d'hyver, où la Lune ocieuse
Tourne si lentement son char tout à l'entour,
Où le coq si tardif nous annonce le jour,
Où la nuict semble un an à l'ame soucieuse,
      Je fusse mort d'ennuy sans ta forme douteuse,
Qui vient par une feinte alleger mon amour,
Et faisant toute nue entre mes bras sejour,
Me pipe doucement d'une joye menteuse.
      Vraye tu es farouche, et fiere en cruauté.
De toy fausse on jouyst en toute privauté.
Pres ton mort je m'endors, pres de luy je repose:
      Rien ne m'est refusé. Le bon sommeil ainsi
Abuse par le faux mon amoureux souci.
S'abuser en amour n'est pas mauvaise chose.

Sonnets pour Helene (XLIII)

Quand vous serez bien vieille, au soir, à la chandelle,
Assise auprès du feu, dévidant en filant,
Direz, chantant mes vers, en vous esmerveillant:
"Ronsard me celebroit du temps que j'estois belle."
      Lors vous n'aurez servante oyant telle nouvelle,
Desja sous le labeur à demy sommeillant,
Qui au bruit de mon nom ne s'aille resveillant,
Benissant vostre nom de louange immortelle.
      Je seray sous la terre, et fantôme sans os
Par les ombres myrteux je prendray mon repos;
Vous serez au fouyer une vieille accroupie,
      Regrettant mon amour et vostre fier desdain.
Vivez, si m'en croyez, n'attendez à demain:
Cueillez dés aujourdhuy les roses de la vie.

Sonnets for Helen (XLII)

THOSE endless Winter nights when the moon reined
Her car with languor round the usual way,
When late the cock announced the coming day,
And night would last a year for the troubled mind,
   I died with longing for your undefined
Dream shape, which came to soothe my love in play
And, naked in my arms while she would stay,
Piped softly all the lies for which I pined.
   In real life you are cruel, fierce, and proud.
Your phantom every secret joy allowed.
The real you dead, this phantom helped me sleep.
   Nothing was banned. The best repose deceived
My dreams with bliss I could not have believed.
To be deceived in love let none hold cheap.

Sonnets for Helen (XLIII)

WHEN you are old and sitting by the fire,
The candle lit at nightfall for your weaving,
You'll say, singing my verses, scarcely believing:
"Ronsard wrote this of me when I was fair."
   Then you will have no servant unaware,
Though she be half asleep with all her slaving,
It was in truth my name she just heard leaving
Your lips, and she will bless that deathless air.
   Beneath the earth, an unsubstantial ghost
Among the myrtles, I shall take my rest;
You, crouched beside the fire, an ancient crone,
   Will mourn my love at last and your disdain.
Believe me, live—tomorrow comes in vain:
Gather today the rose so quickly blown.

Sonnets pour Helene (XLIX)

LE soir qu'Amour vous fist en la salle descendre
Pour danser d'artifice un beau ballet d'Amour,
Vos yeux, bien qu'il fust nuict, ramenerent le jour,
Tant ils sceurent d'esclairs par la place respandre.

Le ballet fut divin, qui se souloit reprendre,
Se rompre, se refaire, et tour dessus retour
Se mesler, s'escarter, se tourner à l'entour,
Contre-imitant le cours du fleuve de Meandre.

Ores il estoit rond, ores long, or' estroit,
Or' en poincte, en triangle en la façon qu'on voit
L'escadron de la Gruë evitant la froidure.

Je faux, tu ne dansois, mais ton pied voletoit
Sur le haut de la terre; aussi ton corps s'estoit
Transformé pour ce soir en divine nature.

Amours de Cassandre (XI)

AH! traistre Amour, donne moy paix ou trêve,
Ou choisissant un autre trait plus fort,
Tranche ma vie, et m'avance la mort;
Douce est la mort d'autant plus qu'elle est bréve.

Un soing fecond en mon penser s'eleve,
Qui mon sang hume, et l'esprit me remord,
Et d'Ixion me fait egal au sort,
De qui jamais la peine ne s'acheve.

Que doy-je faire? Amour me fait errer
Si hautement, que je n'ose esperer
De mon salut qu'une langueur extréme.

Puis que mon Dieu ne me veut secourir,
Pour me sauver il me plaist de mourir,
Et de tuer la mort par la mort mesme.

Sonnets for Helen (XLIX)

THAT evening when Love brought you down to the hall
To dance so well a perfect love ballet,
Your eyes, though it was night, brought back the day
By shedding all that light upon us all.
The ballet was divine, each interval:
The linking, breaking back and drawing away,
The mingling, circling, lingering delay,
As though Meander were a madrigal.
Now it was round, now narrow, long and straight,
Triangular, or shaping like a flight
Southward of cranes that flee the cold in line.
Oh, I am wrong, you did not dance, my sweet,
But hovered over the ground with winged feet.
Your body for that evening was divine.

Loves of Cassandra (XI)

AH! traitorous Love, truce grant me if not peace,
Or, setting me a more remorseless date,
Cut off my life, my death anticipate,
Since death's the sweeter for its quickened pace.
My fertile thought gives care a large increase
By leaching on my blood, my soul to eat,
And bind me on a wheel—Ixion's fate,
Whose endless pain could never find surcease.
What can I do? Love draws me to an air
So perilously thin I would not dare
To hope for any but a languid health.
Since God will not consent to help me, I
Must save myself, contented thus to die
And kill this death in life by death itself.

Amours de Cassandre (CCXXII)

QUE dites-vous, que faites-vous, mignonne?
Que songez-vous? pensez-vous point en moy?
Avez-vous point soucy de mon esmoy,
Comme de vous le soucy m'espoinçonne?
De vostre amour tout le cueur me bouillonne,
Devant mes yeux sans cesse je vous voy,
Je vous entens, absente je vous oy,
Et mon penser d'autre amour ne resonne.
J'ay vos beautez, vos graces et vos yeux
Gravez en moi, les places et les lieux,
Où je vous vy danser, parler, et rire.
Je vous tien mienne, et si ne suis pas mien,
Vous estes seule en qui mon cueur respire,
Mon œil, mon sang, mon malheur et mon bien.

A sa maistresse
(Ode XVII)

MIGNONNE, allons voir si la rose
Qui ce matin avoit desclose
Sa robe de pourpre au Soleil,
A point perdu ceste vesprée
Les plis de sa robe pourprée,
Et son teint au vostre pareil.
Las! voyez comme en peu d'espace,
Mignonne, elle a dessus la place
Las! las! ses beautez laissé cheoir!
O vrayment marastre Nature,
Puis qu'une telle fleur ne dure
Que du matin jusques au soir!
Donc, si vous me croyez, mignonne,
Tandis que vostre âge fleuronne
En sa plus verte nouveauté,
Cueillez, cueillez votre jeunesse:
Comme à ceste fleur, la vieillesse
Fera ternir vostre beauté.

Loves of Cassandra (CCXXII)

WHAT are you saying, my sweet, what do you do?
What are you dreaming? Do you think of me?
Devote one thought to my tranquillity,
When every thought of you will stab me through?
    My heart is simmering with love of you;
Your face without a break I always see;
I hear you, never mind how far you be;
There is no other love that I pursue.
    I have your beauties, graces, and your eyes
Engraved in me, the places I surmise
That you are dancing, speaking—that you smile.
    I hold you mine, and so am not my own;
Within my heart you live and breathe alone—
My eyes, my blood, my good luck and my vile.

To his mistress
(Ode XVII)

DARLING, come see if the rose
Which this morning had unclosed
Crimson garments to the sun
Has not by this evening lost
Folds that redden earliest
In the tints resembling thine.
    Hours so swift they were to pass,
Darling, ere it shed, alas!
Petals flourishing so gay!
Mother Nature's hard, for sure,
If such beauty can't endure
More than for a single day.
    Then believe me, darling, while
Youth for thee may flourish still
In its greenness, gather this,
Gather this thy heritage,
Ere yet, like the flower, old age
Wither soon thy loveliness.

Sur la mort de Marie (IV)

COMME on voit sur la branche au mois de may la rose,
En sa belle jeunesse, en sa premiere fleur,
Rendre le ciel jaloux de sa vive couleur,
Quand l'Aube de ses pleurs au poinct du jour l'arrose;
La grace dans sa fueille, et l'amour se repose,
Embasmant les jardins et les arbres d'odeur;
Mais batue ou de pluye, ou d'excessive ardeur,
Languissante elle meurt, fueille à fueille déclose.
Ainsi en ta premiere et jeune nouveauté,
Quand la Terre et le Ciel honoraient ta beauté,
La Parque t'a tuee, et cendre tu reposes.
Pour obseques reçoy mes larmes et mes pleurs,
Ce vase plein de laict, ce panier plein de fleurs,
Afin que vif et mort ton corps ne soit que roses.

Dialogue de l'autheur et du mondain

EST-CE tant que la Mort? est-ce si grand mal-heur
Que le vulgaire croit? Comme l'heure premiere
Nous faict naistre sans peine, ainsi l'heure derniere,
Qui acheve la trame, arrive sans douleur.
Mais tu ne seras plus? Et puis, quand la paleur
Qui blesmist nostre corps, sans chaleur ne lumiere,
Nous perd le sentiment! quand la main filandiere
Nous oste le desir, perdans nostre chaleur!
Tu ne mangeras plus? Je n'auray plus envie
De boire ne manger: c'est le corps qui sa vie
Par la viande allonge, et par refection.
L'esprit n'en a besoin. Venus, qui nous appelle
Aux plaisirs, te fuira? Je n'auray soucy d'elle:
Qui ne desire plus, n'a plus d'affection.

On the death of Mary (IV)

As on a branch we see the rose in May,
With all its lovely youth and blossoms new,
Making the red sky jealous of its hue,
Its petals wet with tears at break of day,
    Grace hiding in its leaves, love in the bouquet
Scenting the trees, the garden, with rose dew,
But beaten down with rain, or seared with too
Much heat, repining leaf by leaf away,
    So, in the freshness of your early youth,
Your beauty glorified by heaven and earth,
Fate withered you and in the dust disposes.
    Accept for obsequy these tears of ours,
This vase of milk, this basket full of flowers,
That you, in life and death, be only roses.

Dialogue between the author and the world

Is Death so much? Is it so great a woe
As people seem to think? Just as the first
Moment of birth was painless, so the last,
Which shall complete the plot, is likewise so.
    But you will be no more? And then, when slow
Disruption lacking heat or light, shall rust
Our limbs, we feel no more! The hands of lust
Spin out the last desire, and warmth will go!
    You'll eat no more? Then no more shall I long
To eat or drink, since what can still prolong
The lust for life, the loss of life must steal.
    The spirit needs not that. Venus, who snared
Us for these pleasures, flies? I could not care.
He who can want no more, no more can feel.

97

Ode X
(de *Second livre*)

FAY refraischir mon vin de sorte
Qu'il passe en froideur un glaçon;
Fay venir Janne, qu'elle apporte
Son luth pour dire une chanson:
Nous ballerons tous trois au son;
Et dy à Barbe qu'elle vienne,
Les cheveux tors à la façon
D'une follastre Italienne.
   Ne vois-tu que le jour se passe?
Je ne vy point au lendemain.
Page, reverse dans ma tasse,
Que ce grand verre soit tout plain.
Maudit soit qui languit en vain,
Ces vieux Medecins je n'appreuve:
Mon cerveau n'est jamais bien sain,
Si beaucoup de vin ne l'abreuve.

Les derniers vers (VI)

IL faut laisser maisons et vergers et jardins,
Vaisselles et vaisseaux que l'artisan burine,
Et chanter son obseque en la façon du Cygne
Qui chante son trespas sur les bors Mæandrins.
   C'est fait, j'ay devidé le cours de mes destins,
J'ay vescu, j'ay rendu mon nom assez insigne:
Ma plume vol au Ciel pour estre quelque signe,
Loin des appas mondains qui trompent les plus fins.
   Heureux qui ne fut onc, plus heureux qui retourne
En rien comme il estoit, plus heureux qui sejourne,
D'homme, fait nouvel ange, au pres de Jesus-Christ,
   Laissant pourrir çà-bas sa despouille de boüe,
Dont le Sort, la Fortune, et le Destin se joüe,
Franc des liens du corps pour n'estre qu'un esprit.

Ode X
(from *Second livre*)

HAVE my wine be chilled to suit,
Colder than an icicle;
Have Joan come and bring her lute
To perform a canticle:
We shall dance, all three, and tell
Barbara too we'll wait for her,
Hair done in the braided style
Wild Italian girls prefer.
    Don't you note the passing time?
Tomorrow doesn't interest me.
Come, page, fill it to the brim,
Taller let the glasses be.
Curse on languid vanity
Senile doctors deem benign:
Mine's a brain with sanity
Only when awash with wine.

Last verses (VI)

HOMES, orchards, gardens, it is time to leave,
Vessels and vases graved by the artisan,
Time now to sing one's passing, as the swan
Sings its own death beside Meander's wave.
    It's over now, my raveled fate I leave,
I've lived and flourished with enough renown:
My quill, to flash a sign in heaven, has flown
Far from the lures most subtle to deceive.
    Happy who never was, happier who returns
To nothing again, happiest who sojourns,
Transformed from man to angel, close to Christ,
    Leaving to rot below his body of clay,
The sport of luck and fate, who breaks away
From bonds of flesh, to be pure spirit at last.

Louise Labé

1524 - 1566

Sonnet XII
(de *Elégies*)

OH, si j'estois en ce beau sein ravie
De celui là pour lequel vois mourant:
Si avec luy vivre le demeurant
De mes cours jours ne m'empeschoit envie:
    Si m'acollant me disoit: chere Amie,
Contentons nous l'un l'autre! s'asseurant
Que ja tempeste, Euripe, ni Courant
Ne nous pourra desjoindre en notre vie:
    Si, de mes bras le tenant acollé,
Comme du Lierre est l'arbre encercelé,
La mort venoit, de mon aise envieuse,
    Lors que, souef, plus il me baiseroit,
Et mon esprit sur ses levres fuiroit,
Bien je mourrois, plus que vivante, heureuse.

Sonnet XVII
(de *Elégies*)

BAISE m'encor, rebaise-moy et baise:
Donne m'en un de tes plus savoureux,
Donne m'en un de tes plus amoureus:
Je t'en rendray quatre plus chaus que braise.
    Las, te pleins tu? ça que ce mal j'apaise,
En t'en donnant dix autres doucereus.
Ainsi, meslans nos baisers tant heureus,
Jouissons nous l'un de l'autre à notre aise.
    Lors double vie à chacun en suivra.
Chacun en soy et son ami vivra.
Permets m'Amour penser quelque folie:
    Tousjours suis mal, vivant discrettement,
Et ne me puis donner contentement,
Si hors de moy ne fay quelque saillie.

Louise Labé

1524 - 1566

Sonnet XII
(from *Elégies*)

Oн, if I could be ravished in his breast
For whom I languish, if despiteful charms
Did not prevent me living in his arms,
So that my brief remaining days be blessed:
    If, clasping me, he said, "Belovedest,
Let us content each other, that no harms,
By stream, or Straight of Erebus, or storms,
Might cleave our lives asunder till we rest":
    If, while my arms should hold him close to me,
Even as ivy twines about a tree,
Death came because made envious by my bliss,
    While softly he would kiss me all the more,
And on his lips my fleeting spirit soar,
Gladly I'd die, since more than life were this.

Sonnet XVII
(from *Elégies*)

Kiss me again—once more, and then the refrain:
Give me the kisses that taste best to us;
Then give me one of your most amorous:
I'll come back, hotter than coals, with four again.
    There, does it hurt you? Let me soothe the pain
By giving you ten times the softest kiss.
So, mingling kisses to each other's bliss,
Let us enjoy each other's sweetest gain.
    Then there will be a double life for both,
Each loving in his own the dear one's troth.
Allow me, Love, to think a little folly:
    Living discreetly always makes me ill,
Nor can I find content in what I will,
Unless sometimes beyond myself I sally.

Sonnet VIII
(de *Elégies*)

Tout aussi tot que je commence à prendre
Dens le mol lit le repos desiré,
Mon triste esprit hors de moi retiré,
S'en va vers toi incontinent se rendre.

 Lors m'est avis que dedans mon sein tendre
Je tiens le bien, où j'ay tant aspiré,
Et pour lequel j'ay si haut souspiré
Que de sanglots ay souvent cuidé fendre.

 O dous sommeil, o nuit à moy heureuse!
Plaisant repos, plein de tranquilité,
Continuez toutes les nuiz mon songe:

 Et si jamais ma povre ame amoureuse
Ne doit avoir de bien en verité,
Faites au moins qu'elle en ait en mensonge.

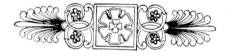

Sonnet VIII
(from *Elégies*)

As soon as I will lay me down to take
The rest I long for in my downy bed,
My restless spirit, from the body fled,
Rushes to you, who keep me wide awake.
    There it would seem, within me where I ache,
The sighs on which my tender bosom fed,
The sobs that rend me like a thunderhead,
My absent bliss dissembling, present make.
    O gentle sleep, dear dark most kind to me!
Pleasant repose alive with fictive joy,
Replenish every night these saving dreams;
    And if my yearning soul can never see
The living likeness of this fond decoy,
Let me believe the lie is what it seems.

Jean de Sponde

1557 - 1595

Qui sont, qui sont ceux-là...

Qui sont, qui sont ceux-là, dont le cœur idolâtre,
Se jette aux pieds du Monde, et flatte ses honneurs?
Et qui sont ces valets, et qui sont ces Seigneurs?
Et ces Ames d'Ebène, et ces Faces d'Albastre?

Ces masques desguisez, dont la troupe folastre,
S'amuse à caresser je ne sçay quels donneurs
De fumées de Court, et ces entrepreneurs
De vaincre encor le Ciel qu'ils ne peuvent combattre?

Qui sont ces lovayeurs qui s'esloignent du Port?
Hommagers à la Vie, et felons à la Mort,
Dont l'estoille est leur Bien, le Vent leur Fantasie?

Je vogue en mesme mer, et craindroy de perir,
Si ce n'est que je sçay que ceste mesme vie
N'est rien que le fanal qui me guide au mourir.

Jean de Sponde

1557 - 1595

Who are they, pray...

Who are they, pray, who are these parasites,
Licking the world's feet, ogling its awards?
Who are these lackeys and who are these lords—
Black souls with faces alabaster white?

These playboys dressed up for a giddy night,
Who spend their time pandering to some court bawd
And think once more their schemes have overpowered
A heaven which they are powerless to fight?

These drifters, tacking off from port afar,
Fawners on life, traitors to death, their star
Nothing but gain, their wind a fitful sigh?

I sail that sea, and if I did not know
This life of ours directs the way to die
By flashing beacons, I would dread to go.

Gabrielle de Coignard

? - 1594

Ces jours me sont si doux...

CES jours me sont si doux en ce beau lieu champêtre,
Voyant d'un fer tranchant fendre le long guéret,
Et enterrer le blé jaunissant, pur et net,
Puis le voir tôt après tout verdoyant renaître.
Mon Dieu, le grand plaisir de voir sur l'herbe paître
La frisée brebis portant son agnelet,
Et le cornu bélier, qui marche tout seulet
Au devant du troupeau, comme patron et maître.
L'air est délicieux, sans pluies ni chaleurs,
Un petit vent mollet fait ondoyer les fleurs,
Les bois portent encor leur superbe couronne;
      L'on n'oit point la rumeur d'un vulgaire babil,
Sinon des oiselets le ramage gentil:
Loué soit l'Eternel qui tous ces biens nous donne.

Gabrielle de Coignard

? - 1594

So sweet to me here...

So sweet to me here are these country days,
Long furrows cleft by the sharp ploughshare,
The yellow grain inserted clean and fair,
And then how soon and green it grows and sways!
    My God, the sheer delight in seeing graze
The curly ewe, big with her lamb to bear,
And the horned ram, strutting with all his flair
For lord and master, leading the flock always.
    The air's delicious, with no rain or heat;
A soft breeze makes the flowers undulate;
Again the woods don their green diadem.
    No vulgar noise of babbling can be heard,
Only the gentle warbling of a bird:
For all these gifts praised be the Eternal Name.

Lyrical Decline

The Swing, by Jean Honoré Fragonard
Courtesy of the Wallace Collection

Lyrical Decline
Seventeenth and Eighteenth Centuries

Rigor mortis of the arts tends to set in when the creative momentum conforms to acceptable arrangement of words, shapes, colors, sounds, instead of these forms responding directly to inspiration. It is true that the forms can be so drenched with borrowed light that for a space, as with organized religion, the delusively luminous prism may be transfused mistakably for the power source. But in translations, especially faithful ones, the failure of primary inspiration and consequent standardization of the medium have accentuated the visibility of the fade, thus becoming diagnostic of artifice and transience.

To infiltrate the vitals of so many different poets in order to assume the color of so many different poems requires more than a chameleon or properly sophisticated aesthete. It calls for some sort of voracious but discriminating parasite that, with the phoenix, recreates what it devours. But there has to be the life there to recreate. Translation of poetry may well be the deepest, most exact history; for poetry aspires to be contemporary expression at the highest level of which a period is capable. If the poetry being translated refuses to live again in our own poetry, this may signify some paralysis or ineptitude in what we are and what we can do, but it is quite as likely to point to something defunct or moribund in the poetry we seek to restore.

We all know about how nations rise and fall, and how the culture of a state has its bloom-tide of music, drama, the space arts. We acknowledge the ethos and élan of a period as it affects the national spirit or is affected by it. But we manage to forget that the arts can and do freeze in a country for a long time, during which the prestige of a style, while resisting transplants, may endure and even seem to flourish, in such a way that nothing very different can live in its shadow.

Now there is a certain stately rhetoric belonging to French which is virtually untransplantable to the soil of the English language, an *air*, displayed most nobly by Racine and Corneille, whose almost complete absence from this book represents no logical loss, since great as these poets were, it is the lyric strain that we are trying to decant, and the dramatic only as it enters the lyric. But after the best of the *Pléiade*, that marble rigor, which produced something of a Pygmalion act in the great French dramatists, reverts to the statuesque in the majority of French

111

poets, up to and even including one side of André Chénier (1762-1794), whom we have assigned as a forerunner of "the New Sound," in the next section.[1]

Something of the same stiltedness as is endemic with eighteenth-century poets on their dignity surfaced, at least a century earlier, in the poetry of which Malherbe's was typical, as evidenced by the hard glitter of his "Dessein de Quitter une Dame." Such poems should be translated only to expose the divergent genius of a foreign poetry, which is scarcely reason enough for them to survive abroad. Take Malherbe's "Paraphrase of the 146th Psalm," a powerful tour de force, presenting an equivocal challenge to match a magnificent artifice with a comparable weight. There might come some help from the sound and stride of one incomparable English poem, James Shirley's "Death the Leveller":

> The glories of our blood and state
> Are shadows, not substantial things;
> There is no armour against fate;
> Death lays his icy hands on kings. . . .

Here, almost rivaling Shirley, is the first stanza of Malherbe's psalm:

> N'espèrons plus, mon âme, aux promesses du monde!
> Sa lumière est un verre, et sa faveur une onde,
> Que toujours quelque vent empêche de calmer;
> Quittons ces vanités, lasson-nous de les suivre:
> C'est Dieu qui nous fait vivre,
> C'est Dieu qu'il faut aimer.

This might become:

> Rely no more, my soul, on what the world can give;
> Its light is but a glass, its favor as a wave,
> Tossed ever by some wind, doomed to eternal strife;
> Forsake these vanities and follow them no more:
> It's God we should adore,
> It's God who gives us life.

But already there's a faltering transposition in deference to the rhyme, whilst it becomes doubtful whether that clangorous stride could be sustained much longer without tedium, in any translation.

Well, come to that, it is just as much a question whether the stiff majesty of Malherbe could be any better matched in modern French than in modern English. In fact, of the two, the French by now are probably even more averse to dressing up in "the Grand Style," as it was once proudly called. By English poetry, for the last century or more, which is to say, since the influence of Wordsworth was felt, that lordly gait and panoply would almost invariably be rejected to favor "language of real men in a state of vivid sensation"; and by French poetry, since Voltaire at least, to favor the dry light of a logical lucidity.

Few reputations can have been higher than that of Malherbe, of whom no less a critic than Boileau said, "Enfin Malherbe vint," ("finally came Malherbe") a pronunciamento with the same assurance and finality as Samuel Johnson's concerning the matching supremacy of Pope for his age: "If Mr. Pope be not a poet, I know not where poetry may be found."[2] These are comfortless reminders that lyricism, together with the recognition of it, may and does curl up and die, without knowing it, for a whole century, during which a book with the title of this one would find precious little that sings in French, hence even less in translation. The same is true of English poetry throughout an almost identical period, that is, in the period between Andrew Marvell and William Collins, when Davenport's dreary adaptations were invariably preferred to the way Shakespeare wrote his plays. We should be the less surprised by such prolonged lapses in taste and passion, who, in the mid-twentieth century, are undergoing a similar decline of melody in poetry. It is better to leave "cuts" in our selection that are half a century long or worse (Viau to Thomas to Chénier) than simulate a lyricism which isn't there.

In case it is thought we are drawing too much discouragement from a single poem by Malherbe, I shall advance, pretty much at random, one more magniloquent poem of the period and species which, in translation, fails, and, according to this contention, must be expected to fail. It is the poem by Jean Ogier de Gombaul (1570-1666) which Walter Savage Landor, in an "Imaginary Conversation," singled out as being, though a sonnet, the "best ode in the language." Here it is, complete with original spelling:

> La voix qui retentit de l'vn à autre Pole,
> La terreur & l'espoir des viuans & des morts,
> Qui du rien sçait tirer les esprits & les corps
> Et qui fit l'Uniuers, d'vne seule parole:
>   La voix du Souuerain, qui les cedres desolé,
> Cependant que l'espine estale ses trésors;
> Qui contre la cabane espargne ses efforts,

Et réduit à neant l'orgueil du Capitole:
Ce tonnerre esclatant, cette diuine voix,
A qui sçavent respondre & les monts, & les bois,
Et qui fait qu'à leur fin toutes choses se rendent.
Que les Cieux les plus hauts, que les lieux les plus bas,
Que ceux qui ne sont point, & que les morts entendent,
Mon âme, elle t'appelle, & tu ne l'entens pas.

The best that I could do with this masterpiece would have to sound like something on this order, even when it were better done:

The voice reverberating pole to pole,
The hope and terror of the quick and the dead,
Creating body and soul, with one word said,
From nothing made the universe unroll:
Voice of the Lord, that makes the cedars fall
And flaunts the treasures of the thorn instead,
Spares the mean hut and brings the vaunted head
Of state to nothing in the Capitol:
The echoing thunder of God's voice will sound
Till every mountain and the woods resound,
Directing all things to their proper end.
Voice heard by highest heaven and deepest hell
The dead and unbegotten comprehend;
It calls you, yet you hear not, O my soul.

Although not all of the sonority is gone from the translation, the sound of the lines in English betrays the same sense of artifice as Keats tried to escape in the second *Hyperion*, when he asked his friend Reynolds to place an "X" beside the lines with the "Miltonic, Latinized intonation," and added characteristically, "English must be kept up."[3] But more discouragingly, the translated *piety* betrays the artifice of the original, now felt more uncomfortably. "The voice of God" becomes stentorian with a megaphone, whilst the soul's deafness to it, instead of being resoundingly contumacious, as Gombaul clearly intended, might be little more than the stalwart refusal to be brow-beaten by monarchical or presidential prerogatives.

It was because the intensity of the sixteenth and early seventeenth century was gradually cooling that the progress of the Muse towards and into the Age of Reason worked such hardships on lyrical poetry. It can bear to be said again: as it was in France, so it was in England; and so it is in the last half of the twentieth century for both, and even more for America. In each case, almost imperceptibly until we are well into it, we see coming closer an age of prose—an age in which Condorcet was a better philosopher and mathematician than J.-B. Rousseau was a thrush, or J.-F. Ducis an adapter of Shakespeare, although perhaps we should acknowledge in Ducis something of the same hardihood, at least, as possessed Davenport, his English counterpart in self-confidence.

Now it is not quite enough to write off whole stretches of a great nation's poetry as predisposed to be less than lyrical in translation, or to discount such stretches as exhibiting primarily qualities of poetic malnutrition or overweight, unless we also make some show of going behind style to the "Spirit of the Forms," and asking some more questions concerning typical originals and what happens to them in transit.

A difficulty occurs right away, in that the two main movements that we have to consider seem on the surface to run counter to each other. One is the baroque; and the other, *préciosité:* the first being moist, heavy, and gorgeous; the second, dry, light, and pretty. It is as though we were asking Poussin and Watteau to keep joint house, before making light of them both. But in poetry, it is something like this that happened. At least we may say that the two tendencies, besides overlapping in time, both suffered from a parallel lapse of directness in their inspiration, a comparable rule of a school, code of a mode.

In each case, deeper than the formal difficulties confronting a translator lies the spirit of the age. In the seventeenth century, religion, or rather, Christianity, (except for those saints and mystics who earn the right to be luminously articulate) became more a cloud than an illumination, whilst as we move into the eighteenth century, religion began to lose its grip on poetry altogether, which turned from the cloister to the salon.

In the seventeenth century, the baroque, which achieved such splendors in music, did not fare so well by the morbidities to which the language of words is prone. Imagine a reader of the seventeenth century, reading the following all too typical lines by the Catholic poet, Jean de la Ceppède:

> . . .O Christ, ô Saint Agneau, daigne-toi de cacher
> Tous mes rouges péchés, brindelles des abîmes,
> Dans les sanglants replis du manteau de ta chair.

> . . .O Christ, O Holy Lamb, hide my red sins,
> As faggots to ignite the fires of hell,
> Within the bleeding mantle of your flesh.

And then these by the Protestant poet, Agrippa d'Aubigné:

> . . .Tu as tout l'univers, où ta gloire on contemple,
> Pour marche pied la terre et le ciel pour un temple:
> Où te chassera l'homme, ô Dieu victorieux?
> Tu possèdes le ciel et les cieux des hauts cieux!

> . . .Thou hast the universe thy fame to greet;
> Heaven is thy temple, the world beneath thy feet:
> Whither shall men pursue thee, God of victory,
> When heavens above heavens blaze thy glory!

Let us assume that this reader would be undisturbed by the lyrical decline here evinced. Then he might also be expected to be oblivious that both poets were under hypnosis to fanatical doctrines, whether of Substitutionary Atonement, or of the monarchical First Person of the Trinity; but he would have understood without the slightest difficulty that the poetic gift of neither might have inhibited him from countenancing death by torture for the heresy of the other.

Do we never escape, then, from the twang of these rather bloody-minded conventicles? Certainly, but not very often. We are scarcely to expect an entire period to be totally excluded from the two avenues by which the lyric may escape from *odium theologicum* and the rigid mold. These avenues are opened by the instinct for simple devotion and that for the sublime, respectively.

The first of these, which in England spoke a little earlier by George Herbert (1593-1633), has counterparts for France, after the sweetbrier quality of Gabrielle de Coignard, in a few surviving poems of Paul Pellison-Fontanier (1624-1693). Here is the last of three "Stanzas" of a prayer, which if given complete, might fail to support the refrain.

> Qui vous mène à la mer, belles et claires ondes?
>   Et vous, charmantes fleurs,
> Où prenez-vous cet ambre et ces tiges fécondes,
> Et ce divers feuillage et ces riches couleurs?
> Arbres, fleurs et ruisseaux, dévote solitude,
> Vous m'en dites assez pour des siècles d'étude.

Clear, beauteous waves, who leads you where you break?
And you, enchanting flowers,
Whence came that amber and that fecund stalk,
Those varied leaves, the colors that are yours?
Trees, flowers, and streams, secluded in devotion,
You speak whole centuries worth of meditation.

There must be other such mementos of steady intimacy, here rather tepidly translatable (with from Traherne an assist, not to be refused from anywhere), but the fact remains, it is a trickle, surviving from a hyperbolical and an arid land.

And what of the instinct for the sublime? This can always *utilize* a doctrine, however sectarian in origin; and if we have learned a little of how to pick our way through the baroque, again we may find at rare intervals the scattered *O Altitudo's* which do not embarrass the love of poetry.

Take Martial de Brives, a Capuchin friar, of whom nothing is known, not even his dates, except that they lie somewhere between 1600 and 1700. This recluse wrote an immensely long "paraphrase" of the "Song of the Three Young Men," in the apochryphal book of Daniel, a canticle of unnumbered *disjecta membra poetae,* each stanza drawn up as dizains and ascribed in Latin to respective participants in an exalted choir of universal glorifiers: Angels, Virtues, Stars of Heaven, Clouds, Seas, Denizens of the Deep, Growing Things, Fowls of the Air, Cattle, other Beasts—on and on, until at last, *Benedice filii hominum Domino:* i.e., Humanity joins the chorus. One rather despairs of conveying these psalms in English. Here is a stammering version of the angels:

Anges, substances immortelles,
Dépendantes divinités,
Du flambeau des eternités
Intelligents étincelles,
Esprits en qui sans mouvement
Pendant un éternel moment
Dieu prend plaisir de se répandre,
Bénissez les saintes beautés
Que vous ne pouvez pas comprendre,
Et portez vos ardeurs plus loin que vos clartés. . .

Angels, substances immortal,
You divinities dependent,
Sparks endowed with mind resplendent
From the torch of the eternal,
Souls in whom, redeemed from movement
During one perpetual moment,
God delights to be expanding,
Praise ye the supernal radiance
High above our understanding,
And let your zeal outreach your shining glance.

Glance? It is "vos clartés"—the light, or lights, of your intelligence: distortion solicited by the pulse of the verse, perhaps, but still distortion. Try with another. Here is the climax, the final explosion of this chain reaction of concerted laudation:

Homme, en qui ces diverse choses
Dont ce vaste monde est rempli,
Comme en un monde recuelli
Sont délicatement closes,
Pierre et plante conjointement
Par l'être, et par l'accroissement,
Bête en la chair, en l'esprit ange,
Puisque tous êtres sont en vous,
Honorez Dieu d'une louange
Qui seule ait la vertu de le bénir pour vous.

Mankind, in whom each wondrous thing
Throughout this vast world is contained,
As though in miniature constrained,
Each with its proper voice, to sing,
The stone and plant in essence joined,
In growth and being together bound,
Beast in the flesh, angel in soul,
Since every being lives in you,
Give glory to the Lord for all,
Who by your voice alone give glory due.

Ah! closer in sense, perhaps, and metaphysically unexceptionable, no doubt,—but where now has fled that exaltation without which the baroque must lose whatever "glory" it might hope to keep? Where is fled the magical incantation? And without the magic, where the poetry? Sucked down by the wiredrawn syntax. Reader, would *you* read upwards of twenty stanzas in English like that? And I assure you that, translated or not, with one exception, they are a lot better than most of the poetry of the period. But it is not twenty stanzas, or twenty poems, that we are talking about, but at least twenty poets, just among those remembered. There is Jean de la Ceppède, Agrippa d'Aubigné, François Maynard, Jacques Davy (Cardinal du Perron), Jean Baptiste Chassignet, Pierre Le Moyne, Du Bois Hus, et al. Some of them can be good. They just won't "go."

Except one, as I have just allowed. This is Claude Hopil and his "Of the Divine Dungeon," which leaps out from the seventeenth century with the same isolated splendor as Antoine-Léonard Thomas's "Ode to Time" from the eighteenth. That is, it rings and burns and aspires and shakes loose from all sectarian cramp and assails the empyrian. And though I despaired of it at first, if one is able to be as theologically neutral as Hopil seems essentially to be (though he'd be shocked to hear this), if one can yield to it as to a Pindaric ode, then it even translates, or such is the hope.

As it is with the failure of Baroque, so it is, for different reasons, with the *"préciosité."* Préciosité was associated, of course, with the highbrows satirized by Molière in "Les Précieuses Ridicules": ladies the actual originals of whom accorded their favors to speech and writing consisting of far-fetched circumlocutions and euphemisms. They would make, for example, the words *"terriblement"* and *"furieusement"* fashionable; and, just as among the English Augustans in the age of Pope, it was preferred that *coffee* be promoted to "Mocha's berry brown," so these ladies would be enraptured by the description of *feet* as "the dear suffering ones." But this *recherché* infection went further than in England, and it would be fair to say that all the poetry most favored in the late seventeenth and early eighteenth century suffered from it. The ground began to be most propitious when Corneille and Racine were elected to the nascent Académie Française, not for their great plays, but because they excelled in writing inscriptions for commemorative medals! Voltaire was considered the greatest *poet* of his age because he was considered the wittiest, which all too often meant the most epigramatically nasty. He is shown a bust of the Abbé de Saint-Pierre which is so faithful a likeness that he stands stunned with perplexity as to which is which, man or statue. Suddenly (and the rhyme makes it strike like a bolt) he knows. If it had not been stone (his victim's name, of course, *means* stone) it would have made a stupid remark. End of poem and, I must say, par for the course.

Translating this sort of thing is a diverting game. If you can find clinching rhymes, and you usually can, go ahead. But how much does it matter? At first, I was collecting quite a few of these wisecracks, which Voltaire did so well; he did them well partly because, as Emerson says, "all the eyes looked one way," and Tennyson, I believe, says, " 'twas his at last who said it best." When it gets down to Jacques de Cailly making a "poem" out of the conclusion that, since he (presumably) has a low boiling point, and since he has taken to hating fools, he finds that he hates nearly everybody ("Je haïs presque tout le monde. . .")—well, today we would be more inclined to say, "Consult a psychiatrist" than to promote this bitter quip to an epigram.

The target of the spite is more often women, whose main crime is that they are deemed cold to sexual advances. Georges de Scudéry (mid-seventeenth century) has an admired sonnet which culminates in the conclusion that Phyllis (they are usually Phyllis) can't help being cold because she is marble, and it is in his role of Pygmalion that she is killing him. The renowned Tristan l'Hermite has an interminable poem of spasmodic charm about a grotto, where he will set up all the luxurious preparations which his divine Phyllis deserves. (This one gets also quite baroque. . .) Cosmetics are the subject of a rather nasty little poem, also much anthologized, by George de Brébeuf (1618-1681), about how *Olinda,* this time, is dependent on beauty aids, drawn from various regions of the world, a listing of which constitutes the poem.

But *Les Précieux* (translatable as either "the Felicitous School" or "the Mannered Ones") can also be nice to women, if in a rather transparent fashion. They love to pay women compliments, and they do it with the flourish that was expected of them. This began as far back as the "conceits" of the Pléiade poets, swarming among the obscure, as well as famous. Let the Phyllis of Oliver de Magny (1529-1561), though he calls her just "Mêsme," stand for all the later ones dubiously exalted by the aspirants for their favors:

> En esté, dans un val, quand le chaut est estresme,
> J'aime à baiser sa bouche et toucher son testin
> Et, sans autre effet, faire un petit festin,
> Non de chair, mais de fruit, de fraises et de crême.

> In summer, in a valley, the heat being extreme,
> I love to kiss her mouth and touch her breast,
> And, other outcome lacking, to have a little feast,
> Not of flesh, but of fruit: in fact, strawberries and cream.

Occasionally, the honey and the sting may come together, as in the elegant Madrigals of Antoine Rambouillet, Marquis de la Sablière (1624-1679), addressed to a lady for whom the original was a Dutch banker's daughter, named Manon van Ghangelt, something of whose attractions traverse the centuries; and in view of the prolonged prevalence of Phyllis (here the virus is Iris) and the present book's studious neglect of her, a further sample might here serve to establish the standard temperature of these perennial *fêtes gallantes.* The following is more *au naturel* than the common run:

> Que mon Iris me plaît lorsqu'elle est négligée,
>   Et que je la vois dégagéee
> De tous les ornements qui cachent ses beautés!
>   La Belle les a tous quittés;
>   Une jupe de simple toile
> Aux plus secrets appas sert à peine de voile;
> On lui voit à plaisir et les bras et la main;
>   Et rien ne cache son beau sein.
> Sur un lit de repos cette belle est couchée,
> La tête dans la main nonchalamment penchée
>   Les yeux tournés vers son Amant.

> How Iris charms me when she casts aside
>   Her finery, and in naked pride
> Discards adornments that her form conceal!
>   The Fair One has removed them all;
>   A simple linen petticoat
> To veil her shape is scarcely adequate;
> Her arms and hand at least are manifest;
>   And nothing hides her lovely breast.
> This gorgeous girl upon a bed reclines
> And, head in hand, indifferently leans;
>   Her eyes upon her lover rest.

Charming! But two madrigals later, be on your guard for the lurking mischief of the Marquis, who is no more about to be deluded than a discotheque sophisticate today.

> Elle est coquette, sotte et belle;
> Assez belle pour le plaisir;
> Assez sotte pour mal choisir;

> Assez coquette enfin pour n'être pas cruelle,
> Elle aura la foule chez elle.

> She is a coquette, foolish and beautiful;
> Lovely enough for pleasure's way
> Foolish enough for choice to stray;
> And yet coquette enough to be uncruel,
> She'll have the crowd where'er she dwell.

Not that all this poetry was confined to blends of barbed complaint and sugared compliment. Thus, Paul Scarron, who, like Pope, lived and died a hopeless cripple, derives the clinching couplet of the epitaph he wrote for himself from the poignant appeal that, since his arthritis kept him awake with constant pain while living, the passerby might tread softly now that for the first time he could sleep. Or the thought may, within limits, achieve a certain valid philosophical point, as distinct from merely a "turn." In fact, the further back we go for progenitors of this wit-poetry, the more real point it is likely to have, as distinct from swagger. Here, for example, is a telling stroke of stoicism by Maturin Régnier (1573-1613):

> J'ai vécu sans nul pensement,
> Me laissant aller doucement
> A la bonne loy naturelle,
> Et si m'étonne fort pourquoy
> La mort osa songer à moy,
> Qui ne songeay jamais à elle.

> I lived without consideration,
> Proceeding in a gentle fashion
> By laws both natural and fit,
> And so I am astonished why
> Death deigned to think of me, when I
> Have never deigned to think of it.

But I decline to retail, like smoke-room jokes, the many vapid smart-aleckisms into which the "wit" can degenerate later on—in Vincent Voiture (to whose memory Pope inscribed an honorific effusion), Isaac de Benserade, Charles de Dalibray, Jean-François Sarasin, Alexis Piran, Charles-François Panard, Charles-Simon Favart. . . .

Let us remain intransigent, then, about the alarming lacunae in our text. Literature should never be intimidated by history. In the end, as we see, there were few poems after Ronsard and before Nerval which could be made to feel at home in this book. Already, by Louis XIII, fluency and ease are not truly the strong points of the second Pléiade which they aspired to be. After that, let other translators couple with the sedate couplets of Pierre le Moyne and Nicholas Boileau, Saint-Amand and Saint-Lambert, plotting in their beds to circumvent pastiches of pastiches by Epigoni at best. Readers will make proper allowance for my aversion to poetry on stilts, including rejection of the idea that "lyrical poetry" should assert property rights on all those endless rhymed couplets—unless, of course, they boil like Baudelaire's, as these do not.

The fact is that, after the biting Sponde and the soaring Hopil, and until Chénier—that "cut branch which might have grown full straight"—the only poets who were willing and able to get off their high horse were La Fontaine, part of the time, and Théophile de Viau, whose "Ode" is saved for lyrics by sounding a little crazy. Was that a nightmare that the poet had? But then he also had the anachronistic daring to make a poem out of it, which resulted in a bit of anticipatory surrealism worthy of Hieronymous Bosch. If we could stretch his lively verse letter to his brother to come under "lyric," we would. Certainly his "Le Matin" would be here if it were a little shorter and we could bring it off, although there too, alas! amid all its freshness, the ingrained inclination for masquerading Endymions and Irises shows up: and, sure enough, in the last stanza, we are invited into the garden to see if it is sprinkled with roses—*"like Phyllis's face"!* I think it is the occasional breeze of his bawdry, for one thing, that lifts him, as when he spoofs the dreaming lovers of the Pléiade (see his sonnet!). It is a breeze which surely ventilates the airlessness of those endless epigrams of the salon. Here is one of his somewhat more ambiguous quips:

> Cette femme a fait comme Troie:
> De braves gens sans aucun fruit
> Furent dix ans à cette proie
> Un cheval n'y fut qu'une nuit.

> This woman has behaved like Troy:
> It took brave men ten years of fight
> To ply without success this prey,
> Which one horse brought down in a night.

Through Louis XIV, XV, and XVI, our search will continue; but at present, it would seem that throughout the Grande Siècle and its postscripts, anything profitably negotiable by a lyric in English practically went away, until we are left with—well, what? The smile and bow of the admirable La Fontaine; some intriguing quirks of Viau; a cut version of Antoine Thomas's magnificent, if too long, ode; and Chénier's death fragments. La Fontaine is graceful and wise, but does not match the lace of the corresponding court music (Lully and Lalande). Viau? Occasionally sparkling quirks, never suggesting a large poet. Thomas is a metaphysical flash in the dark; and Chénier, so often assigned to this period, will for us inaugurate another. For the rest, remember that we have not been saying anything so sweeping as that the rest is silence, but simply that, from our unavoidably eclectic standpoint, the rest, including those poets whom critics have recently tried to rescue from the ruck, appear to be basically "more of the same."[4]

But now a concession: when they complained to James Thurber that the women in his cartoons were unattractive, he answered, "Not to my men";[5] and it is well to remember that we do not easily taste old preciosities with the *gout* that prepared them. After all, it is the tone of the time, more than of the tongue, that grows alien. In all translation, especially of poetry, we seek to match tones; and these problems support the need for constantly reassessing our poetics, as both criterion and corrective for our own *style* of writing, as well as for our painting, composing, dancing, building. This need today is especially formulated by the drift towards formlessness. It is a need that lies more heavily than at any time since the revaluations signalized by "Mauberly," "Prufrock," and the essay entitled "Tradition and the Individual Talent." It is not being suggested that translating lyric masterpieces written long ago will suffice alone as corrective, but if it is done as best we can, this may well play its part.

To sum it up, there is the verse which sooner or later will translate, and the verse, like that quoted of Malherbe's and Gombaul's, which will continue to resist translation, for intrinsic reasons. It is the more stringent verse, susceptible of living translation, that perhaps serves best to sharpen the understanding of what may be utilized to good effect by our own verse manners today—unless we are content to take sides with those manners to the point of ascribing only obsolescence to the behavior of the past. Is it magisterial to remind ourselves that the dynamic evolution of art, as of law, broadens, down from precedent to precedent, not narrows from novelty to novelty?

1. This is not to forget a third figure, not inflated at all: that equable narrator of un-

fading fame, Jean de la Fontaine. He too displays the period's preference for rhymed couplets, whose alexandrines do not sound happiest in English, though he varies his measures more than the rest. He certainly has not suffered from translator's neglect. We are not obligated to share with passion the world's love for all the well beloved. It may be, in part, La Fontaine's period-proclivity for moralizing, however inoffensively, that has deserved my own and other translators' taint of laboriousness with him. The main fault, however, lies probably with us, with the language gap, and with something in his courtliness which insulates us from his smile.

2. Not quite so unconsciously funny as Boileau's *mot*. It is doubtful if the entire corpus of Malherbe contains lines on the level, for example, of "Elegy to the Memory of an Unfortunate Lady," by Pope: "Yet shall thy grave with rising flowers be dress'd, / And the green turf lie lightly on thy breast. . ." But how many swallows make a summer?

3. ". . .surely we don't need any *new* antique vases, or any new epics in the classical style." From a review by Peter S. Prescott, *Newsweek,* June 25, 1973.

4. I did find one other refreshing exception, unconvertible in its completed form to our purpose. This was the somewhat obscure Etienne Pavillon (1632-1705), whose poem, "Letter from the Other World," is best described by its title. There the narrator wanders observantly among dead lovers, at the same time displaying a singular understanding of what ails his time. Encountering a beauty, "triste et misérable," whom he observes tearing her hair at the end of "une sombre allée," he confronts her, rather in the style of Dante and Vergil, and having caused the narrator to enquire tenderly concerning her grief ("Qu'est-ce qui te tourmente tant?"), he abruptly takes leave of us, as follows:

> Chez les morts, sans cérémonie,
> On se parle ainsi librement,
> Et, dès qu'on sort de cette vie,
> On ne fait plus de compliment.

> Among the dead, no ceremony
> Obstructs the freedom of what's meant,
> And souls who from this life win free
> No longer deal in compliment.

If only his contemporaries had got the point!

5. Similarly, William Wycherly (1640-1716) was sticking up for this, his own, period when he wrote: "It is a pleasant, well-bred, free, frolic, pretty age; and if you do not like it, leave it to us who do." I don't like it much, but well said!

125

Claude Hopil

c.1585 - after 1633

Du cachot divin

DANS ce cachot divin, j'entrevois la lumière
En ce lieu sur tout lieu,
Non, l'ombre j'entrevois de ma cause première
Qui n'est autre que Dieu.

C'est tout voir que le voir, c'est assez voir encore
— A l'ombre d'entrevoir —
Que du Roi glorieux que tout le Ciel adore
L'homme ne peut rien voir.

Il faut être ravi dans le cachot céleste
Pour savoir ce que c'est,
C'est un trésor caché plus il se manifeste
Et moins on le connaît.

Quand sa douce lumière à nos yeux se révèle
En ce terrestre lieu,
L'esprit tombe en extase, et la trouve si belle
Qu'il voit bien que c'est Dieu.

Alors étant sans yeux, sans esprit, sans mémoire
Il l'adore caché;
Confessant que son Dieu n'est que lumière et gloire
Lui qu'ombre et que péché.

Mon Dieu, n'est-ce pas vous qui dès ma faible enfance
Révéliez à mes yeux
Ce cachot lumineux, caché sous l'apparence
D'un brouillard gracieux?

Oui? sans doute c'est vous, Seigneur, c'est vous encore
Qui dans un petit bois
Enflammâtes mon cœur de ce feu qui dévore
Les cœurs mêmes des Rois.

Claude Hopil

c. 1585 - after 1633

Of the divine dungeon

In this divine duress I glimpse a purer light
    Than elsewhere any could,
Nay, 'tis the shade of my first cause that comes in sight,
    Which is none else than God.

Seeing this is seeing all, it is a gift as rare
    —To glimpse this fleeting shade—
As that great King of Glory whom the Heavens adore
    But who from man is hid.

In this celestial cell great rapture needs must pour
    For one who knows it best:
Treasure become more dark as manifest the more,
    Which is to know it least.

When his sweet radiance breaks upon our dazzled eyes
    In this terrestrial place,
Such beauty's there, the spirit falls in ecstacies
    To see it is God's face.

He being thus reft of eyes and spirit and memory,
    Adores the secret won,
Confessing that his God is solely light and glory,
    Himself but shadow and sin.

Was it not, Lord, thyself, from my first infancy,
    Who did my gaze assist
To know this radiant dungeon hiding latency
    With a complaisant mist?

Lord, 'tis thou, 'tis thou, who—coming nigher
    In my life's wanderings—
In a little wood, inflamed my heart with that same fire
    Which burns the hearts of kings.

J'étais ravi d'amour, ma pauvre âme pâmée
　　Dans cette obscurité
Ne voyait en ce lieu qu'une épaisse fumée
　　Sans aucune clarté.

Mais sans voir la lumière elle sentait la flamme
　　Du céleste séjour
Qui par le Saint Esprit si bien le cœur enflamme
　　Qu'il n'est plus rien qu'Amour.

Amour, je ne vous vois, voilà toutes mes peines,
　　Saint Amour je vous sens,
Je vous sens sans sentir, vos odeurs souveraines
　　Tous les cœurs ravissants.

Je vous vois sans vous voir, je ne vous vois encore
　　Comme on vous voit aux Cieux,
Mais au prix des mondains je vous vois et j'adore
　　D'un œil mystérieux.

Quel est cet œil divin? est-ce point la prunelle
　　De la céleste foi?
Ou le sommet de l'âme où mon Dieu se révèle
　　Pour me tirer à soi?

Je ne sais ce que c'est, je ne vois que des ombres
　　Dans cette vision,
Mais je suis tout ravi dans ces cachettes sombres
　　En contemplation.

Plus je vois (non pas Dieu) mais de Dieu dans mon âme
　　Tant moins je vois de moi,
Tant plus Dieu se révèle et tant plus je me pâme
　　Et moins je l'entrevois.

Cachot dessus cachot, et voile dessus voile
　　Couvre le Saint des Saints.
Devant ce grand Soleil, comme une obscure Etoile
　　J'adore, admire et crains.

Transported by this love, my mind fell in a swoon
  That sealed my eyes with night
And made them here below see only thickening gloom
  Without a gleam of light.

Yet without seeing the light I still could feel the fires
  Which heavenly dwellings have,
By whose pure flame the Holy Spirit so inspires
  The heart, there's only love.

Yet, Love, I see you not, and hence is all my pain;
  I sense your sacred art:
Sense beyond sense, that finds your fragrance sovereign
  To ravish every heart.

I see you without seeing you, yet do not descry
  As you're descried in Heaven,
I see you and adore with that mysterious eye
  That worldlings here are given.

What is that eye divine? The vision, is it not,
  Of faith, by which we climb
To summits of the mind, where God reveals a thought
  To draw us back to him?

I know not what it is, I can see only shade
  In this supernal vision,
But in my somber hiding place I'm blessed and made
  Ready in contemplation.

The more I see, not God, but God within the mind,
  The less I see of me;
The more God shows himself, the more I'm faint and blind,
  The less him too to see.

Veil upon veil and prison upon prison blur
  The Holy of Holies here,
Before that mighty Sun, like a diminished star,
  I worship, wonder, fear.

Je ne suis pas étoile, mais une ombre funèbre
 Au regard de ses yeux.
Devant ce pur Soleil, l'Ange n'est que ténèbre.
 Dieu seul luit glorieux.

L'Ange luit bien en Dieu, mais Dieu seul en lui-même
 En toute éternité.
J'adore en ce cachot le mystère suprême
 De la simple unité.

No shining star am I, but a funereal shade
    In His supernal sight.
Before that Sun, the Angel must to darkness fade.
    God flames in His own light.

The Angel shines in God, God sole in his own glory
    Is the eternal sun.
In this dark keep I praise the crowning mystery
    Of pure unmingled One.

Théophile de Viau

1590 - 1626

Ode

Un corbeau devant moi croasse,
Une ombre offusque mes regards;
Deux belettes et deux renards
Traversent l'endroit où je passe;
Les pieds faillent à mon cheval,
Mon laquais tombe du haut mal;
J'entends craqueter le tonnerre;
Un esprit se présente à moi;
J'ois Charon qui m'appelle à soi,
Je vois le centre de la terre.

Ce ruisseau remonte à sa source;
Un bœuf gravit sur un clocher;
Le sang coule de ce rocher;
Un aspic s'accouple d'une ourse;
Sur le haut d'une vieille tour
Un serpent déchire un vautour;
Le feu brûle dedans la glace;
Le soleil est devenu noir;
Je vois la lune qui va choir;
Cet arbre est sorti de sa place.

Théophile de Viau

1590 - 1626

Ode

In front of me, a raven's cry:
A shadow shocks my vision loose;
Two weasels and two foxes cross
The bridle-path I travel by;
My horse is plunging off its feet;
My servant falls into a fit;
I hear a sudden thunder clap;
Before my face a spectre rears;
The voice of Charon in my ears,
And see! earth's entrails open up.

That stream flows backward to its source;
Climbing a belfry is an ox;
The blood is flowing from those rocks;
Viper and bear have intercourse;
Writhing atop an ancient tower,
A snake has torn and will devour
A vulture; fire consumes in ice;
The color of the sun turns black;
I see the moon will soon fall back;
That tree has shifted from its place.

Ode à Monsieur de L.
sur la mort de son père

OTE-TOI, laisse-moi rêver:
Je sens un feu se soulever
Dont mon âme est toute embrasée.
O beaux prés, beaux rivages verts,
O grand flambeau de l'univers,
Que je trouve ma veine aisée!
Belle aurore, douce rosée,
Que vous m'allez donner de vers!

Le vent s'enfuit dans les ormeaux,
Et, pressant les feuillus rameaux,
Abat le reste de la nue;
Iris a perdu ses couleurs;
L'air n'a plus d'ombre ni de pleurs;
La bergère, aux champs revenue,
Mouillant sa jambe toute nue,
Foule les herbes et les fleurs.

Ces longues pluies dont l'hiver
Empêchait Tircis d'arriver
Ne seront plus continuées;
L'orage ne fait plus de bruit;
La clarté dissipe la nuit,
Ses noirceurs sont diminuées;
Le vent emporte les nuées,
Et voilà le soleil qui luit.

Mon Dieu, que le soleil est beau!
Que les froides nuits du tombeau
Font d'outrages à la nature!
La Mort, grosse de déplaisirs,
De ténèbres et de soupirs,
D'os, de vers et de pourriture,
Etouffe dans sa sépulture
Et nos forces et nos désirs.

Ode to Monsieur de L.
on the death of his father

LEAVE me alone and let me dream:
I feel within myself a flame,
Wherewith my mind is wrapped around.
O beauteous meadows, fair green shores,
O mighty flame of the universe,
How lightened now is my despond!
Fair dawn, fresh dew upon the ground,
Be you the impulse of my verse!

A rushing wind in the elms now heaves
The branches still unstripped of leaves
And downs the bare ones in the mold;
Iris has lost the tints of showers;
Air sheds no tears, nor the sky lowers;
The shepherdess who tends the fold,
Her bare legs moistened by the field,
Tramples upon the grass and flowers.

Those lengthy rains that saturate
The winter to make Tircis late
His coming will no more delay;
The fury of the storm is gone,
And in the dark a light has shone
To turn the blackness into day;
The wind has swept the clouds away,
And lo, the shining of the sun.

My God, the sun, how fair it is!
How in the tomb the nights will freeze
And make all nature hideous!
Death, fat with what we most despise,
With Stygian darkness and with sighs,
With bones and worms and dust of us,
Stifles in a sarcophagus
The strength we flourish, lust we prize.

Chez elle les géants sont nains;
Les Mores et les Africains
Sont aussi glacés que le Scythe;
Les dieux y tirent l'aviron;
César, comme le bûcheron,
Attendant que l'on ressuscite,
Tous les jours aux bords du Cocyte
Se trouve au lever de Charon.

Tircis, vous y viendrez un jour;
Alors les Grâces et l'Amour
Vous quitteront sur le passage,
Et dedans ces Royaumes vains*
Effacé du rang des humains,
Sans mouvement et sans visage,
Vous ne trouverez plus l'usage
Ni de vos yeux ni de vos mains.

Votre père est enseveli,
Et, dans les noirs flots de l'oubli
Où la Parque l'a fait descendre,
Il ne sait rien de votre ennui,
Et, ne fût-il mort qu'aujourd'hui,
Puisqu'il n'est plus qu'os et que cendre,
Il est aussi mort qu'Alexandre,
Et vous touche aussi peu que lui.

Saturne n'a plus ses maisons,
Ni ses ailes ni ses saisons:
Les Destins en ont fait une ombre.
Ce grand Mars n'est-il pas détruit?
Ses faits ne sont qu'un peu de bruit.
Jupiter n'est plus qu'un feu sombre
Qui se cache parmi le nombre
Des petits flambeaux de la nuit.

---

*In all but one version known to me this line is unaccountably omitted, thus resulting in a shrunk stanza.

Giants are dwarfs in that dark fold;
Moors, Africans, they're all as cold
As any Scythian you can think;
There the gods too must ply the oar;
Caesar, like any woodcutter,
Waiting to rise, whate'er their rank,
Each day, beside Cocytes' bank,
Muster with Charon to confer.

Tircis, one day you'll come to this;
The Lord of Love and every Grace
Will then desert you in the race
And in this Kingdom of the Blind,
Eliminate you from mankind,
Subtract your motion and your face,
For which you'll have no further use,
Nor for your eyes, nor for your hand.

Your father's buried in his grave,
And, in oblivion's black wave,
Where Destiny has brought him under,
Knows nought of your anxiety;
If but today he ceased to be,
Since he is only bone and cinder,
He's still as dead as Alexander
And touches you no more than he.

Saturn commands no more his mansions,
Nor yet his wings, nor yet his sanctions:
The Fates have thrust all that in shade.
How far is fallen Mars's might,
His deeds too noiseless to recite!
Jupiter's fire, now somber made,
Conceals itself amid the crowd
Of feeble flambeaux of the night.

Le cours des ruisselets errants,
La fière chute des torrents,
Les rivières, les eaux salées,
Perdront et bruit et mouvement:
Le soleil, insensiblement
Les ayant toutes avalées,
Dedans les voûtes étoilées
Transportera leur élément.

Le sable, le poisson, les flots,
Le navire, les matelots,
Tritons, et Nymphes, et Neptune,
A la fin se verront perclus:
Sur leur dos ne se fera plus
Rouler le char de la Fortune,
Et l'influence de la lune
Abandonnera le reflus.

Les planètes s'arrêteront,
Les éléments se mêleront
En cette admirable structure
Dont le Ciel nous laisse jouir.
Ce qu'on voit, ce qu'on peut ouïr,
Passera comme une peinture:
L'impuissance de la Nature
Laissera tout évanouir.

Celui qui, formant le soleil,
Arracha d'un profond sommeil
L'air et le feu, la terre et l'onde,
Renversera d'un coup de main
La demeure du genre humain
Et la base où le ciel se fonde;
Et ce grand désordre du monde
Peut-être arrivera demain.

The wandering course of little rills,
The proud descent of waterfalls,
The rivers, waters with mud lip,
Will lose their murmuring sound and movement;
The sun, with lingering deferment,
These features having swallowed up
Within the interstellar deep,
Will bear away their element.

The fish, the waves dashing on sand,
The sea-going ships, the sailors, and
The Nymphs and Tritons, yea, Neptune,
Will see the end of their domain.
Never upon their backs again
Will roll the chariot of Fortune,
And influences of the moon
Exert no more its wax and wane.

The planets will no more revolve,
Imploding atoms will dissolve
In this most excellent creation,
Wherein Heaven grants us to delight.
All things for hearing or for sight
Will fade, like paint of long duration:
Nature, in impotent prostration,
Will let it all evaporate.

He who, in fashioning the sun,
Recovered from oblivion
The air, the fire, the earth, the wave,
Will counter with a stroke of the hand
The dwelling place of humankind
And coping stone of heaven above;
This tremor in the architrave
Tomorrow could the world unbind.

Cette nuit je songeais...

CETTE nuit je songeais que Philis revenue
Belle, comme elle était à la clarté du jour,
Voulait que son fantôme encore fît l'amour
Et que, comme Ixion, j'embrassasse une nue!
    Son ombre dans mon lit se glisse toute nue
Et me dit: Cher Damon, me voici de retour!
Je n'ai fait qu'embellir en ce triste séjour
Où, depuis mon départ, le sort m'a retenue.
    Je viens pour rebaiser le plus beau des amants!
Je viens pour remourir dans tes embrassements!
Alors, quand cette idole eut abusé ma flamme,
    Elle me dit: Adieu! Je m'en fais chez les morts;
Comme tu t'es vanté d'avoir f----- mon corps
Tu pourras te vanter d'avoir f----- mon âme.*

*First appeared in Book II of *Delices satyriques* (1620). The ellipses were in the text, *Les Chefs-d'œuvre du rêve*, edited by François Gachot, Anthologie Planète, 1969. That the poet was spoofing all those wispy dream poems of the Pléiade school seems as certain as that he had a dream.

Last night I dreamed…

LAST night I dreamed that Phyllis was restored
As lovely as she was beneath the sun,
Desiring to engage in phantom fun
Where like Ixion I embraced a cloud!

    Her ghost all naked slipped into my bed
And spoke: Dear Damon, here I am again!
Only more beautiful you see I've grown
Where fate has held me since I left your side.

    I come once more my handsome one to kiss.
I come to die again in your embrace.
Then, when this idol had abused my flame,

    She said: Goodbye! I go home to the dead;
Whatever to my body once you did
Now for my soul your boast can be the same.

Deux epigrammes

Pour être divine et humaine,
Il faut en jeunesse sentir
Les plaisirs de la Magdeleine,
Et puis, vieille, s'en repentir.

*

Je nasquis au monde tout nu,
Je ne sais combien je vivrai;
Si je n'ai rien quand je mourrai
Je n'aurai gagné, ny perdu.

De *Philandre sur la maladie de Tircis*

...Notre destin est assez doux,
Et, pour n'être pas immortelle,
Notre nature est assez belle
Si nous savons jouir de nous.
Rien que nous-mêmes ne nous blesse,
Notre mal, c'est notre faiblesse.
Le sot glisse sur les plaisirs,
Mais le sage y demeure ferme
En attendant que ses désirs
Ou ses jours finissent leur terme.

Two epigrams

To be both human and divine,
We have to know, ere youth is spent,
The pleasures of the Magdalene
And then in time, when old, repent.

*

Naked into the world came I,
Not knowing how long my life would last;
If I have nothing when I die,
I shall have neither gained nor lost.

From *Philander concerning the sickness of Tircis*

...Our destiny is sweet enough;
Our nature not, 'tis true, immortal;
Yet this too would be beautiful
If we could learn to savor life.
There's nothing but ourselves to hurt us;
Only our feebleness can thwart us.
To flit by pleasures stamps the fool;
The wise man firmly will appraise
His wants and, gaining them, there dwell,
Or gain the limit of his days.*

---

*This forms the fifth, last, and best composed stanza. It is eminently isolable as a statement of the philosophy by which Théophile lived and died.

Jean de la Fontaine
1621 - 1695

Le renard et les raisins

CERTAIN renard gascon, d'autres disent normand,
Mourant presque de faim, vit au haut d'une treille
Des raisins, mûrs apparemment,
Et couverts d'une peau vermeille.
Le galant en eût fait volontiers un repas.
Mais comme il n'y pouvait atteindre,
Ils sont trop verts, dit-il, et bons pour des goujats.

Fit-il pas mieux que de se plaindre?

Jean de la Fontaine
1621 - 1695

The fox and the grapes

A CERTAIN Gascon fox—or Norman, could be—
Was almost starving when, way up on a vine,
    He saw a bunch of grapes that should be
    Ripe, judging by the rosy skin.
The rogue was more than ready for a fill.
    But since he could not reach that high,
"Too green," he said; "good for the rank and file."

    Well, wasn't it better than to cry?

La mort et le mourant

La mort ne surprend point le sage:
Il est toujours prêt à partir,
S'étant su lui-même avertir
Du temps où l'on se doit résoudre à ce passage.
Ce temps, hélas! embrasse tous les temps:
Qu'on le partage en jours, en heures, en moments,
Il n'en est point qu'il ne comprenne
Dans le fatal tribut; tous sont de son domaine;
Et le premier instant où les enfants des rois
Ouvrent les yeux à la lumière
Est celui qui vient quelquefois
Fermer pour toujours leur paupière.
Défendez-vous par la grandeur,
Alléguez la beauté, la vertu, la jeunesse:
La mort ravit tout sans pudeur;
Un jour, le monde entier accroîtra sa richesse.
Il n'est rien de moins ignoré,
Et, puisqu'il faut que je le die,
Rien où l'on soit moins préparé.
Un mourant, qui comptait plus de cent ans de vie,
Se plaignait à la Mort que précipitamment
Elle le contraignait de partir tout à l'heure,
Sans qu'il eût fait son testament,
Sans l'avertir au moins. "Est-il juste qu'on meure
Au pied levé? dit-il; attendez quelque peu:
Ma femme ne veut pas que je parte sans elle;
Il me reste à pourvoir un arrière-neveu;
Souffrez qu'à mon logis j'ajoute encore une aile.
Que vous êtes pressante, ô déesse cruelle!"
— "Vieillard, lui dit la Mort, je ne t'ai pas surpris;
Tu te plains sans raison de mon impatience:
Eh! n'as-tu pas cent ans? Trouve-moi dans Paris
Deux mortels aussi vieux; trouve-m'en dix en France.
Je devais, ce dis-tu, te donner quelque avis
˙ Qui te disposât à la chose:
J'aurais trouvé ton testament tout fait,
Ton petit-fils pourvu, ton bâtiment parfait.

Death and the dying

DEATH can't astonish one who's wise:
He's always ready to set forth,
Having resolved upon the path
Before the time to take it shall arise.
       This time, alas! embraces every time:
Whether by days or hours or less it chime,
       None is exempt in this domain;
The fatal levy falls on every man.
The moment when the infants of a king
       First open eyelids to the light
       May be the one when everything
       Is lost for ever to their sight.
       Defend yourself by a great name;
       Allege your beauty, virtue, youth and health;
       Death snatches all and feels no shame;
One day the world will go to swell her wealth.
       Nothing we know more sure than this;
       And, since the truth must now be told,
       Nothing in which we're more remiss.
A dying man, more than a century old,
Complained to Death how swiftly she would tell
Her victim to depart, how suddenly,
       Without a chance to make his will,
Or warning him at least. "Ought one to die
So fast?" he said; "please make the event less soon;
My wife can't bear me leaving without her;
I still must make provision for my grandson;
Just let me add a wing to my house here;
Goddess, you're pushing this, be pleasanter!"
"Old man," said Death, "I'm not surprising you;
You have no right to charge me with impatience:
What! aren't you a hundred? Find me in Paris two
Mortals so ancient; find me ten in France.
I ought, you say, to have given you a clue
       Which would prepare you for this thing:
       I then would find your will all drawn up neat,
Grandson provided for, building complete.

Ne te donna-t-on pas des avis, quand la cause
    Du marcher et du mouvement,
    Quand les esprits, le sentiment,
Quand tout faillit en toi? Plus de goût, plus d'ouïe;
Toute chose pour toi semble être évanouie;
Pour toi l'astre du jour prend des soins superflus;
Tu regrettes des biens qui ne te touchent plus.
    Je t'ai fait voir tes camarades,
    Ou morts, ou mourants, ou malades:
Qu'est-ce que tout cela, qu'un avertissement?
    Allons, vieillard, et sans réplique,
    Il n'importe à la République
    Que tu fasses ton testament."

La Mort avait raison. Je voudrais qu'à cet âge
On sortît de la vie ainsi que d'un banquet,
Remerciant son hôte, et qu'on fît son paquet:
Car de combien peut-on retarder le voyage?
Tu murmures, vieillard! Vois ces jeunes mourir,
    Vois-les marcher, vois-les courir
A des morts, il est vrai, glorieuses et belles,
Mais sûres cependant, et quelquefois cruelles.
J'ai beau te le crier; mon zèle est indiscret:
Le plus semblable aux morts meurt le plus à regret.

But were you given no clues when the inner spring
   By which you walk, by which you move,
   Your spirits, your capacity to love,
All failed you? When you lost your taste and hearing?
When everything for you seemed disappearing?
For you the sun squanders in vain his care:
You hanker for the joys that are no more.
   I've had you look at many a friend
   That's sick and dying or has reached his end:
If these are not your clues, what are they all?
   Come on, old man, let's hear no more;
   Your country doesn't give a straw
   Whether or not you made your will."

Death was quite right: I'd wish at such an age
To take my leave of life as from a banquet,
Thanking my host and making a prompt exit:
For how long can we lengthen out the voyage?
Old man, you grumble! See those young ones die;
   See them walk and see them fly
To deaths, I grant you, glorious, beautiful,
But certain none the less, and sometimes cruel.
I waste my breath; my zeal is indiscreet:
The one most deathly dies with most regret.

149

Paul Pellisson-Fontanier
1624 - 1693

Durant le grand vent à la Bastille.

Vous ne battez que ma prison,
Rudes vents, terribles orages,
Quand sur la mer avec raison
On craint les plus cruels naufrages.

Tu me l'apprends, céleste foi
Dont l'ardeur m'élève et m'enflamme:
Ce faible corps n'est pas à moi,
C'est la demeure de mon âme.

Qu'un autre avec quelque raison
Craigne les plus cruels naufrages:
Vous ne battez que ma prison,
Rudes vents, terribles orages.

Paul Pellisson-Fontanier

1624 - 1693

During the great wind at the Bastille

You only beat against my prison,
You stormy winds, to tear that down,
When if it were the sea, with reason
We'd fear by such a gale to drown.

Celestial faith, you teach hereby
With flames that burn and make me whole:
This feeble body is not I,
It is the dwelling of the soul.

Let someone else fear with good reason
In such a cruel gale to drown:
You only beat against my prison,
You stormy winds to tear that down.

Molière
1622 - 1673

Croyez-moi, hâtons-nous, ma Sylvie…

CROYEZ-MOI, hâtons-nous, ma Sylvie,
Usons bien des moments précieux;
Contentons ici notre envie,
De nos ans le feu nous y convie:
Nous ne saurions, vous et moi, faire mieux.
Quand l'hiver a glacé nos guérets,
Le printemps vient reprendre sa place,
Et ramène à nos champs leurs attraits;
Mais, hélas! quand l'âge nous glace,
Nos beaux jours ne reviennent jamais.

Ne cherchons tous les jours qu'à nous plaire,
Soyons-y l'un et l'autre empressés;
Du plaisir faisons notre affaire,
Des chagrins songeons à nous défaire:
Il vient un temps où l'on en prend assez.
Quand l'hiver a glacé nos guérets,
Le printemps vient reprendre sa place,
Et ramène à nos champs leurs attraits;
Mais, hélas! quand l'âge nous glace,
Nos beaux jours ne reviennent jamais.

Molière

1622 - 1673

Believe me, Sylvia, we should haste…

BELIEVE me, Sylvia, we should haste
To make the best of precious moments;
    Let not this longing go to waste;
Fire of our years bids to the feast:
We two shall never better this bestowment.
    When winter hath our lands congealed,
    Spring cometh soon to take its place,
    Restoring fairness to the field;
        But when age freezes us, alas!
    Our fairest days for ever are repealed.

    Let us not think all days must please us,
    But gladly to each day come home,
        Making of pleasure what may ease us,
    Unmaking grievances that tease us,
Whereof will be enough in time to come.
    When winter hath our lands congealed,
    Spring cometh soon to take its place,
    Restoring fairness to the field,
        But when age freezes us, alas!
    Our fairest days for ever are repealed.

Jean Racine
1639 - 1699

Hymne tiré du Bréviaire

Tandis que le sommeil, réparant la nature,
    Tient enchaînés le travail et le bruit,
Nous rompons ses liens, ô clarté toujours pure!
    Pour te louer dans la profonde nuit.

Que dès notre réveil notre voix te bénisse;
    Qu'à te chercher notre cœur empressé
T'offre ses premiers vœux; et que par toi finisse
    Le jour par toi saintement commencé.

L'astre dont la présence écarte la nuit sombre
    Viendra bientôt recommencer son tour:
O vous, noirs ennemis qui vous glissez dans l'ombre,
    Disparaissez à l'approche du jour.

Nous t'implorons, Seigneur: tes bontés sont nos armes;
    De tout péché rends-nous purs à tes yeux;
Fais que, t'ayant chanté dans ce séjour de larmes,
    Nous te chantions dans le repos des cieux.

Jean Racine

1639 - 1699

Hymn drawn from the Breviary

WHILE sleep that keeps all nature in repair
　　Holds toil and noise in bondage tight,
We break these bonds, O radiance ever pure,
　　To praise thee in the depth of night.

May our voice wake to worship thee straightway,
　　Heart hasten with thy will to blend,
And pledge our vows that, even as the day
　　Begins with thee, so shall it end.

The star whose presence banishes the dark
　　Soon comes to start his round again;
All ye black foes who in the shadows lurk,
　　Be gone at the approach of dawn.

Lord, by whose grace, we're armed against all fears,
　　Grant here our sins may be forgiven,
That we who praise thee in this vale of tears,
　　May praise thee in the peace of heaven....*

*As in other poems of Racine's "Breviary," this exalted hymn sinks by
the weight of its own orthodoxy, the fifth and final stanza, here
omitted, being hardly poetry in French, and unconvertible into English
lyric. The poem previous, by France's greatest comic dramatist, is in
conception the most superficial *carpe diem*, in execution hard to better;
whilst, conversely, this one, by her greatest tragic dramatist, is clearly
conceived on an elevated level, whilst being in expression uneven. The
two poems may stand for the period's "merits and defects," which are
discussed in the Introduction, and according to which critics belonging
to the period, whilst themselves sharing these merits and defects, were
prone to draw up the account.

Mme. Guyon

1648 - 1717

Foi sans assurance

Pour contempler l'essence nue,
Il faut la nue et pure foi;
Lorsqu'en Dieu l'âme est parvenue,
Il ne reste plus rien de moi.

Si je me faisais quelque forme,
Si je me figure un objet,
Je rends mon Dieu semblable à l'homme
Et me trompe dans mon sujet.

Si c'est Jésus que je contemple,
D'un œil simple autant qu'épuré;
Si je me forme à son exemple,
Mon état est très assuré.

Sans me former aucune image
Avec lui me perdant en Dieu,
Je la trouve sans nul partage,
Sans différence, temps ni lieu.

Tel qu'il est au sein de son Père,
Je le trouve et m'abîme en lui:
Tel qu'il était sur la terre
Il règle ma vie aujourd'hui.

Lorsque l'âme est redevenue
Simple comme un petit enfant,
C'est alors que l'Essence nue
Est sa force et son aliment.

Divin moteur de toute chose,
Principe de la Vérité,
Qu'en toi seul mon esprit repose
Et s'abîme en l'immensité.

Mme. Guyon

1648 - 1717

Faith without assurance

To contemplate the essence bare,
Faith must have bareness, purity;
When unto God our souls repair,
Nothing remaineth then of me.

If I within some form constrain,
Or if I summon up an object,
I make my God resemble man,
Betraying object with the subject.

But if to Jesus I would turn
With eyes direct as they are pure,
By his divine example learn,
My state is then completely sure.

Nought apprehending with my vision,
Losing myself in God with him,
I find the form without division,
Or difference of place and time.

As he within his Father's breast,
So I in him commit my way;
Such as he was on earth at first,
He rules my life unto this day.

When once the soul becomes again
As simple as a little child,
It is the Essence bare will then
Sustain and by its strength uphold.

Divine artificer of all,
Thou Principle of Verity,
Grant that in thee I rest my soul
And plunge in the immensity.

Ah! que ce langage est barbare
Pour exprimer ce qu'on conçoit!
Car ce qu'on éprouve est si rare
Que rien en nous ne l'aperçoit.

Là, transporté hors de soi-même,
On entre en un pays nouveau,
Où Dieu qu'on adore et qu'on aime
Sert de sépulcre et de berceau.

Là les puissances suspendues,
Sans discerner ni mal ni bien,
Là les âmes en Dieu perdues
Ne voient plus même leur rien.

Là l'on vit et l'on meurt sans cesse,
On trouve la vie et la mort;
La douleur devient allégresse;
Si je disais tout, j'aurais tort.

O rayon ténébreux d'une immense clarté!
O nuit! ô torrent de lumière,
Pur amour, simple vérité,
Source de bien, cause première!

Doux centre du repos, céleste volupté,
Sacré monument de la gloire,
Doux nœud d'une pure unité,
Absorbement de la mémoire!

Nul objet singulier, un abîme profond
Environne toute notre âme:
Ce qui la perd et la confond,
C'est une mer toute de flamme....

How gross this language to declare
All of the things that we conceive!
For what we've proved is, Ah! so rare,
Nothing in us may this perceive.

Transported there to realms above
This self, we enter a new land,
Where God whom we adore and love
Is cradle and grave, beginning and end.

There hung suspended are the powers,
Without discerning good or ill;
There, lost in God, the minds once ours
Not even see their nothing still.

There endlessly we live and die,
Find life and death as both belong;
The pain converted into joy;
If I told all, it would be wrong.

Dark ray of radiance immense!
O night! O light streaming aflood,
Pure love, truth stripped of all pretense,
First cause and source of all that's good!

Heart of repose and heaven's joy,
Celestial monument of glory,
Sweet knot of oneness sans alloy,
Absorbing every memory!

Unplumbed abyss, devoid of things,
That grasps in its embrace the soul,
Confounding that to which it clings,
A sea of flame enfolding all....

Voltaire

Adieux à la vie

ADIEU; je vais dans ce pays
D'où ne revint point feu mon père:
Pour jamais adieu, mes amis,
Qui ne me regretterez guère.
Vous en rirez, mes ennemis,
C'est le *requiem* ordinaire.
Vous en tâterez quelque jour;
Et, lorsque aux ténébreux rivages
Vous irez trouver vos ouvrages,
Vous ferez rire à votre tour.

Quand sur la scène de ce monde
Chaque homme a joué son rôlet,
En partant il est à la ronde
Reconduit à coups de sifflet.
Dans leur dernière maladie,
J'ai vu des gens de tous états,
Vieux évêques, vieux magistrats,
Vieux courtisans à l'agonie.
Vainement en cérémonie
Avec sa clochette arrivait

L'attirail de la sacristie:
Le curé vainement oignait
Notre vieille âme à sa sortie;
Le public malin s'en moquait;
La satire un moment parlait
Des ridicules de sa vie;
Puis à jamais on l'oubliait:
Ainsi la farce était finie.
Le purgatoire ou le néant
Terminait cette comédie.

Voltaire

1694 - 1778

Farewells to life

FAREWELL; I'm going to that land
Whence my late father comes no more:
And so, goodbye for good, my friends,
This absence you will scarce deplore.
For you, my enemies, you'll find
That requiems are what laughter's for.
Some day you too the sting may learn,
Arriving on the banks of Styx
To suffer for your vaunted works
Laughter that hurts you in your turn.

When in this theatre of the round
Each man has played his little role,
He makes his exit to the sound
Of hisses for the curtain call.
I've seen in their extremity
People of every known estate,
Old bishops and old magistrates,
Old courtesans in agony.
In vain for them that ceremony
Of sacristan with little bell.

No village priest can soothe our pain
By ointment for the parting soul.
Grey hairs are eloquent in vain
Against derision to prevail;
One moment of this ridicule
And, after that, oblivion:
And so, to play it to the full,
We terminate the comic scene
In limbo, or no place at all.

Petits papillons d'un moment,
Invisibles marionnettes,
Qui volez si rapidement
De Polichinelle au néant,
Dites-moi donc ce que vous êtes.
Au terme où je suis parvenu
Quel mortel est le moins à plaindre?
C'est celui qui ne sait rien craindre,
Qui vit et qui meurt inconnu.

Frail, momentary butterfly,
Poor inconspicuous marionette,
At such a rapid pace to fly
From Punchinello to the pit,
Inform me what you signify.
Arrived at partings like my own,
What mortal here makes least complaint?
'Tis he who fears no known event,
Because he lives and dies unknown.

Antoine-Léonard Thomas

1732 - 1785

Ode sur le temps

Le compas d'Uranie a mesuré l'espace.
O Temps, être inconnu que l'âme seule embrasse,
Invisible torrent des siècles et des jours,
Tandis que ton pouvoir m'entraîne dans la tombe,
    J'ose, avant que j'y tombe,
M'arrêter un moment pour contempler ton cours.

Qui me dévoilera l'instant qui t'a vu naître?
Quel œil peut remonter aux sources de ton être?
Sans doute ton berceau touche à l'éternité.
Quand rien n'était encore, enseveli dans l'ombre
    De cet abîme sombre,
Ton germe y reposait, mais sans activité.

Du chaos tout à coup les portes s'ébranlèrent;
Des soleils allumés les feux étincelèrent;
Tu naquis; l'Eternel te prescrivit ta loi.
Il dit au mouvement: "Du Temps sois la mesure."
    Il dit à la nature:
"Le Temps sera pour vous, l'Eternité pour moi."

Dieu, telle est ton essence: oui, l'océan des âges
Roule au-dessous de toi sur tes frêles ouvrages,
Mais il n'approche pas de ton trône immortel.
Des millions de jours qui l'un l'autre s'effacent,
    Des siècles qui s'entassent,
Sont comme le néant aux yeux de l'Eternel.

Mais moi, sur cet amas de fange et de poussière,
En vain contre le Temps je cherche une barrière;
Son vol impétueux me presse et me poursuit.
Je n'occupe qu'un point de la vaste étendue,
    Et mon âme éperdue
Sous mes pas chancelants voit ce point qui s'enfuit.

Antoine-Léonard Thomas

1732 - 1785

Ode on time

URANIA'S compasses have measured space.
O Time, known only to the soul's embrace,
Torrent unseen of ages and of days,
While yet your power sweeps me toward the tomb,
  Before I face that doom,
I dare to pause and contemplate your ways.

Who will reveal the moment of your birth?
What eye can reach to that first coming forth?
Your cradle surely touched eternity.
When yet was nought, still buried in the night
  Of that abysmal pit,
Your germ was there, but fixed in nullity.

The doors of chaos suddenly burst apart;
The furnaces of kindled suns flashed out;
You were born; the Eternal gave you your decree.
He said to motion: "Be of Time the measure."
  And then He said to nature:
"Time is for you, Eternity for me."

And such, God, is your essence: yes, the ocean
Of ages rolls across your frail creation
But never can approach your deathless throne.
Millions of days, effacing one another,
  Age after age, together
Are nothing in the gaze of the Alone.

Yet I upon this heap of dust and slime
In vain would seek a rampart against Time,
Which drives me, hunts me with its eager flight.
I occupy one point throughout the whole,
  And my bewildered soul
Sees that point slip away beneath my feet.

De la destruction tout m'offre des images.
Mon œil épouvanté ne voit que des ravages:
Ici de vieux tombeaux que la mousse a couverts,
Là des murs abattus, des colonnes brisées,
    Des villes embrasées:
Partout les pas du Temps empreints sur l'univers.

Cieux, terres, éléments, tout est sous sa puissance.
Mais tandis que sa main, dans la nuit du silence,
Du fragile univers sape les fondements,
Sur des ailes de feu loin du monde élancée,
    Mon active pensée
Plane sur les débris entassés par le Temps.

Siècles qui n'êtes plus, et vous qui devez naître,
J'ose vous appeler: hâtez-vous de paraître.
Au moment où je suis venez vous réunir.
Je parcours tous les points de l'immense durée
    D'une marche assurée:
J'enchaîne le présent, je vis dans l'avenir.

Le soleil épuisé dans sa brûlante course
De ses feux par degrés verra tarir la source,
Et des mondes vieillis les ressorts s'useront.
Ainsi que des rochers qui du haut des montagnes
    Roulent sur les campagnes,
Les astres l'un sur l'autre un jour s'écrouleront.

Everything shows me emblems of decay.
My eyes, appalled, see worlds in disarray:
Here ancient tombs are covered up with moss;
There, walls reduced to rubble, columns smashed,
    Whole cities burned to ash:
Time's footsteps printed on the universe.

Worlds, heavens, elements obey his beck;
But while his hands, in silent darkness, shake
The frail foundations of this vault sublime,
My active thought is borne on wings of fire,
    Beyond earth soaring higher,
Far from the ruins that are heaped by Time.

Eras long dead, and you still to be born,
I dare to summon you: make haste, return,
Assemble at the moment where I am.
I visit every point throughout the depths
    Of time with steadfast steps:
I grasp the present, grope in future time.

The sun, exhausted in his burning course,
Shall witness light quenched slowly at the source,
And aging worlds, their fuel squandered, smother,
Until, like rocks that from a mountain wall
    Upon the meadows fall,
The stars at last shall hurtle on each other.

Là, de l'Eternité commencera l'empire,
Et dans cet océan où tout va se détruire,
Le Temps s'engloutira comme un faible ruisseau.
Mais mon âme immortelle, aux siècles échappée,
Ne sera point frappée,
Et des mondes brisés foulera le tombeau...

Then will commence to reign Eternity,
Until that ocean where all things must die
Time's feeble rivulet at length absorbs;
Whilst my immortal soul, from cycles free,
      Will not go down with me
But trample on the grave of shattered orbs . . .*

*I incline to the view that Mr. Brereton, who edited *The Penguin Book of French Verse, 2: Sixteenth to Eighteenth Centuries,* was justified in breaking the poem off here; for the remaining eight of its eighteen stanzas tend to decline into the stately moralizing of the period, the best remaining stanza being, perhaps, the thirteenth:

> Trop aveugles humains, quelle erreur vous enivre!
> Vous n'avez qu'un instant pour penser et pour vivre,
> Et cet instant qui fuit est pour vous un fardeau!
> Avare de ses biens, prodigue de son être,
>   Dès qu'il peut se connaître
> L'homme appelle la mort et creuse son tombeau.

Of this the least unsatisfactory translation I have patience for at present is:

> Mankind too blind, what folly makes you drunk!
> You have one instant left to live and think;
> That fleeting instant is your load of doom!
> Stingy of wealth, extravagant of being,
>   Man learns some inward seeing
> In time for death to bid him dig his tomb.

Evariste-Désiré de Parny
1753 - 1814

Chanson madécasse

NAHANDOVE, ô belle Nahandove! l'oiseau nocturne a commencé ses cris, la pleine lune brille sur ma tête, et la rosée naissante humecte mes cheveux. Voici l'heure: qui peut t'arrêter, Nahandove, ô belle Nahandove?

Le lit de feuilles est préparé; je l'ai parsemé de fleurs et d'herbes odoriférantes; il est digne de tes charmes, Nahandove, ô belle Nahandove!

Elle vient. J'ai reconnu la respiration précipitée que donne une marche rapide; j'entends le froissement de la pagne qui l'enveloppe: c'est elle, c'est Nahandove, la belle Nahandove!

Reprends haleine, ma jeune amie; repose-toi sur mes genoux. Que ton regard est enchanteur! que le mouvement de ton sein est vif et délicieux sous la main qui le presse! Tu souris, Nahandove, ô belle Nahandove!

Tes baisers pénètrent jusqu'à l'âme; tes caresses brûlent tous mes sens: arrête, ou je vais mourir. Meurt-on de volupté, Nahandove, ô belle Nahandove?

Le plaisir passe comme un éclair; ta douce haleine s'affaiblit, tes yeux humides se referment, ta tête se penche mollement, et tes transports s'éteignent dans la langueur. Jamais tu ne fus si belle, Nahandove, ô belle Nahandove!

Que le sommeil est délicieux dans les bras d'une maîtresse! moins délicieux pourtant que le réveil. Tu pars, et je vais languir dans les regrets et les désirs; je languirai jusqu'au soir; tu reviendras ce soir, Nahandove, ô belle Nahandove!

Evariste-Désiré de Parny

1753 - 1814

Madagascan song

NAHANDOVE, O beautiful Nahandove! the bird of night has tuned its song, the full moon shines on my head, and the early dew moistens my hair. It is the hour: who is it keeps you, Nahandove, O beautiful Nahandove?

The bed of leaves is made; I have strewn it with fragrant flowers and grass; it is worthy of your charms, Nahandove, O beautiful Nahandove!

She comes. I would always know her fast breathing when she hurries; I hear the rustling pagne that clings to her loins: it is she, it is Nahandove, O beautiful Nahandove!

Catch your breath, my young friend; rest on my knees. How your glance enchants me! How deliciously alive the movement of your breast beneath my hand! You smile, Nahandove, O beautiful Nahandove!

Your kisses pierce even to my soul; your caresses burn my every sense: stop, or I shall die. Does one die of pleasure, Nahandove, O beautiful Nahandove?

The pleasure passes like a flash of lightning; your sweet breath slows, your swimming eyes are closed, your head droops, and your transports are quenched with fatigue. Never were you so beautiful, Nahandove, O beautiful Nahandove!

How delicious is sleep in the arms of a mistress! but less delicious than waking. You go away, and I shall languish with longing till evening; then you will come back, Nahandove, O beautiful Nahandove!

A New Sound

Baudelaire, by Henri Fantin-Latour
  Courtesy of the Louvre

A New Sound
Eighteenth and Nineteenth Centuries

That André Chénier, guillotined in 1794, was not published till 1819 presents us with a posthumous development comparable to what happened with Gerard Hopkins: a new sound in poetry, occurring at least three decades before it was heard. There are two possible criteria for this "newness," either of which may be traceable in the forerunners of a literary movement. The focus may be upon a new sensibility; or upon a shift of style, reflecting that sensibility. *Sensibilité*—for it should be said in French—bespoke a range of feelings by which readers were newly excited, making its first impact by English imports, themselves a curious mix, compacted of Ossian, Sir Walter Scott, Mrs. Radcliffe, Monk Lewis and, presently, Lord Byron: prevailingly a gothic-romantic mix, whose exaggerations may raise eyebrows now, when we have not been subjected to a century of artifice. We should always allow for the swing of the pendulum from one excess to its opposite. One who crawls dying of thirst to a well, real or mirage, does not greet it with great poise or sangfroid.

Such were the more sensational English sources to which moods were at first to accommodate themselves. If you were callous about it, you could say that French poetry was lucky in the horror of the inspiration behind that portion of Chénier's poetry which I believe most counts. This, for me, is found, not in the sculptured lines of "La Jeune Tarantine" or "L'Aveugle," a style which may be seen as the apotheosis of the "marble rigor" of Malherbe, a style which lies somewhere between Milton, Dryden, and the less playful side of Pope, but rather in passages of "A Charlotte Cordray," and more unmistakably in the "Iambes," which Chénier wrote in the Bastille, on the brink of his execution. This grim circumstance made it easier for a genius like his to cut through the ice settling on the heart of poetry, and this he did.

Of course, history, including the history of literature, has no absolute beginnings. It not only leaps forward but turns back on itself. If a vital forerunner, like Chénier, dies prematurely, a second sally, as represented, for example, by Gérard de Nerval, will probably be needed in order to consolidate his gains; and the poets like Lamartine and Vigny, who gained more recognition in their own time, will remain a hindrance to the best progress of poetry.

175

Vigny is instructive; for, as his thought gained a little in reach and flexibility, the wooden note distinctly changed in him, as witnessed by the spirited lines in "Le Mont des Oliviers."[1] Here occurs a moment when it might not be too far-fetched to compare his courtly figure to the whaling-ship captain, at the height of the storm, summoning the Almighty to descend so he could "spit in His eye!" Only for Vigny it is the more effective rejoinder of silence:

> S'il est vrai qu'au Jardin sacré des Ecritures,
> Le Fils de l'homme ait dit ce qu'on voit rapporté;
> Muet, aveugle et sourd au cri des créatures,
> Si le Ciel nous laissa comme un monde avorté,
> Le juste opposera le dédain à l'absence
> Et ne repondra plus que par un froid silence
> Au silence éternel de la Divinité.

> If it is true that, even as Scripture told,
> The Son of Man spoke in Gethsemane;
> If Heaven, that dumped us like a stillborn world,
> Is mute, blind, deaf to every creature's cry,
> The just man will oppose disdain to absence
> And give back nothing but a frosty silence
> To the eternal silence of the sky.

It is regrettable that, because so seldom and intermittently is any level resembling this sustained for more than a few lines in Vigny's interminable poems, the "absence" is one that extends to himself from the ensuing pages. May these stalwart lines serve to paliate our "frosty" neglect.

Also instructive, and in ways not unlike Chénier, is Nerval; for he too had his "sculptured" component in those few great sonnets ("Horus," "El Desdichado," "Anteros," etc.) in which the resounding names defy translation without distortion within the form. But in three of the poems here given, at least, he may be seen as a secular mystic, with far reaches of speculative surmise. In "Golden Verses" he finds a casual angel in the stone; in "The Dark Smudge," laments that he cannot confront the sun's blaze with the steady stare of the eagle; in "Fantasy," experiences an unmistakable "déjà vu," with clear-cut overtones of the rebirth doctrine. Finally, in the third of his "Christ Among the Olives" sonnet sequence, the one in which, together with the Jean-Paul epigraph, the thought concentrates its meaning most clearly and least (for me) untranslatably, he exalts the crucified Savior as representing God less than Mind, or the very capacity for realizing anything.

We speak of new beginnings. We contemplate these repercussions of the storming of the Bastille—repercussions emotional, metaphysical, mystical, as well as political; and we have not introduced the great exile, Victor Hugo. Ah, Hugo! "Hélas, Hugo!" For almost any critical treatment (which this is not), the culminating fixture of this period would certainly have been this formidable man. But must we continue indefinitely to accept his own estimate,[2] or that of his slightly stunned contemporaries, concerning what it was that culminated? They say, "Securus judicat orbis terrarum" (the world judges right in the end); and for the most part, without any conscious attempt at a balancing division of honors, our selections, within the last century-and-a-half anyway, are nevertheless not very far from what other lovers of French poetry have preferred.

But Hugo? The taste for Hugo, including mine, I fear, is still in a slump, certainly as compared with his prodigious reputation: to some extent, the reaction, no doubt, from a time when he was considered beyond criticism. It may be that this was when his greatness as a "freedom fighter" and his majesty in assumption of the role of exiled prophet distracted attention from the exclamatory un-magic which, to this ear, belongs to great lengths of *La Légende de Siècles,* ever since one was assigned it in school. But I would contend that this turning away means something more than "chacun à son goût." Hugo's monotonous reliance on the trumpet, as against the mirror, might entitle him to a solid claim on the Dionysian, vis à vis the Apollonian prerogatives, were it not that his proclamations, whilst being as assertive of their own authority as Isaiah, Milton, or Blake, are drastically less endowed with vision.

Then, to go down a step, what about the vogue of the comic satirist, Pierre-Jean de Béranger? In him the new sound consisted in being a new kind of lampoonist, capable of being funny without the Voltairean vitriol. In 1813, the date of the rollicking but thoroughly subversive "Yvetot," such was Béranger's popularity that the Emperor had little choice but to take the poem in good part. Unfortunately, Béranger was also a model, along with Théodore de Banville later, for the craft of verse of a sort that Gautier and Baudelaire were no longer interested in writing: rejection becoming total in the boy Rimbaud. One wonders again whether his verse would have been served with this disdain at any other time; while as to its *réclame,* people usually like fun and high spirits.

Musset's "swing" was of another sort or sorts. His early poems, like "A Julie," were distinctly startling for their "beat"-type irreverence, and drew the only attempts in this book to a matching vernacular. Its Parisian insouciance is a counter-irritant to the more typical, I fear, "Night of October," from "Nuits," where, without going so far as to say, in Louis Aragon's phrase, that Musset "incorporates the world in his own mediocre anguish," he certainly reveals himself as steeped in the romantic proclivity for confiding his sufferings to paper. If it is asked how the complete lack of detachment with which he weeps on our shoulder here differs from all those "cruel fair" sonnets of the Pléiade, one answer is that Musset's is no convention, but an outpouring that prided itself on spontaneity and rapidity of composition, for he disdained revision. Like Vigny, he changed and advanced, especially in his plays. The surer facility gained from writing those was deployed in the conversational note of his verse, so that this last too became worth remembering.

More important as a progenitor is Théophile Gautier, the father of "art for art's sake," and a kind of hero still, even as late as for Ezra Pound and T.S. Eliot. Eliot mimicked Gautier's "L'Hippopotame" in his own poem of the same title, and in "Whispers of Immortality," quite unconsciously perhaps, imported the very inflection of "Carmen Est Maigre" as "Grishkin Is Nice." Thus two generations after his death, Gautier still threatened as a cult! But there's a paradox here; for alongside these durable anticipations, Gautier is an iron traditionalist, who would have been more perplexed and dismayed by liberties taken in Pound's *Canto's* than would any arbiter since Boileau.

When Gautier wrote "To Zurburan," he would seem to have been reading Dante; and my own attempt was partly to see if I could salvage one of his most ambitious poems from oblivion in English, and partly to determine whether his terza rima would stand up in our language without being forced. But just as with Eliot, such an allegiance as Gautier's to Dante was both cause and consequence of a formulated faith. Thus, in his essay, "On the Excellence of Poetry," this ruthless purist goes so far as to say, "Cadenced periods are not enough; and to be quite verse, for a work to be quite a poem and the speech a song, rhyme alone is still wanted." Then, in his essay on his young friend and idol, Baudelaire (it was somewhat mutual), he recalls what a dim view Baudelaire took of poets "who allow themselves to indulge in libertine sonnets." And what does he mean by "libertine"? Nothing wilder or more dissolute than neglect, not just of rhyme, but of the "law" of the quadruple rhyme, i.e., a-b-b-a, a-b-b-a.

Of the poets remaining here in whom the new sound is heard, two of importance remain to engage our attention, before coming to that "friend and idol," Baudelaire. These are the crowned head and heir apparent, respectively, of the Parnassians: Leconte de Lisle and José-Maria de Hérédia. Here the sound was new, chiefly in the sense that the rigor consciously represented long since by Malherbe, and later proclaimed by Boileau, came into its own in a narrow and perfected gamut. If these poems belong to the past, their patina remains undimmed. Ah! Reader, if you speak no French, get someone who does to read you "Le Rêve du Jaguar" and taste its stealthy terror, or "Le Condor" and hover in its thin, frigid air!

At the same time, these consummate Parnassians, when they wrote of flowers, as Hérédia did in "Floridum Mare," or of cattle browsing in the fields (Lisle's "Midi"), confront us with the question of what happened in France to correspond with the "Return to Nature," fathered by Wordsworth, brothered by Keats and Clare; or in Germany by Goethe, Novalis, Eichendorff? The answer is, nothing. There was, in that sense, no "nature poetry": no soul gathered back into the peace that dwells among the lonely hills; no "sense sublime/Of something far more deeply interfused"; no ". . .schöner, grüner Wald,/Du meiner Lust and Wehen/Andächt'ger Aufenthalt!" (". . .beautiful green forest, pensive refuge of my joys and sorrows").[3]

I hear someone say, "If you were looking for nature poetry, why not translate a champion product from the heartland of romanticism,—like Lamartine's 'Le Lac'?" The more opinionated answer to this objection would be that I find no real communion with nature in this celebrated avatar of French romanticism; the more honest answer, that I do not respond warmly to what affects me as its morbidity, whilst its eloquence happens to strike me as being of the sort whose "neck" Verlaine exhorted us to "wring" ("Art Poétique"). For although this poem may avoid the worst pitfalls of Wordsworthian bombast, it seems also to lack the essential Wordsworthian *experience:* the "unknown modes of being" that give rise to the "grave and serious mood," whilst, on the side of *style,* where does it break into anything resembling Wordsworth's visitations of limpid grace, or into that intensity arising from "the consecration and the poet's dream"? Even the Nature belonging to Rimbaud's *Illuminations* tends to be operatic, or theatrical anyway, and was much indebted to hashish.

So what we have left in French nature poetry are landscapes, where the interest in nature as a companion to the mind of man, or as womb of his soul, is displaced by riots of color, as in the remarkable "Flowers" of

Mallarmé, and (again) Hérédia's "Floridum Mare," where he names eight colors in six lines; or else, if it is not merely "pin-ups," lively or insipid, to which this interest gives rise, it will be self-conscious moody broodings, of the sort which constantly impend with sentimentality throughout Victor Hugo's poetry, and which, in Vigny's too often remain afloat by the buoyancy of inflation.

Or else we are subjected to fascinated and sometimes fascinating revulsions. Pope and his fellow Augustans accustomed us to their active distaste, if not for any landscape wilder than Versailles or Woodstock, then certainly for the "deep and gloomy wood" in which Wordsworth so rejoiced. But not even Pope could have cringed from such uncultivated scenes with a horror equal to that of Baudelaire in the poem which he himself had the good sense to title "Obsession"; or worse, of Verlaine, who boasts of his revulsion ("In the Woods," p. 360). Lacking anything corresponding to the Wordsworthian sense of kinship with the wildwood, what remains is: either the neurotic *frisson* of Verlaine, to which we resist all inclination to play depth psychologist; or, I repeat, the skillful depiction of scenes, or landscapes, where any sense of piercing below the surface belongs less to the pastoral poems, such as Hugo's "June Nights," or Nerval's "April," attractive as they are, than to the somber and devasting city poems of Baudelaire ("Evening Twilight" and "Morning Twilight"), or later of Laforgue ("Winter Sunset").

The voice of Baudelaire himself, however, has a far wider range than anything strictly needed for the mastery of such landscape painting. Sometimes it seems to issue from the distant past. Sometimes it makes our hair rise with intimations of Coleridge, Rimbaud, Poe—even Joyce, Kafka, Beckett. . .who knows what *frissons* still to be? Yet no one could be more individual. To call him a great city poet is one way to classify him, if we have to, but why try? Too many have—even while exalting him as France's greatest, and even though we should have learned by now that true greatness resists classification. Still, it would not hurt and might contribute to the rationale of this book to note certain signal ways in which Baudelaire is most French, especially as they are seen working in one of his greatest poems.

If there is one pretty safe generalization about the French, it is to assert their temperamental inclination for keeping their feet on the ground; and for Baudelaire, by his own confession in "The Albatross," any leaning towards the remote—well, even for poetry itself—"impedes his human gait." Moreover, anything in his nature which draws him to worship is liable to take the form of anti-adoration, as also with Rimbaud: a reversion which not even T.S. Eliot's genuflections before the religiosity which he ascribes to Baudelaire would look pious to other Christians as orthodox as Eliot himself (see "Peter's Denial" and "The Rebel," both breathing a defiance and disdain fully as uncompromising, if not so profane, as passages in Rimbaud's "First Communions").

The poem which, more than any other, pronounces Baudelaire's revolt and affirmation is that instant autobiography of man and dreamer, "Benediction," which he did well to place right after the verses to the reader, in the forefront of *Fleurs du Mal.* What other poem is able to take such long and rapid leaps between pride and scorn, despair and high sense of vocation—and all without breaking stride? For sudden shifts, the English poem that might come closest is Byron's *Don Juan,* where what we have, however, is antic alternation of moods, rather than heated fusion of emotions. Or one might advance "The Waste Land"; but there the "leaps" are interstices, rather, produced by the renowned "sacrifice of intellectual to emotional coherence," with more than lucky debts to Pound's blue pencil.

It is the burning intellect of Baudelaire which, consuming the eviscerated emotions, reaches beyond both intellect and emotion, considered in isolation, and dispenses with "blessedness," in any ordinary meaning of the word. In him, as in so many of the best French poets, it is the intellect which, being in them winged and not shackled by feeling, is able to make the desired leaps, whilst perfectly aware of their footing, and thus is intellect of a kind essentially uncharacteristic of English poetry. When Baudelaire is wallowing in lust, his intellect is most on fire.

Where, in either Byron or Eliot (to take again these two species of something less than major poet) could one find anything resembling the fierce definition given to the embrace of degradation and exaltation witnessed in stanzas ten to fifteen of "Benediction"? There, from impersonating the female harpy who exults in being the idol of abject worship, the speaker leaps to take wing for the heaven of the poet, who weaves the very anguish of this humiliation into his "mystical crown." What prayers and curses and psalms of triumph are pinned down in the fiery focus of such condensed benediction!

This important poem may serve as climactic reminder of how the more characteristic, earthbound preoccupations of Baudelaire blind us to the rarefied components of his genius. In the poems of his here represented, one may observe two distinct orders of mysterious *reciprocity.* The first belongs to the hidden relationships among the manifold of sense (e.g., "Correspondences"); and the second, to the distinctive reciprocal necessity of turmoil and peace exemplified in "Meditation," and even more in "The Void": yes, the same as that word of Hugo and Laforgue, *"le gouffre."* In the last line of Baudelaire's poem by that name we have something like a metaphysical declaration in favor of the void, although, being a poet first, and philosopher, if at all, very much second, Baudelaire himself might have felt a bit uncomfortable to be confronted by so bleak an account of the effect.

The suddenly revealed discomforts of this complex man and poet threaten to shake even the safest generalizations—about his Frenchness or his impiety or his overtness. We need, for example, to be unusually alert in making full allowance for his shyness when he speaks of those matters supernatural for which he does *not* feel scorn. Shyness is not indifference. When, rarely, he does let us into his confidence about this side of him, it is by hints, all the more intriguing for their indirectness or disguise. One clue to his submerged devotion is the surprising way he takes offence at mockery aimed by other authors—for example, by Molière in *Tartuffe;* another is such obiter dicta as that the only professions he found worthy of respect were those of soldier, poet, and priest! Most significant of all were his veiled references to certain covert prepossessions, as when, in *My Heart Laid Bare,* he says: "However, I do possess several convictions, in the highest sense of the word, which cannot be understood by men of my time."

Perhaps the extraordinary popularity of this poet is a fulfilment of that utterance, a sign that it is only now he is beginning to reach us—if indeed he is; for I think he speaks first to poets. But then also, for Baudelaire, as for Donne, for Keats, for Pushkin, for Rilke, there is always the future.

1. These lines occasion an apparent confusion in St. John Lucas's introduction to *The Oxford Book of French Verse,* which seems to be attributing them to "Les Destinées," and without focusing their defiance.

2. There are the disturbing accounts of Hugo's literal self-enthronement for those who took the shoes off their feet to approach him. But also, like Dryden in his "Preface to the Fables," and Wordsworth in his "Preface to the Lyrical Ballads," Hugo, in the preface to his "Cromwell," is the poet-critic, prescribing the criterion by which he expects to be judged.

3. From "Abschied" by Joseph von Eichendorff

"LE VOYAGE": ROBERT LOWELL (The Vogue of "Versions")

Robert Lowell's "Version" of this poem, as of twelve more of Baudelaire's [*The Voyage and Other Versions of Poems by Baudelaire,* by Robert Lowell, Farrar, Strauss, & Giroux, New York, 1958], presents a special problem, one at a level of the philosophy of translation which is at the same time more primary and more advanced than most and to which it would be in the interests of our business to devote some careful attention. First for Robert Lowell comes being true to himself, to his own considerable, if overestimated, talent. Subject to the level of the translator's gift, and the number and audacity of the liberties he takes, this is no mean priority. It is not often that Lowell's popular bowdlerizations (or un-Baudelairizations) of these poems come in danger of being stale, although this is capable of happening too, as when he will say, "time on our hands," for "cette après-midi qui n'a jamais de fin" (for which I decided to fall back on the "always afternoon" of "The Lotus Eaters" (1832), since Baudelaire might conceivably have borrowed it from Tennyson in the first place). But even if we chalk up marks for every resistance to the *flat*, the question would still remain, how profitable will be the result if it is indifferent to the responsibility for retaining the original imagery; for this, more than any other single element, *is* the poetry, so that any radical departure from this element might find it difficult to qualify, even as "imitation."

We need read no further than the third stanza of Lowell's "Version" before encountering an all too typically strong transfusion; for this is where Baudelaire says:

> Les uns, joyeux de fuir une patrie infâme;
> D'autres, l'horreur de leur berceaux, et quelque-uns,
> Astrologues noyés dans les yeux d'une femme,
> La Circé tyrannique aux dangereux parfums.

Here the last two lines, which speak of "Astrologers drowned in a woman's eyes, / The tyrannous Circe with the dangerous perfume. . ." become for Lowell, "With their binoculars on a woman's breast, / reptilian Circe with her junk and wand." What junk? The only possible source of addiction in the verse is Circe's perfume; whilst binoculars, whether or not mounted on a woman's breast, would be of no use to this drowning astrologer, too infatuated to consult his horoscope. If we are, in any sense whatever, going after Baudelaire, we have a duty to direct attention, in this instance, a) to Circe's perfume; and b) to the consultation with stars about the outcome of infatuations. The original idea is much too rich to trifle with. But we run into this sort of thing in very many of the thirty-seven stanzas.

The fourth section of the poem contains an excoriation of the idols of the tribe: the thickening, hardening trunk of the great tree of desire; idols with trumpets, pomp of carved palaces, ruinous dreams of bankers, thrones studded with *shining gems* (which for some reason Lowell translates as *"Slavic saints"*). Lowell has already surprised us in the seventh line of the fourth stanza by converting "Des femmes dont les dents et les ongles sont teints" into "dancers with tattooed bellies and behinds." Baudelaire might let that go with a fleeting grin, though he would see that it does not contribute to the actual biting *sound* of the original, whilst it also gets in the way of Lowell's own rhyme; nor would Baudelaire share the petulant squeamishness about women's "fesses," or buttocks, which sends Lowell so sharply off his text here. But then for the memorable second line of the sixth stanza:

> La femme, esclave vile, orgueilleuse et stupide,
> Sans rire s'adorant et s'aimant sans dégoût;
> L'homme, tyran goulu, paillard, dur et cupide,
> Esclave de l'esclave et ruisseau dans l'égout;

Lowell gives this, where the distortions *really* compound:

there women, servile, peacock-tailed and coarse,
marry for money, and love without disgust
horny pot-bellied tyrants stuffed on lust,
slaves' slaves—the sewer in which their gutter pours!

We have lost the humorless self-adoration of the female and get instead the baffling importation of women marrying for money. Gone is the self-absorbed sadism of the male, who is the female's counterpart. The syntax makes it far from clear that the male provides the gutter spouting into the female sewer (Roy Campbell, usually among the best, this time gets it even more wrong); and instead of Baudelaire's frightful torturers and martyrs, of the next stanza, Lowell's answer feeds his illustrator with the insipid caption, "playboys who live each hour," and gives him permission to depart in other respects from Lowell's "old maids who weep" (itself unlike anything in the French) of the self same line, since this illustrator (Sidney Nolan) feels at liberty to turn the weeping old maid, herself the strangest importation, into a leering aggressor in the uppermost position for the sexual act! Between translator and illustrator, we get further and further away.

The reader will understand that these are not just verbal departures, nor even mere imagistic caprices; Baudelaire's more than Swiftian rage has been reduced to a spite on the rather petty scale of a Gore Vidal or a Truman Capote, so that it should come as no surprise when the departures from Baudelaire's meaning become endemic and systemic. Why, then, the *réclame*, the lavish editions, the dedication to T.S. Eliot (who is not exactly ignorant of French), and so forth? Well, not all of Lowell's "Versions" are a botch. We have some lively *and* faithful verses. Two stanzas later than the above, Eliot, if he ever read it, probably felt at least polite about "O mon semblable, ô mon maître, je te maudis!" being freely rendered, "My image and my lord, I hate your soul!" And the eminent dedicatee might also have responded affably when, two stanzas later again, something of Baudelaire's rhythm is caught with: "Shall we move or rest? Rest, if you can rest;/move if you must. . .," as that rhythm is approximated in other passages, not impossible to find.

But what it comes to is this: If you are·a good poet and lucky, you can improve on some of the lines of a great poem some of the time; but to affect to improve upon any of them you choose at any time you choose, in order to startle or sparkle, will involve you in presumption, or something less than honesty, or both. As to the extent to which the translator of poetry *is* himself a poet, this whole question is a mined no-man's-land; but it is certain that the splendid poet and translator, Robert Fitzgerald, is right about it's not being a question that can be answered by the translator himself, and Robert Lowell has received too much critical acclaim to have to answer it.

It may be that the best safeguard against "versions" that translate "marks of kisses" as "sores of debauchery," and all such pratfalls that have aroused suspicion of the translation of poetry as a con game of the art, would be to do as the estimable poet and Sinologist W. Yip does, and present several aspirants, side by side [*Ezra Pound's Cathay*, Princeton University, 1968]. In fact, one can think of few better disciplines for the student of a) Baudelaire, b) the French language, and c) poetry, than to select several stanzas from, say, "Le Voyage," and then place about seven versions of them side by side: 1) Baudelaire's; 2) Anthony Hartley's literal "blow-by-blow," as printed at the foot of the Penguin page; 3) Roy Campbell's; 4) Robert Lowell's; 5) Joanna Richardson's; 6) Barbara Gibb's (unrhymed); and 7) the student's own, either literal, or, if there has been assurance that he is a poet, in the best and closest verse that he himself can make. He may well end having a right to feel better satisfied with his own than with any other outside the original.

André Chénier

1762 - 1814

Iambes (VIII)

Oɴ vit; on vit infâme. Eh bien? il fallut l'être;
    L'infâme après tout mange et dort.
Ici même, en ses parcs, où la mort nous fait paître,
    Où la hache nous tire au sort,
Beaux poulets sont écrits; maris, amants sont dupes;
    Caquetage, intrigues de sots.
On y chante; on y joue; on y lève des jupes;
    On y fait chansons et bons mots;
L'un pousse et fait bondir sur les toits, sur les vitres,
    Un ballon tout gonflé de vent,
Comme sont les discours des sept cents plats bélitres,
    Dont Barère est le plus savant.
L'autre court; l'autre saute; et braillent, boivent, rient
    Politiques et raisonneurs;
Et sur les gonds de fer soudain les portes crient.
    Des juges tigres nos seigneurs
Le pourvoyeur paraît. Quelle sera la proie
    Que la hache appelle aujourd'hui?
Chacun frissonne, écoute; et chacun avec joie
    Voit que ce n'est pas encor lui...

André Chénier

1762 - 1814

Iambes (VIII)

We live, we live in shame. And so? And so it is;
    Shame after all must eat and sleep.
Here even, in these pens, where death puts us to graze,
    And where an ax conducts the sweep,
Love notes are passed, husbands and lovers duped by flirts;
    Intrigues of fools and chitter-chat.
They sing here, and they gamble; or they lift their skirts;
    They make up songs and bandy wit;
Someone sends up, to bounce on roof and window pane,
    A toy balloon, blown up with air
Like speeches of the seven hundred rogues inane,
    Of whom the wisest is Barère.*
One runs, another jumps; the wiseacres intone,
    Or politicians drink, laugh, bray—
Till, on their iron hinges, doors abruptly groan.
    Our masters' turnkey makes entrée,
A caterer for tigers. Who now will it be
    The waiting ax today will get?
We listen, shudder—till each one with joy may see
    His turn has not come up just yet . . .

*A member of the Convention Nationale, whose name Chénier ciphers, whilst himself waiting in prison for the lot to fall of the guillotine's "sweepstake." Doubtless the poet's turn came whilst working on this satire. For this information, as also for the selection of this fragment entire, I am indebted to Geoffrey Brereton's *The Penguin Book of French Verse, 2: Sixteenth to Eighteenth Centuries.*

Iambes (Saint-Lazare, 1794)

QUAND au mouton bêlant la sombre boucherie
  Ouvre ses cavernes de mort;
Pâtre, chiens et moutons, toute la bergerie
  Ne s'informe plus de son sort!
Les enfants qui suivaient ses ébats dans la plaine,
  Les vierges aux belles couleurs
Qui le baisaient en foule, et sur sa blanche laine
  Entrelaçaient rubans et fleurs,
Sans plus penser à lui, le mangent s'il est tendre.
  Dans cet abîme enseveli,
J'ai le même destin. Je m'y devais attendre.
  Accoutumons-nous à l'oubli.
Oubliés comme moi dans cet affreux repaire,
  Mille autres moutons, comme moi
Pendus aux crocs sanglants du charnier populaire,
  Seront servis au peuple-roi.
Que pouvaient mes amis? Oui, de leur main chérie
  Un mot, à travers ces barreaux,
A versé quelque baume en mon âme flétrie;
  De l'or peut-être à mes bourreaux....
Mais tout est précipice. Ils ont eu droit de vivre.
  Vivez, amis vivez contents!
En dépit de Bavus, soyez lents à me suivre;
  Peut-être en de plus heureux temps
J'ai moi-même, à l'aspect des pleurs de l'infortune,
  Détourné mes regards distraits;
A mon tour, aujourd'hui, mon malheur importune;
  Vivez, amis, vivez en paix.

Chénier

Iambes (Saint-Lazare, 1794)

WHEN the deathly cavern of the somber abattoir
    Is opened to a bleating lamb,
Shepherds and dogs and other sheep are scarcely aware
    Beyond this of the fate to come.
Children who earlier followed its gambols on the grass,
    The maidens with their lovely skin
Who crowded around to kiss it and in its snowy fleece
    Ribbons and flowers to intertwine,
Without a second thought devour it if it's tender.
    Buried deep in this abyss,
I suffer the same fate. I should have been fonder
    Of facts. Let us get used to this.
Forgotten just like me in this appalling lair,
    Like me a thousand other sheep,
Hanging from bloody hooks in the common larder here,
    Are dished up to the Sovereign People.
What could my friends do? Yes, a word from their dear hand
    Passed to me through these iron bars
Might yet have poured some balm upon my withered mind—
    Or bribed my executioners.
All face a precipice. They had their right to be free.
    Live still, my dear ones, live content.
In spite of Bavus*, don't rush to follow me;
    Myself, before imprisonment,
When seeing, perhaps, the tears of those less fortunate,
    Have closed my eyes to their distress;
Now it's my turn for grief to be importunate.
    Then live, my friends. Live on in peace.

*Fouquier-Tinville, public accuser of the Revolutionary Tribunal.

189

Pierre-Jean de Béranger

1780 - 1857

Le roi d'Yvetot

Il était un roi d'Yvetot
    Peu connu dans l'histoire,
Se levant tard, se couchant tôt,
    Dormant fort bien sans gloire,
Et couronné par Jeanneton
D'un simple bonnet de coton,
    Dit-on.
Oh! oh! oh! oh! ah! ah! ah! ah!
Quel bon petit roi c'était là!
    La, la.

If faisait ses quatre repas
    Dans son palais de chaume,
Et sur un âne, pas à pas,
    Parcourait son royaume.
Joyeux, simple et croyant le bien,
Pour toute garde il n'avait rien
    Qu'un chien.
Oh! oh! oh! oh! ah! ah! ah! ah!
Quel bon petit roi c'était là!
    La, la.

Il n'avait de goût onéreux
    Qu'une soif un peu vive;
Mais, en rendant son peuple heureux,
    Il faut bien qu'un roi vive.
Lui-même, à table et sans suppôt,
Sur chaque muid levait un pot
    D'impôt.
Oh! oh! oh! oh! ah! ah! ah! ah!
Quel bon petit roi c'était là!
    La, la.

Pierre-Jean de Béranger

1780 - 1857

The king of Yvetot *

He was a king of Yvetot,
    Little known in story;
Going to bed early, rising late,
    His head lay eased of glory;
For crown his Jane put on it
A cotton sleeping bonnet:
    He won it.
Ho! ho! ho! ho! hee! hee! hee! hee!
What a good little king was he!
    Hee! hee!

He would take four meals a day
    In a thatched-roof palace grand
And on a donkey stray
    In leisure through the land,
Joyful and simple, trusting in good,
And having not a thing for guard
    But a dog.
Ho! ho! ho! ho! hee! hee! hee! hee!
What a good little king was he!
    Hee! hee!

He had no lavish hobby
    Except a lively thirst;
To make their people happy
    Kings must be happy first.
At table he, without support,
For every barrel levied a quart
    Of import.
Ho! ho! ho! ho! hee! hee! hee! hee!
What a good little king was he!
    Hee! hee!

*Pronounced to rhyme with *heave a pot.*

191

Aux filles de bonnes maisons
    Comme il avait su plaire,
Ses sujets avaient cent raisons
    De le nommer leur père.
D'ailleurs il ne levait de ban
Que pour tirer, quatre fois l'an,
    Au blanc.
Oh! oh! oh! oh! ah! ah! ah! ah!
Quel bon petit roi c'était là!
    La, la.

Il n'agrandit point ses Etats,
    Fut un voisin commode,
Et, modèle des potentats,
    Prit le plaisir pour code.
Ce n'est que lorsqu'il expira
Que le peuple, qui l'enterra,
    Pleura.
Oh! oh! oh! oh! ah! ah! ah! ah!
Quel bon petit roi c'était là!
    La, la.

On conserve encor le portrait
    De ce digne et bon prince :
C'est l'enseigne d'un cabaret
    Fameux dans la province.
Les jours de fête, bien souvent,
La foule s'écrie en buvant
    Devant :
Oh! oh! oh! oh! ah! ah! ah! ah!
Quel bon petit roi c'était là!
    La, la.

Because he liked to honey
    With ladies of good feather,
His subjects had full many
    A cause to call him father.
He rarely went saluting,
Only for target shooting
    Saluting.
Ho! ho! ho! ho! hee! hee! hee! hee!
What a good little king was he!
    Hee! hee!

He sought no lebensraum;
    No neighbor did he goad;
This model monarch came
    With pleasure for his code;
So when at last he died,
His people far and wide
    All cried.
Ho! ho! ho! ho! hee! hee! hee! hee!
What a good little king was he!
    Hee! hee!

This prince who was so fine
    Left portraits that would stand
In bars, or swing on signs,
    Famous throughout the land,
And when the people drink,
They raise a glass and clink,
    And think.
Ho! ho! ho! ho! hee! hee! hee! hee!
What a good little king was he!
    Hee! hee!

Marceline Desbordes-Valmore
1786 - 1859

Souvenir

QUAND il pâlit un soir, et que sa voix tremblante
S'éteignit tout à coup dans un mot commencé;
Quand ses yeux, soulevant leur paupière brûlante,
Me blessèrent d'un mal dont je le crus blessé;
Quand ses traits plus touchants, éclairés d'une flamme
     Qui ne s'éteint jamais,
S'imprimèrent vivants dans le fond de mon âme:
     Il n'aimait pas, j'aimais!

Marceline Desbordes-Valmore

1786 - 1859

Recollection

WHEN he turned pale that night and his voice shook,
Suddenly faltering on the brink of sound,
And when he lifted his eyes with a burning look,
Inflicting what I took for his own wound,
When all's that dear in him flamed up for me,
    And, never to grow dim,
Was printed on my soul, it was not he
    That loved me, I loved him.

La couronne effeuillée

J'IRAI, j'irai porter ma couronne effeuillée
Au jardin de mon père où revit toute fleur;
J'y répandrai longtemps mon âme agenouillée:
Mon père a des secrets pour vaincre la douleur.

J'irai, j'irai lui dire, au moins avec mes larmes:
"Regardez, j'ai souffert..." Il me regardera,
Et sous mes jours changés, sous mes pâleurs sans charmes,
Parce qu'il est mon père il me reconnaîtra.

Il dira: "C'est donc vous, chère âme désolée!
La terre manque-t-elle à vos pas égarés?
Chère âme, je suis Dieu; ne soyez plus troublée;
Voici votre maison, voici mon cœur, entrez."

O clémence! ô douceur! ô saint refuge, ô Père!
Votre enfant qui pleurait vous l'avez entendu!
Je vous obtiens déjà puisque je vous espère
Et que vous possédez tout ce que j'ai perdu.

Vous ne rejetez pas la fleur qui n'est plus belle;
Ce crime de la terre au ciel est pardonné.
Vous ne maudirez pas votre enfant infidèle,
Non d'avoir rien vendu, mais d'avoir tout donné.

The leafless crown

I WILL go, I will go and bear my leafless crown
Unto my father's garden where flowers may live again;
I will pour out there my soul a long time kneeling down:
My father knoweth secrets for conquering all pain.

I'll go, I'll go and tell him—my tears will do no harm—
"See, I have suffered…" And he will look at me,
And under my changed days, my pallor without charm,
Because he is my father, what I am he'll see.

He will say, "And so it's you, my desolated dear!
Does the world fail you on the byways you have been?
Dear heart, I am God; be not troubled any more;
Here is your home, and here's my heart, come in."

O kindness! sweetness! refuge! O Father, I know
You listened, you have heard your weeping child at least!
Because my hope is in you, at last I grasp you now
And you possess already all that I have lost.

You don't reject the flower that is no longer fair;
This evil of the world in heaven is forgiven.
You will not curse your child, unfaithful in despair,
For having nothing sold, because all things were given.

Alphonse Lamartine

1790 - 1869

Vers sur un album

Le livre de la vie est le livre suprême
Qu'on ne peur ni fermer, ni rouvrir à son choix;
Le passage attachant ne s'y lit pas deux fois,
Mais le feuillet fatal se tourne de lui-même;
On voudrait revenir à la page où l'on aime
Et la page où l'on meurt est déjà sous vos doigts!

Alphonse Lamartine

1790 - 1869

Verse in an album

THE book of life above all books is lord,
Closed never nor reopened by our choice;
The most attractive lines are not read twice,
The fatal leaves turn of their own accord:
We yearn back to the page where one adored
And the page already opens where one dies.

Victor Hugo
1802 - 1885

Nuits de Juin

L'ÉTÉ, lorsque le jour a fui, de fleurs couverte
La plaine verse au loin un parfum enivrant;
Les yeux fermés, l'oreille aux rumeurs entr'ouverte,
On ne dort qu'à demi d'un sommeil transparent.

Les astres sont plus purs, l'ombre paraît meilleure;
Un vague demi-jour teint le dôme éternel;
Et l'aube doux et pâle, en attendant son heure,
Semble toute la nuit errer au bas du ciel.

Elle était déchaussée...

ELLE était déchaussée, elle était décoiffée,
Assise, les pieds nus, parmi les joncs penchants;
Moi qui passais par là, je crus voir une fée,
Et je lui dis: Veux-tu t'en venir dans les champs?

Elle me regarda de ce regard suprême
Qui reste à la beauté quand nous en triomphons,
Et je lui dis: Veux-tu, c'est le mois où l'on aime,
Veux-tu nous en aller sous les arbres profonds?

Elle essuya ses pieds à l'herbe de la rive;
Elle me regarda pour la seconde fois,
Et la belle folâtre alors devint pensive.
Oh! comme les oiseaux chantaient au fond des bois!

Comme l'eau caressait doucement le rivage!
Je vis venir à moi, dans les grands roseaux verts,
La belle fille heureuse, effarée et sauvage,
Ses cheveux dans ses yeux, et riant au travers.

Victor Hugo

1802 - 1885

June nights

WHEN day has fled, all covered with flowers, the summer
Drenches the plain with intoxicating scent:
Eyes closed, ears partly open to each rumor,
We are half gone in a sleep to the light transparent.

The stars are purer then, more perfect the shade;
A vague half-day tints the eternal on high;
And the sweet, pale dawn, awaiting her hour to invade,
Seems to wander all night on the verge of the sky.

She wore no stockings...

SHE wore no stockings; she was hatless, wild,
And sat with her naked feet in the bending reeds.
I was passing by, believed her a fairy child,
And said to her: would you come where the meadow leads?

She glanced at me with that triumphant look
That belongs to beauty stooping from above;
And I said, "Would you rather find a shady nook?
Would you? This is the month ordained for love."

She dried her feet in the grass by the river-bank,
She looked at me a second time at her ease,
And the lovely playful one now paused to think.
Oh! how the birds were singing in the trees!

How softly the water caressed the banks of the stream!
Between the tall green reeds I saw her approaching,
This carefree girl, faintly startled, that nothing could tame,
Her hair in her eyes and her laughter sideways arching.

Le vieillard chaque jour...

LE vieillard chaque jour dans plus d'ombre s'éveille;
A chaque aube il est mort un peu plus que la veille.
La vie humaine, ce nœud vil,
Se défait lentement, rongé par l'âme ailée;
Le sombre oiseau lié veut prendre sa volée
Et casse chaque jour un fil.

O front blanc qu'envahit la grande nuit tombante,
Meurs! tour à tour ta voix, ta face succombante,
Ton œil où décroît l'horizon
S'éteignent — ce sera mon destin et le vôtre —
Comme on voit se fermer le soir l'une après l'autre
Les fenêtres d'une maison.

Ave, Dea; moriturus te salutat

A Judith Gautier

LA mort et la beauté sont deux choses profondes
Qui contiennent tant d'ombre et d'azur qu'on dirait
Deux sœurs également terribles et fécondes
Ayant la même énigme et le même secret.
O femmes, voix, regards, cheveux noirs, tresses blondes,
Brillez, je meurs! Ayez l'éclat, l'amour, l'attrait,
O perles que la mer mêle à ses grandes ondes,
O lumineux oiseaux de la sombre forêt!
Judith, nos deux destins sont plus près l'un de l'autre
Qu'on me croirait, à voir mon visage et le vôtre;
Tout le divin abîme apparaît dans vos yeux,
Et moi, je sens le gouffre étoilé dans mon âme;
Nous sommes tous les deux voisins du ciel, madame,
Puisque vous êtes belle et puisque je suis vieux.

Each day the old man...

EACH day the old man wakes in shadow more,
Each dawn more dead than on the day before.
   The life of man, that nest of clay,
Is worn out slowly by the winged mind;
Bound fast, the somber bird, chafing to find
   His freedom, breaks a thread each day.

Pale forehead that the falling night invades,
Die! Each in turn, your voice, your eye where fades
   The distance, and your dwindling face
Are dying down—this is my fate and yours—
Like watching, one by one, at dusk indoors
   The windows closing in a house.

Ave, Dea; moriturus te salutat
       To Judith Gautier

BEAUTY and death are two deep things that tell
Of so much light and shade, one could pronounce
These sisters equal, whether fecund or fell,
The same enigma, same concealed response.
  O women, voices, looks, black hair and yel-
low braids, shine, I must die! Seize radiance,
Love, charm, O pearls the sea hurls in its swell,
O shining birds where somber woods grow dense!
  Judith, our fates are closer than appears
To one another, by my face and yours;
Deep in your eyes all heaven's depths unfold,
  Deep in my soul I feel the starred abyss;
Both you and I to heaven are moving close,
Since you are beautiful and I am old.

Gérard de Nerval

1808 - 1855

Avril

DÉJÀ les beaux jours, — la poussière,
Un ciel d'azur et de lumière,
Les murs enflammés, les longs soirs; —
Et rien de vert: — à peine encore
Un reflet rougeâtre décore
Les grands arbres aux rameaux noirs!

Ce beau temps me pèse et m'ennuie.
— Ce n'est qu'après des jours de pluie
Que doit surgir, en un tableau,
Le printemps verdissant et rose,
Comme une nymphe fraîche éclose,
Qui, souriante, sort de l'eau.

Le relais

EN voyage, on s'arrête, on descend de voiture;
Puis entre deux maisons on passe à l'aventure,
Des chevaux, de la route et des fouets étourdi,
L'œil fatigué de voir et le corps engourdi.

Et voici tout à coup, silencieuse et verte,
Une vallée humide et de lilas couverte,
Un ruisseau qui murmure entre les peupliers, —
Et la route et le bruit sont bien vite oubliés!

On se couche dans l'herbe et l'on s'écoute vivre,
De l'odeur du foin vert à loisir on s'enivre,
Et sans penser à rien on regarde les cieux...
Hélas! une voix crie: "En voiture, messieurs!"

Gérard de Nerval

1808 - 1855

April

FINE days already, dusty blight,
The azure sky ablaze with light,
The lengthening evenings, walls on fire,
With nothing green, and hardly yet
The flushed reflections to offset
Black branches where the trees aspire.

How heavily my heart sustains
This brilliant weather! Only rains
Should usher in the month of May,
A picture turning green and rose,
The way a nymph emerging glows
With water, smiling at her play.

Stagecoach

You reach a stop and climb down from the bus;*
Sick of the traffic's pandemonium,
You risk a short stroll from the terminus,
Eyes stupefied with staring, body numb.

Here suddenly you find silence and green,
A small, damp valley, covered with lilac;
Tall poplars and a murmuring stream between:
Your brutal route has struck a bivouac.

You lie on grass and hear your life go by,
You get a little drunk on the smell of sward,
You think of not one thing except the sky—
And then you hear a voice cry, "All aboard!"

*Would this poetic journalese, scarcely less so in Nerval, qualify as
Lowellian "version"? At least it's loose and gropes for parallel sound?

Fantaisie

Iʟ est un air pour qui je donnerais
Tout Rossini, tout Mozart et tout Weber,
Un air très vieux, languissant et funèbre,
Qui pour moi seul a des charmes secrets !

Or, chaque fois que je viens à l'entendre,
De deux cents ans mon âme rajeunit...
C'est sous Louis treize; et je crois voir s'étendre
Un coteau vert, que le couchant jaunit.

Puis un château de brique à coins de pierre,
Aux vitraux teints de rougeâtres couleurs,
Ceint de grands parcs, avec une rivière
Baignant ses pieds, qui coule entre les fleurs;

Puis une dame, à sa haute fenêtre,
Blonde aux yeux noirs, en ses habits anciens,
Que, dans une autre existence peut-être,
J'ai déjà vue... et dont je me souviens !

Fantasy

Iᴛ is a tune for which I'd gladly give
Rossini, Weber, our entire Mozart,
Tune very old and languishing and grave,
Whose secret charm is only for my heart.

Now, every time I hear that air, my mind
Is younger by two hundred years undone:
Louis the Thirteenth reigns; I seem to find
A green hill yellowed by the setting sun;

Then a chateau, stone-angled, mainly brick,
With rose-glass windows shining in the towers,
A river at its feet and spreading park,
Through which the water flows between its flowers.

And then a lady at a high window,
Blond with black eyes, a dress long obsolete,
Whom in some other life I once did know,
Perhaps, and, having seen do not forget.

Vers dorés

Eh quoi! tout est sensible!

PYTHAGORAS

HOMME! libre penseur — te crois-tu seul pensant
Dans ce monde où la vie éclate en toute chose:
Des forces que tu tiens ta liberté dispose,
Mais de tous tes conseils l'univers est absent.
    Respecte dans la bête un esprit agissant: ...
Chaque fleur est une âme à la Nature éclose;
Un mystère d'amour dans le métal repose:
"Tout est sensible!" Et tout sur ton être est puissant.
    Crains, dans le mur aveugle un regard qui t'épie:
A la matière même un verbe est attaché...
Ne la fais pas servir à quelque usage impie!
    Souvent dans l'être obscur habite un Dieu caché;
Et comme un œil naissant couvert par ses paupières,
Un pur esprit s'accroît sous l'écorce des pierres!

Le point noir

QUICONQUE a regardé le soleil fixement
Croit voir devant ses yeux voler obstinément
Autour de lui, dans l'air une tache livide.

Ainsi, tout jeune encore et plus audacieux,
Sur la gloire un instant j'osai fixer les yeux:
Un point noir est resté dans mon regard avide.

Depuis, mêlée à tout comme un signe de deuil,
Partout, sur quelque endroit que s'arrête mon œil,
Je la vois se poser aussi, la tache noire! —

Quoi, toujours! Entre moi sans cesse et le bonheur!
Oh! c'est que l'aigle seul — malheur à nous! malheur!
Contemple impunément le Soleil et la Gloire.

Golden verses

> What! Everything can feel!
> PYTHAGORAS

WHEN everything with life is bursting out,
Think you, free thinking man, you think alone?
Your liberty can rule the strength you own,
But larger worlds are absent from your thought.
    Respect in every beast an active soul:
A mind unfolds in every waving flower;
In metal too sleeps love's mysterious power;
"All things can feel!" All hold you in control.
    Fear in the sightless wall a watching glance:
Even with matter there's a built-in word.
O never make it serve an evil chance!
    Often the dark of being hides a God;
And, like an eye with shuttered eyelids born,
A pure spirit grows beneath the stone.

The dark smudge

WHOEVER gazes steadfast at the sun
Will always see before his eyes a stain
That trembles black in the surrounding air.

So, while still young and too bold not to try,
I dared into that blaze to dart my eye,
Since when the spot of black is always there.

Mingled with everything, a sign of woe,
No matter where it is my glances go,
I see it settling too, this livid blight.

What! Always this between my joy and me?
Woe to us! Only the eagle, none but he,
Can stare unblinded into that great light.

Le Christ aux oliviers

> Dieu est mort! le ciel est vide...
> Pleurez! enfants, vous n'avez
> plus de père!
>
> JEAN-PAUL

III

"Immobile Destin, muette sentinelle,
Froide Nécessité!... Hasard qui, t'avançant
Parmi les mondes morts sous la neige éternelle,
Refroidis, par degrés, l'univers pâlissant,
   "Sais-tu ce que tu fais, puissance originelle,
De tes soleils éteints, l'un l'autre se froissant...
Es-tu sûr de transmettre une haleine immortelle,
Entre un monde qui meurt et l'autre renaissant?...
   "O mon père! est-ce toi que je sens en moi-même?
As-tu pouvoir de vivre et de vaincre la mort?
Aurais-tu succombé sous un dernier effort
   "De cet ange des nuits que frappa l'anathème?...
Car je me sens tout seul à pleurer et souffrir,
Hélas! et, si je meurs, c'est que tout va mourir!"

Christ in the olive grove

> God is dead! The sky is empty.
> Weep, children, you have no
> more father!
>
> JEAN-PAUL

III

*"UNMOVING Destiny, dumb sentinel,
Cold doom, blind luck amid dead planets hiding,
Beneath whose everlasting winter will
Freeze slowly all existence still abiding,
    "Know you what you are doing, original
Decree, with all your burnt out suns colliding
Against each other?... Are you sure to exhale
A deathless breath for each new world subsiding?
    "My father! is it you in me I feel?
Have you the power to live and conquer death?
Or could you have succumbed, at his last breath,
    "To the angel of night, struck by the curse of hell?
I weep and suffer utterly alone,
And if I die, then all die, all's undone!"

*Christ speaks.

Alfred de Musset
1810 - 1857

A Julie

On me demande, par les rues,
Pourquoi je vais bayant aux grues,
Fumant mon cigare au soleil,
A quoi se passe ma jeunesse,
Et depuis trois ans de paresse
Ce qu'ont fait mes nuits sans sommeil.

Donne-moi tes lèvres, Julie;
Les folles nuits qui t'ont pâlie
Ont séché leur corail luisant.
Parfume-les de ton haleine;
Donne-les-moi, mon Africaine,
Tes belles lèvres de pur sang.

Mon imprimeur crie à tue-tête
Que sa machine est toujours prête,
Et que la mienne n'en peut mais.
D'honnêtes gens, qu'un club admire,
N'ont pas dédaigné de prédire
Que je n'en reviendrai jamais

Julie, as-tu du vin d'Espagne?
Hier, nous battions la campagne;
Va donc voir s'il en reste encor.
Ta bouche est brûlante, Julie;
Inventons donc quelque folie
Qui nous perde l'âme et le corps.

Alfred de Musset

1810 - 1857

To Julie

WHY, they ask me, in the street,
Gape at every tart I meet,
Smoke cigars beneath the sun,
How my youth has been misspent,
Three years lavished to lament
What my sleepless nights have done.

Please, your lips, my Julie! All
Those wild nights that made you pale
Drained the crimson from the bud.
Make it fragrant with your breath;
Give me that sweet Afric mouth
With its purity of blood.

Printer's yelling off his head:
Press all set to go, he said,
Mine the one to show the lack.
Honest club-sustaining folk
Never, when of me they spoke,
Scorned to say I'd not come back.

Julie, have we any wine?
How about that quart from Spain?
Yesterday we drank it all?
Burning up, your mouth is, Julie;
Let's both think up some new folly,
Good to sink us body and soul.

On dit que ma gourme me rentre,
Que je n'ai plus rien dans le ventre,
Que je suis vide à faire peur;
Je crois, si j'en valais la peine,
Qu'on m'enverrait à Sainte-Hélène,
Avec un cancer dans le cœur.

Allons, Julie, il faut t'attendre
A me voir quelque jour en cendre,
Comme Hercule sur son rocher.
Puisque c'est par toi que j'expire,
Ouvre ta robe, Déjanire,
Que je monte sur mon bûcher.

La nuit d'Octobre

LE POETE

... C'ETAIT, il m'en souvient, par une nuit d'automne,
Triste et froide, à peu près semblable à celle-ci;
Le murmure du vent, de son bruit monotone,
Dans mon cerveau lassé berçait mon noir souci.
J'étais à la fenêtre, attendant ma maîtresse;
Et, tout en écoutant dans cette obscurité,
Je me sentais dans l'âme une telle détresse,
Qu'il me vint le soupçon d'une infidélité.
La rue où je logeais était sombre et déserte;
Quelques ombres passaient, un falot à la main;
Quand la bise sifflait dans la porte entr'ouverte,
On entendait de loin comme un soupir humain.
Je ne sais, à vrai dire, à quel fâcheux présage
Mon esprit inquiet alors s'abandonna.

So I'm "reaping what I've sown,"
Gut with nothing but a groan,
Empty too with fear my art;
Were I only worth the pain,
Pack me off to Saint Hélène,
With a cancer in my heart.

Come, my Julie, best be warned,
Some day you will see me burned,
Hercules upon his pyre!
Since by you it is I'm dead,
Deianira's dress be spread:
Let me climb into the fire.

October night

THE POET *
. . . I REMEMBER that it was a night of the Fall,
Cheerless and cold, a little like this one;
The murmur of the wind, with its sad call,
Cradled a black mood in my weary brain.
I stood at the window, waiting for my mistress;
And in the dark, listening with every pulse,
My mind began to feel so much distress,
There came to me the thought that she was false.
The street I lived in was deserted, drear;
Some shadows from a lamp in hand swung by;
When the wind whistled through the door ajar,
It sounded like a distant human sigh.
Of what presentiments I then would feel,
To tell the truth, I know not how to speak.

*This selection in effect commences and concludes the long speech by
"le Poète," which is the heart of the lengthy Dialogue between the Poet
and the Muse. Not enough would be gained by including the rest, which
is very uneven.

Je rappelais en vain un reste de courage,
Et me sentis frémir lorsque l'heure sonna.
Elle ne venait pas. Seul, la tête baissée,
Je regardai longtemps les murs et le chemin, —
Et je ne t'ai pas dit quelle ardeur insensée
Cette inconstante femme allumait en mon sein;
Je n'aimais qu'elle au monde, et vivre un jour sans elle
Me semblait un destin plus affreux que la mort.
Je me souviens pourtant qu'en cette nuit cruelle
Pour briser mon lien je fis un long effort.
Je la nommai cent fois perfide et déloyale,
Je comptai tous les maux qu'elle m'avait causés.
Hélas! au souvenir de sa beauté fatale,
Quels maux et quels chagrins n'étaient pas apaisés!
Le jour parut enfin. — Las d'une vaine attente,
Sur le bord du balcon je m'étais assoupi;
Je rouvris la paupière à l'aurore naissante,
Et je laissai flotter mon regard ébloui.
Tout à coup, au détour de l'étroite ruelle,
J'entends sur le gravier marcher à petit bruit...
Grand Dieu! préservez-moi! je l'aperçois, c'est elle;
Elle entre. — D'où viens-tu? Qu'as-tu fait cette nuit?
Réponds, que me veux-tu? qui t'amène à cette heure?
Ce beau corps, jusqu'au jour, où s'est-il étendu?
Tandis qu'à ce balcon, seul, je veille et je pleure,
En quel lieu, dans quel lit, à qui souriais-tu?
Perfide! audacieuse! est-il encore possible
Que tu viennes offrir ta bouche à mes baisers?
Que demandes-tu donc? par quelle soif horrible
Oses-tu m'attirer dans tes bras épuisés?
Va-t'en, retire-toi, spectre de ma maîtresse!
Rentre dans ton tombeau, si tu t'en es levé;
Laisse-moi pour toujours oublier ma jeunesse,
Et, quand je pense à toi, croire que j'ai rêvé!...

I trembled and in vain my heart would steal
A glint of hope each time the clock would strike.
She did not come. Alone, head hanging low,
For long I stared at the walls and watched the street,
And still I have not told what crazy glow
That faithless woman kindled in my heart;
I loved her, only her; beyond her sight
To live one day seemed harder than to die.
But I recall how on that cruel night
I made prolonged attempts to break the tie.
I counted all the evils she had caused;
A hundred times I called her false and mean.
Yet as the pain and wrong rose unappeased,
Alas! her fatal beauty came between.
At length the day appeared. My hopeless hope
Had crushed me till I drowsed on the balcony.
I came to as the sun was coming up
And cast about me with a dazzled eye.
Suddenly, round the corner where we were,
I heard advancing down the lane a light
Footstep. And then I saw—God help me!—her.
She entered. "Where were *you*? What was it tonight?
What brings you here this hour? Where have you slept
With that sweet body of yours all this long while?
Whilst I, alone and sleepless, watched and wept,
Where, in what bed, and whom for did you smile?
Perfidious! brash! Is it still possible
You come back here for kisses with those charms?
What can you want? What thirst's so horrible
That you would draw me to your jaded arms?
Ghost of a mistress, get out, get you gone!
If ever you left it, climb back in your tomb;
Let me forget for good my youth undone
And, when I think of you, believe I dream.''. . .

217

Charles Cros
1842 - 1888

Scherzo

SOURIRES, fleurs, baisers, essences,
Après de si fades ennuis,
Après de si ternes absences,
Parfumez le vent de mes nuits!

Illuminez ma fantaisie,
Jonchez mon chemin idéal,
Et versez-moi votre ambroisie,
Longs regards, lys, lèvres, santal!

*

Car j'ignore l'amour caduque
Et le dessillement des yeux,
Puisqu'encor sur ta blanche nuque
L'or flamboie en flocons soyeux.

Et cependant, ma fière, amie,
Il y a longtemps, n'est-ce pas?
Qu'un matin tu t'es endormie,
Lasse d'amour entre mes bras.

*

Ce ne sont pas choses charnelles
Qui font ton attrait non pareil,
Qui conservent à tes prunelles
Ces mêmes rayons de soleil.

Charles Cros

1842 - 1888

Scherzo

SMILES, flowers, and kisses—essences—
After such a boring blight,
After such dismal absences,
Perfume for me the wind of night!

Light up my fancy, make ideal
My path by sprinkling it with good,
Pour everything ambrosial,
Long looks, lips, lilies, sandalwood!

*

I have no skill with love that's sick
And lives by sealing off the sight,
Not while the hair flames on your neck,
That golden fleece against the white.

And yet how long is it, proud friend,
Since that one morning when your charms
Grew weary of our loving and
Sank into sleep between my arms?

*

It isn't just the carnal touch
That makes your beauty past compare
And keeps your eyes reflecting such
Lights from the sunbeams playing there.

Car les choses charnelles meurent,
Ou se fanent à l'air réel.
Mais toujours tes beautés demeurent
Dans leur nimbe immatériel.

*

Ce n'est plus l'heure des tendresses
Jalouses, ni des faux serments.
Ne me dis rien de mes maîtresses,
Je ne compte pas tes amants.

*

A toi, comète vagabonde
Souvent attardée en chemin,
Laissant ta chevelure blonde
Flotter dans l'éther surhumain,

Qu'importent quelques astres pâles
Au ciel troublé de ma raison,
Quand tu viens à longs intervalles
Envelopper mon horizon?

*

Je ne veux pas savoir quels pôles
Ta folle orbite a dépassés,
Tends-moi tes seins et tes épaules;
Que je les baise, c'est assez.

For carnal things can simply die,
Or fade upon the air that's real,
While haloed still your beauties lie
And flourish immaterial.

*

We're past the time for old distresses
Or jealousies or lies for cover.
Speak not of all my mistresses,
I do not count your every lover.

*

For you, my astral vagabond,
Late-comer at a loitering pace,
Letting your hair float wide and blond
Across the interstellar space,

What do a few pale starlets mean
In the vexed heaven of my reason,
When you, at seasons far between,
Come to envelop my horizon?

*

I do not want to know your least
Mad orbit over polar ice:
Give me your shoulders and your breast,
Only to kiss these will suffice.

221

Leconte de Lisle

1818 - 1894

Midi

MIDI, roi des étés, épandu sur la plaine,
Tombe en nappes d'argent des hauteurs du ciel bleu.
Tout se tait. L'air flamboie et brûle sans haleine;
Le terre est assoupie en sa robe de feu.

L'étendue est immense, et les champs n'ont pas d'ombre
Et la source est tarie où buvaient les troupeaux;
La lointaine forêt, dont la lisière est sombre,
Dort là-bas, immobile, en un pesant repos.

Seuls, les grands blés mûris, tels qu'une mer dorée,
Se déroulent au loin, dédaigneux du sommeil;
Pacifiques enfants de la terre sacrée,
Ils épuisent sans peur la coupe du soleil.

Parfois, comme un soupir de leur âme brûlante,
Du sein des épis lourds qui murmurent entre eux,
Une ondulation majestueuse et lente
S'éveille, et va mourir à l'horizon poudreux.

Non loin, quelques bœufs blancs, couchés parmi les herbes,
Bavent avec lenteur sur leurs fanons épais,
Et suivent de leurs yeux languissants et superbes
Le songe intérieur qu'ils n'achèvent jamais.

Homme, si, le cœur plein de joie ou d'amertume,
Tu passais vers midi dans les champs radieux,
Fuis! la nature est vide et le soleil consume:
Rien n'est vivant ici, rien n'est triste ou joyeux.

Mais si, désabusé des larmes et du rire,
Altéré de l'oubli de ce monde agité,
Tu veux, ne sachant plus pardonner ou maudire,
Goûter une suprême et morne volupté,

Leconte de Lisle

1818 - 1894

Noon

Noon, spreading over the plain, the king of summers,
Falls down in silver sheets from the azure height.
All's still. The breathless weather flames and simmers;
Earth drowses in a dress of burning light.

The expanse is vast where fields enjoy no shade,
The spring is dry that watered flocks of sheep;
The forest, crouched behind its bordering glade,
Sinks motionless into a heavy sleep.

Only the fields of grain, like seas of gold,
Reach far away this slumber to disdain;
Untroubled children of the sacred mold,
Fearless they drain the chalice of the sun.

Sometimes a sigh heaves from their burning soul,
To send a murmuring sound from blade to blade;
Then slow, majestic undulations roll
Towards the dusty distance, where they fade.

Not far away, some white cattle lying
In the grass, drool slowly down their great dewlaps,
Languidly with their haughty eyes descrying
The trail of inner dreams that never lapse.

Man, if towards noon you tread these blazing fields,
Your heart possessed with grief or joy, oh! leave!
The sun devours you; nature, empty, yields
Nothing to gladden, nothing to bereave.

But if you're sick of laughter and of tears,
Thirsty for Lethe in this restless world,
If, paralysed between a curse and cheers,
You long some last, sad rapture to behold,

Viens! Le soleil te parle en paroles sublimes;
Dans sa flamme implacable absorbe-toi sans fin;
Et retourne à pas lents vers les cités infimes,
Le cœur trempé sept fois dans le néant divin.

Le rêve du jaguar

Sous les noirs acajous, les lianes en fleur,
Dans l'air lourd, immobile et saturé de mouches,
Pendent, et, s'enroulant en bas parmi les souches,
Bercent le perroquet splendide et querelleur,
L'araignée au dos jaune et les singes farouches.
C'est là que le tueur de bœufs et de chevaux,
Le long des vieux troncs morts à l'écorce moussue,
Sinistre et fatigué, revient à pas égaux.
Il va, frottant ses reins musculeux qu'il bossue;
Et, du mufle béant par la soif alourdi,
Un souffle rauque et bref, d'une brusque secousse,
Trouble les grands lézards, chauds des feux de midi,
Dont la fuite étincelle à travers l'herbe rousse.
En un creux du bois sombre interdit au soleil
Il s'affaisse, allongé sur quelque roche plate;
D'un large coup de langue il se lustre la patte;
Il cligne ses yeux d'or hébétés de sommeil;
Et, dans l'illusion de ses forces inertes,
Faisant mouvoir sa queue et frissonner ses flancs,
Il rêve qu'au milieu des plantations vertes,
Il enfonce d'un bond ses ongles ruisselants
Dans la chair des taureaux effarés et beuglants.

Come, the sun speaks to you in words sublime;
Be drawn into that fierce light unalloyed;
Then walk back slowly to the streets of crime,
Your heart bathed sevenfold in the divine void.

The jaguar's dream

UNDER the trees of black mahogany, dangle
The flowering vines in an air drenched with flies,
And, twining down the trunks, the vines disguise
Jeweled parakeets that swing and wrangle,
Spiders with yellow backs, wild monkeys' eyes.
It's there this killer of the horse and ox
Returns with steady pace along dead trunks,
Baleful and weary from his bloody works,
Scraping his sinewy loins, humping his flanks;
And from his gaping muzzle, heavy with drouth,
A short harsh breath, exploding with a shock,
Startles great lizards basking in noon's mouth
That dart along the brown grass like a spark.
In a crotch of the somber wood, hid from the glare,
He sinks down stretched out on a level spot,
With a broad stroke of his tongue to polish his foot,
And blink his golden eyes still half aware.
And now, his sluggish forces lulled asleep,
Moving his tail, quivering his sides, he dreams
Of how in green plantations he will leap
On bellowing bulls and, bathing in their streams
Of blood, plunge his claws deeper in their screams.

Le sommeil du condor

Par delà l'escalier des roides Cordillères,
Par delà les brouillards hantés des aigles noirs,
Plus haut que les sommets creusés en entonnoirs
Où bout le flux sanglant des laves familières,
L'envergure pendante et rouge par endroits,
Le vaste Oiseau, tout plein d'une morne indolence,
Regarde l'Amérique et l'espace en silence
Et le sombre soleil qui meurt dans ses yeux froids.
La nuit roule de l'Est, où les pampas sauvages
Sous les monts étagés s'élargissent sans fin;
Elle endort le Chili, les villes, les rivages,
Et la Mer Pacifique et l'horizon divin;
Du continent muet elle s'est emparée;
Des sables aux coteaux, des gorges aux versants,
De cime en cime, elle enfle, en tourbillons croissants,
Le lourd débordement de sa haute marée.
Lui, comme un spectre, seul, au front du pic altier,
Baigné d'une lueur qui saigne sur la neige,
Il attend cette mer sinistre qui l'assiège:
Elle arrive, déferle et le couvre en entier.
Dans l'abîme sans fond la Croix australe allume
Sur les côtes du ciel son phare constellé.
Il râle de plaisir, il agite sa plume,
Il érige son cou musculeux et pelé,
Il s'enlève en fouettant l'âpre neige des Andes,
Dans un cri rauque il monte où n'atteint pas le vent,
Et, loin du globe noir, loin de l'astre vivant,
Il dort dans l'air glacé, les ailes toutes grandes.

The condor's sleep

BEYOND the Cordilleras' beetling steps,
Beyond the fogs haunted by swarthy eagles,
Soaring higher than summits scooped in funnels,
Where bleeding lava laps familiar slopes,
His spread wings slack and streaked with scarlet hues,
The vast bird, full of mournful indolence,
Stares at America and space in silence,
The somber sun sinking in his cold eyes.
Night rolls down from the East, where spreads the sweep
Of savage pampas under the range on high
And wraps all Chile, towns and shores, in sleep,
To where the sea's divine horizons lie.
It grips the silent continent so wide,
From sands to foothills, glens to soaring crags;
From peak to peak its eddying ground swell drags
The heavy flood of that encroaching tide.
As for this ghost, alone on the lofty spur,
Bathed with a glow that reddens the snow-cap, he
Awaits that sinister, besieging sea:
It comes, unfurls, and covers him entire.
The Southern Cross, hung in the bottomless vault,
Above the coasts of heaven trims its wick.
He shakes his feathers, croaking to exult,
And cranes the sinews of his glabrous neck.
Whipping the Andes' bitter snow, to soar
Where no winds stir, he hurls a raucous cry;
And far from the dark globe, the living star,
His great wings spread, he sleeps in the frozen sky.

José-Maria de Hérédia

1842 - 1905

Floridum mare

La moisson débordant le plateau diapré
Roule, ondule et déferle au vent frais qui la berce;
Et le profil, au ciel lointain, de quelque herse
Semble un bateau qui tangue et lève un noir beaupré.

Et sous mes pieds, la mer, jusqu'au couchant pourpré,
Céruléenne ou rose ou violette ou perse
Ou blanche de moutons que le reflux disperse,
Verdoie à l'infini comme un immense pré.

Aussi les goëlands qui suivent la marée,
Vers les blés murs que gonfle une houle dorée,
Avec de cris joyeux, volaient en tourbillons;

Tandis que, de la terre, une brise emmiellée
Eparpillait au gré de leur ivresse ailée
Sur l'Océan fleuri des vols de papillons.

Antoine et Cléopâtre

Tous deux ils regardaient, de la haute terrasse,
L'Egypte s'endormir sous un ciel étouffant
Et le Fleuve, à travers le Delta noir qu'il fend,
Vers Bubaste ou Saïs rouler son onde grasse.

Et le Romain sentait sous la lourde cuirasse,
Soldat captif berçant le sommeil d'un enfant,
Ployer et défaillir sur son cœur triomphant
Le corps voluptueux que son étreinte embrasse.

Tournant sa tête pâle entre ses cheveux bruns
Vers celui qu'enivraient d'invincibles parfums,
Elle tendit sa bouche et ses prunelles claires;

Et sur elle courbé, l'ardent Imperator
Vit dans ses larges yeux étoilés de points d'or
Toute une mer immense où fuyaient des galères.

José-Maria de Hérédia
1842 - 1905

Floridum mare

THE harvest, washing over the dappled plain,
Rolls and unfurls in the cool, cradling wind;
Some harrow, against the distant sky outlined,
Heaves a dark bowsprit on a sea of grain.

    This sea underfoot, right to the purple screen
In the west, is azure, pink, or violet-veined,
Or aqua, or white steeds by the ebb-tide reined,
And turning to a field of infinite green.

    The sea-gulls too, that over the billows glide
Toward ripened corn aflood with its own gold tide,
Fly round in whirlwinds with their joyful cries;

    While, from the land, across the ocean's bed
Of flowers, a honeyed breeze would spread
Flights, winged with ecstacy, of butterflies.

Antony and Cleopatra

THE two of them looked down from a high terrace
On Egypt asleep beneath a stifling heaven
And the Stream, by which the black Delta is cloven,
Spreading smooth waves to Bubastis or Sais.

    And the triumphing Roman, under his bronze cuirass
A captive soldier, lulled in the sleep that's given
To infants, feels on his heart succumb and soften
The urgent body that his arms embrace.

    Turning her head, by the dark hair obscured,
Towards him her stealthy scent deranged and lured,
She yields her mouth and her pupils brimmed with light;

    And, bending over her, the burning king
Sees in those eyes gold meteors scattering:
A boundless sea, galleys in headlong flight.

Théophile Gautier

1811 - 1872

A une robe rose

Que tu me plais dans cette robe
Qui te déshabille si bien,
Faisant jaillir ta gorge en globe,
Montrant tout nu ton bras païen!

Frêle comme une aile d'abeille,
Frais comme un cœur de rose-thé,
Son tissu, caresse vermeille,
Voltige autour de ta beauté.

De l'épiderme sur la soie
Glissent des frissons argentés,
Et l'étoffe à la chair renvoie
Ses éclairs roses reflétés.

D'où te vient cette robe étrange
Qui semble faite de ta chair,
Trame vivante qui mélange
Avec ta peau son rose clair?

Est-ce à la rougeur de l'aurore,
A la coquille de Vénus,
Au bouton de sein près d'éclore,
Que sont pris ces tons inconnus?

Ou bien l'étoffe est-elle teinte
Dans les roses de ta pudeur?
Non; vingt fois modelée et peinte,
Ta forme connaît sa splendeur.

Jetant le voile qui te pèse,
Réalité que l'art rêva,
Comme la princesse Borghèse
Tu poserais pour Canova.

Théophile Gautier

1811 - 1872

To a rose dress

How I like you in that dress
Which undresses all your forms,
Springing out to hold your breast,
Stripping bare your pagan arms!

Flimsy as a queen bee's wing,
Fresh as tea-roses in texture,
Fabric a caressing thing,
Clinging rose about each feature.

Rose reflected from your dress
Quivers with a silver sheen,
Glistens on your surfaces,
Sending rose back to your skin.

Where did this mysterious gown
Come from, modeled, I suppose,
From the flesh that is your own:
Living weft suffused with rose?

Are those tints from Venus' shell?
Are they from the rosy dawn?
Or from where the nipples swell,
Bursting out as if just born?

Is the bodice colored rose
By the flush of modesty?
No; since twenty times you've posed,
You should know your figure's beauty.

If you dropped that tiresome veil,
Like Canova we should bless
Art's enduring dream made real
In the live Princess Borghèse.

Et ces plis roses sont les lèvres
De mes désirs inapaisés,
Mettant au corps dont tu les sèvres
Une tunique de baisers.

Carmen

CARMEN est maigre, — un trait de bistre
Cerne son œil de gitana.
Ses cheveux sont d'un noir sinistre,
Sa peau, le diable la tanna.

Les femmes disent qu'elle est laide,
Mais tous les hommes en sont fous:
Et l'archevêque de Tolède
Chante la messe à ses genoux;

Car sur sa nuque d'ambre fauve
Se tord un énorme chignon
Qui, dénoué, fait dans l'alcôve
Une mante à son corps mignon.

Et, parmi sa pâleur, éclate
Une bouche aux rires vainqueurs;
Piment rouge, fleur écarlate,
Qui prend sa pourpre au sang des cœurs.

Ainsi faite, la moricaude
Bat les plus altières beautés,
Et de ses yeux la lueur chaude
Rend la flamme aux satiétés.

Elle a, dans sa laideur piquante,
Un grain de sel de cette mer
D'où jaillit, nue et provocante,
L'âcre Vénus du gouffre amer.

Like my lips, each rosy fold,
Tunic of unslaked desire,
Clothing secrets you withhold,
Clings with kisses of bright fire.

Carmen

CARMEN is thin—a touch of bister
Surrounds her gipsy eye with sin.
Black of her hair is sinister;
The devil tints her tawny skin.

The women say her looks are sick,
Whereof men's wits contract disease;
Prelate of one archbishopric
Conducts the mass before her knees.

For on her nape of amber pale
Her chignon piles a heavy weight,
Which, let fall in her bedroom, will
Wrap her slight body to her feet.

Amid this pallor will explode
A mouth with victory in its laugh.
Red pigment for a scarlet bud
That drinks of hearts their purple life.

A blackamoor made in this wise
Will beat our haughty beauties down,
And the hot glitter of her eyes
Burn up each boring paragon.

In all her gamey flaws there glows
The acrid element she keeps
Of that salt sea from which arose
Nude Venus of the bitter deep.

A Zurbaran

MOINES de Zurbaran, blancs chartreux qui, dans l'ombre,
Glissez silencieux sur les dalles des morts,
Murmurant des *Pater* et des *Ave* sans nombre,

Quel crime expiez-vous par de si grands remords?
Fantômes tonsurés, bourreaux à face blême,
Pour le traiter ainsi, qu'a donc fait votre corps?

Votre corps, modelé par le doigt de Dieu même,
Que Jésus-Christ, son fils, a daigné revêtir,
Vous n'avez pas le droit de lui dire: "Anathème!"

Je conçois les tourments et la foi du martyr,
Les jets de plomb fondu, les bains de poix liquide,
La gueule des lions prête à vous engloutir,

Sur un rouet de fer les boyaux qu'on dévide,
Toutes les cruautés des empereurs romains;
Mais je ne comprends pas ce morne suicide!

Pourquoi donc, chaque nuit, pour vous seuls inhumains,
Déchirer votre épaule à coups de discipline,
Jusqu'à ce que le sang ruisselle sur vos reins?

Pourquoi ceindre toujours la couronne d'épine,
Que Jésus sur son front ne mit que pour mourir,
Et frapper à plein poing votre maigre poitrine?

Croyez-vous donc que Dieu s'amuse à voir souffrir,
Et que ce meurtre lent, cette froide agonie,
Fassent pour vous le ciel plus facile à s'ouvrir?

Cette tête de mort entre vos doigts jaunie,
Pour ne plus en sortir, qu'elle rentre au charnier!
Que votre fosse soit par un autre finie!

To Zurbaran

CARTHUSIAN monks of Zurbaran, white in the shade,
Murmuring Ave's and Pater's till you're hoarse,
Gliding quietly over the slabs of the dead,

What crime do you atone with such remorse?
Tonsured phantoms, tortured pale with hunger,
What has your body done to earn this curse?

The body modelled by God's very finger,
That Jesus Christ, His son, has deigned to wear,
You have no right to curse it any longer.

I can conceive the martyr's pain and prayer,
The death by pitch, the drops of melted lead,
The jaws of lions ravenous to tear,

The iron wheels that ripped their bowels wide,
And all the imperial cruelties of Rome,
But cannot grasp this mournful suicide!

Why, then each night, inhuman and alone,
Lash your bare shoulders with such penal zest,
Until upon your loins the blood runs down?

Why always with the crown of thorn be dressed,
When Jesus only put it on to die?
Why beat with clenched hand at your meager chest?

Do you believe God likes to hear you cry,
That this cold pain, this murder drawn out slow,
Opens an easier passage to the sky?

That skull between your pale hands—let it go
Down to its charnel house and never come out!
Then let some other spade your rites bestow!

L'esprit est immortel, on ne peut le nier;
Mais dire, comme vous, que le chair est infâme,
Statuaire divin, c'est te calomnier!

Pourtant quelle énergie et quelle force d'âme
Ils avaient, ces chartreux, sous leur pâle linceul,
Pour vivre, sans amis, sans famille et sans femme,

Tout jeunes, et déjà plus glacés qu'un aïeul,
N'ayant pour horizon qu'un long cloître en arcades,
Avec une pensée, en face de Dieu seul!

Tes moines, Lesueur, près de ceux-là sont fades:
Zurbaran de Séville a mieux rendu que toi
Leurs yeux plombés d'extase et leurs têtes malades,

Le vertige divin, l'enivrement de foi
Qui les fait rayonner d'une clarté fiévreuse,
Et leur aspect étrange, à vous donner l'effroi.

Comme son dur pinceau les laboure et les creuse!
Aux pleurs du repentir comme il ouvre des lits
Dans les rides sans fond de leur face terreuse!

Comme du froc sinistre il allonge les plis;
Comme il sait lui donner les pâleurs du suaire,
Si bien que l'on dirait des morts ensevelis!

Qu'il vous peigne en extase au fond du sanctuaire,
Du cadavre divin baisant les pieds sanglants,
Fouettant votre dos bleu comme un fléau bat l'aire,

Vous promenant rêveurs le long des cloîtres blancs,
Par file assis à table au frugal réfectoire,
Toujours il fait de vous des portraits ressemblants.

Deux teintes seulement, clair livide, ombre noire;
Deux poses, l'une droite et l'autre à deux genoux,
A l'artiste ont suffi pour peindre votre histoire.

The soul can't die, of this there is no doubt,
But thus to assert that flesh is infamous
Calumniates the heavenly sculptor's art.

Yet what sheer energy and mental force
These pale Carthusians hid beneath their shroud,
To give up friends and family intercourse,

While still so young, be colder than some old clod,
With no horizon past the cloistered shade
And but one thought, confronting only God!

Your monks, Le Sueur, beside these pictures, fade.
Zurbaran of Seville showed with more truth
The glazed eyes in those sick heads that he made,

The giddy holiness, the drunken faith,
Which makes them radiate a feverish light,
And that queer look that frightens one to death.

How his stern brush ploughs them, hollows them out,
And grooves their ashen faces for the tears
That cut unfathomed wrinkles in their route!

How he draws folds in the frock so it appears
Longer, to give the pallor of shrouds on the slain,
So true it could be dead men he inters!

Whether he paints your raptures in the shrine,
Kissing the bleeding feet of the crucified Lord,
Whipping, as flails might thresh, your livid spine,

Or dreaming, strolling along the white arcade,
Or seated in straight rows at the frugal meal—
Your likeness always is precisely made.

Only two hues—black shade with high-lights dull:
Two postures—either upright or kneeling down,
Sufficed the artist to relate your tale.

Forme, rayon, couleur, rien n'existe pour vous;
A tout objet réel vous êtes insensibles,
Car le ciel vous enivre et la croix vous rend fous,

Et vous vivez muets, inclinés sur vos bibles,
Croyant toujours entendre aux plafonds entr'ouverts
Eclater brusquement les trompettes terribles!

O moines! maintenant, en tapis frais et verts,
Sur les fosses par vous à vous-mêmes creusées,
L'herbe s'étend. — Eh bien! que dites-vous aux vers?

Quels rêves faites-vous? quelles sont vos pensées?
Ne regrettez-vous pas d'avoir usé vos jours
Entre ces murs étroits, sous ces voûtes glacées?

Ce que vous avez fait, le feriez-vous toujours?

Real light and form and color you've never known;
You are insensible of what exists.
Made drunk by heaven, and by the cross insane;

Heads bowed above your bibles like deaf mutes,
You are always dreaming that a sudden burst
Of frightful trumpets through the roof will burst!

O monks! even now, like carpets green and warm,
Fresh grass adorns the pits dug by your spade
For your own tombs; and what are you telling the worms?

What are the thoughts and dreams you don't parade?
Do you deplore that you have lived your span
Walled in behind these frozen colonnades?

What you have done, would you do over again?

Charles Baudelaire

1821 - 1867

La beauté

JE suis belle, ô mortels! comme un rêve de pierre,
Et mon sein, où chacun s'est meurtri tour à tour,
Est fait pour inspirer au poëte un amour
Eternel et muet ainsi que la matière.

Je trône dans l'azur comme un sphinx incompris;
J'unis un cœur de neige à la blancheur des cygnes;
Je hais le mouvement qui déplace les lignes,
Et jamais je ne pleure et jamais je ne ris.

Les poëtes, devant mes grandes attitudes,
Que j'ai l'air d'emprunter aux plus fiers monuments,
Consumeront leurs jours en d'austères études;

Car j'ai, pour fasciner ces dociles amants,
De purs miroirs qui font toutes choses plus belles:
Mes yeux, mes larges yeux aux clartés éternelles!

Les plaintes d'un Icare

LES amants des prostituées
Sont heureux, dispos et repus;
Quant à moi, mes bras sont rompus
Pour avoir étreint des nuées.

C'est grâce aux astres nonpareils,
Qui tout au fond du ciel flamboient,
Que mes yeux consumés ne voient
Que des souvenirs de soleils.

En vain j'ai voulu de l'espace
Trouver la fin el le milieu;
Sous je ne sais quel œil de feu
Je sens mon aile qui se casse;

Charles Baudelaire

1821 - 1867

Beauty

My beauty, mortals, is a stony one
To dream; my breast, where each is bruised in turn,
Is formed to make the hearts of poets burn
With love as mute and durable as stone.

Enthroned in azure, like a sphinx asleep,
Inscrutable, with heart of snow like swans,
I hate the movement that deranges lines,
And so I never laugh and never weep.

The poets, in thralldom to my stately ways,
Ways borrowed maybe from a marble pride,
Will waste in stringent trials all their days,

Because, to keep these docile lovers tied,
My eyes, pure mirrors of transfiguring light,
My eyes make all things lovelier by their sight.

Lament of an Icarus

THE lovers of a harlot's charms
Are smugly glutted with the chase;
But as for me, my close embrace
Of clouds has broken both my arms.

Thanks to the matchless stars that blaze
Deep at the bottom of the sky,
My withered eyes may now descry
Suns only that are memories.

In vain my yearning flight would spring
To reach the utmost ends of space,
The fiery eye in that strange face
Consumes my unavailing wing,

Et brûlé par l'amour du beau,
Je n'aurai pas l'honneur sublime
De donner mon nom à l'abîme
Qui me servira de tombeau.

L'albatros

SOUVENT, pour s'amuser, les hommes d'équipage
Prennent des albatros, vastes oiseaux des mers,
Qui suivent, indolents compagnons de voyage,
Le navire glissant sur les gouffres amers.

A peine les ont-ils déposés sur les planches,
Que ces rois de l'azur, maladroits et honteux
Laissent piteusement leurs grandes ailes blanches
Comme des avirons traîner à côté d'eux.

Ce voyageur ailé, comme il est gauche et veule!
Lui, naguère si beau, qu'il est comique et laid!
L'un agace son bec avec un brûle-gueule,
L'autre mime, en boitant, l'infirme qui volait!

Le Poëte est semblable au prince des nuées
Qui hante la tempête et se rit de l'archer;
Exilé sur le sol au milieu des huées,
Ses ailes de géant l'empêchent de marcher.

Till love of beauty is my doom;
Nor will that burning nemesis
Inscribe my name in the abyss
Which now must serve me as a tomb.

The albatross

OFTEN a crew, to wile away the hour,
Will trap an albatross, huge birds that keep
Indolent company with ships that scour
The waves, like comrades on the bitter deep.

No sooner dropped on deck than these great kings
Of the sky, deposed, unwieldy now and maimed,
Trail piteously beside them great white wings,
Like broken oars, as if they were ashamed.

Oh! this winged traveler! What a lame one now!
Lately so lovely, he is an ugly freak.
One sailor, lurching, apes that speed made slow;
Another sticks a pipe inside his beak.

Haunting the storm, deriding the archer's bow,
This potentate of clouds is like the poet;
Exiled on earth, amid cat-calls below,
His giant wings impede him when afoot.

Le crépuscule du soir

Voici le soir charmant, ami du criminel;
Il vient comme un complice, à pas de loup; le ciel
Se ferme lentement comme une grande alcôve,
Et l'homme impatient se change en bête fauve.

O soir, aimable soir, désiré par celui
Dont les bras, sans mentir, peuvent dire: Aujourd'hui
Nous avons travaillé! — C'est le soir qui soulage
Les esprits que dévore une douleur sauvage,
Le savant obstiné dont le front s'alourdit,
Et l'ouvrier courbé qui regagne son lit.
Cependant des démons malsains dans l'atmosphère
S'éveillent lourdement, comme des gens d'affaire,
Et cognent en volant les volets et l'auvent.
A travers les lueurs que tourmente le vent
La Prostitution s'allume dans les rues;
Comme une fourmilière elle ouvre ses issues;
Partout elle se fraye un occulte chemin,
Ainsi que l'ennemi qui tente un coup de main;
Elle remue au sein de la cité de fange
Comme un ver qui dérobe à l'Homme ce qu'il mange.
On entend çà et là les cuisines siffler,
Les théâtres glapir, les orchestres ronfler;
Les tables d'hôte, dont le jeu fait les délices,
S'emplissent de catins et d'escrocs, leur complices,
Et les voleurs, qui n'ont ni trêve ni merci,
Vont bientôt commencer leur travail, eux aussi,
Et forcer doucement les portes et les caisses
Pour vivre quelques jours et vêtir leurs maîtresses.

Recueille-toi, mon âme, en ce grave moment,
Et ferme ton oreille à ce rugissement.
C'est l'heure où les douleurs des malades s'aigrissent!
La sombre Nuit les prend à la gorge; ils finissent
Leur destinée et vont vers le gouffre commun;
L'hôpital se remplit de leurs soupirs. — Plus d'un
Ne viendra plus chercher la soupe parfumée,

Evening twilight

HERE comes beguiling dusk, the felon's friend;
It creeps like wolves that hide what they intend;
Sky, a huge closet, closes down for rest,
And man can scarcely wait to be a beast.

Evening, well loved by every man to say
And make it true: these arms worked hard today.
Evening it is that soothes the savage care
Of minds consumed with what they cannot bear,
Whether the scholar's with his weary head,
Or the bent workman dropping into bed.
Meanwhile, like business men who go to work,
Foul demons heavily wake up and knock,
Beating their wings against the porch and shutters;
And where the wind torments the light that flutters,
Street prostitution on a sudden flares;
It opens, like an ant-heap, all its doors;
Like a besieging army that essays
Surprise assaults by secret passageways;
Like worms devouring the intestine's food,
It crawls throughout the filthy city's blood.
Here is the sound of kitchens sizzling; there,
A theater yelping, or a string-band's snore;
Cheap chop-houses, where gambling is the game,
Are packed with pimps, whores, crooks, who have no name
For pity or respite; soon they too begin
Preparing softly for the work they're in,
Unsealing doors and safes to have the means
To live awhile and keep their girls in gowns.

At this grave moment, mind yourself, my soul,
And shut your ears to night's infernal howl.
It's now that, for the dying, pain grows worse!
Night takes them by the throat; they end their course
And go to gulfs where deeper shadows close;
The hospital is filled with sighs of those
Who will return no more to that dear smell

Au coin du feu, le soir, auprès d'une âme aimée.

Encore la plupart n'ont-ils jamais connu
La douceur du foyer et n'ont jamais vécu!

Le crépuscule du matin

La diane chantait dans les cours des casernes,
Et le vent du matin soufflait sur les lanternes.

C'était l'heure où l'essaim des rêves malfaisants
Tord sur leurs oreillers les bruns adolescents;
Où, comme un œil sanglant qui palpite et qui bouge,
La lampe sur le jour fait une tache rouge;
Où l'âme, sous le poids du corps revêche et lourd,
Imite les combats de la lampe et du jour.
Comme un visage en pleurs que les brises essuient,
L'air est plein du frisson des choses qui s'enfuient,
Et l'homme est las d'écrire et la femme d'aimer.

Les maisons çà et là commençaient à fumer.
Les femmes de plaisir, la paupière livide,
Bouche ouverte, dormaient de leur sommeil stupide;
Les pauvresses, traînant seins maigres et froids,
Soufflaient sur leurs tisons et soufflaient sur leurs doigts,
C'était l'heure où parmi le froid et la lésine
S'aggravent les douleurs des femmes en gésine;
Comme un sanglot coupé par un sang écumeux
Le chant du coq au loin déchirait l'air brumeux;
Une mer de brouillards baignait les édifices,
Et les agonisants dans le fond des hospices
Poussaient leur dernier râle en hoquets inégaux.
Les débauchés rentraient, brisés par leurs travaux.

L'aurore grelottante en robe rose et verte
S'avançait lentement sur la Seine déserte,
Et le sombre Paris, en se frottant les yeux,
Empoignait ses outils, vieillard laborieux.

Of soup beside the fire they love so well.

But most of them have never known or loved
The sweetness of a home, have never lived!

Morning twilight

IN barrack courtyards reveille was blown,
And on the street-lamps blew the winds of dawn.

It was the hour when striplings in the throes
Of harmful dreams twist sun-tanned on their pillows;
When, like a bleeding eye that throbs in pain,
The lamplight prints on day a scarlet stain;
When mind, beneath the body's sullen sway,
Mimics the combats of the night and day.
The air, a face in tears dried by the breeze,
Is fraught with shudders of whatever flees;
And man is weary of writing, women of loving.

From chimneys here and there smoke began moving.
Women of pleasure, eyelids looking livid,
Mouth open wide, were sunk in sleep of the stupid;
Beggars, that dragged their breasts shrunken and chill,
Blew on their fingers, blew on brands of coal.
It was the hour, among the cold and thin,
When pains grew sharp of women lying in;
Like a heaved sob that blood-choked gullets rend,
A cockcrow tore the mist somewhere beyond;
Fog bathed the buildings. Down in the lowest ward
Of hospitals an anguished rale broke hard
With hiccoughing to strangle dying cries.
The rakes returned, spent with their exercise.

Dawn, shivering in a dress of rose and green,
Slowly advanced on the deserted Seine;
And somber Paris, toil-worn veteran,
Rubbing his eyes, picked up his tools again.

Le soleil

LE long du vieux faubourg, où pendent aux masures
Les persiennes, abri des secrètes luxures,
Quand le soleil cruel frappe à traits redoublés
Sur la ville et les champs, sur les toits et les blés,
Je vais m'exercer seul à ma fantasque escrime,
Flairant dans tous les coins les hasards de la rime.
Trébuchant sur les mots comme sur les pavés,
Heurtant parfois des vers depuis longtemps rêvés.

Ce père nourricier, ennemi des chloroses,
Eveille dans les champs les vers comme les roses;
Il fait s'évaporer les soucis vers le ciel,
Et remplit les cerveaux et les ruches de miel.
C'est lui qui rajeunit les porteurs de béquilles
Et les rend gais et doux comme des jeunes filles,
Et commande aux moissons de croître et de mûrir
Dans le cœur immortel qui toujours veut fleurir!

Quand, ainsi qu'un poëte, il descend dans les villes,
Il ennoblit le sort des choses les plus viles,
Et s'introduit en roi, sans bruit et sans valets,
Dans tous les hôpitaux et dans tous les palais.

The sun

ALONG old suburbs with their tattered blinds,
To hide the lewdness in these people's minds,
While the ferocious sun renews its heat
On town and hedge, on roofs and fields of wheat,
I duel alone, fantastic pantomime,
At every corner fencing with a rhyme,
Stumbling on words—rough curbs to trip a theme—
And strike with lines that flashed once in a dream.

This fostering sun, begrudging pallid woes,
Wakes in the ground alike both worm and rose,
Makes care evaporate into the blue,
With honey fills the hive, and spirit too.
He has old cripples cast away the crutch
And gives them, like young girls, a sprightly touch;
Commands the harvest to grow ripe and tall·
In hearts that long to flourish at his call.

When, like a poet, he settles on the town,
He lends what's vile the glory of his crown
And enters simply, king who needs no thrall,
Each royal palace and each hospital.

Baudelaire

Obsession

Gʀᴀɴᴅs bois, vous m'effrayez comme des cathédrales;
Vous hurlez comme l'orgue; et dans nos cœurs maudits,
Chambres d'éternel deuil où vibrent de vieux râles,
Répondent les échos de vos *De profundis.*
Je te hais, Océan! tes bonds et tes tumultes,
Mon esprit les retrouve en lui; ce rire amer
De l'homme vaincu, plein de sanglots et d'insultes,
Je l'entends dans le rire énorme de la mer.
Comme tu me plairais, ô nuit! sans ces étoiles
Dont la lumière parle un langage connu!
Car je cherche le vide, et le noir, et le nu!
Mais les ténèbres sont elles-mêmes des toiles
Où vivent, jaillissant de mon œil par milliers,
Des êtres disparus aux regards familiers.

Je t'adore…

Jᴇ t'adore à l'égal de la voûte nocturne,
O vase de tristesse, ô grande taciturne,
Et t'aime d'autant plus, belle, que tu me fuis,
Et que tu me parais, ornement de mes nuits,
Plus ironiquement accumuler les lieues
Qui séparent mes bras des immensités bleues.

Je m'avance à l'attaque, et je grimpe aux assauts,
Comme après un cadavre un chœur de vermisseaux,
Et je chéris, ô bête implacable et cruelle!
Jusqu'à cette froideur par où tu m'es plus belle!

Obsession

DARK woods, I dread you like cathedral gloom;
You roar like organs; endless griefs reply,
To shake our stricken hearts, those cells of doom,
And match your *de profundis* with a sigh.
    I loathe you, Ocean!—in myself rehearse
Your leaping tumult; that harsh jubilee
Of bitter men, who sob even as they curse,
Repeats the raucous laughter of the sea.
    How I could love you, Night—without your stars,
Whose light accosts me in a tongue well known!
I seek what's void and black and known of none!
    And yet the very dark of night restores,
Thronging my empty canvas, a great host
With looks familiar, beings for ever lost.

I idolize you...

I IDOLIZE you like the vault of night,
Tall woman, vase of sorrow and of quiet;
The more you flee, the more your beauty moves
My heart to paint the dark with what it loves,
Until this mockery seems to multiply
The leagues between my arms and that far sky.

So I advance against your ghostly bed,
Like swarms of worms that batten on the dead,
And cherish, O my sweet relentless beast,
That cruel ice which makes you loveliest!

Les bijoux

La très-chère était nue, et, connaissant mon cœur,
Elle n'avait gardé que ses bijoux sonores,
Dont le riche attirail lui donnait l'air vainqueur
Qu'ont dans leurs jours heureux les esclaves des Mores.

Quand il jette en dansant son bruit vif et moqueur,
Ce monde rayonnant de métal et de pierre
Me ravit en extase, et j'aime à la fureur
Les choses où le son se mêle à la lumière.

Elle était donc couchée et se laissait aimer,
Et du haut du divan elle souriait d'aise
A mon amour profond et doux comme la mer,
Qui vers elle montait comme vers sa falaise.

Les yeux fixés sur moi, comme un tigre dompté,
D'un air vague et rêveur elle essayait des poses,
Et la candeur unie à la lubricité
Donnait un charme neuf à ses métamorphoses;

Et son bras et sa jambe, et sa cuisse et ses reins,
Polis comme de l'huile, onduleux comme un cygne,
Passaient devant mes yeux clairvoyants et sereins;
Et son ventre et ses seins, ces grappes de ma vigne,

S'avançaient, plus câlins que les Anges du mal,
Pour troubler le repos où mon âme était mise,
Et pour la déranger du rocher de cristal
Où, calme et solitaire, elle s'était assise.

Je croyais voir unis par un nouveau dessin
Les hanches de l'Antiope au buste d'un imberbe,
Tant sa taille faisait ressortir son bassin.
Sur ce teint fauve et brun le fard était superbe!

The jewels

THE darling was naked, but knowing how to snare
My heart, she only wore her rich array
Of chiming jems that gave the conquering air
Of Moorish slave girls on a holiday.

For when it dances with keen mocking sound,
This scintillating world of steel and stone
Gives rapture, for if light and sound can blend,
I love it so that I am scarcely sane.

So there she lay and let herself be loved,
And from the divan's height she smiled, as if
Glad that my rising passion gently moved
Towards her as the sea towards a cliff.

Her eyes, like a tame tiger's fixed on me,
She tried new postures with a dreamy air;
The candor joined to the lubricity
Gave a new charm to all her changes there.

Her arm, her leg, her thigh, her loins' wide sweep,
Glossy as oil and sinuous as a swan,
Passed by my gaze, serene but unasleep,
And then her belly and breasts, my clusters of vine,

Advanced, more coaxing than an evil angel,
To spoil the peace wherein my mind was stayed
And shake it reeling from the rock of crystal
On which it sat, alone and undismayed.

I thought I saw a new form to preserve
The haunches of a queen of Amazon
With boyish bust, to stress the pelvic curve.
The rouge was stunning on her skin of fawn.

— Et la lampe s'étant résignée à mourir,
Comme le foyer seul illuminait la chambre,
Chaque fois qu'il poussait un flamboyant soupir,
Il inondait de sang cette peau couleur d'ambre!

Les promesses d'un visage

J'AIME, ô pâle beauté, tes sourcils surbaissés,
    D'où semblent couler des ténèbres;
Tes yeux, quoique très-noirs, m'inspirent des pensers
    Qui ne sont pas du tout funèbres.

Tes yeux, qui sont d'accord avec tes noirs cheveux,
    Avec ta crinière élastique,
Tes yeux, languissamment, me disent: "Si tu veux,
    Amant de la muse plastique,

Suivre l'espoir qu'en toi nous avons excité,
    Et tous les goûts que tu professes,
Tu pourras constater notre véracité
    Depuis le nombril jusqu'aux fesses;

Tu trouveras au bout de deux beaux seins bien lourds,
    Deux larges médailles de bronze,
Et sous un ventre uni, doux comme du velours,
    Bistré comme la peau d'un bonze,

Une riche toison qui, vraiment, est la sœur
    De cette énorme chevelure,
Souple et frisée, et qui t'égale en épaisseur,
    Nuit sans étoiles, Nuit obscure!"

And now, because the lamp resolved to die,
The room was lighted by the fire alone,
And every time the flames would breathe a sigh,
They flushed blood-red the amber of her skin.

Promises in a face

I LOVE, O lovely pale one, how your brows
    Level their arch above a wave
Of pouring dark; your eyes, though black, arouse
    No thoughts in me about the grave.

Your eyes give back the blackness of your hair,
    That mane so lambent to the touch;
Your languid eyes say to me, "If you dare,
    Loving the tactile muse so much,

"To follow hopes that we inspired in you,
    And every taste you have defined,
You can confirm the truth of all we knew,
    From navel to the curves behind;

"You'll find, where beautiful full breasts grow steep,
    Two bronze medallions at the crown,
And soft as velvet, under the belly's sweep,
    Like skin of Buddhist monks, red-brown,

"A dusky fleece, rich as the sister sight
    Of that huge other mass of hair,
Supple and curled and thick as you, dark Night,
    When utterly without a star!"

Le beau navire

Je veux te raconter, ô molle enchanteresse!
Les diverses beautés qui parent ta jeunesse;
      Je veux te peindre ta beauté
Où l'enfance s'allie à la maturité.

Quand tu vas balayant l'air de ta jupe large,
Tu fais l'effet d'un beau vaisseau qui prend le large,
      Chargé de toile, et va roulant
Suivant un rhythme doux, et paresseux, et lent.

Sur ton cou large et rond, sur tes épaules grasses,
Ta tête se pavane avec d'étranges grâces;
      D'un air placide et triomphant
Tu passes ton chemin, majestueuse enfant.

Je veux te raconter, ô molle enchanteresse!
Les diverses beautés qui parent ta jeunesse;
      Je veux te peindre ta beauté
Où l'enfance s'allie à la maturité.

Ta gorge qui s'avance et qui pousse la moire,
Ta gorge triomphante est une belle armoire
      Dont les panneaux bombés et clairs
Comme les boucliers accrochent des éclairs;

Boucliers provoquants, armés de pointes roses!
Armoire à doux secrets, pleine de bonnes choses,
      De vins, de parfums, de liqueurs
Qui feraient délirer les cerveaux et les cœurs!

Quand tu vas balayant l'air de ta jupe large,
Tu fais l'effet d'un beau vaisseau qui prend le large,
      Chargé de toile, et va roulant
Suivant un rhythme doux, et paresseux, et lent.

Tes nobles jambes sous les volants qu'elles chassent,
Tourmentent les désirs obscurs et les agacent
      Comme deux sorcières qui font

The beautiful boat

I WOULD recount for you, sweet witch, the truth
Concerning various charms that dress your youth;
         And I would paint your beauty true,
Where child and woman blend as one in you.

When, as they sweep the air, your skirts swing free,
You're like a beauteous ship that stands to sea,
         Crowding on sail and rolling along,
To follow a rhythm sweet and lazy and long.

Flaunting above round neck and shoulders wide,
Your head with alien grace parades its pride;
         With air triumphant and serene,
You go your royal way, an infant queen.

I'd draw you up a list, soft sorceress,
Of beauties that your youth deserves to dress;
         I want to paint your beauty true,
Where child and woman meet as one in you.

Your breast advancing thrusts the silken gown,
Triumphant breast, sweet closet of renown,
         Embossed with convex panels bright,
That catch, like bucklers, every flash of light;

Provoking bucklers, armed with rosy stings,
Secret recess that hides enticing things,
         Wines and liqueurs, perfumes mysterious,
To render all our brains and hearts delirious.

When with ballooning skirt you heel away,
You favor a fair vessel, anchors aweigh,
         Full-rigged, in canvas, dipping along,
To hold a rhythm indolent, smooth and long.

Your noble thighs that bend to chase your skirt
Excite obscure desires and make them hurt,
         Like two dark sorcerers who stir

Tourner un philtre noir dans un vase profond.

Tes bras, qui se joueraient des précoces hercules,
Sont des boas luisants les solides émules,
  Faits pour serrer obstinément
Comme pour l'imprimer dans ton cœur, ton amant.

Sur ton cou large et rond, sur tes épaules grasses,
Ta tête se pavane avec d'étranges grâces;
  D'un air placide et triomphant
Tu passes ton chemin, majestueuse enfant.

Hymne

A LA très-chère, à la très-belle
Qui remplit mon cœur de clarté,
A l'ange, à l'idole immortelle,
Salut en immortalité!

Elle se répand dans ma vie
Comme un air imprégné de sel,
Et dans mon âme inassouvie
Verse le goût de l'éternel.

Sachet toujours frais qui parfume
L'atmosphère d'un cher réduit,
Encensoir oublié qui fume
En secret à travers la nuit,

Comment, amour incorruptible,
T'exprimer avec vérité?
Grain de musc qui gis, invisible,
Au fond de mon éternité!

A la très-bonne, à la très-belle
Qui fait ma joie et ma santé,
A l'ange, à l'idole immortelle,
Salut en immortalité!

An inky philter in a cavernous jar.

Your arms, which might have thrown young Hercules,
Behave like gleaming pythons that would squeeze
      Your lover with relentless art,
As if to print him helpless on your heart.

Your lusty neck and shoulders flaunt your face,
That sways above them with exotic grace;
      Placid and playing sure to win,
You go your way, a child and yet a queen.

Hymn

To her most dear, most beautiful,
Who brims my heart with light to pour,
Angel, my immortal idol,
Salutations evermore!

She spreads in all the life I bless,
As salty airs infuse a gale,
And pours the taste of timelessness
Into a thirst that will not fail.

Sachet forever fresh to bring
Sweet perfume to a dear retreat,
Forgotten censer smoldering
In secret through the hours of night,

Undying love, how can I tell
The truth about you, that sublime
Minim of musk invisible,
Deep in my time beyond all time!

To her most dear, most beautiful,
Who makes my health and joy endure,
Angel, everlasting idol,
Salutations evermore!

Chant d'automne

I

Bientot nous plongerons dans les froides ténèbres;
Adieu, vive clarté de nos étés trops courts!
J'entends déjà tomber avec des chocs funèbres
Le bois retentissant sur le pavé des cours.

Tout l'hiver va rentrer dans mon être: colère,
Haine, frissons, horreur, labeur dur et forcé,
Et, comme le soleil dans son enfer polaire,
Mon cœur ne sera plus qu'un bloc rouge et glacé.

J'écoute en frémissant chaque bûche qui tombe;
L'échafaud qu'on bâtit n'a pas d'écho plus sourd.
Mon esprit est pareil à la tour qui succombe
Sous les coups du bélier infatigable et lourd.

Il me semble, bercé par ce choc monotone,
Qu'on cloue en grande hâte un cercueil quelque part.
Pour qui? – C'était hier l'été; voici l'automne!
Ce bruit mystérieux sonne comme un départ.

II

J'aime de vos longs yeux la lumière verdâtre,
Douce beauté, mais tout aujourd'hui m'est amer,
Et rien, ni votre amour, ni le boudoir, ni l'âtre,
Ne me vaut le soleil rayonnant sur la mer.

Et pourtant aimez-moi, tendre cœur! soyez mère,
Même pour un ingrat, même pour un méchant;
Amante ou sœur, soyez la douceur éphémère
D'un glorieux automne ou d'un soleil couchant.

Courte tâche! La tombe attend; elle est avide!
Ah! laissez-moi, mon front posé sur vos genoux,
Goûter, en regrettant l'été blanc et torride,
De l'arrière-saison le rayon jaune et doux!

Song of autumn

I

Soon we shall plunge into the frigid shades;
Farewell, bright light of summers too soon gone!
I hear already thudding on the yards
The winter woodpiles with their mournful din.

All winter will reenter me: the gall,
The hate and shivering, horror, joyless work,
Till, like the sun within his polar hell,
My heart will be a red and frozen block.

Trembling, I hear each log that rumbles down;
A scaffold being built would sound the same.
My mind is like the bastion of a town
Which is demolished by a battering ram.

Here, as I listen, stupified by blows,
They could be rushing to nail up a hearse.
For whom? The summer gone, now autumn goes:
That eerie noise sounds like an exodus.

II

I love the green light your long eyes give forth,
Sweet beauty, though today is sour for me,
And nothing, not your love, nor bed, nor hearth,
Is worth the sunlight shining on the sea.

Yet love me still, bad ingrate that I am!
Dear heart, be mother, sister, lover—be mine;
The sweetness is ephemeral; be the same
As Autumn's glory or the sun's decline.

Brief task! The hungry tomb awaits us all.
Ah! let me taste, brow resting on your knees,
The gentle yellow light of fading Fall,
And hanker still for summer's burning seas!

Mœsta et errabunda

Dis-moi, ton cœur parfois s'envole-t-il, Agathe,
Loin du noir océan de l'immonde cité,
Vers un autre océan où la splendeur éclate,
Bleu, clair, profond, ainsi que la virginité?
Dis-moi, ton cœur parfois s'envole-t-il, Agathe?

La mer, la vaste mer, console nos labeurs!
Quel démon a doté la mer, rauque chanteuse
Qu'accompagne l'immense orgue des vents grondeurs,
De cette fonction sublime de berceuse?
La mer, la vaste mer, console nos labeurs!

Emporte-moi, wagon! enlève-moi, frégate!
Loin! loin! ici la boue est faite de nos pleurs!
— Est-il vrai que parfois le triste cœur d'Agathe
Dise: Loin des remords, des crimes, des douleurs,
Emporte-moi, wagon, enlève-moi, frégate?

Comme vous êtes loin, paradis parfumé,
Où sous un clair azur tout n'est qu'amour et joie,
Où tout ce que l'on aime est digne d'être aimé!
Où dans la volupté pure le cœur se noie!
Comme vous êtes loin, paradis parfumé!

Mais le vert paradis des amours enfantines,
Les courses, les chansons, les baisers, les bouquets,
Les violins vibrant derrière les collines,
Avec les brocs de vin, le soir, dans les bouquets,
— Mais le vert paradis des amours enfantines,

L'innocent paradis, plein de plaisirs furtifs,
Est-il déjà plus loin que l'Inde et que la Chine?
Peut-on le rappeler avec des cris plaintifs,
Et l'animer encor d'une voix argentine,
L'innocent paradis plein de plaisirs furtifs?

Mœsta et errabunda*

Does your heart, Agatha, sometimes fly away,
Far from the dark sea of the filthy city,
Toward that bright water where the splendors play,
Ocean of blue, clear, deep virginity?
Does your heart, tell me, sometimes yearn away?

The sea, the mighty sea will soothe our pain!
What demon is it that has given the sea,
Hoarse singer while the piping winds complain,
A lullaby of such sublimity?
The sea, the mighty sea to calm our pain!

Wheels, carry me off! Ah! frigate, take me away!
Far, far away! Here mud is made with tears!
—Does the sad heart of Agatha still say:
Far from remorse and crime and dismal fears,
Coach, carry me off! Ship, take me far away!

How far you are, sweet smelling paradise,
Where under clear blue skies all's love and joy,
Where all we love is worthy of love's price,
Where hearts are drowned in bliss without alloy!
How far you are, my fragrant paradise!

All the green heaven of our childish loves,
The races, kisses, songs, flowers with sweet smells,
The jugs of wine at evening in the groves,
The violins that throbbed behind the hills—
All that green paradise of childish loves,

The guileless paradise of secret joys,
Is it now further than India or Cathay?
Can we recover it with plaintive cries
And raise with silvery voice a vanished day,
Innocent paradise of hidden joys?

*This and the three pairs of repeating stanzas in "Le beau navire"
request in English a degree of modulation.

Le voyage

A Maxime du Camp

I

Pour l'enfant, amoureux de cartes et d'estampes,
L'univers est égal à son vaste appétit.
Ah! que le monde est grand à la clarté des lampes!
Aux yeux du souvenir que le monde est petit!

Un matin nous partons, le cerveau plein de flamme,
Le cœur gros de rancune et de désirs amers,
Et nous allons, suivant le rhythme de la lame,
Berçant notre infini sur le fini des mers:

Les uns, joyeux de fuir une patrie infâme;
D'autres, l'horreur de leurs berceaux; et quelques-uns,
Astrologues noyés dans les yeux d'une femme,
La Circé tyrannique aux dangereux parfums.

Pour n'être pas changés en bêtes, ils s'enivrent
D'espace et de lumière et de cieux embrasés;
La glace qui les mord, les soleils qui les cuivrent,
Effacent lentement la marque des baisers.

Mais les vrais voyageurs sont ceux-là seuls qui partent
Pour partir; cœurs légers, semblables aux ballons,
De leur fatalité jamais ils ne s'écartent,
Et, sans savoir pourquoi, disent toujours: Allons!

Ceux-là dont les désirs ont la forme des nues,
Et qui rêvent, ainsi qu'un conscrit le canon,
De vastes voluptés, changeantes, inconnues,
Et dont l'esprit humain n'a jamais su le nom!

II

Nous imitons, horreur! la toupie et la boule
Dans leur valse et leurs bonds; même dans nos sommeils
La Curiosité nous tourmente et nous roule,

The voyage

To Maxime du Camp

I

FOR the eager child crazy on maps and stamps
The universe equals his appetite.
Ah! how the world is wide by the light of lamps,
And yet to eyes of memory how slight!

One morning we set forth, our brains on fire,
Hearts full of cravings, bitter enmities,
And riding the rhythm of the waves, we fare,
Rocking infinity on finite seas:

Some, glad to leave a country they despise;
Others, the horror of their birth; and some—
Their horoscope drowned in a woman's eyes—
The tyrant Circe with her fell perfume.

Not to be changed to beasts, their drinking turns
To space and light and the consuming skies;
The ice that gnaws them and the suns that bronze
Slowly efface the kisses that were lies.

But the true travelers leave just to be leaving;
Hearts like balloons, lighter than air they fly;
They never call their destiny deceiving;
They say, "Let's go!" and yet they don't know why.

These are the ones whose wants are shaped like clouds,
Who dream, as draftees dream about a gun,
Of vast delights with strange and changing modes,
Whose name the human mind has never known!

II

Horrors! the way we bounce about like a ball
Or waltz around like a top! Even in sleep,
The urge to know torments us, makes us roll

Comme un Ange cruel qui fouette des soleils.

Singulière fortune où le but se déplace,
Et, n'étant nulle part, peut être n'importe où!
Où l'Homme, dont jamais l'espérance n'est lasse,
Pour trouver le repos court toujours comme un fou!

Notre âme est un trois-mâts cherchant son Icarie;
Une voix retentit sur le pont: "Ouvre l'œil!"
Une voix de la hune, ardente et folle, crie:
"Amour... gloire... bonheur!" Enfer! c'est un écueil!

Chaque îlot signalé par l'homme de vigie
Est un Elderado promis par le Destin;
L'Imagination qui dresse son orgie
Ne trouve qu'un récif aux clartés du matin.

O le pauvre amoureux des pays chimériques!
Faut-il le mettre aux fers, le jeter à la mer,
Ce matelot ivrogne, inventeur d'Amériques
Dont le mirage rend le gouffre plus amer?

Tel le vieux vagabond, piétinant dans la boue,
Rêve, le nez en l'air, de brillants paradis;
Son œil ensorcelé découvre une Capoue
Partout où la chandelle illumine un taudis.

III

Etonnants voyageurs! quelles nobles histoires
Nous lisons dans vos yeux profonds comme les mers!
Montrez-nous les écrins de vos riches mémoires,
Ces bijoux merveilleux, faits d'astres et d'éthers.

Nous voulons voyager sans vapeur et sans voile!
Faites, pour égayer l'ennui de nos prisons,
Passer sur nos esprits, tendus comme une toile,
Vos souvenirs avec leurs cadres d'horizons.

Dites, qu'avez-vous vu?

Like suns, urged by an angel with a whip.

Strange fate, the goal is always over the hill,
And being nowhere, anywhere is best,
Whilst man, whose sense of hope is never still,
Runs like a madman always looking for rest!

Bound for Acaria, our soul is a three-master;
A voice is heard to sound "Alert" on deck,
A wild voice from the crows-nest giving the muster:
"Love... glory... happiness!" Hell! it's a rock!

Each islet hailed aloft from the look-out station
Is some new Eldorado, offering relief,
And then this orgy of the imagination
By morning light turns out to be a reef.

O the poor lover of unheard of strands!
Do you clap him in irons or toss him in the ocean,
This drunken sailor, mapping American lands,
The actual gulf more bitter for the notion?

Thus the old vagabond, wading in the mud,
Dreams, his nose in the air, of a heavenly kingdom;
His spellbound eye reveals a Capuan abode
Wherever a candle may light up a slum.

III

Astounding travelers! what exalted stories
We read in your eyes, as deep as ocean streams!
Show us the coffers where you keep your memories,
Composed of stars and ether, marvelous gems.

We want to travel without steam or sails!
To brighten the long boredom of our prisons,
Paint on the stretched canvas of our souls
Your memories, framed only by far horizons.

Tell us, what have you seen?

IV

"Nous avons vu des astres
Et des flots; nous avons vu des sables aussi;
Et, malgré bien des chocs et d'imprévus désastres,
Nous nous sommes souvent ennuyés, comme ici.

La gloire du soleil sur la mer violette,
La gloire des cités dans le soleil couchant,
Allumaient dans nos cœurs une ardeur inquiète
De plonger dans un ciel au reflet alléchant.

Les plus riches cités, les plus grands paysages,
Jamais ne contenaient l'attrait mystérieux
De ceux que le hasard fait avec les nuages.
Et toujours le désir nous rendait soucieux!

— La jouissance ajoute au désir de la force.
Désir, vieil arbre à qui le plaisir sert d'engrais,
Cependant que grossit et durcit ton écorce,
Tes branches veulent voir le soleil de plus près!

Grandiras-tu toujours, grand arbre plus vivace
Que le cyprès? — Pourtant nous avons, avec soin,
Cueilli quelques croquis nour votre album vorace,
Frères qui trouvez beau tout ce qui vient de loin!

Nous avons salué des idoles à trompe;
Des trônes constellés de joyaux lumineux;
Des palais ouvragés dont la féerique pompe
Serait pour vos banquiers un rêve ruineux;

Des costumes qui sont pour les yeux une ivresse;
Des femmes dont les dents et les ongles sont teints,
Et des jongleurs savants que le serpent caresse."

V

Et puis, et puis encore?

IV

          "We have seen stars
And waves; we have seen dunes of yellow sand;
In spite of shocks and unforeseen disasters,
We were often bored, as here in our own land.

"Glory of sunlight on the violet wave,
Glory of cities when the sunset's in action,
Lit in our hearts a burning rage to dive
Into a sky with such a soft reflection.

"The richest cities, landscapes opening wide,
Never had such mysterious allure
As what a freak of chance makes with a cloud.
Always there's want, to make us insecure!

"Enjoyment gives a new strength to desire.
Desire, old tree where pleasures fructify,
Even as your bark grows thick and tough each year,
Your branches move closer to light's supply!

"Great flowering tree, have you more life to spend
Than the cypress? Brothers, we have saved with care
Sketches for your fond album, since you find
All things more beautiful that come from far.

"We have saluted idols with the sound
Of trumpets, thrones glittering with gems,
Finely carved palaces, whose fairyland
Of pomp would give a banker ruinous dreams;

"Clothes that are for the eyes a drunkenness,
Women that dye their teeth and nails with stains,
Deft jugglers wooed by snakes with a caress."

V

And then, and then what next?

VI

"O cerveaux enfantins!

Pour ne pas oublier la chose capitale,
Nous avons vu partout, et sans l'avoir cherché,
Du haut jusques en bas de l'échelle fatale,
Le spectacle ennuyeux de l'immortel péché:

La femme, esclave vile, orgueilleuse et stupide,
Sans rire s'adorant et s'aimant sans dégoût;
L'homme, tyran goulu, paillard, dur et cupide,
Esclave de l'esclave et ruisseau dans l'égout;

Le bourreau qui jouit, le martyr qui sanglote;
La fête qu'assaisonne et parfume le sang;
Le poison du pouvoir énervant le despote,
Et le peuple amoureux du fouet abrutissant;

Plusieurs religions semblables à la nôtre,
Toutes escaladant le ciel; la Sainteté,
Comme en un lit de plume un délicat se vautre,
Dans les clous et le crin cherchant la volupté;

L'Humanité bavarde, ivre de son génie,
Et, folle maintenant comme elle était jadis,
Criant à Dieu, dans sa furibonde agonie:
"O mon semblable, ô mon maître, je te maudis!"

Et les moins sots, hardis amants de la Démence,
Fuyant le grand troupeau parqué par le Destin,
Et se réfugiant dans l'opium immense!
— Tel est du globe entier l'éternel bulletin."

VII

Amer savoir, celui qu'on tire du voyage!
Le monde, monotone et petit, aujourd'hui,
Hier, demain, toujours, nous fait voir notre image:

VI

"O childish brains!

"But not to overlook the main affair,
We've seen it all, no need to search again,
From top to bottom of the fatal stair,
The whole dull pageant of immortal sin:

"Woman, a mean slave, stupid and arrogant,
Adoring herself—no laughter or self-disdain;
Man, hard and greedy—gluttonous, lecherous tyrant,
Slave to the slave, and gutter brimming the drain;

"The laughing hangman and the sobbing saint,
The feast all spiced and redolent of blood;
The despot sapped with power's venomous taint,
And the common people in love with the brutal goad;

"Several religions, very like our own,
All scaling heaven, whose Sanctity entails,
Like sybarites who wallow in beds of down,
The search for thrills in a hair shirt, and nails;

"Babbling humanity, drunk on its own great brain,
And just as crazy today as hitherto,
Cries out to God in its infuriate pain,
'Dear Lord, made in my image, my curse on you!'

"And those less foolish, outright lovers of madness,
Who shun the mighty herd penned in by fate,
And turn for help to opium's boundlessness!
—Such is the timeless news of the total planet."

VII

What bitter truth to draw from all these travels!
The world, for ever and ever monotonous,
Tomorrow, yesterday, shows nothing but ourselves:

Une oasis d'horreur dans un désert d'ennui!

Faut-il partir? rester? Si tu peux rester, reste;
Pars, s'il le faut. L'un court, et l'autre se tapit
Pour tromper l'ennemi vigilant et funeste;
Le Temps! Il est, hélas! des coureurs sans répit,

Comme le Juif errant et comme les apôtres,
A qui rien ne suffit, ni wagon ni vaisseau,
Pour fuir ce rétiaire infâme; il en est d'autres
Qui savent le tuer sans quitter leur berceau.

Lorsque enfin il mettra le pied sur notre échine,
Nous pourrons espérer et crier: En avant!
De même qu'autrefois nous partions pour la Chine,
Les yeux fixés au large et les cheveux au vent,

Nous nous embarquerons sur la mer des Ténèbres
Avec le cœur joyeux d'un jeune passager.
Entendez-vous ces voix, charmantes et funèbres,
Qui chantent: "Par ici! vous qui voulez manger

Le Lotus parfumé! c'est ici qu'on vendange
Les fruits miraculeux dont votre cœur a faim;
Venez vous enivrer de la douceur étrange
De cette après-midi qui n'a jamais de fin!"

A l'accent familier nous devinons le spectre;
Nos Pylades là-bas tendent leurs bras vers nous.
"Pour rafraîchir ton cœur nage vers ton Electre!"
Dit celle dont jadis nous baisions les genoux.

VIII

O Mort, vieux capitaine, il est temps! levons l'ancre!
Ce pays nous ennuie, ô Mort! Appareillons!
Si le ciel et la mer sont noirs comme de l'encre,
Nos cœurs que tu connais sont remplis de rayons!

Oasis of horror in deserts of tediousness!

Then should we go or stay? Stay if you can;
Go if you must. One runs; and one, to deceive
His sharp and sinister enemy, crouches down:
Time! Alas! some runners have no reprieve,

Like the apostles, like the Wandering Jew,
For whom no ship or coach, nothing can flee
This black retiary. Yet there were those who knew
The way to kill him from their infancy.

And when at last he plants his foot on our spine,
We can take hope and say, "Let's go beyond!"
Just like when going to China was the plan,
Eyes far away and hair stirred by the wind,

We shall embark upon the Sea of Gloom
With a young passenger's exultant heart.
Oh! can you hear those charming tones of doom
That sing: "This way all those who want to eat

The scented Lotus: here is that marvelous fruit
Gathered by all whose hearts have craved the boon;
Come to the harvest, get drunk on the sweet
Exotic draft of always afternoon!"

By this familiar voice we guess the ghost;
There our Pylades hail us, arms held out.
And she whose knees we long ago have kissed
Cries, "Swim for your Electra. It will cool your heart!"

VIII

Old captain Death, it's time to sail, I think.
This country bores us: come on, Death, let's go!
Even if the sky and sea are black as ink,
Our hearts are filled with sunbeams, as you know!

Verse-nous ton poison pour qu'il nous réconforte!
Nous voulons, tant ce feu nous brûle le cerveau,
Plonger au fond du gouffre, Enfer ou Ciel, qu'importe?
Au fond de l'Inconnu pour trouver du *nouveau!*

Le gouffre

Pascal avait son gouffre, avec lui se mouvant.
— Hélas! tout est abîme, — action, désir, rêve,
Parole! et sur mon poil qui tout droit se relève
Mainte fois de la Peur je sens passer le vent.
En haut, en bas, partout, la profondeur, la grève,
Le silence, l'espace affreux et captivant...
Sur le fond de mes nuits Dieu de son doigt savant
Dessine un cauchemar multiforme et sans trêve.
　　　J'ai peur du sommeil comme on a peur d'un grand trou,
Tout plein de vague horreur, menant on ne sait où;
Je ne vois qu'infini par toutes les fenêtres,
　　　Et mon esprit, toujours du vertige hanté,
Jalouse du néant l'insensibilité.
— Ah! ne jamais sortir des Nombres et des Etres!

274

Pour out for us your poison to console!
So fiercely does this fire devour the brain,
We'd plunge, no matter what, to Heaven or Hell,
For something *new* in the depth of the Unknown!

The void

PASCAL had moving with him an abyss,
Which is, alas! all things—action, desire,
Dream, word!— which makes my hair stand up with fear;
I often feel the chilling wind of this.

    Above, below, on all sides, far and near,
Silence and space, most frightful, will oppress;
And, looming on a background of black mass,
God's learned hands weave endless nightmare.

    I fear sleep as I would a giant hole
Of horrors leading to a place untold;
All windows face the same infinity;

    Haunted for ever by vertigo, my mind
Envies the emptiness benumbed and blind.
Ah! never from Numbers and Beings to break free!

Recueillement

Sois sage, ô ma Douleur, et tiens-toi plus tranquille.
Tu réclamais le Soir; il descend; le voici:
Une atmosphère obscure enveloppe la ville,
Aux uns portant la paix, aux autres le souci.
Pendant que des mortels la multitude vile,
Sous le fouet du Plaisir, ce bourreau sans merci,
Va cueillir des remords dans la fête servile,
Ma Douleur, donne-moi la main; viens par ici,
    Loin d'eux. Vois se pencher les défuntes Années,
Sur les balcons du ciel, en robes surannées;
Surgir du fond des eaux le Regret souriant;
    Le Soleil moribond s'endormir sous une arche,
Et, comme un long linceul traînant à l'Orient,
Entends, ma chère, entends la douce Nuit qui marche.

Correspondances

La Nature est un temple où de vivants piliers
Laissent parfois sortir de confuses paroles;
L'homme y passe à travers des forêts de symboles
Qui l'observent avec des regards familiers.
    Comme de longs échos qui de loin se confondent
Dans une ténébreuse et profonde unité,
Vaste comme la nuit et comme la clarté,
Les parfums, les couleurs et les sons se répondent.
    Il est des parfums frais comme des chairs d'enfants,
Doux comme les hautbois, verts comme les prairies,
— Et d'autres, corrompus, riches et triomphants,
    Ayant l'expansion des choses infinies,
Comme l'ambre, le musc, le benjoin et l'encens,
Qui chantent les transports de l'esprit et des sens.

Meditation

Be wise, my grief, and keep yourself more calm.
You prayed for evening; it comes down; it's here:
A dimness falls, as though it would embalm
The town, with peace for some, for others care.
While the vile multitude of mortals swarm
Beneath the whip of Pleasure and that drear
Hangman wrings penance in the servile game,
Give me your hand, my sorrow; now come near,
Far from all those. See how the dead years lean
On balconies of heaven, with tattered mien;
Regret, sprung from the depth of waters, smiles;
The dying sun asleep beneath an arch;
And like a lingering shroud that eastward trails,
Beloved, hear, O hear Night's soft approach.

Correspondences

Nature abides, a shrine where columns stay
Alive and give forth words confused at times;
Man roves a forest of symbolic names
That gaze at him in a familiar way.
Like echoes mingling with a distant reach
Into a deep and shadowy completeness,
Wide as the dark and ranging like all brightness,
Sounds, scents, and colors answer each to each.
There are some scents as fresh as children's skin,
Sweet as oboes, green as a field of grass,
And others, rich, corrupt, potent as sin,
Expanding without end through infinite space,
Like ambergris, musk, benjamin, incense,
That sing the rhapsodies of soul and sense.

Le rebelle

Un Ange furieux fond du ciel comme un aigle,
Du mécréant saisit à plein poing les cheveux,
Et dit, le secouant: "Tu connaîtras la règle!
(Car je suis ton bon Ange, entends-tu?) Je le veux!
Sache qu'il faut aimer, sans faire la grimace,
Le pauvre, le méchant, le tortu, l'hébété,
Pour que tu puisses faire à Jésus, quand il passe,
Un tapis triomphal avec ta charité.

Tel est l'Amour! Avant que ton cœur ne se blase,
A la gloire de Dieu rallume ton extase;
C'est la Volupté vraie aux durables appas!"

Et l'Ange, châtiant autant, ma foi! qu'il aime,
De ses poings de géant torture l'anathème;
Mais le damné répond toujours: "Je ne veux pas!"

Le reniement de Saint Pierre

Qu'est-ce que Dieu fait donc de ce flot d'anathèmes
Qui monte tous les jours vers ses chers Séraphins?
Comme un tyran gorgé de viande et de vins,
Il s'endort au doux bruit de nos affreux blasphèmes.

Les sanglots des martyrs et des suppliciés
Sont une symphonie enivrante sans doute,
Puisque, malgré le sang que leur volupté coûte,
Les cieux ne s'en sont point encore rassasiés!

— Ah! Jésus, souviens-toi du Jardin des Olives!
Dans ta simplicité tu priais à genoux
Celui qui dans son ciel riait au bruit des clous
Que d'ignobles borreaux plantaient dans tes chairs vives.

Lorsque tu vis cracher sur ta divinité
La crapule du corps de garde et des cuisines,
Et lorsque tu sentis s'enfoncer les épines
Dans ton crâne où vivait l'immense Humanité;

The rebel

An angry angel, plunging from the sky,
Secured the sinner, hawk-like, by his hair,
Shook him, and shouted, "Would you now defy
Your Guardian Angel? Listen—and beware!

 Know well that you must love, without a fuss,
The poor, the wicked, the deformed, the dull,
That you may spread, when Christ returns to us,
A welcome mat of kindness triumphal.

 For such is Love! Before your heart grows tame,
Rekindle to God's glory your low flame,
And enter lasting bliss without a blot!"

 The angel then, most chastening when most kind,
Tortured the damned soul in his giant hand,
But he would always answer, "I will not!"

Peter's denial

What does God do with this diurnal spate
Of curses mounting toward His seraphim?
He's lulled by that sweet sound when we blaspheme,
For He's a tyrant, gorged with wine and meat.

The sobs of martyrs and men doomed in jails
Must certainly intoxicate the skies,
A symphony that never satisfies,
In spite of all the blood their mirth entails.

Ah! Jesus, think now of Gethsemane!
You knelt, too innocent to understand,
Before that Being who, while they pierced your hands,
Heard the vile hangmen with a laugh of glee.

When drunken guardsmen and the scullery scorn
Mocked you and spat on your divinity,
And when your head, home of Humanity,
Had felt them press on it the crown of thorn,

279

Quand de ton corps brisé la pesanteur horrible
Allongeait tes deux bras distendus, que ton sang
Et ta sueur coulaient de ton front pâlissant,
Quand tu fus devant tous posé comme une cible,

Rêvais-tu de ces jours si brillants et si beaux
Où tu vins pour remplir l'éternelle promesse,
Où tu foulais, monté sur une douce ânesse,
Des chemins tout jonchés de fleurs et de rameaux,

Où, le cœur tout gonflé d'espoir et de vaillance,
Tu fouettais tous ces vils marchands à tour de bras,
Où tu fus maître enfin? Le remords n'a-t-il pas
Pénétré dans ton flanc plus avant que la lance?

— Certes, je sortirai, quant à moi, satisfait
D'un monde où l'action n'est pas la sœur du rêve;
Puissé-je user du glaive et périr par le glaive!
Saint Pierre a renié Jésus... il a bien fait!

Bénédiction

LORSQUE, par un décret des puissances suprêmes,
Le Poëte apparaît en ce monde ennuyé,
Sa mère épouvantée et pleine de blasphèmes
Crispe ses poings vers Dieu, qui la prend en pitié:

— "Ah! que n'ai-je mis bas tout un nœud de vipères,
Plutôt que de nourrir cette dérision!
Maudite soit la nuit aux plaisirs éphémères
Où mon ventre a conçu mon expiation!

Puisque tu m'as choisie entre toutes les femmes
Pour être le dégoût de mon triste mari,
Et que je ne puis pas rejeter dans les flammes,
Comme un billet d'amour, ce monstre rabougri,

When, dragging out your arms, the ghastly weight
Unhinged your broken body, down which flowed
From waning forehead mingled sweat and blood;
When you were targeted for public hate,

Did you then dream about the brilliant times
When, to fulfill the eternal word of God,
Mounted upon a gentle ass, you trod
The roads bestrewn with flowers and with palms,

When, with a heart made great by gallant trust,
You lashed those traffickers with all your force,
Their master at last? And did not this remorse
Pierce your side deeper than the lance's thrust?

—For me, I choose in such a world to dwell
Where action is not sister to a dream;
Could I but live by the sword and die by its gleam!
Peter denied his Master. . . He did well!

Benediction

WHEN, by a mandate of the powers supreme,
The Poet is born into a world that's bored,
His mother, moved by horror to blaspheme,
Clenches her fist to call a pitying Lord:

"If only I had spawned a viper's brood,
Rather than suckle this poor joke of doom!
God curse the night in which a lustful mood
Visited expiation on my womb!

"Since, of all women, thou hast fixed the blame
On me for my disgusted husband's woe,
And since I cannot fling back in the flame,
Like a love letter, this foul embryo,

Je ferai rejaillir ta haine qui m'accable
Sur l'instrument maudit de tes méchancetés,
Et je tordrai si bien cet arbre misérable,
Qu'il ne pourra pousser ses boutons empestés!''

Elle ravale ainsi l'écume de sa haine,
Et, ne comprenant pas les desseins éternels,
Elle-même prépare au fond de la Géhenne
Les bûchers consacrés aux crimes maternels.

Pourtant, sous la tutelle invisible d'un Ange,
L'Enfant déshérité s'enivre de soleil,
Et dans tout ce qu'il boit et dans tout ce qu'il mange
Retrouve l'ambroisie et le nectar vermeil.

Il joue avec le vent, cause avec le nuage,
Et s'enivre en chantant du chemin de la croix;
Et l'Esprit qui le suit dans son pèlerinage
Pleure de le voir gai comme un oiseau des bois.

Tous ceux qu'il veut aimer l'observent avec crainte,
Ou bien, s'enhardissant de sa tranquillité,
Cherchent à qui saura lui tirer une plainte,
Et font sur lui l'essai de leur férocité.

Dans le pain et le vin destinés à sa bouche
Ils mêlent de la cendre avec d'impurs crachats;
Avec hypocrisie ils jettent ce qu'il touche,
Et s'accusent d'avoir mis leurs pieds dans ses pas.

Sa femme va criant sur les places publiques:
''Puisqu'il me trouve assez belle pour m'adorer,
Je ferai le métier des idoles antiques,
Et comme elles je veux me faire redorer;

Et je me soûlerai de nard, d'encens, de myrrhe,
De génuflexions, de viandes et de vins,
Pour savoir si je puis dans un cœur qui m'admire
Usurper en riant les hommages divins!

"I'll make thy crushing hate rebound upon
The misbegotten agent of thy spite
And twist this tree before it has begun
To sprout, that all its buds be gnawed with blight."

And so she swallows down the froth of hate
And, baffled by the heavenly designs,
Rears, at the bottom of hell's deepest pit,
The stake devoted to maternal crimes.

And all the while, in an unseen Angel's care,
Drunk on the sun, this changeling child would roam,
Quaff crimson nectar, feast on ambrosial fare,
The food and drink of his eternal home.

He plays with the wind, converses with a cloud,
Rejoices singing on his way to the cross,
The Spirit that follows him along this road
Weeping to see him gay as a bird got loose.

All those whom he would love watch him with fear,
Or else, made bold by his tranquillity,
Contrive who can extort from him a tear
And try upon him their ferocity.

The bread and wine intended for his mouth
They mix with filthy sputum or with ash,
Denounce themselves for treading in his path,
And what he touched affect to throw in the trash.

His woman, flaunting scorn of him in the street,
Cries, "Since he finds me fair enough to adore,
I'll be the idol that he prates about
And do myself in gold, like shrines before.

"I'll take my fill of incense, nard, and myrrh,
Of genuflections, of choice food and wine,
To see if, while I'm laughing, I can spur
Him to prostrations meant for the divine.

Et, quand je m'ennuierai de ces farces impies,
Je poserai sur lui ma frêle et forte main;
Et mes ongles, pareils aux ongles des harpies,
Sauront jusqu'à son cœur se frayer un chemin.

Comme un tout jeune oiseau qui tremble et qui palpite,
J'arracherai ce cœur tout rouge de son sein,
Et, pour rassasier ma bête favorite,
Je le lui jetterai par terre avec dédain!"

Vers le Ciel, où son œil voit un trône splendide,
Le Poëte serein lève ses bras pieux,
Et les vastes éclairs de son esprit lucide
Lui dérobent l'aspect des peuples furieux:

— "Soyez béni, mon Dieu, qui donnez la souffrance
Comme un divin remède à nos impuretés
Et comme la meilleure et la plus pure essence
Qui prépare les forts aux saintes voluptés!

Je sais que vous gardez une place au Poëte
Dans les rangs bienheureux des saintes Légions,
Et que vous l'invitez à l'éternelle fête
Des Trônes, des Vertus, des Dominations.

Je sais que la douleur est la noblesse unique
Où ne mordront jamais la terre et les enfers,
Et qu'il faut pour tresser ma couronne mystique
Imposer tous les temps et tous les univers.

Mais les bijoux perdus de l'antique Palmyre,
Les métaux inconnus, les perles de la mer,
Par votre main montés, ne pourraient pas suffire
A ce beau diadème éblouissant et clair;

Car il ne sera fait que de pure lumière,
Puisée au foyer saint des rayons primitifs,
Et dont les yeux mortels, dans leur splendeur entière,
Ne sont que des miroirs obscurcis et plaintifs!"

"And when this impious joke exhausts applause,
My fragile hand will demonstrate its art;
My nails will tear him like a harpy's claws
And dig a bloody pathway to his heart.

"Like a young bird that trembles in his hand,
I'll snatch that heart out bleeding from his breast,
Throw it disdainfully upon the ground,
And gorge with it the hound that I like best."

The Poet beholds in the sky a shining throne,
To which, arms raised, his worship is in pledge,
And the wide lightning of his lucid brain
Strips off distractions of the rabble's rage:

"Praise be to thee, O Lord, by whom we endure
Suffering as balm for our impurities,
Which, like an essence most refined and pure,
Strengthens our hearts for sacred ecstacies.

"I know thou guardest, high among the bless'd,
A place transcendent which the Poet owns,
Inviting him to that eternal feast
Of Principalities and Powers and Thrones.

"I know how pain is that rare gift and noble
Which neither earth nor hell can ever debase,
That weaving this strange crown as I am able
Demands all time and every universe.

"But not Palmyra's jewels of long ago,
Nor undiscovered gold, nor pearls of the sea,
As mounted by thy hand, would ever show
Like this bright diadem that shines for me;

"For it shall be composed of purest light,
Drawn from the holiest hearth of primal fire,
Of which these mortal eyes, with clearest sight,
Are but a misty mirror, blurred with care."

The Future Drags Its Feet

Le Cimetière Marin, by G. Zeltins

The Future Drags Its Feet
Nineteenth Century

The title of this section translates part of a line from Valéry's "Graveyard by the Sea." It is intended to suggest that the poetry wavers between the past and the future. The resulting sustained impression receives its initial character from the two dominant poets at the head of the list, who will engage most of our attention here.

The first, Stephane Mallarmé, in the spirit of his forms, reaches towards the past, with a mysterious vision, in small compass, of great originality and splendor, which had slow but lasting influence. The second, Arthur Rimbaud, may be the most extraordinary phenomenon of genius in the history of poetry, commencing with sedulous formal fidelity to the past, but quickly smashing every idol in sight in the baffling breakthrough he projected, before spurning poetry and taking flight from the scene, *aetat* nineteen. His subsequent impact was also a delayed fuse but explosive enough. It is the contention here that the opposing lights emitted by these two shoot off reflexively to the rest, major to minor, minor to less, till they climax again in Valéry, a disciple of the first.

Remembering that history has no absolute beginnings, nor endings either, then side by side with the inveterate impetus of the status quo, we are going to see the compensating tendency of that momentum to exhaust itself and seek renewal by a new impulse or direction. This propensity is perfectly reconcilable with the fact that the present unit, at the end of its manifold explorative ventures, bows out with two first-rate poets having strong traditional leanings, and that the last poem, Valéry's, seems greater than any written since. Throughout the section we witness the wavering between fidelity to tradition and varieties of probative groping, sometimes quite unconscious as such.

It is easy to observe parallels in England: the cultivated decadence of Verlaine and Swinburne, Moréas and Dowson; deployment of the vernacular in Corbière and Browning; "honest doubt" of Prudhomme and Arnold; pure passion of Catherine Pozzi[1] and Emily Bronte. We could go on accumulating such counterparts, some of them more susceptible than others of focus on particular poems. Could it be that in both countries there were failures, either of nerve or of talent, on the verge of poetry trembling to be born? In Prudhomme and Noailles, we see the hesitations of the sensitive agnostic, who exhibits the same reluctance to abandon accustomed verse forms as accustomed faith. In Toulet (as in the versatile Charles Cros earlier), the swing forward, if so it may be dignified, takes the form of a rather self-conscious truancy of manners, hard to be thought of as forward according to any standards accepted by our own notorious "sexual revolution"—about which Catherine Pozzi or even Jacques Prévert, favorite of nightclubs, would have known little and cared less. And conversely, Francis Jammes' devoutness as a Catholic is matched by his nostalgic style, to the point of threatening sentimentality, notwithstanding the charm.

But then these retrospective loyalties are not safe from the intensely French smile of Levet, not to speak of the nimble impudence of Corbière, and the open derision of Laforgue, both of whom reach forward all the way to Eliot and Pound, who, as Edmund Wilson showed, were not ashamed to assimilate them two generations later. And poetry redolent of a twilight charm must reckon with reservations from another quarter: the conscious experimentation of the tribe of Moréas, by whom our selections might have done better, if only because of his prominence in a *movement,* that of the symbolists, no less.

The paradox of diverging conservatism and change becomes for us a distinct and compact mélange, that fits the scheme almost too neatly. In the figure of Paul Fort, who, immersed in the poetry of the folk, contributed a voluminous ballad literature, we see at the same time a slightly naive experimentalism, which led him to conceal the regularity of his rhythms and rhymes in what are ostensibly prose paragraphs—instead of the reverse, as is expected of us today: that is, disguising prose as verse.

And where does Emile Verhaeren belong in this succession? Were it not for the strongest argument of all, that he wrote in French, there could be a case for excluding him altogether, not only because he was Belgian, but because he does not *feel* French. There are, however, the further considerations that he has real greatness, and that, without our having to go beyond the scope of his own work, he wonderfully vindicates this pattern of reaching two ways. He revels with the exuberance of *Leaves of Grass.* He recoils from the encroaching urban miasma with at least as sharp a revolt as Ruskin or William Morris. At the same time his verses run and leap in liberated alexandrines.

It is through Verlaine that we shall trace this winding movement back to its visible source in the twin peaks, Mallarmé and Rimbaud. The gift that survives as self-sufficient in Verlaine is his melody, in which there lurks a weakness of luxury. It doesn't make that much difference whether his dreams are sacred or profane: they share the same diffuse eroticism and the same slightly tremulous narcissism. "Art Poétique" was to be read by numberless neophyte symbolists as a capsule "platform," one that was to program much mimicry. Here we find vagueness apotheosized, and music given pride of place in the making of a poem: "De la musique avant toute chose,. . ." (Yes, but what sort of music?). It is a slogan which may be seen as the rival of "L'image avant tout." But neither the neophytes of Verlaine nor those who draw attention to their repudiation of what his poetry stands for have seen that to encourage one of these preoccupations, whether with music or imagery, at the expense of the other, is to promote a moribund poetry.

It is significant if sad that Rimbaud's trenchant programs make no reference to the elder poet who was, until the break between them, his intimate companion. Instead, his homage is to Baudelaire, "the first visionary," and "the king of poets." Side by side with this exaltation of Baudelaire is a disdainful assault on the Parnassians, who preceded and succeeded him, and whom he has every intention of leaving out on a limb.

When Verlaine used the word "decadent" for himself, Rimbaud, and Mallarmé, he had little understanding that to such an ill-assorted trio the misnomer could apply only in contrast to the chill "hard edge" of the Parnassians, and less idea still of the glancing humor that draws Rimbaud together with Corbière and Laforgue, to liberate these last three (leaving Verlaine out) from the solemnity of the card-carrying surrealists, who would claim Rimbaud as one of themselves!

Rimbaud is not only one of the two fountainheads of decisive change in the practice of poetry in this era, but a crucial challenge for the translator. How are we going to set about rendering poems like "First Communions," "Seven-Year-Old Poets," and "Memory," which last Wallace Fowlie had some good reason, short as it is, to describe as Rimbaud's finest poem? The first problems concern form, and specifically the question whether we are to abandon the attempt to salvage the melody of these poems, in our competing fidelity to such considerations as syntax, conforming change of pace, and something that might be called "dash." My own answers have been influenced by what we are now to see that Rimbaud himself said, as well as did.

It is the exceptional freedom of imaginative movement, within the equally arresting formal rigor, that presents in these poems the most daunting obstacles to lyrical transposition. Let us suppose ourselves to be among those who proclaim, or concede, that (in Rimbaud's own words) "music and rhymes are games and pastimes"—except, he said, for

Greece, where "verses and lyres give rhythm to action."[2] But even if such a concession is made, it could not be said that, as regards form, Rimbaud ever faltered in playing the game strictly according to the sternest rules of French verse, from Ronsard to Banville. To quote Rimbaud again, "If what he [the poet] brings back from *down there* has form, he gives form" (italics Rimbaud's). And it is in this same letter to Paul Demery that his flipness underscores his loyalties: "I would give you my *Lovers of Paris,* one hundred hexameters, sir, and my *Death of Paris,* two hundred hexameters!" There too, speaking seriously now of the poets of the future (who have never lost an opportunity to offer him their fealty, even when they have not possessed what it took to follow his example), he says, "Always filled with Number and Harmony, these poems will be made to endure." Then, and as if to clinch his point: "Let me close with a pious hymn!"—having said which, he flings at his bewildered mentor the torrential, surrealistic piece, "Accroupisse-ments" ("Squattings"), composed in faultless alexandrines, arranged in equally meticulous quintuplets, rhyming a-b-a-b-a. It may be objected that I have conveniently forgotten how, after Rimbaud said, "If it has form, he gives form," he adds, "If it is formless, he gives formlessness." But what should settle the matter is that the "formlessness" never trespasses upon Rimbaud's *verse,* which wells up from "down there" where form is required; for that matter, does not get into any French verse of consequence previous to André Breton's "Les Champs Magnétiques" (1921), if verse this may be called—after which comes the deluge of formlessness, and not only in France, of course.

The contention behind what we are saying is that poetry's widespread and uncompromising revolt against form, revolt of which poor Rimbaud has frequently been proclaimed as the (innocent) focal hierophant, or "voyant," can never be at the cost of those laws of "harmony" by which the poetry of verse lives and moves; and that Rimbaud's poetic practice, in actuality, consistently bears this out. Well was it that he said, "I never lose step";[3] for whatever may have been his "departures into new loves and new sounds,"[4] the "Numbers" had no wish to be novel, any more than the stones, the leaves, and the tides are novel. Dancing may be as liberated as you please without being walking.

Are we not, then, to regard the shooting lights of *Illuminations* as poems? Not really. Rimbaud himself is most unlikely ever to have thought of them as such. They are stunning notes for poems, rather than poems: notes for which he had yet to discover the finally appropriate form, the perfect "Number and Harmony," in the brief time before, at the age of nineteen, he renounced poetry altogether—possibly from a shrewd fear of madness, such as, whether from drugs or not, afflicted Collins and Clare, Hölderlin and Nietzsche, Nerval, Utrillo, Artaud, et al. We might say that the forms, vacant and expectant, awaited the plunge of drastic poetic renewal; that the plunge took place, and we are witness to it; but that we still await the emergence of the swimmer *with his strokes,* or forms of movement. Thus, it is the haunting suggestions, "indistinguishable from what is foreseen but not yet formulated," as Réné Char says, the potential rather than the achievement of *Illuminations,* which has subsequently helped to hypnotize two generations of poets and critics to suppose that formlessness in poetry is equal or superior to form.

It is these amazing visions that Rimbaud may conceivably have been hoping to vindicate as resurrections from what he called "melodies and forms dying."[5] In that unlikely case, "the hope was drunk in which he dressed himself." They are still but gestures towards melodies and forms yearning to be born. Or let Rimbaud himself say it: "All the *possibilities* of harmony and architecture will be in commotion at your center"[6] (italics mine). If the melodies turn out to be "impossible," there can be no substitute for these melodies, or for the "fraternal awakening of all choral and orchestral energies and their immediate application."[7] It is these energies which are to bring "abolition of all clamorous and turbulent pain *(toutes souffrances sonores et mouvantes)* in more intense music."[8]

If we ask, with the speaker in Eliot's "Portrait of a Lady": "Are these ideas right or wrong?" the answer is likely to be decisive as to our evaluation of new poetry and our own practice of it.

In his poems proper, it is sometimes quite exceptionally difficult to get at Rimbaud's thought. For me the most elusive poem in the book is "Eternity," here, as by other translators, still unsolved, but the fresh attempt is indispensable. At the age of seventeen, Rimbaud had glimpsed, this once at least, that eternity is not endless time, but a breakthrough into dimensions that nullify time altogether, the absolute now; and that he found a way, in those tight, eliptical stanzas, to communicate this awareness without a trace of didacticism: first, through an arcane fusion of sun, night, and sea; and then, through the self-denial of specious hopes, in favor of something resembling what we might attribute to the existential self-reliance, a gesture which, incidentally, becomes less subtle, more clamorously overt in Corbière's "Pariah." It is not an epiphany to recommend itself to simpler faiths. We shall not wish to make claims for it either mystical or prophetical. Nevertheless, it reaches into regions where many a simpler faith might falter, for its very ellipses glitter with intimations of translogical consciousness, or, to put it in abstractions even more alien to poetry, anticipates perceptions and affirmations which we are still unready to recognize as sacred in such secular disguise.

In "Golden Age," we have angels, but they are made even more in Rimbaud's image than Rilke's angels in Rilke's. Enid Starkie seems to see it as a religious limitation that this was so.[9] Should it be seen as such? Our thematic ordering (see Introduction, pp. 12-13) would have grouped this poem and "Eternity," together with "Memory" and "First Communions," among poems of Divinity. The famous blasphemies of the latter (perhaps the most emotionally complex, as well as stylistically formative, poem in this collection), blaspheme less from perversity than from this extraordinary youth's subjection so early to a transcending "Illumination" of a more personal and primary order. This illumination was one which, by Enid Starkie's own account, returned to Rimbaud on his deathbed, after the long years of "infidelity"; but, as she conjectures from Isabelle Rimbaud's mystified account of the poet's utterances in his penultimate hours, an illumination which returned *previous* to the celebrated conversion. The conversion, then, may be understood as a last-moment deposit of exhaustion, despair, and surrender, in loving gratitude for the devoted ministrations of the poet's sister; and poems like "Eternity" and "Golden Age" as clues to his sporadic, disinherited mystical strain. Or, if it is preferred, he might, at the end, have "come home" to such a strain in clothing familiar to his childhood.

Finally, we should take another look at the wonderful "Memory," but this time from the standpoint, less of its form than of its vision. It is a peculiarly elusive poem, and one which, notwithstanding its characteristic strain of the sardonic, belongs nevertheless with poems of Divinity by its persistent suggestions of another world, a world of timeless ramparts and reachless flowers, of mysterious resorts "far beyond the mountain" and of "thousands of angels!" These encroach with surprising intimations on the sky and trees and water, on the grass and children and busy mowers and hilarious Madame, who stands too upright in the grain field; and then, debouching without warning on the joyful boatyards and the flowers bordering the still water—suddenly, there is the putrescence and the mud. (Were it not so artless, it would be hard to think that Rimbaud, even *aetat* seventeen, had no knowledge of the mantric lotus, rooted in mud and mounting through water to blossom in the air.) And that magical old dredger in his motionless punt, padlocked by the mother, no doubt, lest he turn a harmless skiff into a *Bateau Ivre* and drown himself! It is a world, and it is more than a world.

"Encroach," we said; "overshadow," it might be; but never does it *displace* the world of mud and sweat: fusion scarcely believable without the clear, close, terse *music* of the lines, only forty, and all so deceptively casual. For if poetry gives us mementos of otherness, it is not, at best, by appealing away from the everyday world and conjuring in its place a hypostatized, hallowed symbol, such as the lotus, the mustard seed, the grail; but by contriving that the many-colored manifold itself, in all its multifariousness—the water, the children, the maid, the mud—shall make a leap beyond the normal acceptation of the light of common day.

Swimming upstream, as it were, to Mallarmé, the second of our "twin peaks," we find that in him language itself becomes a most peculiar burning-glass. It is language which may appear, at first glance, to identify itself with the stylistic fetishism from which emerged the most brilliant results of Leconte de Lisle and the Parnassians; but though it is an answer which may spring from a kindred verbal elevation, the result flows, for Mallarmé, into a more enchanted vale. English poetry too has its Shelley and Yeats, who, like Mallarmé, do more than enunciate the rationale of this answer, since their poems exemplify it. Mallarmé was always a theorist; but it is not by his theories, it is by the wondrous enacted language of his poems that he becomes such an authentic example of that *voyant* which, in different ways, Rimbaud, even Balzac,[10] together with many others of that period, aspired to be—sometimes only pretended to be, though this pretense would be when they were not content or able to let their poetry speak for their vision.

Being a *voyant* was a craze which, in these writers, but especially in Mallarmé, differs in root and flower from preoccupations characteristic of either the critic or the theologian, to both of whom language will be a conceptual or, at best, devotional *instrumentality*. To Mallarmé, language becomes a *mantric finality*: a system of spells, which enabled him, in Jacob Boehme's words, to "bud forth again and receive the first life, a purgation from creation." The words, the syntax have an evocatory force, such as is conveyed by the Sanskrit word *bija*: locutions by which real powers may be elicited from heaven. Mallarmé himself thought of it much in this way.

Paralleling thus in far-out contrivance Rimbaud's celebrated "deréglement de tous les sens," Mallarmé in his poems gives us terminological audacities, syntactical dislocations, and soft aural explosions, such as flourish in the unassailable (for me) in English verse, *Hommages et Tombeaux,* or (likewise, as yet, alas!) *L'Après Midi d'un Faune,* not to speak of *Un Coup de Dés,* if that is verse.

Belonging to a similar elusiveness, however, are familiar traces among those of his poems, limpid if hermetic, whose translation is here attempted: the parenthetical postponement of resolution in the closing tercet of the sonnet, "O si chère de loin. . ."; the intoxication with negation of ". . .des vols qui n'ont pas fui. . ." in the opening quatrain of "Le Vierge, le Vivace, et le Bel Aujourd'hui," but this mania evinced in a hundred other places; the weird apostrophe to poetry, addressed as "la Berceuse," in "Don du Poème," where, in the closing lines, that mother-goddess is conjured to press her breast for the milk of inspiration, and in doing so yields a shower of milky music of the strangest order![11]

Then there is the risk of ultimate spiritual disaster if the poet is stripped of those persistent wings of his, as in the closing stanza of "Les Fenêtres"; above all, perhaps, the involvement of the very luminosity of our festive planet itself with the potent mirage of poetry, in the powerful "Quand l'ombre menaça. . . ." May these too few, too random instances witness to the *order* of contrivance that I speak of, though they will so little suffice to convey the idea of its magic and reach. It is an anarchical manipulation, effecting that disturbance of usage which in Mallarmé disposes certain readers towards the free flight of "the Alone to the Alone," when his own poetry, consciously or unconsciously, does not itself engage in this flight.

The despairingly beautiful "Le Vierge, le Vivace, et le Bel Aujourd'hui" might, without bending too far, be read as resting, however remotely, on a doctrine of metempsychosis, subject to metamorphosis. At least, here, as in certain of Yeats's poems, notably "The Wild Swans of Coole," the symbolism is such as derives ultimately from the same source as the Svetasvatara Upanishad, where the swan is the "jiva," or individual soul, that must wander far from home so long as it still conceives itself distinct from the absolute self. But the poem itself is singularly undoctrinal: the poet-swan hovers, a transient embodiment of timelessness, to draw the earthbound heart upward. The same poet's "Little Tunes," trembling as they do on the very verge of a sense beyond sense, never to be rescued except by word music, seem to be pitched on purpose to catch any drifting wind of inspiration on *our* part: inspiration, or aspiration, that might, like those Aeolian harps beloved of Shelley, blow through us from what the poems almost, but not quite, say.

Is it hoping too much that these tiny "Tunes," together with this swan, may enable a far guess at what Mallarmé meant when he wrote: "Every sacred thing that wishes to remain sacred surrounds itself with mystery"?[12] It is only when he sinks from the level of this mystery, that he enters what he himself called, "the terrible struggle with this wicked old bundle of feathers, fortunately overthrown, named [i.e., by us] God" (". . .la lutte terrible avec ce vieux et méchant plumage, terrassé, heureusement, Dieu"). But it remains true that most of his poetry, whatever may be its doctrinal non-commitment, takes place on the level of complex *rites*.

Valéry's genius is very quiet to be so close in time. It's fine that France's pride in him should have gone to the opposite of quietness in lavishing beautiful editions and devout tributes. What other nation would have so treasured a philosopher poet only less inaccessible than Mallarmé, or even bestowed recognition beyond a *recherché élite?* The kinship between his creation and Mallarmé's is in some ways closer than those weekly reunions on the Rue de Rome; and yet their work is perfectly distinct, both in the silence and the breaking of it.

Mallarmé always, and with agonizing delay, presides over his poem; with Valéry, notwithstanding the disrespect he claimed for it, the poem becomes the sacred instrument by which he clues in on the mysteries, and the technical headaches themselves are the divine opportunity, until presently the poem takes control of the poet's meditative fervor. With Mallarmé, the movement is inward towards a mysterious center. But observe how "The Graveyard by the Sea," with a tidal movement, like the sea it contemplates, responds to that "mass of calm and visible reserve," to the roof above, the grove of pines around, the sailing ships on the horizon and sailing doves above, telescoped as one, the burning heat of the sun, the stupendous power of the waves, which at the end sweep away his pages, himself, and us, who stand listening stunned to these rites, as awesome as those of his master.

It can only be translated with a comparable turbulence and surreptitious calm control. It is a poem of great range for its length; it is contemplative metaphysics and ethics; it is many seascapes in calm and storm; it is reflections on its own craft; but more persistently than these sources of inspiration, it is a love poem to death, in which death has the ruling voice. The same thematic complexity extends to so seemingly slight a poem as "The Footsteps," on the face of it a still, impassioned love poem, which is, however, absorbed in the breathless visitations of the poet's craft. But here, as in all Valéry's poems, there is something that suffuses all the branching emotions and interlocking themes. It is the *music,* so inevitable as to seem governed purely by impulse, yet so sensitively disciplined that his poetry takes leave of one age and ushers in another with sounds as insidious as Debussy's.

1. Apropos of the traditional overtones of Catherine Pozzi's two great love poems, "Ave" and "Vale," I should like to quote the remarks of Dr. Michael Channing of San Diego State University; "I agree that, as you said, it renders 'passion without what the Buddha meant by craving.' And in so doing it reminds me of certain Troubadour poems, especially those by Jaufre Rudel, which express the theme of 'Amors de terra lonhdana' ('Love from a far-away land'). As you know, there is a school of interpretation which sees these and other Troubadour poems as inspired by the Catharist 'heresy,' in which, to pick up your terms, because it belongs to the world of matter and the flesh, is sinful, while 'passion' is pure, since it is really directed beyond the beloved to the Divine, of whom the Lady is a symbol. With a few adjustments, it seems that these poems of Pozzi might be at home in a collection of medieval Troubadour poems."

2. Letter to Paul Demery. May 15, 1871.

3. *Illuminations.* "Morning of Drunkenness."

4. Ibid., "Departure."

5. Ibid., "Youth III. Twenty Years Old."

6. Ibid., "Youth IV."

7. Ibid., "Sale."

8. Ibid., "Genius."

9. *Arthur Rimbaud,* Norton, 1947. See, especially, "Conclusion," and page 415, although it would not be a less valuable book because the point I am here making would not quite be for Miss Starkie.

10. I say "even" because we do not normally associate a "visionary" with the *Comédie Humaine;* but I doubt it was only of *Serafita* and *Louis Lambert* that Baudelaire was thinking when he referred to Balzac as "above all else a passionate visionary. . .more angelic in devotion than the people who act out the dramas of this real world." (Article on Théophile Gautier.)

11. Let this poem provide, for once, a staple sample of back-stage props, that is to say, of those countless Philistine considerations besetting any acceptable solution in utmost translating. Here, the insufficiently colorless rhyme at line 2 is conditioned by the necessity to preserve, as intact as possible, the queer and famous magic of the first line. Such alternatives as the English jaw-breaker "Idumean Night" would probably have to set up something like "stripped of feathers quite," essentially a comic opera rhyme and a phrase which is also stripped of Mallarmé's special thought suggesting the poem's original plastic (plumed) state, previous to its no longer airborne condition in "black" ink. For although, of course, it is ostensibly the dawn that is pale, bloody, and featherless, yet dawn and poem are telescoped, in the Mallarmé manner. On the other hand, "plucked of freedom," though true to the thought, is a shade looser than one's fussier strategies would choose—with consequent pale, black questioning the poem's inclusion. This hesitation was neutralized, however, by partial preservation of the complex spell exerted by the closing lines, where the outlandish act of poetic composition is

conveyed by the damnedest blend of paternity, senility, sensuality, purity, piety, and sanctity—all heavily infused with the sardonic (lines 6, 7, 11, and—well, everywhere). Besides, we have to ask again, ''Where else, not French, may the poem's total effect be guessed at?''

12. ''Toute chose sacrée et qui veut demeurer sacrée s'enveloppe de mystère.'' Quoted also by Anthony Hartley in the introduction to his edition of Mallarmé (*Penguin Poets,* 1965). It is to be found in *l'Artiste,* September 15, 1862.

Stephane Mallarmé

1842 - 1898

Le sonneur

CEPENDANT que la cloche éveille sa voix claire
A l'air pur et limpide et profond du matin
Et passe sur l'enfant qui jette pour lui plaire
Un angélus parmi la lavande et le thym,
Le sonneur effleuré par l'oiseau qu'il éclaire,
Chevauchant tristement en geignant du latin
Sur la pierre qui tend la corde séculaire,
N'entend descendre à lui qu'un tintement lointain.
Je suis cet homme. Hélas! de la nuit désireuse,
J'ai beau tirer le câble à sonner l'Idéal,
De froids péchés s'ébat un plumage féal,
Et la voix me vient que par bribes et creuse!
Mais, un jour, fatigué d'avoir en vain tiré,
O Satan, j'ôterai la pierre et me pendrai.

Don du poème

JE t'apporte l'enfant d'une nuit d'Idumée!
Noire, à l'aile saignante et pâle, déplumée,
Par le verre brûlé d'aromates et d'or,
Par les carreaux glacés, hélas! mornes encor,
L'aurore se jeta sur la lampe angélique.
Palmes! et quand elle a montré cette relique
A ce père essayant un sourire ennemi,
La solitude, bleue et stérile a frémi.
O la berceuse, avec ta fille et l'innocence
De vos pieds froids, accueille une horrible naissance:
Et ta voix rappelant viole et clavecin,
Avec le doigt fané presseras-tu le sein
Par qui coule en blancheur sibylline la femme
Pour les lèvres que l'air du vierge azur affame?

Stephane Mallarmé

1842 - 1898

The bell-ringer

WHILE the bell wakes its voice to the pure air
Of deep and limpid morning, passing over
The child, who flings, to give the joy his share,
An angelus for lavender and clover,
　　The bell-ringer is brushed by the brightened flare
Of a bird. He mutters Latin, hauling ever
The stone that weights the ancient cord, aware
Of distant tintinnabulary fever.
　　I am that man. On the cord of anxious night
In vain I haul away for the ideal sound,
Cold sins with loyal plumage play around,
　　The voice comes only halt and thin from the height!
But one day, sick of the futile tug and clang,
O Satan, I shall loose the stone and hang.

Gift of the poem

I BRING you the infant of a night in Edom!
Black, with pale, bleeding wing and plucked of freedom,
In by the window burning with gold and spice
Burst dawn, alas! through mournful panes of ice,
Hurling itself upon the angel lamp.
Palms! and when to this father essaying a damp
Unfriendly smile, the dawn revealed that wrack,
The blue and sterile solitude shrank back.
O lullaby nurse with your daughter and innocent
Cold feet, a horrid birth you now confront:
Your voice a viol and harpsichord at least,
With shriveled finger will you squeeze the breast
Of woman streaming sibylline whiteness there
To lips athirst for the sky's blue virgin air?

Quand l'ombre menaça...

QUAND l'ombre menaça de la fatale loi
Tel vieux Rêve, désir et mal de mes vertèbres,
Affligé de périr sous les plafonds funèbres
Il a ployé son aile indubitable en moi.

Luxe, ô salle d'ébène où, pour séduire un roi
Se tordent dans leur mort des guirlandes célèbres,
Vous n'êtes qu'un orgueil menti par les ténèbres
Aux yeux du solitaire ébloui de sa foi.

Oui, je sais qu'au lointain de cette nuit, la Terre
Jette d'un grand éclat l'insolite mystère,
Sous les siècles hideux qui l'obscurcissent moins.

L'espace à soi pareil qu'il s'accroisse ou se nie
Roule dans cet ennui des feux vils pour témoins
Que s'est d'un astre en fête allumé le génie.

Toute l'âme résumée...

TOUTE l'âme résumée
Quand lente nous l'expirons
Dans plusieurs ronds de fumée
Abolis en autres ronds

Atteste quelque cigare
Brûlant savamment pour peu
Que la cendre se sépare
De son clair baiser de feu

Ainsi le chœur des romances
A la lèvre vole-t-il
Exclus-en si tu commences
Le réel parce que vil

Le sens trop précis rature
Ta vague littérature.

When the shade crept...

WHEN the shade crept, by fatal ordering,
Toward that old Dream, my bones' desire and rheum,
Condemned to pine roofed in as by a tomb
It folded in me its unerring wing.
     Black hall of surfeit where, to lure a king,
Garlands of fame twist dying as they bloom,
Nothing but pride you are, mirage of the gloom,
Bright faith to which bedazzled hermits cling.
     Yes, I know well that far off in this night,
The Earth gives forth a vast mysterious light,
Darkened by hideous ages all the less.
     Space always space, expand it or ignore,
In boredom spins base fires for witnesses
To the lit genius of one festive star.

The soul summed up entire...

THE soul summed up entire
When, slowly vanishing,
We make the smoke aspire
Ascending ring in ring

Gives proof of some cigar
That smoothly burns, unless
The ash creep up too near
The lit tip's fiery kiss;

So choirings of romance
To singing lips will rush.
Exclude the real, if once
Begun, because it's trash.

Your mystery you deface
By meaning too precise.

Les fleurs

Des avalanches d'or du vieil azur, au jour
Premier et de la neige éternelle des astres
Jadis tu détaches les grands calices pour
La terre jeune encore et vierge de désastres,

Le glaïeul fauve, avec les cygnes au col fin,
Et ce divin laurier des âmes exilées
Vermeil comme le pur orteil du séraphin
Que rougit la poudeur des aurores foulées,

L'hyacinthe, le myrte à l'adorable éclair
Et, pareille à la chair de la femme, la rose
Cruelle, Hérodiade en fleur du jardin clair,
Celle qu'un sang farouche et radieux arrose!

Et tu fis la blancheur sanglotante des lys
Qui roulant sur des mers des soupirs qu'elle effleure
A travers l'encens bleu des horizons pâlis
Monte rêveusement vers la lune qui pleure!

Hosannah sur le cistre et dans les encensoirs,
Notre Dame, hosannah du jardin de nos limbes!
Et finisse l'écho par les célestes soirs,
Extase des regards, scintillement des nimbes!

O Mère qui créas en ton sein juste et fort,
Calices balançant la future fiole,
De grandes fleurs avec la balsamique Mort
Pour le poëte las que la vie étiole.

The flowers

FROM golden avalanches of old azure,
On the first day and one time from the stars'
Eternal snow, you took great sepals for
The earth still young and virgin from disasters,

The tawny gladiolus, with the bow-
Necked swans, and that divine rose laurel bush
Of souls in exile, pink as the seraph's toe
Whom modesty of trodden dawns made blush,

The hyacinth, the myrtle's lovely sheen,
And, like a woman's flesh, the cruel rose,
Flowering Herodias, of gardens queen,
Watered with wild and radiant blood it grows!

You made the whiteness of the lilies' tears
That skims on seas of sighs across the blue
Incense of pale horizons, mounting sheer
Dreamily towards the moon that's weeping too.

Hosanna on the cithern with incense
To you, Our Lady, from this garden limbo,
Hosannas new with each ecstatic glance
Through heavenly evenings to the final echo!

O Mother in whose bosom strong and just
Grew calyxes the future phial to sway,
Great flowers to soothe, with Death's assuaging rest,
The weary poet wilted by decay.

Sonnet

O si chère de loin et proche et blanche, si
Délicieusement toi, Mary, que je songe
A quelque baume rare émané par mensonge
Sur aucun bouquetier de cristal obscurci
    Le sais-tu, oui! pour moi voici des ans, voici
Toujours que ton sourire éblouissant prolonge
La même rose avec son bel été qui plonge
Dans autrefois et puis dans le futur aussi.
    Mon cœur qui dans les nuits parfois cherche à s'entendre
Ou de quel dernier mot t'appeler le plus tendre
S'exalte en celui rien que chuchoté de sœur
    N'était, très grand trésor et tête si petite,
Que tu m'enseignes bien toute une autre douceur
Tout bas par le baiser seul dans tes cheveux dite.

Rondels

I

Rien au réveil que vous n'ayez
Envisagé de quelque moue
Pire si le rire secoue
Votre aile sur les oreillers

Indifféremment sommeillez
Sans crainte qu'une haleine avoue
Rien au réveil que vous n'ayez
Envisagé de quelque moue.

Tous les rêves émerveillés
Quand cette beauté les déjoue
Ne produisent fleur sur la joue
Dans l'œil diamants impayés
Rien au réveil que vous n'ayez.

Sonnet

So dear far off and near and O so white,
Deliciously yourself, Mary, I dream
Of some deluding redolence of balm
Upon a crystal vase bedimmed of light,
    You know, yes! and for years that dazzling bright
Perennial smile prolongs for me the same
Rose now that every summer came
To plunge into the past then future sight.
    My heart which sometimes seeks to reach accord
With you at night or by what tenderest word
To call you, only "sister" whispering said
    Except you teach me some more gentle care,
So vast a treasure in so small a head,
Told softly by the sole kiss for your hair.

Rondels

I

Nothing when you wake you have not
Thought of with a little pouting
Worse if laughter while you're dreaming
Shake your wing though pillows move not.

Sleep indifferently and fear not
Breath that soon could be confessing
Something when you wake you have not
Thought of with a little pouting.

All the dazzled dreams contrive not
When this beauty baffles dreaming
On the cheek such flowers blooming
In the eyes the gems they price not
Anything you waking have not.

Rondels

II

Si tu veux nous nous aimerons
Avec tes lèvres sans le dire
Cette rose ne l'interromps
Qu'à verser un silence pire

Jamais de chants ne lancent prompts
Le scintillement du sourire
Si tu veux nous nous aimerons
Avec tes lèvres sans le dire

Muet muet entre les ronds
Sylphe dans la pourpre d'empire
Un baiser flambant se déchire
Jusqu'aux pointes des ailerons
Si tu veux nous nous aimerons.

Brise marine

La chair est triste, hélas! et j'ai lu tous les livres.
Fuir! là-bas fuir! Je sens que des oiseaux sont ivres
D'être parmi l'écume inconnue et les cieux!
Rien, ni les vieux jardins reflétés par les yeux
Ne retiendra ce cœur qui dans la mer se trempe
O nuits! ni la clarté déserte de ma lampe
Sur le vide papier que la blancheur défend,
Et ni la jeune femme allaitant son enfant.
Je partirai! Steamer balançant ta mâture,
Lève l'ancre pour une exotique nature!

Un Ennui, désolé par les cruels espoirs,
Croit encore à l'adieu suprême des mouchoirs!
Et, peut-être, les mâts, invitant les orages
Sont-ils de ceux qu'un vent penche sur les naufrages
Perdus, sans mâts, sans mâts, ni fertiles îlots...
Mais, ô mon cœur, entends le chant des matelots!

Rondels

II

Iғ you want we'll love each other
With your lips but without speaking
What this rose says never smother
Save by lesser silence seeking

Songs can never make smiles gather
In the sudden gleam partaking
If you want we'll love each other
With your lips but never speaking

Soft between rounds sung together
Sylph that royal crimson teaching
Kiss of torn fire will be reaching
To the very tip of feather
If you want we love each other.

Sea breeze

Tнe flesh is sad, and I've read all the words.
To flee! To fly away! I think the birds
Are drunk to be with unknown foam and skies!
Nothing, not even old gardens caught in the eyes,
Can hold this heart from plunging out to sea,
O nights! not even the lamp alone with me,
Keeping the page white from the words that infest,
Nor infant suckled at my own wife's breast.
I will away! You ship with swaying mast,
Raise anchor for exotic lands at last!

A tedium, edged with cruel hope of relief,
May still believe a waving handkerchief.
What if, inviting storms, men tempest-tossed
Ride with bent masts above the ships long lost—
No masts, no masts, and no green isles to spring.
Hear still, my heart, the song the sailors sing!

Les fenêtres

Las du triste hôpital, et de l'encens fétide
Qui monte en la blancheur banale des rideaux
Vers le grand crucifix ennuyé du mur vide,
Le moribond sournois y redresse un vieux dos,

Se traîne et va, moins pour chauffer sa pourriture
Que pour voir du soleil sur les pierres, coller
Les poils blancs et les os de la maigre figure
Aux fenêtres qu'un beau rayon clair veut hâler.

Et la bouche, fiévreuse et d'azur bleu vorace,
Telle, jeune, elle alla respirer son trésor,
Une peau virginale et de jadis! encrasse
D'un long baiser amer les tièdes carreaux d'or.

Ivre, il vit, oubliant l'horreur des saintes huiles,
Les tisanes, l'horloge et le lit infligé,
La toux; et quand le soir saigne parmi les tuiles,
Son œil, à l'horizon de lumière gorgé,

Voit des galères d'or, belles comme des cygnes,
Sur un fleuve de pourpre et de parfums dormir
En berçant l'éclair fauve et riche de leurs lignes
Dans un grand nonchaloir chargé de souvenir!

Ainsi, pris du dégoût de l'homme à l'âme dure
Vautré dans le bonheur, où ses seuls appétits
Mangent, et qui s'entête à chercher cette ordure
Pour l'offrir à la femme allaitant ses petits,

Je fuis et je m'accroche à toutes les croisées
D'où l'on tourne l'épaule à la vie, et, béni,
Dans leur verre, lavé d'éternelles rosées,
Que dore le matin chaste de l'Infini

The windows

WEARY of that sad hospital, the stale
Incense, climbing up the same pale drape
To the huge crucifix so sick of its wall,
The dying man with cunning straightens up

And drags himself to warm his dregs (though less
Than watch the sun reflected on the stones)
Toward windows where he flattens his thin face
On glass a lovely sunbeam longs to bronze.

His fevered mouth would drink the sky's blue bowl;
The mouth that once inhaled a virgin's skin,
In his lost youth, now only can make foul
With a bitter kiss the warm gold window pane.

Drunken, he lives, forgetting holy oils,
Physic and cough, the clock, and that doomed bed;
When evening bleeds among the shining tiles,
His eye, fixed on horizons gorged with red,

Sees golden galleys, beautiful as swans,
Asleep on a river of purple perfumery,
Rocking the tawny lightning of their lines
In a large indifference charged with memory!

So, caught in horror of man's callous soul,
Who bathes in joys of appetite alone
And always searches for the same offal
To offer his wife suckling her little one,

I flee and to the casements cling from whence
We turn our back on life and all its pain;
Enshrined in that bright glass that has been rinsed
With timeless dews gilded with endless dawn,

Je me mire et me vois ange! et je meurs, et j'aime
— Que la vitre soit l'art, soit la mysticité —
A renaître, portant mon rêve en diadème,
Au ciel antérieur où fleurit la Beauté!

Mais, hélas! Ici-bas est maître: sa hantise
Vient m'écœurer parfois jusqu'en cet abri sûr,
Et le vomissement impur de la Bêtise
Me force à me boucher le nez devant l'azur.

Est-il moyen, ô Moi qui connais l'amertume,
D'enfoncer le cristal par le monstre insulté
Et de m'enfuir, avec mes deux ailes sans plume
— Au risque de tomber pendant l'éternité?

Tristesse d'été

LE soleil, sur le sable, ô lutteuse endormie,
En l'or de tes cheveux chauffe un bain langoureux
Et, consumant l'encens sur ta joue ennemie,
Il mêle avec les pleurs un breuvage amoureux.
    De ce blanc flamboiement l'immuable accalmie
T'a fait dire, attristée, ô mes baisers peureux,
"Nous ne serons jamais une seule momie
Sous l'antique désert et les palmiers heureux!"
    Mais ta chevelure est une rivière tiède,
Où noyer sans frissons l'âme qui nous obsède
Et trouver ce Néant que tu ne connais pas!
    Je goûterai le fard pleuré par tes paupières,
Pour voir s'il sait donner au cœur que tu frappas
L'insensibilité de l'azur et des pierres.

I look and see myself an angel there!
Whether the glass be art or myth, I love,
I die—to live—and as a bright crown wear
My earlier heaven that flowered in realms above.

Alas! the world below is master still:
Its specter haunts me even to this high
Retreat, where vomitings of folly will
Force me to hold my nose at the blue sky.

O Self, familiar with this bitterness,
How smash the glass insulted by the fiend
And fly away, my twin wings featherless,
Risking a fall through time without an end?

Sadness of summer

O SLEEPING wrestler, sunlight on the sand
Foments a languorous bath in the gold of your hair,
Burns on your angry cheek the incense, and
Mingles with tears to make a love draught there.
    The changeless calm of this white blaze saddened
You, after my fearful kissing, to declare,
"We'll never under happy palm trees blend,
Embalmed as one, a desert tomb to share!"
    And yet the soul that haunts us in that river
Of yellow hair is drowned without a shiver
And finds the nothingness beyond your art.
    I'll taste the shadow weeping from your eyes,
To see if that can give my stricken heart
The indifference of stones and azure skies.

Angoisse

JE ne viens pas ce soir vaincre ton corps, ô bête
En qui vont les péchés d'un peuple, ni creuser
Dans tes cheveux impurs une triste tempête
Sous l'incurable ennui que verse mon baiser:
    Je demande à ton lit le lourd sommeil sans songes
Planant sous les rideaux inconnus du remords,
Et que tu peux goûter après tes noirs mensonges,
Toi qui sur le néant en sais plus que les morts.
    Car le Vice, rongeant ma native noblesse
M'a comme toi marqué de sa stérilité,
Mais tandis que ton sein de pierre est habité
    Par un cœur que la dent d'aucun crime ne blesse,
Je fuis, pâle, défait, hanté par mon linceul,
Ayant peur de mourir lorsque je couche seul.

Le vierge, le vivace et le bel aujourd'hui...

LE vierge, le vivace et le bel aujourd'hui
Va-t-il nous déchirer avec un coup d'aile ivre
Ce lac dur oublié que hante sous le givre
Le transparent glacier des vols qui n'ont pas fui!
    Un cygne d'autrefois se souvient que c'est lui
Magnifique mais qui sans espoir se délivre
Pour n'avoir pas chanté la région où vivre
Quand du stérile hiver a resplendi l'ennui.
    Tout son col secouera cette blanche agonie
Par l'espace infligée à l'oiseau qui le nie,
Mais non l'horreur du sol où le plumage est pris.
    Fantôme qu'à ce lieu son pur éclat assigne,
Il s'immobilise au songe froid de mépris
Que vêt parmi l'exil inutile le Cygne.

Anguish

Not to subdue your body am I here
Tonight, O victim beast, whom the world's vice
Invades, nor stir a sad storm in your hair,
Impure below sick boredom of my kiss;
    Hovering beneath the curtains of remorse,
After your lurid lies, I ask of your bed
The heavy, dreamless sleep you taste perforce,
Who fathom more of nothing than the dead.
    For Vice, devouring my so noble name,
Like you has stamped me with its sterile shame,
But while your heart within a breast of stone
    Remains unwounded by the tooth of crime,
I flee, pale, haggard, haunted by my tomb,
Afraid of dying when I sleep alone.

Will the virginal, lovely and lively day...

Will the virginal, lovely and lively day
Tear for us the forgotten lake with a blow
Of its drunken wing? The water is haunted below
Its frost by the crystalline ice of flights that stay!
    A languished swan remembers his previous way
Sublime but has no hope in escape, for no,
He never sang of lands to journey to
When tedium of dead winter shed its ray.
    All of his neck will shake off this white pain
That space inflicts on the bird to his disdain,
But not the horror of earth his trapped wings learn.
    Phantom assigned here by his shining elan,
He is fastened in the frigid dream of scorn
Worn in his empty exile by the Swan.

Petit air

I

QUELCONQUE une solitude
Sans le cygne ni le quai
Mire sa désuétude
Au regard que j'abdiquai

Ici de la gloriole
Haute à ne la pas toucher
Dont maint ciel se bariole
Avec les ors de coucher

Mais langoureusement longe
Comme de blanc linge ôté
Tel fugace oiseau si plonge
Exultatrice à côté

Dans l'onde toi devenue
Ta jubilation nue.

Little tune

I

Sᴏᴍᴇ design of loneliness
Lacking any swan or quay
Mirrors its own emptiness
In the glance I threw away

Down from the vainglory there
Too aloof for touch of clay
Skies resplendent everywhere
Golden with the dying day

Yet will languorously range
Like white linen tossed away
If such fleeting bird should plunge
Where exultantly you play

Merging with you in the sea
One in naked ecstacy.

Petit air

II

INDOMPTABLEMENT a dû
Comme mon espoir s'y lance
Eclater là-haut perdu
Avec furie et silence,

Voix étrangère au bosquet
Ou par nul écho suivie,
L'oiseau qu'on n'ouït jamais
Une autre fois en la vie.

Le hagard musicien,
Cela dans le doute expire
Si de mon sein pas du sien
A jailli le sanglot pire

Déchiré va-t-il entier
Rester sur quelque sentier!

Le cantonnier
(de *Chansons Bas*)

CES cailloux, tu les nivelles
Et c'est, comme troubadour,
Un cube aussi de cervelles
Qu'il me faut ouvrir par jour.

Little tune

II

As my longing mounts on high
A voice must there have burst its bounds
Far out imperturbably
Lost in fury without sound,

Stranger to the thorny wood
Followed by no echo heard,
Voice that never more here could
Come from any living bird.

Gaunt musician, voice in doubt
Dying if 'twas from my heart
Not from his the grief burst out
With a sob of deeper hurt

Torn he is but will remain
Whole upon some path again.

The roadmender
(from *Vulgar Songs*)

You are leveling all these stones:
I, since I'm a troubadour,
Opening up a cube of brains
Every morning for my chore.

Arthur Rimbaud

1854 - 1891

Sensation

Par les soirs bleus d'été, j'irai dans les sentiers,
Picoté par les blés, fouler l'herbe menue:
Rêveur, j'en sentirai la fraîcheur à mes pieds.
Je laisserai le vent baigner ma tête nue.

Je ne parlerai pas, je ne penserai rien:
Mais l'amour infini me montera dans l'âme,
Et j'irai loin, bien loin, comme un bohémien,
Par la Nature, — heureux comme avec une femme.

Alchimie du verbe
(de "Délires II")

Loin des oiseaux, des troupeaux, des villageoises,
Que buvais-je, à genoux dans cette bruyère
Entourée de tendres bois de noisetiers,
Dans un brouillard d'après-midi tiède et vert?

Que pouvais-je boire dans cette jeune Oise,
— Ormeaux sans voix, gazon sans fleurs, ciel couvert! —

Boire à ces gourdes jaunes, loin de ma case
Chérie? Quelque liqueur d'or qui fait suer.

Je faisais une louche enseigne d'auberge.
— Un orage vint chasser le ciel. Au soir
L'eau des bois se perdait sur les sables vierges,
Le vent de Dieu jetait des glaçons aux mares;

Pleurant, je voyais de l'or — et ne pus boire. —

Arthur Rimbaud

1854 - 1891

*Sensation**

In the blue summer evenings I will stroll,
Pricked by the wheat, on paths soft to the tread;
Dreaming, while underfoot the grass is cool;
Letting the wind break over my bare head.

I'll speak of nothing, think of nothing too:
But boundless love will rise up in my soul,
And, like a gipsy, I will wander through
The land in joy, as if I'm with a girl.

Alchemy of the word
(from "Délires II")

What did I drink, knee-deep in a patch of furze,
Far from the birds, the flocks, the village girls,
Deep in a wood of sapling hazel trees,
Warm and green in a misty afternoon world?

What could I have been drinking from this young Oise?
—Still elms, unflowering turf, the skies rain-filled!

And what from these yellow gourds, far away from my house
So dear?—To make me sweat, a liquor of gold.

I must have looked like a squinting tavern sign.
—Down came an evening storm; the heavens shrank,
God's wind flung icicles on pools of rain,
In virgin sand the woodland waters sank;

Some gold I saw and wept—and could not drink.

*The lyric sounds mature. The author was fifteen.

Roman

I

On n'est pas sérieux, quand on a dix-sept ans.
— Un beau soir, foin des bocks et de la limonade,
Des cafés tapageurs aux lustres éclatants!
— On va sous les tilleuls verts de la promenade.

Les tilleuls sentent bon dans les bons soirs de juin!
L'air est parfois si doux, qu'on ferme la paupière;
Le vent chargé de bruits, — la ville n'est pas loin, —
A des parfums de vigne et des parfums de bière...

II

— Voilà qu'on aperçoit un tout petit chiffon
D'azur sombre, encadré d'une petite branche,
Piqué d'une mauvaise étoile, qui se fond
Avec de doux frissons, petite et toute blanche...

Nuit de juin! Dix-sept ans! — On se laisse griser.
La sève est du champagne et vous monte à la tête...
On divague; on se sent aux lèvres un baiser
Qui palpite là, comme une petite bête...

III

Le cœur fou Robinsonne à travers les romans,
— Lorsque, dans la clarté d'un pâle réverbère,
Passe une demoiselle aux petits airs charmants,
Sous l'ombre du faux col effrayant de son père...

Et, comme elle vous trouve immensément naïf,
Tout en faisant trotter ses petites bottines,
Elle se tourne, alerte et d'un mouvement vif...
— Sur vos lèvres alors meurent les cavatines...

Love Story

I

No one is serious when he's seventeen.
—It's a fine evening, beer and lemonade
Be darned! Bright lights can have the café scene!
—You take green lindens by the promenade.

Lindens feel good in the good June evenings!
The air can be so sweet you close your eyes;
The wind is charged with sounds the city brings,
And mingled smells of beer and vineyards rise…

II

Look, you can see a tiny little belt
Of dark blue cloth that in a branch is caught,
Pricked by a wicked star that softly melts,
A quivering diamond, small, completely white…

June night! Seventeen!—You may be in your cups.
The sap is champagne and a heady thing…
You ramble on; you feel a kiss on your lips
That quivers like a humming-bird on wing…

III

The crazy heart Crusoes through all romance,
—When, passing underneath a pale street light,
A young miss with those charming airs, perchance,
Strolls, overawed by Father's false cravat.

She finds you just incredibly naive;
Trotting along in small boots, ankle high,
Alert, She turns, with movements so alive
That on your lips the cavatinas die…

IV

Vous êtes amoureux. Loué jusqu'au mois d'août.
Vous êtes amoureux. — Vos sonnets La font rire.
Tous vos amis s'en vont, vous êtes *mauvais goût.*
— Puis l'adorée, un soir, a daigné vous écrire...!

— Ce soir-là,... — vous rentrez aux cafés éclatants,
Vous demandez des bocks ou de la limonade...
— On n'est pas sérieux, quand on a dix-sept ans
Et qu'on a des tilleuls verts sur la promenade.

Ophélie

II

O PALE Ophélie! belle comme la neige!
Oui tu mourus, enfant, par un fleuve emporté!
— C'est que les vents tombant des grands monts de Norwège
T'avaient parlé tout bas de l'âpre liberté;

C'est qu'un souffle, tordant ta grande chevelure,
A ton esprit rêveur portait d'étranges bruits;
Que ton cœur écoutait le chant de la Nature
Dans les plaintes de l'arbre et les soupirs des nuits;

C'est que la voix des mers folles, immense râle,
Brisait ton sein d'enfant, trop humain et trop doux;
C'est qu'un matin d'avril, un beau cavalier pâle,
Un pauvre fou, s'assit muet à tes genoux!

IV

You are in love. Hired out until next August.
You are in love. Your sonnets make Her laugh.
Your friends all leave you flat, you're in bad taste.
Then dream-girl deigns to send a letter off.

—That evening—you rejoin the café scene,
You order beers or else a lemonade...
—No one is serious when he's seventeen
And linden trees are green on the promenade.

Ophelia*

II

O PALE Ophelia! beautiful as snow!
Yes, swept off by a river, child, you drowned!
Because from cliffs of Norway winds spoke low
To you with a fierce freedom in the sound;

Because a wind that tore at your long hair
Possessed your dreaming mind with phantom cries,
And it was Nature's song your heart would hear
In wailing of the trees and midnight sighs;

Because huge rattling voices of mad seas
Bruised your child heart, too human and too sweet;
Because, one April morning, at your knees,
A pale and handsome prince, poor fool, sat mute!

*Written by an even younger fifteen-year-old than was "Roman"—by
four months. Here, however, I did reluctantly cut the first section,
which adds nothing to the tuneful effect of this, Rimbaud's only
entirely romantic lyric.

Ciel! Amour! Liberté! Quel rêve, ô pauvre Folle!
Tu te fondais à lui comme une neige au feu:
Tes grandes visions étranglaient ta parole
— Et l'Infini terrible effara ton œil bleu!

III

— Et le Poète dit qu'aux rayons des étoiles
Tu viens chercher, la nuit, les fleurs que tu cueillis,
Et qu'il a vu sur l'eau, couchée en ses longs voiles,
La blanche Ophélia flotter, comme un grand lys.

Ma bohème

Je m'en allais, les poings dans mes poches crevées;
Mon paletot aussi devenait idéal;
J'allais sous le ciel, Muse! et j'étais ton féal;
Oh! là! là! que d'amours splendides j'ai rêvées!
　　　Mon unique culotte avait un large trou.
— Petit-Poucet rêveur, j'égrenais dans ma course
Des rimes. Mon auberge était à la Grande-Ourse.
— Mes étoiles au ciel avaient un doux frou-frou
　　　Et je les écoutais, assis au bord des routes,
Ces bons soirs de septembre où je sentais des gouttes
De rosée à mon front, comme un vin de vigueur;
　　　Où, rimant au milieu des ombres fantastiques,
Comme des lyres, je tirais les élastiques
De mes souliers blessés, un pied près de mon cœur!

Love! Freedom! Heaven! What dreams, you foolish child!
You melted towards him like the snow in a fire:
Your words all strangled by those visions wild,
Blue eyes appalled by Infinite Desire!

III

And that at night she comes, the poet says,
To gather flowers by the stars' pale light,
And that the water in her long veil sways
And floats Ophelia like a lily white.

My Bohemia

I went my way, my fists in pockets torn;
My topcoat too became a dreamy sight;
I rode beneath the sky, dear Muse, your knight:
My, my! what splendid dreams of love were worn!
　　My only trousers had a giant hole:
A Tom-Thumb dreamer, rhymes strewn everywhere.
For lodging I put up at the Great Bear,
And all my sky with rustling stars was full:
　　I listened by the roadside to each new
September eve, so drenched with drops of dew
I felt my forehead wet with vintage tart;
　　While lurking shadows rhymed with fantasies,
I plucked my dream lyre, strung with shoe-laces,
Pressing a wounded sole close to my heart!

Les poètes de sept ans

Et la Mère, fermant le livre du devoir,
S'en allait satisfaite et très fière, sans voir,
Dans les yeux bleus et sous le front plein d'éminences,
L'âme de son enfant livrée aux répugnances.

Tout le jour il suait d'obéissance; très
Intelligent; pourtant des tics noirs, quelques traits
Semblaient prouver en lui d'âcres hypocrisies.
Dans l'ombre des couloirs aux tentures moisies,
En passant il tirait la langue, les deux poings
A l'aine, et dans ses yeux fermés voyait des points.
Une porte s'ouvrait sur le soir: à la lampe
On le voyait, là-haut, qui râlait sur la rampe,
Sous un golfe de jour pendant du toit. L'été
Surtout, vaincu, stupide, il était entêté
A se renfermer dans la fraîcheur des latrines:
Il pensait là, tranquille et livrant ses narines.

Quand, lavé des odeurs du jour, le jardinet
Derrière la maison, en hiver, s'illunait,
Gisant au pied d'un mur, enterré dans la marne
Et pour des visions écrasant son œil darne,
Il écoutait grouiller les galeux espaliers.
Pitié! Ces enfants seuls étaient ses familiers
Qui, chétifs, fronts nus, œil déteignant sur la joue,
Cachant de maigres doigts jaunes et noirs de boue
Sous des habits puant la foire et tout vieillots,
Conversaient avec la douceur des idiots!
Et si, l'ayant surpris à des pitiés immondes,
Sa mère s'effrayait, les tendresses, profondes,
De l'enfant se jetaient sur cet étonnement.
C'était bon. Elle avait le bleu regard, — qui ment!

Seven-year-old poets

AND then the Mother, closing the lesson book,
Went off content and proud, without a look
In her child's blue eyes beneath the bumpy brow
To see him shrink from what she would allow.

All day he sweated docile. He was bright;
But certain ugly habits showed a blight
Of venomous pretension taking shape.
In darkened passage-ways, behind a drape,
He would put out his tongue, stick his fist hot
In his groin, and shut his eyes to see the dots.
A door would open on evening: by the flare
Of lamps you'd see him stifling high on a stair,
Beneath a gulf of day which hung from the roof.
In summer, specially, he'd stay aloof,
Abortive, dumb, locked in a cool latrine,
Sniffing his thoughts, serene because unseen.

In winter when, behind the house, the yard
Was washed of daytime smells by moonlight poured,
Stretched at the foot of a wall, buried in mud,
Squeezing his eye to make the visions flood,
He'd fantasize the trellise being swarmed.
Pity? The only young to whom he warmed
Were puny, with blank foreheads, eyes inert,
Hiding thin fingers, yellow and black with dirt,
In rags that pitifully stank of shit,
Conversing meek as any idiot;
And if his mother caught him in compassion,
She winced away from such a filthy fashion
Of tenderness, which smote her with surprise.
And that was good. She had the blue look—that lies!

A sept ans, il faisait des romans, sur la vie
Du grand désert, où luit la Liberté ravie,
Forêts, soleils, rives, savanes! — Il s'aidait
De journaux illustrés où, rouge, il regardait
Des Espagnoles rire et des Italiennes.
Quand venait, l'œil brun, folle, en robes d'indiennes,
— Huit ans, — la fille des ouvriers d'à côté,
La petite brutale, et qu'elle avait sauté,
Dans un coin, sur son dos, en secouant ses tresses,
Et qu'il était sous elle, il lui mordait les fesses,
Car elle ne portait jamais de pantalons;
— Et, par elle meurtri des poings et des talons,
Remportait les saveurs de sa peau dans sa chambre.

Il craignait les blafards dimanches de décembre,
Où, pommadé, sur un guéridon d'acajou,
Il lisait une Bible à la tranche vert-chou;
Des rêves l'oppressaient chaque nuit dans l'alcôve.
Il n'aimait pas Dieu; mais les hommes, qu'au soir fauve,
Noirs, en blouse, il voyait rentrer dans le faubourg
Où les crieurs, en trois roulements de tambour,
Font autour des édits rire et gronder les foules.
— Il rêvait la prairie amoureuse, où des houles
Lumineuses, parfums sains, pubescences d'or,
Font leur remuement calme et prennent leur essor!

Et comme il savourait surtout les sombres choses,
Quand, dans la chambre nue aux persiennes closes,
Haute et bleue, âcrement prise d'humidité,
Il lisait son roman sans cesse médité,
Plein de lourds ciels ocreux et de forêts noyées,
De fleurs de chair aux bois sidérals déployées,
Vertige, écroulements, déroutes et pitié!
— Tandis que se faisait la rumeur du quartier,
En bas, — seul, et couché sur des pièces de toile
Ecrue, et pressentant violemment la voile!

At seven he wrote novels about living
In deserts where charmed Liberty is thriving,
Suns, forests, shores, savannas—all with lush
Ideas from Illustrateds, where he'd blush
At laughing girls of Italy and Spain.
When, brown-eyed, mad, in cotton frock rough-spun,
That eight-year-old from working folk next door,
The little brute, had jumped him to the floor,
Bringing him down beneath her, shaking a braid,
He bit her buttocks, always on parade,
Because she wore no panties; having blessed
The bruises from her heels as well as fist,
He took back to his room the smell of her skin.
He feared December evenings closing in,
When, all spruced up, at a small mahogany table,
He had to read a sprout-green covered Bible.
Dreams troubled him each night in the alcove.
It was not God but men that he could love,
Dark men in blouses whom at dusk he'd see
Returning to the suburbs, where the three
Drum-rolls of the town criers make the crowd
Lament or laugh at mandates read aloud.
Then he would dream of loving fields where bright
Pubescences heave golden in their flight.

And yet in somber things he reveled most,
When, in the empty room, with shutters closed,
Lofty and blue, damp with an acrid bite,
He read the novel that he dreamt about,
The heavy ochroid skies, the forests drowned,
The heavenly woods where flowers of flesh abound,
The reelings, fallings, utter rout, the pity!
—While dim below came rumors of the city—
He lying alone on strips of unbleached sail,
With violent premonitions of the gale!

Les chercheuses de poux

QUAND le front de l'enfant, plein de rouges tourmentes,
Implore l'essaim blanc des rêves indistincts,
Il vient près de son lit deux grandes sœurs charmantes
Avec de frêles doigts aux ongles argentins.

Elles assoient l'enfant devant une croisée
Grande ouverte où l'air bleu baigne un fouillis de fleurs,
Et dans ses lourds cheveux où tombe la rosée
Promènent leurs doigts fins, terribles et charmeurs.

Il écoute chanter leurs haleines craintives
Qui fleurent de longs miels végétaux et rosés,
Et qu'interrompt parfois un sifflement, salives
Reprises sur la lèvre ou désirs de baisers.

Il entend leurs cils noirs battant sous les silences
Parfumés; et leurs doigts électriques et doux
Font crépiter parmi ses grises indolences
Sous leurs ongles royaux la mort des petits poux.

Voilà que monte en lui le vin de la Paresse,
Soupir d'harmonica qui pourrait délirer;
L'enfant se sent, selon la lenteur des caresses,
Sourdre et mourir sans cesse un désir de pleurer.

The lice hunters

WHEN the child's forehead, full of torments red,
Craves the white swarm of dreams that sleep unveils,
Come two big charming sisters to his bed,
With fragile fingers and with silver nails.

They set the boy down with a window view,
Where clumps of flowers are washed with the blue air,
And through his thick hair, damp with falling dew,
Stroll their slim fingers, magical with fear.

He hears the singing of their timid breath
That smells of honey slowly drawn from roses,
With intermittent hissing sounds beneath
Saliva sucked on the lip, or longed-for kisses.

He hears their dark eye-lashes beating back
The scented hush; soft, rapid fingers slice
Into his leaden indolence, make crack
With royal nails the death of little lice.

Now mounts in him the wine of laziness,
Threat of delirium in a mouth-organ's sigh;
And with the languor of that slow caress,
Springs up, dies down, the constant need to cry.

Le dormeur du val

C'est un trou de verdure où chante une rivière
Accrochant follement aux herbes des haillons
D'argent; où le soleil, de la montagne fière,
Luit: c'est un petit val qui mousse de rayons.

Un soldat jeune, bouche ouverte, tête nue
Et la nuque baignant dans le frais cresson bleu,
Dort: il est étendu dans l'herbe, sous la nue,
Pâle dans son lit vert où la lumière pleut.

Les pieds dans les glaïeuls, il dort. Souriant comme
Sourirait un enfant malade, il fait un somme:
Nature, berce-le chaudement: il a froid.

Les parfums ne font pas frissonner sa narine;
Il dort dans le soleil, la main sur sa poitrine
Tranquille. Il a deux trous rouges au côté droit.

Qu'est-ce pour nous, mon cœur...

Qu'est-ce pour nous, mon cœur, que les nappes de sang*
Et de braise, et mille meurtres, et les longs cris
De rage, sanglots de tout enfer renversant
Tout ordre; et l'Aquilon encor sur les débris;

Et toute vengeance? Rien!... — Mais si, tout encor,
Nous la voulons! Industriels, princes, sénats,
Périssez! puissance, justice, histoire, à bas!
Ça nous est dû. Le sang! le sang! la flamme d'or!

Tout à la guerre, à la vengeance, à la terreur,
Mon Esprit! Tournons dans la Morsure: Ah! passez,
Républiques de ce monde! Des empereurs,
Des régiments, des colons, des peuples, assez!

*The autographed copy has no title. The title "Vertige," accepted by the usually reliable Alan Boase, was dreamed up by Bérichon for his 1912 edition.

The sleeper of the valley

A VERDANT hollow where a river sings
And idly in the silver grass delays,
Where the warm sun from the proud mountain flings
Its light: the little valley foams bright rays.
    A soldier, young, mouth open and bared head,
His neck bathing in blue water cress,
Sleeps on the grass, so pale in his green bed,
Below the cloud, where rains the light's caress.
    Feet wrapped in gladiolus, fast asleep,
He smiles, a sickly child that takes a nap:
Cradle him warmly, Nature: he is cold.
    No perfumes now can make his nostril stir;
With hand on breast, he sleeps in sunlight there,
At peace. And in his right side, two red holes.

What's it to us, my heart...

WHAT'S it to us, my heart, the sheets of blood
And flame, a million murders, frantic wails,
Sobs from all hell to uproot the ordered good,
While over the ruins the north wind prevails;

And what's with all this vengeance? Nothing! Yet still
We crave it. Magnates, kings, and senates: damn
Them! Power, justice, history: down with them all!
This is our due. Blood! Blood! The golden flame!

Let's be for war, my soul, vengeance, and terrors!
Let's writhe in the festering bite of war! Ah! may
Republics of this world all vanish! Emperors,
Regiments, colonists, peoples, enough I say!

Qui remuerait les tourbillons de feu furieux,
Que nous et ceux que nous nous imaginons frères?
A nous! Romanesques amis: ça va nous plaire.
Jamais nous ne travaillerons, ô flots de feux!

Europe, Asie, Amérique, disparaissez.
Notre marche vengeresse a tout occupé,
Cités et campagnes! — Nous serons écrasés!
Les volcans sauteront! et l'océan frappé...

Oh! mes amis! — mon cœur, c'est sûr, ils sont des frères:
Noirs inconnus, si nous allions! allons! allons!
O malheur! je me sens frémir, la vieille terre,
Sur moi de plus en plus à vous! la terre fond.

Ce n'est rien! j'y suis! j'y suis toujours.

Les premières communions

I

VRAIMENT, c'est bête, ces églises des villages
Où quinze laids marmots encrassant les piliers
Ecoutent, grasseyant les divins babillages,
Un noir grotesque dont fermentent les souliers:
Mais le soleil éveille, à travers des feuillages,
Les vieilles couleurs des vitraux irréguliers.

La pierre sent toujours la terre maternelle.
Vous verrez des monceaux de ces cailloux terreux
Dans la campagne en rut qui frémit solennelle,
Portant près des blés lourds, dans les sentiers ocreux,
Ces arbrisseaux brûlés où bleuit la prunelle,
Des nœuds de mûriers noirs et de rosiers fuireux.

Tous les cent ans on rend ces granges respectables
Par un badigeon d'eau bleue et de lait caillé:

Who should stir up the furnace of desire
But we and brothers that we fantasize?
Rally to us, all you dream friends, arise!
Rejoice! we'll toil no more, Oh waves of fire!

Europe, America, Asia—let none remain,
For our avenging march has stormed them all,
City and country! We shall be crushed and fall!
Volcanoes will explode! The smitten main...

Ah! friends!—My heart, they're brothers, that is sure:
If we could leave, dark strangers! Go today!
Curse on this trembling self, yours more and more,
On me the ancient earth is falling away.

It's nothing! I am here! I am still here.

First communions

I

REALLY, it's crass, these little village shrines,
Where fifteen runty marmosets befoul
The plinths and, burbling sanctimonious lines,
Attend a black grotesque with shoes that smell:
But through the leaves outside, the sunlight shines
To wake the faded tales the windows tell.

Still the bricks smell of the maternal earth.
You see the hillocks of this earthy stone
Our countryside in rut will bring to birth,
That quivers solemnly beside the corn,
Bearing scorched blackberry shrubs on the ochre path,
Where sloes are blue and fleeting roses burn.

They spruce up those old barns each century
With a blue wash and curdled milk for tint;

Si des mysticités grotesques sont notables
Près de la Notre-Dame ou du Saint empaillé,
Des mouches sentant bon l'auberge et les étables
Se gorgent de cire au plancher ensoleillé.

L'enfant se doit surtout à la maison, famille
Des soins naïfs, des bons travaux abrutissants;
Ils sortent, oubliant que la peau leur fourmille
Où le Prêtre du Christ plaqua ses doigts puissants.
On paie au Prêtre un toit ombré d'une charmille
Pour qu'il laisse au soleil tous ces fronts brunissants.

Le premier habit noir, le plus beau jour de tartes,
Sous le Napoléon ou le Petit Tambour
Quelque enluminure où les Josephs et les Marthes
Tirent la langue avec un excessif amour
Et que joindront, au jour de science, deux cartes:
Ces seuls doux souvenirs lui restent du grand Jour.

Les filles vont toujours à l'église, contentes
De s'entendre appeler garces par les garçons
Qui font du genre après messe ou vêpres chantantes.
Eux qui sont destinés au chic des garnisons,
Ils narguent au café les maisons importantes,
Blousés neuf, et gueulant d'effroyables chansons.

Cependant le Curé choisit pour les enfances
Des dessins; dans son clos, les vêpres dites, quand
L'air s'emplit du lointain nasillement des danses,
Il se sent, en dépit des célestes défenses,
Les doigts de pied ravis et le mollet marquant;
— La Nuit vient, noir pirate aux cieux d'or débarquant.

II

Le Prêtre a distingué parmi les catéchistes,
Congrégés des Faubourgs ou des Riches Quartiers,
Cette petite fille inconnue, aux yeux tristes,
Front jaune. Les parents semblent de doux portiers.

And if those gargoyle shapes of mystery
Do crowd Our Lady and the bulging Saint,
Yet flies smell good of stalls and hostelry
And crawl on the sunny roof to eat wax paint.

The child is bound by home ties over all,
The simple family cares, the harsh work done;
They leave mass, mindless how their skins would crawl
Where Christ's priest laid his potent fingers on.
The priest is paid a roof, to shade his hall
A bower, that all these brows may bronze in the sun.

The blessed day of cakes, the first black coat,
Beneath Napoleon and the Little Drummer
Joseph and Martha, colored anecdote,
Extend their tongues to the Host with love for ever:
These and two catechism cards denote
For him of that great Day the sole survivor.

The girls will go to church, and not a frown
For boys abusing them as bitch or worse;
Soon they will set the style in a garrison town
Who now chant vespers, show off after mass,
In cafés scoff at families well-known,
Tricked in new blouses howl their songs of brass.

Meantime the Curé for the children chose
Some drawings; in his yard the air was bold
With hum of distant dancing, after close
Of vespers: even though the heavens would scold,
His calf beat time, he itched in all his toes.
Night, a black pirate, beached on skies of gold.

II

Among the catechists who there converged
To be confirmed, suburban overflow
Of wealthier folk, the parson has observed
Some quiet *portier's* child with eyes of woe:

"Au grand Jour, le marquant parmi les Catéchistes,
Dieu fera sur ce front neiger ses bénitiers."

III

La veille du grand Jour, l'enfant se fait malade.
Mieux qu'à l'Eglise haute aux funèbres rumeurs,
D'abord le frisson vient, — le lit n'étant pas fade —
Un frisson surhumain qui retourne: "Je meurs..."

Et, comme un vol d'amour fait à ses sœurs stupides,
Elle compte, abattue et les mains sur son cœur,
Les Anges, les Jésus et ses Vierges nitides
Et, calmement, son âme a bu tout son vainqueur.

Adonaï!... — Dans les terminaisons latines,
Des cieux moirés de vert baignent les Fronts vermeils
Et tachés du sang pur des célestes poitrines,
De grands linges neigeux tombent sur les soleils!

— Pour ses virginités présentes et futures
Elle mord aux fraîcheurs de ta Rémission,
Mais plus que les lys d'eau, plus que les confitures,
Tes pardons sont glacés, ô Reine de Sion!

IV

Puis la Vierge n'est plus que la vierge du livre.
Les mystiques élans se cassent quelquefois...
Et vient la pauvreté des images, que cuivre
L'ennui, l'enluminure atroce et les vieux bois;

Des curiosités vaguement impudiques
Epouvantent le rêve aux chastes bleuités
Qui s'est surpris autour des célestes tuniques,
Du linge dont Jésus voile ses nudités.

"On the great Day, God, seeing her, will reserve
For this pale brow His holiest chrism to snow."

III

On the eve of the great Day, the child feels bad.
Worse than in that tall church with its doleful sighing;
First comes a fever fit—not just her bed
Being damp—that monstrous fit again: "I'm dying..."

As if from her dull sisters stealing love,
Cast down she counts, with hands upon her heart,
The Angels, Christs, and snowy Virgins of
Her soul, which calmly drank what conquered it.

Adonai!... In the Latin terminations,
Green-watered skies baptize the flushing brow,
Pure bosom blood of heavenly incarnations
To stain great cloths that fall on suns like snow!

—For her virginities, or late or soon,
She gnaws at thy cool mercy that forgives,
But colder are thy pardons, Queen of Sion,
Than any water-lilies or preserves!

IV

The Virgin then is only she in the book.
Those mystic flights may haply break and fall...
Then come dull figures with the copper look
That bores, cheap colored prints, woodcuts that pall;

Vague curiosities bereft of shame
Surprise the chaste blue dream with deep distress
To find itself confronted by the same
Tunic that covers Jesus' nakedness.

Elle veut, elle veut, pourtant, l'âme en détresse,
Le front dans l'oreiller creusé par les cris sourds,
Prolonger les éclairs suprêmes de tendresse,
Et bave... — L'ombre emplit les maisons et les cours.

Et l'enfant ne peut plus. Elle s'agite, cambre
Les reins et d'une main ouvre le rideau bleu
Pour amener un peu la fraîcheur de la chambre
Sous le drap, vers son ventre et sa poitrine en feu...

V

A son réveil, — minuit, — la fenêtre était blanche.
Devant le sommeil bleu des rideaux illunés,
La vision la prit des candeurs du dimanche;
Elle avait rêvé rouge. Elle saigna du nez,

Et se sentant bien chaste et pleine de faiblesse
Pour savourer en Dieu son amour revenant,
Elle eut soif de la nuit où s'exalte et s'abaisse
Le cœur, sous l'œil des cieux doux, en les devinant;

De la nuit, Vierge-Mère impalpable, qui baigne
Tous les jeunes émois de ses silences gris;
Elle eut soif de la nuit forte où le cœur qui saigne
Ecoule sans témoin sa révolte sans cris.

Et faisant la victime et la petite épouse,
Son étoile la vit, une chandelle aux doigts,
Descendre dans la cour où séchait une blouse,
Spectre blanc, et lever les spectres noirs des toits.

VI

Elle passa sa nuit sainte dans des latrines.
Vers la chandelle, aux trous du toit coulait l'air blanc,
Et quelque vigne folle aux noirceurs purpurines,
En deçà d'une cour voisine s'écroulant.

She wants and wants again, her soul distraught,
The furrowed pillow silencing her moans,
To lengthen the last flash of tender thought:
She drools... The shadow fills the yards and homes.

And she can stand no more. She plants her feet
And, arching her loins, she reaches out to pull
The blue bed curtain, that, beneath the sheet
Fresh air might keep her chest and stomach cool.

V

When she awoke—midnight—the casement white:
Bathed in the moonlit curtains' sleep of blue,
A vision seized her of pure Sabbath light;
She had dreamed red. Her nose was bleeding too,

And feeling her chastity and feebleness,
That she might savor love for God once more
She craved the night's soft skies where heart may guess,
Exalted or cast down, heaven's secret lore:

The night, mysterious Virgin-Mother, who loves
Young passions in her silences of grey,
Strong night that keeps no witness, this she craves,
Where hearts may dumbly bleed their wrath away.

Her star observes her, candle in her hand,
Playing the victim and the little wife,
Down to the courtyard filled with ghosts descend,
White ghost for a drying blouse, black for that roof.

VI

She spent her holy night in the latrine.
White air through roof holes on her candle poured,
And steeped in purple blackness, a wild vine,
Collapsing down this side a neighbor yard.

La lucarne faisait un cœur de lueur vive
Dans la cour où les cieux bas plaquaient d'ors vermeils
Les vitres; les pavés puant l'eau de lessive
Soufraient l'ombre des murs bondés de noirs sommeils.

VII

Qui dira ces langueurs et ces pitiés immondes,
Et ce qu'il lui viendra de haine, ô sales fous
Dont le travail divin déforme encor les mondes,
Quand la lèpre à la fin mangera ce corps doux?

VIII

Et quand, ayant rentré tous ses nœuds d'hystéries,
Elle verra, sous les tristesses du bonheur,
L'amant rêver au blanc million des Maries,
Au matin de la nuit d'amour, avec douleur:

"Sais-tu que je t'ai fait mourir? J'ai pris ta bouche,
Ton cœur, tout ce qu'on a, tout ce que vous avez;
Et moi, je suis malade: Oh! je veux qu'on me couche
Parmi les Morts des eaux nocturnes abreuvés!

"J'étais bien jeune, et Christ a souillé mes haleines.
Il me bonda jusqu'à la gorge de dégoûts!
Tu baisais mes cheveux profonds comme les laines
Et je me laissais faire... ah! va, c'est bon pour vous,

"Hommes! qui songez peu que la plus amoureuse
Est, sous sa conscience aux ignobles terreurs,
La plus prostituée et la plus douloureuse,
Et que tous nos élans vers vous sont des erreurs!

"Car ma Communion première est bien passée.
Tes baisers, je ne puis jamais les avoir sus:
Et mon cœur et ma chair par ta chair embrassée
Fourmillent du baiser putride de Jésus!"

The red-gold panes reflect a heart-shaped splash
On courtyards where the light from the low sky falls;
The paving stones, sulphured with suds from the wash,
Pollute the shadows of dark, sleep-crammed walls.

VII

These languors, this soiled pity who can tell,
Or, when her lovely body rots in the end
With leprosy, the hate she will compel,
From fools whose piety deforms the land?

VIII

And when hysteria tightens on her mind,
She'll see, on the morning of love's night supreme,
Her lover, in the transports sad and blind,
Embrace white million Marys in a dream:

"You know I made you die? I took your mouth,
Your heart, all that you have, all that you might,
And I am sick: Oh! plunge me in the drouth
Of the thirsty dead, quenched with waters of night!

"My breath was young when Christ had soured my peace.
He stuffed me to the throat enough to spew!
You kissed my hair below, deep as a fleece:
I let you do it... That's all right for you,

"You men! who little dream that she most fond,
Beneath her craven conscience and its ache,
Is most degraded, deepest in despond,
And every impulse towards you a mistake!

"My first Communion is long since past.
Your kisses always were the absent bliss:
Always my heart and flesh, by yours bound fast,
Crawl with putrescence of the Jesus kiss!"

IX

Alors l'âme pourrie et l'âme désolée
Sentiront ruisseler tes malédictions.
— Ils auront couché sur ta Haine inviolée,
Echappés, pour la mort, des justes passions.

Christ! ô Christ, éternel voleur des énergies,
Dieu qui pour deux mille ans vouas à ta pâleur,
Cloués au sol, de honte et de céphalalgies,
Ou renversés, les fronts des femmes de douleur.

Mémoire

I

L'EAU claire; comme le sel des larmes d'enfance,
L'assaut au soleil des blancheurs des corps de femmes;
la soie, en foule et de lys pur, des oriflammes
sous les murs dont quelque pucelle eut la défense;

l'ébat des anges; — Non... le courant d'or en marche,
meut ses bras, noirs, et lourds, et frais surtout, d'herbe. Elle
sombre, ayant le Ciel bleu pour ciel-de-lit, appelle
pour rideaux l'ombre de la colline et de l'arche.

II

Eh! l'humide carreau tend ses bouillons limpides!
L'eau meuble d'or pâle et sans fond les couches prêtes.
Les robes vertes et déteintes des fillettes
font les saules, d'où sautent les oiseaux sans brides.

Plus pure qu'un louis, jaune et chaude paupière
le souci d'eau — ta foi conjugale, ô l'Epouse! —
au midi prompt, de son terne miroir, jalouse
au ciel gris de chaleur la Sphère rose et chère.

IX

Then the soul putrid, the soul desolate,
Drenched with the curse from your corrupted breath,
Prostrate on your inviolable Hate,
Will have lost real passion for a mask of death.

O Christ, Christ! deathless thief of the fire unbound,
God who for two milleniums pledged your pale stain
On brows of grieving women, nailed to the ground
By shame or migraine, or thrown back in pain.

Memory

I

CLEAR water; like the salt tears children shed;
Whiteness of women's bodies assaulting the sun;
the silk of massed flags and pure lilies under the battlements defended by a maid.

Frolic of angels—No... gold stream on the march
moves heavy arms, black, cool with green grass. She
somber beneath the sky's bed-canopy,
summons for curtains the shadow of hill and arch.

II

Look! a limpid froth on the humid surface spreads!
The beds are prepared for bottomless water pale gold.
Green faded pinafores of willows now unfold
from which leap up in the air unbridled birds.

Purer than a louis, eyelid yellow and warm,
marsh marigold—your conjugal faith, O Spouse—
promptly at noon reflects the dear and rose
Sphere in the hot grey sky with a dimmed form.

347

III

Madame se tient trop debout dans la prairie
prochaine où neigent les fils du travail; l'ombrelle
aux doigts; foulant l'ombelle; trop fière pour elle;
des enfants lisant dans la verdure fleurie

leur livre de maroquin rouge! Hélas, Lui, comme
mille anges blancs qui se séparent sur la route,
s'éloigne par delà la montagne! Elle, toute
froide, et noire, court! après le départ de l'homme!

IV

Regret des bras épais et jeunes d'herbe pure!
Or des lunes d'avril au cœur du saint lit! Joie
des chantiers riverains à l'abandon, en proie
aux soirs d'août qui faisaient germer ces pourritures!

Qu'elle pleure à présent sous les remparts! l'haleine
des peupliers d'en haut est pour la seule brise.
Puis, c'est la nappe, sans reflets, sans source, grise:
un vieux, dragueur, dans sa barque immobile, peine.

V

Jouet de cet œil d'eau morne, je n'y puis prendre,
ô canot immobile! oh! bras trop courts! ni l'une
ni l'autre fleur: ni la jaune qui m'importune,
là; ni la bleue, amie à l'eau couleur de cendre.

Ah! la poudre des saules qu'une aile secoue!
Les roses des roseaux dès longtemps dévorées!
Mon canot, toujours fixe; et sa chaîne tirée
Au fond de cet œil d'eau sans bords, — à quelle boue?

III

Madame in the meadow, too erectly held,
Where snows the busy grain, her parasol in hand,
tramples on flowers too proud for her to stand;
children are reading in the flowery field

their book of red morocco. Alas the day!
with a thousand shining angels fled is he
far off beyond the mountain, while she,
So cold and dark, runs! after the man gone away!

IV

Nostalgia for the thick young arms of grass!
The gold of April moons in that pure bed;
joy of abandoned boatyards, prey to corrod-
ing August nights that bred decay of this.

Let her lament now underneath the walls!
Only tall poplars in the wind's breath sway.
Then this murk surface without springs, and grey:
an ancient dredger in his still barge toils.

V

Toy of this pool's sad eye, beyond my reach,
O moveless boat! Arms too short for need
of either flower: the yellow one that pleads,
or the blue friend in water the color of ash.

Ah! dust of willows shaken by a bird!
Roses of swamp-reeds swallowed long ago!
My boat still motionless and chained below
deep in this water's rimless eye—in what mud?

L'éternité

ELLE est retrouvée.
Quoi? — L'Eternité.
C'est la mer allée
Avec le soleil.

Ame sentinelle,
Murmurons l'aveu
De la nuit si nulle
Et du jour en feu.

Des humains suffrages,
Des communs élans
Là tu te dégages
Et voles selon.

Puisque de vous seules,
Braises de satin,
Le Devoir s'exhale
Sans qu'on dise: enfin.

Là pas d'espérance,
Nul orietur.
Science avec patience,
Le supplice est sûr.

Elle est retrouvée.
Quoi? — L'Eternité.
C'est la mer allée
Avec le soleil.

Eternity

I HAVE found it again.
What?—Eternity.
It is how the sun
Is gone with the sea.

My sentinel soul,
Let us murmur the prayer
Of the night so null
And the day on fire.

From what men approve,
From transports they share,
You burst from this groove
And accordingly soar.

Since by you alone,
Your satin live ember,
Does Duty breathe on,
None calling your number.

No fair expectations,
No orietur,
Knowledge with patience,
The torture is sure.

I have found it again.
What?—Eternity.
It is how the sun
Is gone with the sea.

Age d'or

QUELQU'UNE des voix
Toujours angélique
— Il s'agit de moi, —
Vertement s'explique:

Ces mille questions
Qui se ramifient
N'amènent, au fond,
Qu'ivresse et folie;

Reconnais ce tour
Si gai, si facile:
Ce n'est qu'onde, flore,
Et c'est ta famille!

Puis elle chante. O
Si gai, si facile,
Et visible à l'œil nu...
— Je chante avec elle, —

Reconnais ce tour
Si gai, si facile,
Ce n'est qu'onde, flore,
Et c'est ta famille!... etc...

Et puis une voix
— Est-elle angélique! —
Il s'agit de moi,
Vertement s'explique;

Et chante à l'instant
En sœur des haleines:
D'un ton Allemand,
Mais ardente et pleine:

Le monde est vicieux;
Si cela t'étonne!

Golden age

OF the voices there's one,
Angelic the strain
—All for me it is done—
To chide and arraign:

The questions abound
—A thousand, I think—
Which lead in the end
To madness and drink;

Note how these behave,
So easy, so gay:
Just a flowering, a wave,
Your family they.

Then O she will sing,
So easy and gay.
A naked-eye thing...
—I too sing away—

See how they behave,
So easy and gay:
Just a flowering, a wave,
Your family they!

Then a voice—the same one
Of the angel domain—
For me it is done,
Insisting again,

Singing urgently on,
A sister to breath,
With a strong German tone,
Warm and whole underneath:

The world has no shame,
If that could surprise!

Vis et laisse au feu
L'obscure infortune.

O! joli château!
Que ta vie est claire!
De quel Age es-tu,
Nature princière
De notre grand frère! etc...

Je chante aussi, moi:
Multiples sœurs! voix
Pas du tout publiques!
Environnez-moi
De gloire pudique... etc...

Départ

Assez vu. La vision s'est rencontrée à tous les airs.
Assez eu. Rumeurs des villes, le soir, et au soleil, et toujours.
Assez connu. Les arrêts de la vie. — O Rumeurs et Visions!
Départ dans l'affection et le bruit neufs!

Live, give to the flame
All the dim miseries.

Bright castle, how strong
The life in your hall!
To what age belongs
Your imperial soul,
Our brother so tall?

Myself, I sing too,
You sisters in heaven,
Songs perfectly new!
Shy glory be given
By your secret few.

Departure

ENOUGH seen. The vision encountered in every air.

Enough had. The far sounds of towns, in the evening, in the sunlight, always.

Enough known. Life's suspensions. O far sounds and visions!

Departure in new affection and in the noise made new.

Paul Verlaine
1844 - 1896

Art poétique

A Charles Morice

De la musique avant toute chose,
Et pour cela préfère l'Impair
Plus vague et plus soluble dans l'air,
Sans rien en lui qui pèse ou qui pose.

Il faut aussi que tu n'ailles point
Choisir tes mots sans quelque méprise:
Rien de plus cher que la chanson grise
Où l'Indécis au Précis se joint.

C'est des beaux yeux derrière des voiles,
C'est le grand jour tremblant de midi,
C'est, par un ciel d'automne attiédi,
Le bleu fouillis des claires étoiles!

Car nous voulons la Nuance encor,
Pas la Couleur, rien que la nuance!
Oh! la nuance seule fiance
Le rêve au rêve et la flûte au cor!

Fuis du plus loin la Pointe assassine,
L'Esprit cruel et le Rire impur,
Qui font pleurer les yeux de l'Azur,
Et tout cet ail de basse cuisine!

Prends l'éloquence et tords-lui son cou!
Tu feras bien, en train d'énergie,
De rendre un peu la Rime assagie.
Si l'on n'y veille, elle ira jusqu'où?

Paul Verlaine

1844 - 1896

The art of poetry

To Charles Morice

LET music, of all things, come first,
And first in music the uneven,
That melts vaguely in a thin heaven,
With nothing heavy or held fast.

And you must never choose to write
Words without anything that's wrong;
Nothing more dear than that grey song
Where strict and mutable unite:

Veiling of the lovely eyes,
Daylight shimmering at noon,
Blue crowd of stars that glitter down
From the autumn-mellowed skies.

For nuance we always yearn,
Nuance, not color, is the end,
Only by light and shade we blend
Dream with dream and flute with horn.

Avoid the murderous epigram,
Base laughter, cruel wit that's cheap;
They make the very heavens weep.
Away with kitchen garlic sham!

Take eloquence and wring its neck!
And, while about it, be advised
To keep the rhyme a little wise
Before it goes right off the track.

O qui dira les torts de la Rime?
Quel enfant sourd ou quel nègre fou
Nous a forgé ce bijou d'un sou
Qui sonne creux et faux sous la lime?

De la musique encore et toujours!
Que ton vers soit la chose envolée
Qu'on sent qui fuit d'une âme en allée
Vers d'autres cieux à d'autres amours.

Que ton vers soit la bonne aventure
Eparse au vent crispé du matin
Qui va fleurant la menthe ou le thym...
Et tout le reste est littérature.

J'admire l'ambition du Vers Libre...

J'ADMIRE l'ambition du Vers Libre,
— Et moi-même que fais-je en ce moment
Que d'essayer d'émouvoir l'équilibre
D'un nombre ayant deux rhythmes seulement?

Il est vrai que je reste dans ce nombre
Et dans la rime, un abus que je sais
Combien il pèse et combien il encombre,
Mais indispensable à notre art français.

Autrement muet dans la poésie,
Puisque la langage est sourd à l'accent.
Qu'y voulez-vous faire? Et la fantaisie
Ici perd ses droits: rimer est pressant.

Que l'ambition du Vers Libre hante
De jeunes cerveaux épris de hasards!
C'est l'ardeur d'une illusion touchante.
On ne peut que sourire à leurs écarts.

O who can tell the wrongs of rhyme?
What deaf child or black imbecile
Has forged this gem that under the file
Sounds hollow, scarcely worth a dime.

Always again let music rise!
And let your line soar like a thing
Chased by a spirit on the wing
To other loves and other skies.

Let your line come to pass like pure
Good luck that by the wind is sent,
A morning breath of thyme and mint...
And all the rest is literature.

I must admire the Free Verse aim...

I MUST admire the Free Verse aim:
What do they think I'm trying to do
Right now but make the beat less tame
Of lines that scan by two and two?

It's true I stay within this form
And rhyme, whilst knowing it to hurt,
How tough it is and cumbersome,
But requisite to our French art.

Or else in verse it has no hope,
Because our tongue is deaf to stress.
What's left you? Fancy has no scope:
Without the rhyme it's spiritless.

How much the craze for freedom draws
Young minds who like to take a chance!
So sadly flimsy is the cause
You have to smile at their offence.

Gais poulains qui vont gambadant sur l'herbe
Avec une sincère gravité!
Leur cas est fou, mais leur âge est superbe.
Gentil vraiment, le Vers Libre tenté!

Dans les bois

D'AUTRES, — des innocents ou bien des lymphatiques, —
Ne trouvent dans les bois que charmes langoureux,
Souffles frais et parfums tièdes. Ils sont heureux!
D'autres s'y sentent pris — rêveurs — d'effrois mystiques.

Ils sont heureux! Pour moi, nerveux, et qu'un remords
Epouvantable et vague affole sans relâche,
Par les forêts je tremble à la façon d'un lâche,
Qui craindrait une embûche ou qui verrait des morts.

Ces grands rameaux jamais apaisés, comme l'onde,
D'où tombe un noir silence avec une ombre encor
Plus noire, tout ce morne et sinistre décor
Me remplit d'une horreur triviale et profonde.

Surtout les soirs d'été: la rougeur du couchant
Se fond dans le gris bleu des brumes qu'elle teinte
D'incendie et de sang; et l'angélus qui tinte
Au lointain semble un cri plaintif se rapprochant.

Le vent se lève chaud et lourd, un frisson passe
Et repasse, toujours plus fort, dans l'épaisseur
Toujours plus sombre des hauts chênes, obsesseur,
Et s'éparpille, ainsi qu'un miasme, dans l'espace.

La nuit vient. Le hibou s'envole. C'est l'instant
Où l'on songe aux récits des aïeules naïves...
Sous un fourré, là-bas, là-bas, des sources vives
Font un bruit d'assassins postés se concertant.

Gay ponies gambling on the heath
With a sincerity most grave!
Their aim is rash, but O what youth!
The whole attempt is surely brave!

In the woods

SOME people, whether simple or misled,
Will find in woods a gentle, charming theme,
Fresh breezes and warm perfumes. Lucky for them!
Others, moonstruck, are seized with mystic dread.

Lucky for them! I'm nervous, and a most
Relentless pang, vague but perverse, comes on;
Forests can make me shake like a poltroon,
Who fears an ambush or has seen a ghost.

Those huge boughs never resting, like the sea,
Where falls black silence and a shade that's still
More black, those sinister arrangements fill
My mind with fear not trivial to me.

Especially summer evenings: then the red
Sunset dissolves in blue grey mist with wings
Of fire and blood; the angelus that rings
Far off sounds like a plaintive cry ahead.

The wind stirs, heavy and warm, a shiver to pass
And repass, gradually stronger; darkness heaves,
Spreads and absorbs the oak-trees' denser leaves,
To scatter a miasma over space.

Night falls. The owl takes wing. It is the time
When throngs of old wives' tales come back to mock...
Beneath a hedge, there, there, a rustling brook
Sounds like assassins lurking for a crime.

Mon rêve familier

Je fais souvent ce rêve étrange et pénétrant
D'une femme inconnue, et que j'aime, et qui m'aime,
Et qui n'est, chaque fois, ni tout à fait la même
Ni tout à fait une autre, et m'aime et me comprend.

Car elle me comprend, et mon cœur, transparent
Pour elle seule, hélas! cesse d'être un problème
Pour elle seule, et les moiteurs de mon front blême,
Elle seule les sait refraîchir, en pleurant.

Est-elle brune, blonde ou rousse? — Je l'ignore.
Son nom? Je me souviens qu'il est doux et sonore
Comme ceux des aimés que la Vie exila.

Son regard est pareil au regard des statues,
Et, pour sa voix, lointaine, et calme, et grave, elle a
L'inflexion des voix chères qui se sont tues.

Le ciel est, par dessus le toit...

Le ciel est, par-dessus le toit,
    Si bleu, si calme!
Un arbre, par-dessus le toit,
    Berce sa palme.

La cloche, dans le ciel qu'on voit,
    Doucement tinte.
Un oiseau sur l'arbre qu'on voit
    Chante sa plainte.

Mon Dieu, mon Dieu, la vie est là,
    Simple et tranquille.
Cette paisible rumeur-là
    Vient de la ville.

— Qu'as-tu fait, ô toi que voilà
    Pleurant sans cesse,
Dis, qu'as-tu fait, toi que voilà,
    De ta jeunesse?

My recurrent dream

I OFTEN have this strange and piercing dream
Of one unknown who loves me, whom I love,
Who is and yet is not the woman of
My previous dreams but knows and loves the same.
　　She understands me, and my heart will seem
Lucid, alas! to her alone, will have
For her no problem, while her hand will strive
To cool my brow until her tears will brim.
　　Is she blond, dark, with red hair? I don't know.
Her name? It haunts with hints of long ago,
Like those once loved but banished from our day.
　　Her look reminds me of a statue's look,
Her voice is gentle, calm, and far away,
With tones of those dear voices death once took.

The sky is above the eaves...

The sky is above the eaves,
　　So blue and serene,
The tree is above the eaves,
　　Waving its green.

Bell in the sky for me
　　Tranquilly ringing,
Bird in the tree for me,
　　Plaintively singing.

Ah! God, God! life is there,
　　Tranquil and plain!
That peaceful murmur there
　　Comes from the town.

You who are weeping so,
　　What have you done,
What have you done to
　　Your youth that is gone?

363

Parsifal

PARSIFAL a vaincu les Filles, leur gentil
Babil et la luxure amusante — et sa pente
Vers la Chair de garçon vierge que cela tente
D'aimer les seins légers et ce gentil babil;
　　Il a vaincu la Femme belle, au cœur subtil,
Etalant ses bras frais et sa gorge excitante;
Il a vaincu l'Enfer et rentre sous sa tente
Avec un lourd trophée à son bras puéril,
　　Avec la lance qui perça le Flanc suprême!
Il a guéri le roi, le voici roi lui-même,
Et prêtre du très saint Trésor essentiel.

　　En robe d'or il adore, gloire et symbole,
Le vase pur où resplendit le Sang réel,
— Et, ô ces voix d'enfants chantant dans la coupole!

Parsifal

PARSIFAL has conquered the Girls, their affable
Babble and their diverting lust—and his flair
Of a virgin boy for the flesh that lust ensnares,
To love the wanton breasts and that affable babble;
    He has conquered the beautiful Woman with heart so
        subtle,
Parading her cool arms and her bosom that lures;
He has conquered Hell, and on his arm he bears
Back to his tent the heavy prize of battle,
    The very lance that pierced the Side supreme.
He has healed the king, himself a king become,
And priest of the pure Treasure quintessential.
    In a golden robe he adores the glory and emblem,
The true blood that illumines the holy grail,
—And, O those children's voices singing in the dome!

Jean Moréas

1856 - 1910

Une jeune fille parle

Les fenouils m'ont dit: Il t'aime si
Follement qu'il est à ta merci;
Pour son revenir va t'apprêter.
— Les fenouils ne savent que flatter!
Dieu ait pitié de mon âme.

Les pâquerettes m'ont dit: Pourquoi
Avoir remis ta foi dans sa foi?
Son cœur est tanné comme un soudard.
— Pâquerettes, vous parlez trop tard!
Dieu ait pitié de mon âme.

Les sauges m'ont dit: Ne l'attends pas,
Il s'est endormi dans d'autres bras.
— O sauges, tristes sauges, je veux
Vous tresser toutes dans mes cheveux...
Dieu ait pitié de mon âme.

Jean Moréas

1856 - 1910

A young girl speaks

The fennel said to me: he is so crazy
About you that you have him at your mercy;
Run and get ready for he's coming back.
—The fennel only knows sweet talk!
May God have mercy on my soul.

The Easter daisies said to me: Then why
Upon his good faith did your faith rely?
His heart is tough, a drafted reprobate.
—But daisies, your advice is late!
May God have mercy on my soul.

The sage bloom said to me: don't wait for him,
He's sleeping in another's arms this time.
—O sage, sad sage, if I could choose to wear
Your blossom woven in my hair…
May God have mercy on my soul.

René-François Sully Prudhomme

1839 - 1907

Intus

Deux voix s'élèvent tour à tour
Des profondeurs troubles de l'âme:
La raison blasphème, et l'amour
Rêve un Dieu juste et le proclame.

Panthéiste, athée, ou chrétien,
Tu connais leurs luttes obscures;
C'est mon martyre, et c'est le tien,
De vivre avec ces deux murmures.

L'intelligence dit au cœur:
"Le monde n'a pas un bon père,
Vois, le mal est partout vainqueur."
Le cœur dit: "Je crois et j'espère.

Espère, ô ma sœur, crois un peu,
C'est à force d'aimer qu'on trouve;
Je suis immortel, je sens Dieu."
L'intelligence lui dit: "Prouve!"

René-François Sully Prudhomme

1839 - 1907

Intus

Two voices deep in the mind are heard
With troubled echoes, one by one:
Reason blasphemes, love dreams a Lord
Who's just and strives to make Him known.

Pantheist, atheist, christian shrine,
You know what creeds you struggled through;
It is your martyrdom and mine
To live with murmurs of those two.

Intelligence says to the heart:
"No gentle father governs Earth;
See, evil gains in every part."
The heart says: "I have hope and faith.

"Hope on, my sister, let faith bud,
Till we arrive by dint of love;
I am immortal, I sense God."
Intelligence replies: "Then prove."

Tristan Corbière
1845 - 1875

Do, l'enfant, do

Buona vespre! Dors: Ton bout de cierge,
On l'a posé là, puis on est parti.
Tu n'auras pas peur seul, pauvre petit?...
C'est le chandelier de ton lit d'auberge.

Du fesse-cahier ne crains plus la verge,
Va!... De t'éveiller point n'est si hardi.
Buona sera! Dors: Ton bout de cierge...

Est mort. — Il n'est plus, ici, de concierge:
Seuls, le vent du nord, le vent du midi
Viendront balancer un fil-de-la-Vierge.
Chut! Pour les pieds-plats, ton sol est maudit.
— *Buona notte!* Dors: Ton bout de cierge...

Le mousse

— MOUSSE: il est donc marin, ton père?...
— Pêcheur. Perdu depuis longtemps.
En découchant d'avec ma mère,
Il a couché dans les brisants...
    Maman lui garde au cimetière
Une tombe — et rien dedans. —
C'est moi son mari sur la terre,
Pour gagner du pain aux enfants.
    Deux petits. — Alors, sur la plage,
Rien n'est revenu du naufrage?...
— Son garde-pipe et son sabot...
    La mère pleure, le dimanche,
Pour repos... Moi: j'ai ma revanche
Quand je serai grand — matelot! —

Tristan Corbière

1845 - 1875

Sleep, baby, sleep

Buona vespre! Sleep: Your candle-end
They set beside you when they went away.
Don't be afraid alone, poor little friend...
Just an inn candle, bed-time, close of day.

Don't be afraid of this pen-pusher's hand,
Not to awake's not hard, for all they say.
Buona sera! Sleep: Your candle-end...

Is dead. Mine host no longer will attend:
The north wind and the south, they only play
With gossamer to make it quiver and bend.
Shh! Cursed is this ground for any rogues that stray.
— *Buona notte!* Sleep: Your candle-end...

Cabin boy

"Your Dad's a sailor too, then, right?"
"Fisherman, and long time dead.
Left Mom's bed in the middle of the night,
Sleeps now in the drink instead.
        Now Mom has him in the plot,
Empty coffin for his bed,
Me now all the man she's got
To get the kids a bite of bread:
        Two of them." "Was nothing found
Along the beach where he was drowned?"
"Case for his pipe and one old shoe...
        Mom bawls Sundays now—for rest...
When I'm big I'll know the best
Comeback—be big sailor too."

Paria

Qu'ILS se payent des républiques,
Hommes libres! — carcan au cou —
Qu'ils peuplent leurs nids domestiques!...
— Moi je suis le maigre coucou.

— Moi, — cœur eunuque, dératé
De ce qui mouille et ce qui vibre...
Que me chante leur Liberté,
A moi? toujours seul. Toujours libre.

— Ma Patrie... elle est par le monde;
Et, puisque la planète est ronde,
Je ne crains pas d'en voir le bout...
Ma patrie est où je la plante:
Terre ou mer, elle est sous la plante
De mes pieds — quand je suis debout.

— Quand je suis couché: ma patrie
C'est la couche seule et meurtrie
Où je vais forcer dans mes bras
Ma moitié, comme moi sans âme;
Et ma moitié: c'est une femme...
Une femme que je n'ai pas.

L'idéal à moi: c'est un songe
Creux; mon horizon — l'imprévu —
Et le mal du pays me ronge...
Du pays que je n'ai pas vu.

Que les moutons suivent leur route,
De Carcassonne à Tombouctou...
— Moi, ma route me suit. Sans doute
Elle me suivra n'importe où.

Mon pavillon sur moi frissonne,
Il a le ciel pour couronne:
C'est la brise dans mes cheveux...

Pariah

GIVE them republics for their good,
With liberty!—the neck in yoke—
Give them a nest to hatch their brood!
For me the scrawny cuckoo's luck.

A eunuch, I—no ecstacy!
Deprived of all that pulse and flow,
What is this Freedom song to me,
Alone and free to come and go?

My country being the planet round,
I need not fear to reach its bound.
My country's where I want to be,
Wherever I may stand up straight
And choose a place to plant my feet,
Whether on land or on the sea.

And when I'm laying down my head,
My country is the lonely bed
Where, bruised, I forcibly embrace
My other half, soulless like me;
And that's a woman, naturally...
A woman whom I don't possess.

My dream of good's an empty one;
Horizon—what is unforeseen—
By homesickness I am undone...
Sick for a home I've never seen.

Let the sheep follow where they're led,
From Carcassonne to Timbuctoo...
With me it is the road instead
That follows me—who cares where to.

Above me let my ensign fly,
With nothing for a crown but sky:
And the breezes in my hair...

Et dans n'importe quelle langue;
Je puis subir une harangue;
Je puis me taire si je veux.

Ma pensée est un soufle aride:
C'est l'air. L'air est à moi partout.
Et ma parole est l'écho vide
Qui ne dit rien — et c'est tout.

Mon passé: c'est ce que j'oublie.
La seule chose qui me lie,
C'est ma main dans mon autre main.
Mon souvenir — Rien — C'est ma trace
Mon présent, c'est tout ce qui passe
Mon avenir — Demain... demain.

Je ne connais pas mon semblable;
Moi, je suis ce que je me fais.
— *Le Moi humain est haïssable...*
— Je ne m'aime ni ne me hais.

— Allons! la vie est une fille
Qui m'a pris à son bon plaisir...
Le mien, c'est: la mettre en guenille,
La prostituer sans désir.

— Des dieux?... — Par hasard j'ai pu naître;
Peut-être en est-il — par hasard...
Ceux-là, s'ils veulent me connaître,
Me trouveront bien quelque part.

— Où que je meure: ma patrie
S'ouvrira bien, sans qu'on l'en prie,
Assez grande pour mon linceul...
Un linceul encor: pour que faire?...
Puisque ma patrie est en terre
Mon os ira bien là tout seul...

I can tolerate the chatter,
In what language doesn't matter;
I can keep quiet if I prefer.

My thought's an arid breath of wind:
The air—and that belongs to me.
My words, blank echoes left behind—
And that's the only repartee.

My past is what I have forgot.
The only fear of any knot,
My one hand in the other—so.
My memory—Nothing—It's my track
My present, what will not come back
My future—Tomorrow... tomorrow.

There's none I know to be my fellow;
Me, I am what I make myself.
The word is, Hate the human Ego...
I neither love nor hate myself.

—All right, then: life's the kind of girl
Who took me on to suit her pleasure...
For me to bring about her fall
And prostitute her at my leisure.

—Gods?... It was chance that I was born;
There may be some such things—there may...
If my address they want to learn,
They can just look it up some day.

Wherever I die, my native land
Will open wide without demand,
Enough at least to make a tomb...
Tomb, did I say? Why even that?...
My land being earth, my bones are what,
All by themselves, will find some room...

Jules Laforgue
1860 - 1887

Couchant d'hiver

QUEL couchant douloureux nous avons eu ce soir!
Dans les arbres pleurait un vent de désespoir,
Abattant du bois mort dans les feuilles rouillées.
A travers le lacis des branches dépouillées
Dont l'eau-forte sabrait le ciel bleu-clair et froid,
Solitaire et navrant, descendait l'astre-roi.
O Soleil! l'autre été, magnifique en ta gloire,
Tu sombrais, radieux comme un grand Saint-Ciboire,
Incendiant l'azur! A présent, nous voyons
Un disque safrané, malade, sans rayons,
Qui meurt à l'horizon balayé de cinabre,
Tout seul, dans un décor poitrinaire et macabre,
Colorant faiblement les nuages frileux
En blanc morne et livide, en verdâtre fielleux,
Vieil or, rose-fané, gris de plomb, lilas pâle.
Oh! c'est fini, fini! longuement le vent râle,
Tout est jaune et poussif; les jours sont révolus,
La Terre a fait son temps; ses reins n'en peuvent plus.
Et ses pauvres enfants, grêles, chauves et blêmes
D'avoir trop médité les éternels problèmes,
Grelottants et voûtés sous le poids des foulards
Au gaz jaune et mourant des brumeux boulevards,
D'un œil vide et muet contemplent leurs absinthes,
Riant amèrement, quand des femmes enceintes
Defilent, étalant leurs ventres et leurs seins,
Dans l'orgueil bestial des esclaves divins...

Ouragans inconnus des débâcles finales,
Accourez! déchaînez vos trombes de rafales!
Prenez ce globe immonde et poussif! balayez
Sa lèpre de cités et ses fils ennuyés!
Et jetez ses débris sans nom au noir immense!
Et qu'on ne sache rien dans la grande innocence
Des soleils éternels, des étoiles d'amour,
De ce Cerveau pourri qui fut la Terre, un jour!

Jules Laforgue

1860 - 1887

Winter sunset

WHAT a mournful sunset we have had tonight!
In the trees the crying wind brings down a weight
Of gloom with dead wood on the withered leaves.
Our royal star, distraught and lonely, grieves
Declining in the barren branches' lace,
Etched acid on a sky of pale blue ice.
O sun! when in your summer glory blest,
You went down radiant, like a giant Host
Burning the azure! We behold, these days,
A sickly safron disc, bereft of rays,
Expire on a horizon steeped in red,
A blotch that some consumptive might have bled,
The tinted, tainted clouds convulsed and chill,
A livid white corrupted with green bile,
Dull-gold, lead-grey, sick-lilac, withered-rose:
All finished, finished! The wind prolongs death throes;
Our days are done for, sere, decayed, perplexed.
Earth, having had its day, becomes unsexed;
Its cheerless children, thin and bald and pale
With trying to probe what time will not unveil,
Shiver and stoop beneath a weight of shawls.
While gaslight dies round fog-bound city walls,
They fix their absinthe with a vacant eye,
Deriding pregnant women passing by
Who flaunt their breasts and bellies as they tread
With bestial pride in serfdom to a god...

Impenetrable tempests of our doom,
Unloose the deluge of the wrath to come!
Assault this perishing world! Oh sweep away
Its leprous cities, heirs of its dismay!
Fling down those nameless ruins in endless night!
Where blameless suns burn with eternal light
And stars with love, let nothing more be known
Of onetime Earth, that decomposing Brain!

377

Pour le livre d'amour

Je puis mourir demain et je n'ai pas aimé.
Mes lèvres n'ont jamais touché lèvres de femme,
Nulle ne m'a donné dans un regard son âme,
Nulle ne m'a tenu contre son cœur pâmé.

Je n'ai fait que souffrir, pour toute la nature,
Pour les êtres, le vent, les fleurs, le firmament,
Souffrir par tous mes nerfs, minutieusement
Souffrir de n'avoir pas d'âme encore assez pure.

J'ai craché sur l'amour et j'ai tué la chair!
Fou d'orgueil, je me suis roidi contre la vie!
Et seul sur cette Terre à l'Instinct asservie
Je défiais l'Instinct avec un rire amer.

Partout, dans les salons, au théâtre, à l'église,
Devant ces hommes froids, les plus grands, les plus fins,
Et ces femmes aux yeux doux, jaloux ou hautains
Dont on redorerait chastement l'âme exquise,

Je songeais: tous en sont venus là! j'entendais
Les râles de l'immonde accouplement des brutes!
Tant de fanges pour un accès de trois minutes!
Hommes, soyez corrects! ô femmes, minaudez!

For the book of love

I COULD die tomorrow and have loved not one,
No woman's lips with mine I ever took,
Not one has given her soul up in a look
Or held me on her breast in the final swoon.

My suffering was for nature, that is all,
For beings—the wind, the flowers, the firmament—
Suffering in all my nerves and every moment
To know myself not pure enough of soul.

I killed the flesh and then I spat on love!
Insane with pride, I stiffened against life!
Alone on earth, and with a bitter laugh
I challenged Instinct while I was its slave.

In any salon, theatre, church that's built,
Mixing with these great men so cold and wise,
And women with their sweet, proud, jealous eyes,
Whose tender minds we chastely paint with gilt,

I thought: they all come to it—heard it done—
The vile death-rattle of the coupling brutes!
Such muck, and all for those three-minute fits!
Men, watch your manners! Women, simper on!

Esthétique

LA Femme mûre ou jeune fille,
J'en ai frôlé toutes les sortes,
Des faciles, des difficiles.
Voici l'avis que j'en rapporte:

C'est des fleurs diversement mises,
Aux airs fiers ou seuls selon l'heure,
Nul cri sur elles n'a de prise;
Nous jouissons, Elle demeure.

Rien ne les tient, rien ne les fâche,
Elles veulent qu'on les trouve belles,
Qu'on le leur râle et leur rabâche,
Et qu'on les use comme telles;

Sans souci de serments, de bagues,
Suçons le peu qu'elles nous donnent,
Notre respect peut être vague,
Leurs yeux sont hauts et monotones.

Cueillons sans espoirs et sans drames,
La chair vieillit après les roses;
Oh! parcourons le plus de gammes!
Car il n'y a pas autre chose.

Dimanches

BREF, j'allais me donner d'un "Je vous aime"
Quand je m'avisai non sans peine
Que d'abord je ne me possédais pas bien moi-même.

(Mon Moi, c'est Galathée aveuglant Pygmalion!
Impossible de modifier cette situation.)

Aesthetic

GIRLS? Ripe or young, I've known them all,
I've had a brush with every sort,
Easy and tough, the pure, the frail,
All kinds, and here is my report:

In varied dress, each one's a flower,
Forlorn or proud to suit the day;
No cry of ours has any power;
We take our joy, and there they stay.

Nothing will rile them, nothing rule,
They wish that, endlessly repeated,
We croak at them they're beautiful
And make it true by how they're treated.

Why worry about oath or ring?
Just suck the sweets they may confer;
However vague the vows we bring,
Their eyes preserve the same hauteur.

Gather ye rosebuds without hope,
Don't dramatize or take your pulse;
Play the whole scale throughout its scope—
Because you know there's nothing else.

Sundays

I WAS just about to say "I love you" and give myself
When it came over me, not without some pain,
That, first of all, I didn't possess myself.

(My self is Galatea, blinding Pygmalion!
Impossible to modify this situation.)

Ainsi donc, pauvre, pâle et piètre individu
Qui ne croit à son Moi qu'à ses moments perdus,
Je vis s'effacer ma fiancée
Emportée par le cours des choses,
Telle l'épine voit s'effeuiller,
Sous prétexte de soir sa meilleure rose.

Or, cette nuit anniversaire, toutes les Walkyries du vent
Sont revenues beugler par les fentes de ma porte:
Vae soli!
Mais, ah! qu'importe?
Il fallait m'en étourdir avant!
Trop tard! ma petite folie est morte!
Qu'importe *Vae soli!*
Je ne retrouverai plus ma petite folie.

Le grand vent bâillonné,
S'endimanche enfin le ciel du matin.
Et alors, eh! allez donc, carillonnez!
Toutes cloches des bons dimanches!
Et passez layettes et collerettes et robes blanches
Dans un frou-frou de lavande et de thym
Vers l'encens et les brioches!
Tout pour la famille, quoi! *Vae soli!* C'est certain.

La jeune demoiselle à l'ivoirin paroissien
Modestement rentre au logis.
On le voit, son petit corps bien reblanchi
Sait qu'il appartient
A un tout autre passé que le mien!

Mon corps, ô ma sœur, a bien mal à sa belle âme...
Oh! voilà que ton piano
Me recommence, si natal maintenant!
Et ton cœur qui s'ignore s'y ânonne
En ritournelles de bastringues à tout venant,
Et ta pauvre chair s'y fait mal!...
A moi, Walkyries!
Walkyries des hypocondries et des tueries!

So then, I, a pale and pitiful individual,
Believing in his self but once in a forgotten while,
Saw my fiancée's withdrawal,
Carried away by the drift of things,
As the briar sees its best rose fall,
On the pretext that roses die in the evening.

Now, on this anniversary night, all the valkyries of the wind,
Have come back to bellow through the cracks of my door:
Vae soli!
But ah! why should I care?
They should have dinned it in me time out of mind.
Too late! my little folly is no more!
What's the point of *Vae soli?*
I shall not find again my little folly.

Gag the big wind,
And the morning sky puts on its Sunday splendor.
Hey! let them be well carillonned,
All those good Sunday bells!
Don your baby linen, collarettes, white frocks.
In a swish of thyme and lavender
Towards the incense and breakfast rolls!
Everything for the family, what! *Vae soli!* That's for sure.

The young miss with the ivory book of prayer
Modestly comes home again;
Her little body, made all white again,
Knows it belongs and must incline
To quite a different past from mine!

My body, O my sister, hurts in its beautiful soul...
See how your piano
Renews me now, like being born again!
The while your heart is to itself unknown,
Flutters for every partner at each ravishing refrain,
And every time your poor flesh feels a pain!...
Help, Valkyries!
Valkyries of spleens and butcheries!

Ah! que je te les tordrais avec plaisir,
Ce corps bijou, ce cœur à ténor,
Et te dirais leur fait, et puis encore
La manière de s'en servir
De s'en servir à deux.
Si tu voulais seulement m'approfondir ensuite un peu!

Non, non! C'est sucer la chair d'un cœur élu,
Adorer d'incurables organes
S'entrevoir avant que les tissus se fanent
En monomanes, en reclus!

Et ce n'est pas sa chair qui me serait tout.
Et je ne serais pas qu'un grand cœur pour elle,
Mais quoi s'en aller faire les fous
Dans des histoires fraternelles!
L'âme et la chair, la chair et l'âme,
C'est l'esprit édénique et fier
D'être un peu l'Homme avec la Femme.

En attendant, oh! garde-toi des coups de tête,
Oh! file ton rouet et prie et reste honnête.

— Allons, dernier des poètes,
Toujours enfermé tu te rendras malade!
Vois, il fait beau temps, tout le monde est dehors,
Va donc acheter deux sous d'ellébore,
Ça te fera une petite promenade.

Ah! I'd squeeze them for you with the greatest pleasure,
That jewel body of yours, that heart of a tenor;
I'd tell you all about them and the manner
To put them to use, the two of us together.
If you would only explore *me* a little thereafter!

No, that's sucking the blood of a chosen heart,
Adoring incurable organs, pre-viewing each other
Before the tissues begin to wither
Into the monomania that lives apart!

And it's neither just her body that employs all of my art,
Nor that I'm just for being the great heart that kissed her;
Do we have to play a foolish part
In the drama of brother and sister?
Mind and body, body and mind,
It is in the proud spirit of Eden
To play the man a little with womankind.

Meanwhile, don't throw it all away, but wait!
Oh spin your wheel and pray and live straight.

—Come on, now, you the lowliest of poets,
If you're always a shut-in you'll make yourself sick!
The weather's fine, they're all out of doors,
Go buy a nickel's worth of hellebore,
And that will make you a nice little walk.*

*The rhymes are approximately as loose and displaced as Laforgue's
own, if not invariably in the same position, the main idea being not to
hurt the playful hurt, or hurt playfulness.

L'impossible

Je puis mourir ce soir! Averses, vents, soleil
Distribueront partout mon cœur, mes nerfs, mes moelles.
Tout sera dit pour moi! Ni rêve, ni réveil.
Je n'aurai pas été là-bas, dans les étoiles!

En tous sens, je le sais, sur ces mondes lointains,
Pèlerins comme nous des pâles solitudes,
Dans la douceur des nuits tendant vers nous les mains,
Des Humanités sœurs rêvent par multitudes!

Oui! des frères partout! (Je le sais, je le sais!)
Ils sont seuls comme nous. — Palpitants de tristesse,
La nuit, ils nous font signe! Ah! n'irons-nous, jamais?
On se consolerait dans la grande détresse!

Les astres, c'est certain, un jour s'aborderont!
Peut-être alors luira l'Aurore universelle
Que nous chantent ces gueux qui vont, l'Idée au front!
Ce sera contre Dieu la clameur fraternelle!

Hélas! avant ces temps, averses, vents, soleil
Auront au loin perdu mon cœur, mes nerfs, mes moelles,
Tout se fera sans moi! Ni rêve, ni réveil!
Je n'aurai pas été dans les douces étoiles!

The impossible

I MAY well die to-night. Sun, wind, and rain
Will scatter everywhere my heart, nerves, marrow.
Asleep or waking, nothing will remain.
I shan't have been out there with stars tomorrow.

In those far worlds, I know, wherever sight
Is, pilgrims with the self-same solitudes
Reach us their hands across the gentle night,
Our sister beings in dreamy multitudes.

Yes, siblings everywhere, I know, I know:
Cheerless as we, trembling with loneliness,
They beckon darkling. Shall we never go?
We might console each other in distress!

It's certain that the stars will some day meet!
Then maybe universal dawn will shine,
Which we poor thought-disfigured wretches greet
With brotherly outcry at God's design.

Alas! before that time, sun, wind, and rain
Will far away have lost my heart, nerves, marrow,
And I shall neither sleep nor wake again
To any gentle stars on any morrow!

Eclair de gouffre

J'ETAIS sur une tour au milieu des étoiles.

Soudain, coup de vertige! un éclair où, sans voiles,
Je sondais, grelottant d'effarement, de peur,
L'énigme du Cosmos dans toute sa stupeur!
Tout est-il seul? Où suis-je? Où va ce bloc qui roule
Et m'emporte? — Et je puis mourir! mourir! partir,
Sans rien savoir! Parlez! O rage! et le temps coule
Sans retour! Arrêtez, arrêtez! Et jouir?
Car j'ignore tout, moi! mon heure est là peut-être?
Je ne sais pas! J'étais dans la nuit, puis je nais,
Pourquoi? D'où l'univers? Où va-t-il? Car le prêtre
N'est qu'un homme. On ne sait rien! Montre-toi, parais,
Dieu, témoin éternel! Parle, pourquoi la vie?
Tout se tait! Oh! l'espace est sans cœur! Un moment!
Astres! je ne veux pas mourir! J'ai du génie!
Ah redevenir rien irrévocablement!

Lightning of the abyss

I STAND on a tower surrounded by the stars.

The veils are rent, vertiginous lightning flares,
Where, charged with dread, I sound the utmost height
Of the world's enigma in its stunning night.
Is all, then, one? Where am I? Whither, sphere
That bears me onward when it could destroy?
And I could die without knowing any more,
Die and leave ignorant! O rage, speak out clear!
Time flows unceasing. Cease! And what of joy?
For knowledge I have none. Perhaps fate leased
My hour? I was in night, then I was born,
Why? Whence the universe? Where to? Your priest
Is mere man. Show yourself, God, be you known,
Eternal knower! Speak, has life a why?
Silence. The whole of space is heartless. Wait,
Stars! I have genius, I don't want to die.
Ah! to be nothing again for endless night!

Emile Verhaeren

1855 - 1916

Un matin

Des le matin, par mes grand'routes coutumières
Qui traversent champs et vergers,
Je suis parti clair et léger,
Le corps enveloppé de vent et de lumière.

Je vais, je ne sais où. Je vais, je suis heureux;
C'est fête et joie en ma poitrine:
Que m'importent droits et doctrines,
Le caillou sonne et luit, sous mes talons poudreux;

Je marche avec l'orgueil d'aimer l'air et la terre
Et d'être immense et d'être fou
Et de mêler le monde et tout
A cet enivrement de vie élémentaire.

Oh les pas voyageurs et clairs des anciens dieux!
Je m'enfouis dans l'herbe sombre
Où les chênes versent leurs ombres
Et je baise les fleurs sur leurs bouches de feu.

Les bras fluides et doux des rivières m'accueillent;
Je me repose et je repars,
Avec mon guide: le hasard,
Par des sentiers sous bois dont je mâche les feuilles.

Il me semble jusqu'à ce jour n'avoir vécu
Que pour mourir et non pour vivre:
Oh quels tombeaux creusent les livres
Et que de fronts armés y descendent vaincus!

Dites, est-il vrai qu'hier il existât des choses,
Et que des yeux quotidiens
Aient regardé, avant les miens,
Les vignes s'empourprer et s'exalter les roses?

Emile Verhaeren

1855 - 1916

One morning

Since dawn, by paths familiar to my sight,
  Through fields and where the orchards stood,
  I've set forth feeling bright and good,
My body wrapped in wind and clothed in light.

I'm off, I don't know where. Happy I feel;
  Joyful and festive in my breast:
  Who cares for rights and creeds and the rest?
Stone rings and shines beneath my dusty heel;

I walk with pride in loving earth and air,
  In being tall and being mad,
  Infusing the world and all's that made
With drunk delight in the simple life that's there.

Oh vagrant footprints of old gods still clear!
  I slip away to the dark glade
  Where oak trees on the grass pour shade,
I kiss the flowers on their mouths of fire.

By sweet wet arms of rivers I'm received;
  I sleep secure, for I abide
  With chance, who goes with me as guide
On woodland pathways where I chew the leaves.

I feel that till today my life has all
  Been lived to die and not to live;
  Oh how books dig for us a grave!
What armored fronts they raise up, doomed to fall!

Say, is it true that there existed all
  These things before beneath the sun,
  That eyes have gazed before my own
At vines soon purple, and the rose grown tall?

Pour la première fois, je vois les vents vermeils
Briller dans la mer des branchages,
Mon âme humaine n'a point d'âge;
Tout est jeune, tout est nouveau, sous le soleil.

J'aime mes bras, mes mains, mes épaules, mon torse
Et mes cheveux amples et blonds
Et je voudrais, par mes poumons,
Boire l'espace entier pour en gonfler ma force.

Oh ces marches à travers bois, plaines, fossés,
Où l'être chante et pleure et crie
Et se dépense avec furie
Et s'enivre de soi ainsi qu'un insensé!

Le navire

Nous avancions tranquillement sous les étoiles;
La lune oblique errait autour du vaisseau clair,
Et l'étagement blanc des vergues et des voiles
Projetait sa grande ombre au large sur la mer.

La froide pureté de la nuit embrasée
Scintillait dans l'espace et frissonnait sur l'eau;
On voyait circuler la grande Ourse et Persée
Comme en des cirques d'ombre éclatante, là-haut.

Dans le mât d'artimon et le mât de misaine,
De l'arrière à l'avant où se dardaient les feux,
Des ordres, nets et continus comme des chaînes,
Se transmettaient soudain et se nouaient entre eux.

Chaque geste servait à quelque autre plus large
Et lui vouait l'instant de son utile ardeur,
Et la vague portant la carène et sa charge
Leur donnait pour support sa lucide splendeur.

For the first time I see the winds of dawn
    Shine forth in a bosky sea,
    My human soul from age is free;
All things are young, all new beneath the sun.

I love my arms, hands, shoulders, my full length,
    Yes, and my hair that's blond and long,
    And I am thirsty, with these lungs,
To drink the whole of space into my strength.

But oh these walks through wood and dike and plain,
    Where life will sing and weep and cry out
    And spend itself in wild riot
And get drunk on itself like one insane!

The ship

We moved serenely underneath the stars;
The slanting moon revolved around the ship,
And tier on tier of gleaming sails and spars
Projected their huge shadow on the deep.

The frigid purity embraced by night
Glittered in space and quivered on the wave;
The Great Bear and Perseus wheeled in sight,
Like circus rings, dazzling the dark above.

In mizzen mast and foremast, like a chain,
From stern to prow, where darted tracks of fire,
Commands were passed down ever and again,
With swift response in which all links conspired.

Each gesture served some other still more great
And gave a function to each ardent breath,
Just as the wave buoyed up the keel and freight,
Giving its shining splendor from beneath.

La belle immensité exaltait la gabarre
Dont l'étrave marquait les flots d'un long chemin;
L'homme, qui maintenait à contre-vent la barre,
Sentait vibrer tout le navire entre ses mains.

Il tanguait sur l'effroi, la mort et les abîmes,
D'accord avec chaque astre et chaque volonté,
Et maîtrisant ainsi les forces unanimes,
Semblait dompter et s'asservir l'éternité.

Such beauteous might endowed this hulk with pride;
Its prow laid down a pathway long and straight;
And man, who held the tiller to the tide,
Felt the whole vessel in his hands vibrate.

Each star concerted with each act of will;
Tossed high by fear and death and depths of sea,
Subduing their joint forces by his skill,
He seemed to master all eternity.

Raymond de la Tailhède

1867 - 1938

Ombres

QUAND nous sommes allés vers le soleil levant
Les matins étaient blancs comme des tourterelles;
Des brouillards s'étendaient dans la pourpre du vent
Sur des rivages de roses surnaturelles,
Quand nous sommes allés vers le soleil levant.

Mais, de l'Egypte jusqu'aux îles Baléares,
Quand le ciel fut rempli des clartés de Vénus,
Nous avons oublié les légendes barbares,
Nous avons vu grandir des astres inconnus
Sur la Sicile et les quatre Baléares.

Et c'est la basilique immense de la Nuit,
Les étoiles dans le silence; une par une
Elles ont apparu sur la mer qui reluit,
Toujours plus pâles à travers le clair de lune
Les planètes et les étoiles de la Nuit.

Sur la plaine des mers fauves et virginales
Nous avons regardé des choses d'autrefois;
Notre âme a traversé des fêtes triomphales;
Les dieux retentissaient avec de grandes voix
Sur la forêt des mers fauves et virginales.

Dans le tourment de sa pensée il regardait
L'épanouissement de ce rêve nocturne;
Les larmes de la vie entière qu'il perdait
Montèrent de son cœur ardent et taciturne
Que dans l'effroi de sa pensée il regardait.

Raymond de la Tailhède

1867 - 1938

Shadows

WHEN we advanced towards the rising sun,
The mornings were as white as doves, and mist
Lay stretched out in the purple winds of dawn,
On shores of roses fairer than exist,
When we advanced towards the rising sun.

And yet from Egypt to the Balearic Isles,
When Venus flooded heaven with its light,
We forgot the barbarous legends and descried
Mysterious constellations move in sight
Of Sicily and the four Balearic Isles.

There, in the huge basilica of Night,
The stars stood forth in silence one by one
Above the sea, which gave them back less bright,
Diminished by the rising of the moon,
The planets and the other stars of Night.

On savannas of the tawny, virginal seas
We gazed at the events of long ago;
Our souls passed through triumphal pageantries;
We heard great voices of the gods echo
Above the forest of tawny, virginal seas.

In agony of thought he fixed his gaze
Upon the blossoming of this night dream;
The tears of all his slowly ebbing days
Rose from the silent, stricken heart of him,
While in this fearfulness of thought he gazed.

Alors me reposant entre ses mains si douces
Je lui dis: Pour calmer ton esprit soucieux,
O mon ami, toi qui jamais ne me repousses,
La douceur de ma voix adoucira tes yeux,
La douceur de mes yeux rendra tes larmes douces.

Mais la Nuit et la Mer s'éloignaient lentement;
La lumière montait au-dessus des royaumes,
Et nous n'avons plus vu les dieux en ce moment,
Ni les étoiles, créatrices de fantômes,
Car la Nuit et la Mer s'éloignaient lentement.

Then, resting between his hands of gentleness,
I said to him: To calm your troubled mind,
My friend, who never turned from me your face,
Gentler will be your eyes for how I sound,
Gentler your tears for my eyes gentleness.

But the night and the sea drew slowly far away,
The light ascended above the celestial kingdoms;
Now we could see the gods no more that day,
Nor yet the stars, progenitors of phantoms,
For the night and the sea drew slowly far away.

Paul-Jean Toulet

1867 - 1920

Toi qu'empourprait l'âtre d'hiver...

Toi qu'empourprait l'âtre d'hiver
　　Comme une rouge nue
　　Où déjà te dessinait nue
L'arome de ta chair;

Ni vous, dont l'image ancienne
　　Captive encore mon cœur,
　　Ile voilée, ombres en fleurs,
Nuit océanienne;

Non plus ton parfum, voilier
　　Sous la main qui t'arrose,
　　Ne valent la brûlante rose
Que midi fait plier.

Puisque tes jours ne t'ont laissé...

Puisque tes jours ne t'ont laissé
Qu'un peu de cendre dans la bouche,
Avant qu'on ne tende la couche
Où ton cœur dorme, enfin glacé,
Retourne, comme au temps passé,
Cueillir, près de la dune instable,
Le lys qu'y courbe un souffle amer,
— Et grave ces mots sur le sable:
Le rêve de l'homme est semblable
Aux illusions de la mer.

Paul-Jean Toulet

1867 - 1920

You the winter hearth made flush...

You the winter hearth made flush
  Like a rosy cloud,
Where the perfume of your flesh
  Sketched your body nude;

Not your form which, as of old,
  Still enslaves my sight,
Flowering shadows, island veiled,
  Oceanic night;

Nor your scent—like stocks it flows,
  Watered by my hand—
Could be worth the burning rose
  Closed at noon's command.

Since your days accomplished only...

Since your days accomplished only
In your mouth an ashen taste,
Ere the bed is made that's lonely,
Where your heart sleeps cold at last,
Turn back to the lily broken
Near the shifting dune that's lost;
Gather soon this fragile token,
Match it with man's dream, and grave
In the sand the word MISTAKEN,
Canceled by the oblivious wave.*

---

*This has to have loose elements suggestive of "version" to extract the
essence.

401

La première fois

— "Maman!... Je voudrais qu'on en meure,"
    Fit-elle à pleine voix.
— "C'est que c'est la première fois,
    Madame, et la meilleure."

Mais elle, d'un coude ingénu
    Remontant sa bretelle,
— "Non, ce fut en rêve", dit-elle.
    "Ah! que vous étiez nu..."

The first time

—"Oн Mother!... Of this I could die blest,"
  She cried at the top of her voice.
—"It's because the first time's apt to be choice,
  Madame, and even the best."

But she, replacing her brasiere,
  With a girl's guileless squirm,
Said, "No, it must have been a dream,
  Ah! how nude you were..."

Francis Jammes
1868 - 1938

Il va neiger...

Il va neiger dans quelques jours. Je me souviens
de l'an dernïer. Je me souviens de mes tristesses
au coin du feu. Si l'on m'avait demandé: qu'est-ce?
j'aurais dit: laissez-moi tranquille. Ce n'est rien.

J'ai bien réfléchi, l'année avant, dans ma chambre,
pendant que la neige lourde tombait dehors.
J'ai réfléchi pour rien. A présent comme alors
je fume une pipe en bois avec un bout d'ambre.

Ma vieille commode en chêne sent toujours bon.
Mais moi j'étais bête parce que ces choses
ne pouvaient pas changer et que c'est une pose
de vouloir chasser les choses que nous savons.

Pourquoi donc pensons-nous et parlons-nous? C'est drôle;
nos larmes et nos baisers, eux, ne parlent pas,
et cependant nous les comprenons, et les pas
d'un ami sont plus doux que de douces paroles.

On a baptisé les étoiles sans penser
qu'elles n'avaient pas besoin de nom, et les nombres,
qui prouvent que les belles comètes dans l'ombre
passeront, ne les forceront pas à passer.

Et maintenant même, où sont mes vieilles tristesses
de l'an dernier? A peine si je m'en souviens.
Je dirais: laissez-moi tranquille, ce n'est rien,
si dans ma chambre on venait me demander: qu'est-ce?

Francis Jammes

1868 - 1938

It's going to snow

In a few days it will snow and I recall
Last year my sadness here as I would sit
By the fire. If you had asked me, what is it?
I would have said, forget it. Nothing at all.

I was reflecting last year by this fire,
And thick outside my room the falling snow.
Aimlessly thinking. Just as then, so now,
I sit and smoke an amber-mouthpiece briar.

My old oak chest still has that same good smell.
But I was dumb, because there's many a thing
Will stay unchanged and it's a pose to long
For riddance of the things we know so well.

Why do we think and talk, then? It's so queer;
Our tears and kisses never speak, and yet
These we can understand and find them sweet;
Like a friend's footsteps, they are always clear.

We have baptized the stars without a notion
That they require no name; likewise our numbers,
Which prove the lovely comet still remembers
To pass into the shade, won't force that motion.

And where has all the past year's sadness gone?
I scarcely now recall what made it come.
But if again you ask, in that same room,
What is it? I'd say: Nothing, leave me alone.

Le vieux village

LE vieux village était rempli de roses
et je marchais dans la grande chaleur
et puis ensuite dans la grande froideur
de vieux chemins où les feuilles s'endorment.

Puis je longeai un mur long et usé;
c'était un parc où étaient de grands arbres,
et je sentis une odeur du passé,
dans les grand arbres et dans les robes blanches.

Personne ne devait l'habiter plus...
Dans ce grand parc, sans doute, on avait lu...
Et maintenant, comme s'il avait plu,
les ébéniers luisaient au soleil cru.

Ah! des enfants des autrefois, sans doute,
s'amusèrent dans ce parc si ombreux...
On avait fait venir des plantes rouges
des pays loin, aux fruits très dangereux.

Et les parents, en leur montrant les plantes
leur expliquaient: celle-ci n'est pas bonne...
c'est du poison... elle arrive de l'Inde...
et celle-là est de la belladone.

Et ils disaient encore: cet arbre-ci
vient du Japon où fut votre vieil oncle...
Il l'apporta tout petit, tout petit,
avec des feuilles grandes comme l'ongle.

Ils disaient encore: nous nous souvenons
du jour où l'oncle revint d'un voyage aux Indes;
il arriva à cheval, par le fond
du village, avec un manteau et des armes...

The old village

THE ancient village, redolent with roses,
was very warm, then later bitter cold,
and there along the ancient paths I strolled,
and in the heat and cold the leaves were sleeping.

I went along a lengthy wall, much worn;
it was a park where flourished lofty trees;
the odor that I caught was long since borne
by those great trees and lurked in those white robes.

No one could any more be living there...
In this great park, you will have read, for sure...
And now, as if the rain had cleared the air,
the ebony trees were shining in the glare.

Ah! once it must have been that children played
here where the trees close in to form a shade...
From distant lands had come the crimson plants,
with fruits of which they're told to be afraid.

The parents, when they pointed out those plants,
said to the children: this one isn't good...
it's poisonous... it came to us from India...
and that one's belladonna—never food.

And then again they said: this tree so tall
came from Japan, where your old uncle was...
He brought it back when it was very small,
with great leaves which already looked like claws.

They said again: we can recall the day
the uncle came back from a voyage to India:
He rode a horse from down the village way,
wearing a military cloak and arms...

C'était un soir d'été. Des jeunes filles
couraient au parc où étaient de grands arbres,
des noyers noirs avec des roses blanches,
et des rires sous les noires charmilles.

Et les enfants couraient, criant: c'est l'oncle!
Lui, descendait avec son grand chapeau,
du grand cheval, avec son grand manteau...
Sa mère pleurait: ô mon fils... Dieu est bon...

Lui, répondait: nous avons eu tempête...
L'eau douce a bien failli manquer à bord.
Et la vieille mère le baisait sur la tête
en lui disant: mon fils, tu n'es pas mort...

Mais à présent où est cette famille?
A-t-elle existé? A-t-elle existé?
Il n'y a plus que des feuilles qui luisent,
aux arbres drôles, comme empoisonnés...

Et tout s'endort dans la grande chaleur...
Les noyers noirs pleins de grande froideur...
Personne là n'habite plus...
Les ébéniers luisent au soleil cru.

A summer evening, and some girls, it seems,
were running through the park with those great trees,
white roses twined around black walnut trunks,
bright sounds of laughter under the black hornbeams.

And all the children ran, crying, "It's Uncle!"
And he it was from his great horse got down,
with his great hat, and his great battle gown...
His mother wept: my son... Then: God is good...

And he: we had a storm at sea, he said...
Almost ran out of drinking water aboard.
And his old mother kissed him on the head,
saying, Oh my son, my son, you are not dead...

But now, to-day, where is that family?
Have they existed? Did they ever live?
Nothing remains of the queer trees they said
were poison but the shining of the leaves...

And everything is sleeping in the heat...
Black walnut trees are redolent with a great
cold... No one now lives there...
The ebony trees are shining in the glare.

Emmanuel Signoret

1872 - 1900

Elégie II
(de *La Souffrance des eaux*)

Au cimetière de Tivoli

LA colonnade en marbre éclate sur le ciel:
Sur les cyprès fleuris puisant un sombre miel
Erre un troupeau léger d'abeilles rougissantes,
La source à la clarté joint ses ondes naissantes,
Où maint spectre s'assied d'eau vivante abreuvé.
Quand l'astre couronné de lis sera levé,
Diane aux voiles blancs, l'œil clos sous sa couronne,
Que la brise du fleuve en grondant t'environne!
Nous mettrons aux bergers des flambeaux dans les mains,
Nous leur dirons: "Versez, par torrents, aux chemins
La lumière opulente! Assez d'âmes sont mortes!
De la maison sans joie allez! brisez les portes!
L'œil de l'homme a du ciel les charmantes couleurs,
Les membres parfumés des enfants sont des fleurs
Où, du pollen des dieux, l'homme vrai fructifie!
Des sépulcres brisés jaillit l'aube de vie!"

Emmanuel Signoret

1872 - 1900

Elegy II
(from *The Suffering of the Waters*)

At the Tivoli Cemetery

THE marble columns shine against the sky:
A little flock of reddish bees go by
Sucking dark honey from the cypress blooms;
The brook unites its new-born waves with beams
Of light, to quench the thirst of many a ghost.
When veiled Diana, crowned with lilies, floats
Above, eyes closed beneath her starry crown,
Let the stream's murmuring breeze close you around.
We shall put torches in the shepherds' hands,
Saying, "Pour rich light on every path in the land!
Pour it in torrents! Souls enough are dead.
Go, break down all the doors of the house that's sad!
Man's eye reflects the lovely tints of the sky,
The children smell of flowers that never die,
Where blooms with pollen of gods the real man.
From sepulchres burst open flows the dawn."

411

Paul Fort

1872 - 1960

Le bercement du monde

Du coteau, qu'illumine l'or tremblant des genêts, j'ai vu
jusqu'au lointain le bercement du monde, j'ai vu ce peu de
terre infiniment rythmée me donner le vertige des distances
profondes.

L'azur moulait les monts. Leurs pentes alanguies
s'animaient sous le vent du lent frisson des mers. J'ai vu,
mêlant leurs lignes, les vallons rebondis trembler jusqu'au
lointain de la fièvre de l'air.

Là, le bondissement au penchant du coteau des terres
labourées où les sillons se tendent, courbes comme des arcs
où pointent les moissons avant de s'élancer vers le ciel dans
l'air tendre.

Là se creuse un vallon, sous des prés en damier, que blesse
en un repli la flèche d'un clocher; ici des roches rouges aux
arêtes brillantes se gonflent d'argent pur où croule une eau
fumante.

Plus loin encor s'étage une contrée plus belle, où luisent
des pommiers près de leur ombre ronde. Là dans un creux
huileux de calme, le soleil, où vit une prairie, fait battre une
émeraude.

Et je voyais des terres et des terres plus loin, en marche
vers le ciel et qui semblaient plus pures; l'une où tremblait
le fard gris-perle des lointains; les autres au bord du ciel,
étaient déjà l'azur.

Je restai jusqu'au soir à contempler cette œuvre, à suivre
l'ondulation de cette mer, et je sentais très doucement
faiblir mon cœur au bercement sans fin des vagues de la
terre.

Paul Fort

1872 - 1960

The cradling of the world

FROM a hill illumined with broom that trembles with gold,
I have watched from afar the world's rocking motion, the
rhythm of earth with its infinite manifold, that made me reel
with vistas deep as ocean.

The sky molded the hills. Their fading slopes sprang live
beneath the wind from tumbling seas. I have seen the rounded
valleys mingle their shapes and shimmer remotely in the
fervid breeze.

The country rebounding along the pitch of the hill, where
the furrows expose the ploughed curvature bare, is like a bow
with harvest drawn, until the shoots are aimed at the sky in
the tender air.

A valley is carven out under checkered fields, fissure
arrowed by chimes that a steeple yields; dark scarlet escarp-
ments on the ridges swell with limpid silver misting a water-
fall.

There, further and fairer still, the land shelves down, where
apples glimmer in their own round shade; and there, in an
oily hollow of calm, the sun hammers an emerald where lives
a glade.

And I saw the lands beyond lands yet further away, purer
with distance, sky their rendezvous: one where the paint
vibrates with a pearl-grey, others beyond the horizon, merged
in blue.

I stayed till evening, witnessing this work, following those
undulations yonder beneath, and slowly I could feel my
heart go slack in the endless rocking of the waves of
earth.

Comme un bouillonnement de vagues déchaînées, devant moi jusqu'aux grèves en feu du soleil, je vis vallons et monts, nuages, ciel d'été, remonter l'infini des clartés et s'y perdre.

Je me tenais debout entre les genêts d'or, dans le soir où Dieu jette un grand cri de lumière... et je levais tremblant la palme de mon corps vers cette grande Voix qui rythme l'Univers.

Cette fille, elle est morte...

CETTE fille, elle est morte, et morte dans ses amours.

Ils l'ont portée en terre, en terre au point du jour.

Ils l'ont couchée toute seule, toute seule en ses atours.

Ils l'ont couchée toute seule, toute seule en son cercueil.

Ils sont rev'nus gaîment, gaîment avec le jour.

Ils ont chanté gaîment, gaîment: "Chacun son tour.

"Cette fille, elle est morte, est morte dans ses amours."

Ils sont allées aux champs, aux champs comme tous les jours...

Like waves unchained when they convulse and simmer, stretching towards the strands on fire with the sun, I saw valleys and mountains, clouds, the sky of summer, climb to that infinite splendor and be gone.

I stood up straight amid the golden broom, in the evening when God hurls a light sublime… trembling, erect, like a tall palm my form, to hail that Voice which beats celestial time.*

This light girl here has died…

THIS light girl here has died, has died in the midst of her loves.

They have borne her into the earth, the earth at break of day.

They have laid her to rest alone, alone in her garments gay.

They have laid her to rest alone, all alone in her grave.

They have come back home merrily, merrily with the day.

They have sung merrily, merrily: "Each in turn this way.

This light girl, she has died, died in the midst of her loves."

They have gone to the fields, to the fields, like any other day.

---

* In most of his poems, as here, Fort preferred to hide his rhymes and measures, however rigorous, in ostensible prose paragraphs.

Henry J.M. Levet

1874 - 1906

République Argentine — La Plata

Ni les attraits des plus aimables Argentines,
Ni les courses à cheval dans la pampa,
N'ont le pouvoir de distraire de son spleen
Le Consul général de France à la Plata!

On raconte tout bas l'histoire du pauvre homme:
Sa vie fut traversée d'un fatal amour,
Et il prit la funeste manie de l'opium;
Il occupait alors le poste à Singapoore...

— Il aime à galoper par nos plaines amères,
Il jalouse la vie sauvage du gaucho,
Puis il retourne vers son palais consulaire,
Et sa tristesse le drape comme un poncho...

Il ne s'aperçoit pas, je n'en suis que trop sûre,
Que Lolita Valdez le regarde en souriant,
Malgré sa tempe qui grisonne, et sa figure
Ravagée par les fièvres d'Extrême-Orient...

416

Henry J.M. Levet

1874 - 1906

Argentine republic — La Plata

Neither the charms of the loveliest Argentine,
Nor horse races on the pampas, for that matter,
Were able to distract from feeling mean
The Consul General of France assigned to La Plata!

Under their breath they tell of this poor man:
The fact is that his heart was hopelessly lost,
And he was incurably hooked on heroin
At the time he held the Singapore post.

He loves to gallop on our arid plains,
For he affects the wild life of the gaucho;
But then towards the consulate he turns,
And melancholy drapes him like a poncho.

He never once perceives that Lola Valdez
Is smiling at him, though too manifest,
And this in spite of greying hair, and face
Ravaged by fevers caught in the Far East.

Anna-Elizabeth de Noailles

1876 - 1933

Si vous parliez, Seigneur...

Si vous parliez, Seigneur, je vous entendrais bien,
Car toute humaine voix pour mon âme s'est tue,
Je reste seule auprès de ma force abattue,
J'ai quitté tout appui, j'ai rompu tout lien.

Mon cœur méditatif et qui boit la lumière
Vous aurait absorbé, si, transgressant les lois,
Comme le vent des nuits qui pénètre les pierres
Votre verbe enflammé fût descendu sur moi!

Nul ne vous souhaitait avec tant d'indigence;
Je vous aurais fêté au son du tympanon
Si j'avais, dans mon triste et studieux silence,
Entendu votre voix et connu votre nom.

Si forte qu'eût été l'ombre sur vos visages,
Sublime Trinité! j'eusse écarté la nuit,
Mon esprit vous aurait poursuivie sans ennui,
Et j'aurais abordé à votre clair rivage.

Mais jamais rien à moi ne vous a révélé,
Seigneur! ni le ciel lourd comme une eau suspendue,
Ni l'exaltation de l'été sur les blés,
Ni le temple ionien sur la montagne ardue;

Ni les cloches qui sont un encens cadencé,
Ni le courage humain, toujours sans récompense,
Ni les morts, dont l'hostile et pénétrant silence
Semble un renoncement invincible et lassé;

Ni ces nuits où l'esprit retient comme une preuve
Son aspiration au bien universel;
Ni la lune qui rêve et voit passer le fleuve
Des baisers fugitifs sous les cieux éternels.

Anna-Elizabeth de Noailles

1876 - 1933

Lord, if you spoke...

LORD, if you spoke, I'd hear your every sound,
All human voices silenced in my mind,
And I to my sole battered strength confined,
All aid abandoned, loosened every bond.

My meditative heart that drinks the sun,
You could have made your own if, flouting laws,
Like the night wind that penetrates a stone,
Your flaming word stooped to consume my flaws.

No one has longed for you with such distress;
To fete you I'd put dulcimers to shame,
If, in my sad and studious quietness,
I could have heard your voice and known your name.

However dark your faces might have grown,
Bright Trinity, I would have charged the night,
My spirit would have followed without fright,
Until your shining shore had been made known.

But touching you, Lord, nothing helped me learn,
Neither the heavens, heavy with their spill,
Nor summer's rapture in the ears of corn,
Nor Attic temple on the hard won hill;

Nor cadenced incense in the sound of bells,
Nor human fortitude that stays unpaid,
Nor that stern, piercing silence of the dead,
Renunciation weary but unquelled;

Nor yet those nights when, like a proof, the mind
Retains its yearning for the common weal,
Nor moon that dreams and sees the river wind,
To flee the kisses that the heavens steal.

Hélas! ni ces matins de ma brûlante enfance,
Où, dans les prés gonflés d'un nuage d'odeur,
Je sentais, tant l'extase en moi jetait sa lance,
Un ange dans les cieux qui m'arrachait le cœur!

Pourtant, ayez pitié! Que votre main penchante
Vienne guider mon sort douloureux et terni;
J'aspire à vous, Splendeur, Raison éblouissante!
Mais je ne vous vois pas, ô mon Dieu! et je chante
A cause du vide infini!

Alas! nor mornings when my childhood burned
In fields with cloudy perfume spread apart:
Such rapture hurled its lance in me, I learned
An angel in the skies had seized my heart!

Have mercy still, and may your sovereign hand
Incline my tarnished destiny to guide!
I crave you, Splendor, flower of Reason, and
I do not see you. So, my God, I stand
            And sing into the endless void!

Catherine Pozzi

1882 - 1934

Ave

Très haut amour, s'il se peut que je meure
Sans avoir su d'où je vous possédais,
En quel soleil était votre demeure,
En quel passé votre temps, en quelle heure
Je vous aimais,

Très haut amour qui passez la mémoire,
Feu sans foyer dont j'ai fait tout mon jour,
En quel destin vous traciez mon histoire,
En quel sommeil se voyait votre gloire,
O mon séjour...

Quand je serai pour moi-même perdue
Et divisée à l'abîme infini,
Infiniment, quand je serai rompue,
Quand le présent dont je suis revêtue
Aura trahi,

Par l'univers en mille corps brisée,
De mille instants non rassemblés encor,
De cendre aux cieux jusqu'au néant vannée,
Vous referez pour une étrange année
Un seul trésor,

Vous referez mon nom et mon image
De mille corps emportés par le jour,
Vive unité sans nom et sans visage,
Cœur de l'esprit, ô centre du mirage
Très haut amour.

Catherine Pozzi

1882 - 1934

Ave

O SOVEREIGN love, if I should die
Possessing you and blind to whence,
Under what sun you passed me by,
In what lost age and hour and sky,
　　I loved you once,

O love surpassing memory,
Fire that made all my day a flame,
What destiny bestowed my story,
In what strange sleep appeared your glory,
　　My only home…

When lost to me, I shall have wandered,
Cloven, to the abysmal shade,
When I am infinitely sundered,
When by this Now, whose clothing hindered,
　　I am betrayed,

Torn in a thousand fragments, tossed
Through space, and winnowed to thin air,
You will restore from all that's past,
From ash of a thousand moments lost,
　　One treasured year.

My name and face you will restore
From a thousand shreds the day unwove,
Nameless and faceless, single the more,
Heart of my soul, mirage's core,
　　My sovereign love.

Vale

Lᴀ grande amour que vous m'aviez donnée
Le vent des jours a rompu ses rayons —
Où fut la flamme, où fut la destinée
Où nous étions, où par la main serrée
    Nous nous tenions

Notre soleil, dont l'ardeur fut pensée
L'orbe pour nous de l'être sans second
Le second ciel d'une âme divisée
Le double exil où le double se fond

Son lieu pour vous apparaît cendre et crainte,
Vos yeux vers lui ne l'ont pas reconnu
L'astre enchanté qui portait hors d'atteinte
L'extrême instant de notre seule étreinte
    Vers l'inconnu.

Mais le futur dont vous attendez vivre
Est moins présent que le bien disparu.
Toute vendange à la fin qu'il vous livre
Vous la boirez sans pouvoir être qu'ivre
    Du vin perdu.

J'ai retrouvé le céleste et sauvage
Le paradis où l'angoisse est désir
Le haut passé qui grandit d'âge en âge
Il est mon corps et sera mon partage
    Après mourir.

Quand dans mon corps ma délice oubliée
Où fut ton nom, prendra forme de cœur
Je revivrai notre grande journée,
Et cette amour que je t'avais donnée
    Pour la douleur.

Vale

Of that great love which you have given me
The wind of days dispersed the light we found,
Where dwelt the flame, where ruled our destiny,
Where once we lived, where clasped in unity
          Our hands were bound:

Our sun, in whose great heat we did deny
That there could be for us a state beyond,
A second heaven when the parted die,
The double exile doubly so marooned,

It seemed to you a dreadful ashen place
Your eyes that gazed towards it looked not on
The enchanted star which bore beyond all loss
The instant of our uttermost embrace
          Towards the unknown.

The life which in the future marks your fate
Is present less than gladness that is gone.
There'll be no vintage for you soon or late
Will have the power to intoxicate
          Of that lost wine.

I have regained the rapture and the rage
The paradise where anguish is desire
The towering past that grows from age to age
This is my body and shall be my wage
          When I expire.

When in that body my forgotten joy
Bearing your name, the heart's own form shall take
I will relive our day without alloy,
The love I gave you nothing can destroy,
          For sorrow's sake.

Scopolamine

LE vin qui coule dans ma veine
A noyé mon cœur et l'entraîne
Et je naviguerai le ciel
A bord d'un cœur sans capitaine
Où l'oubli fond comme du miel.

Mon cœur est un astre apparu
Qui nage au divin nonpareil.
Dérive, étrange devenu!
O voyage vers le Soleil —
Un son nouvel et continu
Est la trame de ton sommeil.

Mon cœur a quitté mon histoire
Adieu Forme je ne sens plus
Je suis sauvé je suis perdu
Je me cherche dans l'inconnu
Un nom libre de la mémoire.

Scopolamine

THE wine that's flowing in my vein
Has borne away my heart to drown
And I shall navigate the skies
On board a heart where, captain gone,
Honeyed oblivion melting lies.

My heart's exposed, a sailing star,
Launched in the nonpareil divine.
Set forth, my heart, whate'er you are!
O journey onward toward the sun—
A ceaseless sound new to the ear
Is weft whereby your sleep is spun.

My heart has left my history
Farewell to Form I feel no more
I'm lost and saved and I explore
To find on that mysterious shore
A name that's free from memory.

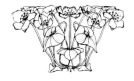

Paul Valéry

1871 - 1945

Le vin perdu

J'AI, quelque jour, dans l'Océan,
(Mais je ne sais plus sous quels cieux),
Jeté, comme offrande au néant,
Tout un peu de vin précieux...
    Qui voulut ta perte, ô liqueur?
J'obéis peut-être au devin?
Peut-être au souci de mon cœur,
Songeant au sang, versant le vin?
    Sa transparence accoutumée
Après une rose fumée
Reprit aussi pure la mer...
    Perdu ce vin, ivres les ondes!...
J'ai vu bondir dans l'air amer
Les figures les plus profondes...

Les pas

TES pas, enfants de mon silence,
Saintement, lentement placés,
Vers le lit de ma vigilance
Procèdent muets et glacés.

Personne pure, ombre divine,
Qu'ils sont doux, tes pas retenus!
Dieux!... tous les dons que je devine
Viennent à moi sur ces pieds nus!

Si, de tes lèvres avancées,
Tu prépares pour l'apaiser,
A l'habitant de mes pensées
La nourriture d'un baiser,

Paul Valéry

1871 - 1945

The lost wine

Upon a day, I cast from me
(But I forget beneath what sign),
Oblation to the oblivious sea,
A vestige of my precious wine…
    Choice vintage, who might want you spilled?
Perhaps I did what heaven would?
Perhaps it was my heart that willed
To pour the wine and dream of blood?
    Stained briefly with a smoke of rose,
The sea recovered its repose,
Transparent once again and pure…
    Lost was the wine, drunken the wave!…
And tossing in the briny air
I saw the forms unfathomed move…

The footsteps

Born of my quiet, your footsteps steal,
Sacred and slow, to where I lie,
Watching how they, like ice, congeal
The still approach they sanctify.

Being most pure, my shade divine,
Your hesitating steps are sweet.
Lord! every gift that I divine
Comes to me on those naked feet!

If it is true that you propose
To give with your advancing mouth,
Here where my thoughts of you repose,
The drink of kisses for my drouth,

Ne hâte pas cet acte tendre,
Douceur d'être et de n'être pas,
Car j'ai vécu de vous attendre,
Et mon cœur n'était que vos pas.

Le bois amical

Nous avons pensé des choses pures
Côte à côte, le long des chemins,
Nous nous sommes tenus par les mains
Sans dire... parmi les fleurs obscures;
Nous marchions comme des fiancés
Seuls, dans la nuit verte des prairies;
Nous partagions ce fruit de féeries
La lune amicale aux insensés
Et puis, nous sommes morts sur la mousse,
Très loin, tout seuls parmi l'ombre douce
De ce bois intime et murmurant;
Et là-haut, dans la lumière immense,
Nous nous sommes trouvés en pleurant
O mon cher compagnon de silence!

La distraite

Daigne, Laure, au retour de la saison des pluies,
Présence parfumée, épaule qui t'appuies
Sur ma tendresse lente attentive à tes pas,
Laure, très beau regard qui ne regarde pas,
Daigne, tête aux grands yeux qui dans les cieux t'égares,
Tandis qu'à pas rêveurs, tes pieds voués aux mares
Trempent aux clairs miroirs dans la boue arrondis,
Daigne, chère, écouter les choses que tu dis...

No need to rush this gentle move,
Dear for what is and what is not,
Since waiting for you made me live,
Only your footsteps were my heart.

The friendly wood

SIDE by side along the road,
We held each other by the hand;
With all things pure our thoughts remained;
The unseen flowers we speechless trod.

    Like two who are betrothed we strayed
Through the green night of fields, alone.
We shared the fairy fruit of the moon
That gives her friendship to the mad.

    Then on the moss we were as dead,
Alone and far in the gentle shade,
Of this secluded, murmuring wood,

    And there on high, in the mighty light,
Found weeping in the quietude,
Dear comrade of the silent night.

The distracted one

DEIGN, Laura, now the rainy days return,
Sweet smelling presence, shoulder that will lean
On my slow care at every step you take,
Laura, who look so lovely and do not look,
Deign, head with large eyes lost in the sky,
While dreamy feet, stepping in pools near by,
Disturb the sky's clear mirrors, ringed with clay,
Deign, dear, to listen to the things you say...

Hélène

Azur! c'est moi... Je viens des grottes de la mort
Entendre l'onde se rompre aux degrés sonores,
Et je revois les galères dans les aurores
Ressusciter de l'ombre au fil des rames d'or.

Mes solitaires mains appellent les monarques
Dont la barbe de sel amusait mes doigts purs;
Je pleurais. Ils chantaient leurs triomphes obscurs
Et les golfes enfuis aux poupes de leurs barques.

J'entends les conques profondes et les clairons
Militaires rythmer le vol des avirons;
Le chant clair des rameurs enchaîne le tumulte,

Et les Dieux, à la proue héroïque exaltés
Dans leur sourire antique et que l'écume insulte,
Tendent vers moi leurs bras indulgents et sculptés.

Neige

Quel silence, battu d'un simple bruit de bêche!...

Je m'éveille, attendu par cette neige fraîche
Qui me saisit au creux de ma chère chaleur.
Mes yeux trouvent un jour d'une dure pâleur
Et ma chair langoureuse a peur de l'innocence.
Oh! combien de flocons, pendant ma douce absence,
Durent les sombres cieux perdre toute la nuit!
Quel pur désert tombé des ténèbres sans bruit
Vint effacer les traits de la terre enchantée
Sous cette ample candeur sourdement augmentée
Et la fondre en un lieu sans visage et sans voix,
Où le regard perdu relève quelques toits
Qui cachent leur trésor de vie accoutumée
A peine offrant le vœu d'une vague fumée.

Helen

AZURE! it's me… I issue from death's shores
To hear the waves break with their pacing din
And see once more those galleys in the dawn
Rise from the shades, on banks of golden oars.
    My lonely hands are beckoning the kings
Whose salty beards amused my shining fingers;
I wept. These once were the triumphant singers
Whose tall prows gave the fleeing waves their wings.
    The sounding clarion and the deep-toned conch
Control the rowers toiling on the bench,
From whom bright songs arise to chain the tumult;
    And the gods, uplifted high above the storms,
Calm, smiling still whom the spindrift would insult,
Gently hold out to me their sculptured arms.

Snow

SUCH silence, broken by the stroke of a spade!

I wake, and all this fresh snow waits there, laid
To pluck me from the hollow of my warm nest.
My eyes reveal a light of pallid crust,
My drowsy flesh recoils from the innocent day.
How many flakes, while I slipped softly away,
The somber dark has squandered in the skies!
I wake and to what a pure desert rise,
Which silently effaced the spellbound earth
To bring this vast white secrecy to birth,
Without a voice, without a lineament;
For the lost gaze few roofs are evident
To hide the treasured daily life of folk,
Yielding no tribute but a wraith of smoke.

Le cimetière marin

Μή, φίλα ψυχά, βίον ἀθάνατον
σπεῦδε, ταν δ'ἔμπρακτον ἄντλει
μαχανάν.

Pindare, *Pythiques, III.*

CE toit tranquille, où marchent des colombes,
Entre les pins palpite, entre les tombes;
Midi le juste y compose de feux
La mer, la mer, toujours recommencée!
O récompense après une pensée
Qu'un long regard sur le calme des dieux!

Quel pur travail de fins éclairs consume
Maint diamant d'imperceptible écume,
Et quelle paix semble se concevoir!
Quand sur l'abîme un soleil se repose,
Ouvrages purs d'une éternelle cause,
Le Temps scintille et le Songe est savoir.

Stable trésor, temple simple à Minerve,
Masse de calme, et visible réserve,
Eau sourcilleuse, Œil qui gardes en toi
Tant de sommeil sous un voile de flamme,
O mon silence!... Edifice dans l'âme, .
Mais comble d'or aux mille tuiles, Toit!

Temple du Temps, qu'un seul soupir résume,
A ce point pur je monte et m'accoutume,
Tout entouré de mon regard marin;
Et comme aux dieux mon offrande suprême,
La scintillation sereine sème
Sur l'altitude un dédain souverain.

Comme le fruit se fond en jouissance,
Comme en délice il change son absence
Dans une bouche où sa forme se meurt,

The graveyard by the sea

> Seek not, O my soul, the life of
> the immortals; rather enjoy what
> falls within thy reach.
>
> Pindar, *Pythics III*

THIS tranquil roof, trodden by sailing doves,
Shimmers among the tombs, the pines above.
Impartial Noon composes out of flame
The sea, the sea, forever new again!
Sweet compensation after thought is done
To fix a steady gaze on the gods' calm!

How pure a feat of lightning to consume
So many a diamond of invisible foam!
What utter peace seems coming into being!
When, resting over the abyss, a sun will pause,
These pure creations of eternal cause,
Time sparkles and the Dream's a way of knowing.

Firm treasure, shrine to heaven's lucid queen,
Dense mass of calm and reticence that's seen,
Proud-lidded water, eye under fiery veils
With so much slumber held in your control,
O silence! Building founded in my soul,
But roofed with golden eaves and a myriad tiles!

Time's temple, summed up in a simple sigh,
To this pure spot I climb, drawn partly by
Dear custom: there I gaze all round at the main
Deep, and, like my utmost sacrifice
To the gods, that calm effulgence will suffice
Only to sow a heavenly disdain.

As fruit dissolves in pleasure, rearranging
Within the mouth its fading feature, changing
The shape to sweetness as the taste prevails,

435

Je hume ici ma future fumée,
Et le ciel chante à l'âme consumée
Le changement des rives en rumeur.

Beau ciel, vrai ciel, regarde-moi qui change!
Après tant d'orgueil, après tant d'étrange
Oisiveté, mais pleine de pouvoir,
Je m'abandonne à ce brillant espace,
Sur les maisons des morts mon ombre passe
Qui m'apprivoise à son frêle mouvoir.

L'âme exposée aux torches du solstice,
Je te soutiens, admirable justice
De la lumière aux armes sans pitié!
Je te rends pure à ta place première:
Regarde-toi!... Mais rendre la lumière
Suppose d'ombre une morne moitié.

O pour moi seul, à moi seul, en moi-même,
Auprès d'un cœur, aux sources du poème,
Entre le vide et l'événement pur,
J'attends l'écho de ma grandeur interne,
Amère, sombre et sonore citerne,
Sonnant dans l'âme un creux toujours futur!

Sais-tu, fausse captive des feuillages,
Golfe mangeur de ces maigres grillages,
Sur mes yeux clos, secrets éblouissants,
Quel corps me traîne à sa fin paresseuse,
Quel front l'attire à cette terre osseuse?
Une étincelle y pense à mes absents.

Fermé, sacré, plein d'un feu sans matière,
Fragment terrestre offert à la lumière,
Ce lieu me plaît, dominé de flambeaux,
Composé d'or, de pierre et d'arbres sombres,
Où tant de marbre est tremblant sur tant d'ombres;
La mer fidèle y dort sur mes tombeaux!

So to my squandered soul the heavens sing
Of shores that change in the tide's murmuring,
And then my future figment I inhale.

Fair, changeless sky, consider me who change!
After so stiff a pride, after so strange
An idleness, and yet imbued with strength,
I can surrender to these shining spaces;
Above the homes of the dead my shadow passes,
Subdues me to its wavering pace and length.

My soul, though scorched by torches of the solstice,
May yet endure the unendurable justice
Of light that comes in pitiless arms arrayed.
O light, I give you back your first domain:
Look at yourself! But to give back light's reign
Presumes a somber moiety of shade.

O for myself alone, close to the heart,
Alone with self, at the source of the poem's art,
Between the dark void and the pure event,
I wait the echo of my tones that dwell
With greatness in a grim, sonorous well,
Tones haunting with some future testament.

Gulf that looks captured by the foliage
While it devours the slim bars of that cage,
Dazzling closed eyes with secrets of the sun,
Who knows what body drags me to its end,
Or brow drags bodies to a bony ground?
There a spark burns for loved ones who are gone.

Closed, sacred, fraught with immaterial fire,
Terrestrial fragment offered to bright air,
This place enchants me, governed by flambeaux,
Composed of gold and stone and somber trees,
Where marble trembles above the shade of these;
Staunch to my tombs, the sea takes her repose.

Chienne splendide, écarte l'idolâtre!
Quand solitaire au sourire de pâtre,
Je pais longtemps, moutons mystérieux,
Le blanc troupeau de mes tranquilles tombes,
Eloignes-en les prudentes colombes,
Les songes vains, les anges curieux!

Ici venu, l'avenir est paresse.
L'insecte net gratte la sécheresse;
Tout est brûlé, défait, reçu dans l'air
A je ne sais quelle sévère essence...
La vie est vaste, étant ivre d'absence,
Et l'amertume est douce, et l'esprit clair.

Les morts cachés sont bien dans cette terre
Qui les réchauffe et sèche leur mystère.
Midi là-haut, Midi sans mouvement
En soi se pense et convient à soi-même...
Tête complète et parfait diadème,
Je suis en toi le secret changement.

Tu n'as que moi pour contenir tes craintes!
Mes repentirs, mes doutes, mes contraintes
Sont le défaut de ton grand diamant...
Mais dans leur nuit toute lourde de marbres,
Un peuple vague aux racines des arbres
A pris déjà ton parti lentement.

Ils ont fondu dans une absence épaisse,
L'argile rouge a bu la blanche espèce,
Le don de vivre a passé dans les fleurs!
Où sont des morts les phrases familières,
L'art personnel, les âmes singulières?
La larve file où se formaient des pleurs.

Les cris aigus des filles chatouillées,
Les yeux, les dents, les paupières mouillées,
Le sein charmant qui joue avec le feu,

Bright watch-dog, keep idolators at bay!
When I'm alone, and, in my shepherd's way,
Smile as I graze my flock the whole day long,
Mysterious white flock of these my tombs,
Keep far away the prudent doves, vain dreams,
And curious angels that do not belong!

Once arrived here, the future drags its feet.
The dainty insect scratches on dry heat;
All is undone, burnt, rendered in the air
To heaven knows what rarefied essence...
For life is huge and drunk with its own absence,
And bitterness is sweet, and the mind clear.

The hidden dead lie easy in this clay,
Which warms and dries their mystery in decay.
Noon high up there, Noon, motionless and strange,
Self-born, self-nurtured, rapt in its own theme...
Most flawless head and perfect diadem,
I am within you the mysterious change.

There's none but me to comprehend your fears!
My doubts, my curbs, and my repentant tears
Of your great diamond are the single flaw...
Yet in their night weighed down with marble, these
Vague people dwelling at the roots of trees
Already slowly have incurred your law.

For they are rendered to a compact void,
White clay is swallowed by the kind that's red,
The gift of life has passed into the flowers.
Where are they now, the individual dead,
The singular grace, the simple things they said?
A worm crawls now where once there trickled tears.

The squeals of tickled girls, their eyes, their teeth,
Their moistened eyelids, pretty breast beneath,
That plays with fire according to their way,

Le sang qui brille aux lèvres qui se rendent,
Les derniers dons, les doigts qui les défendent,
Tout va sous terre et rentre dans le jeu!

Et vous, grande âme, espérez-vous un songe
Qui n'aura plus ces couleurs de mensonge
Qu'aux yeux de chair l'onde et l'or font ici?
Chanterez-vous quand serez vaporeuse?
Allez! Tout fuit! Ma présence est poreuse,
La sainte impatience meurt aussi!

Maigre immortalité noire et dorée,
Consolatrice affreusement laurée,
Qui de la mort fais un sein maternel,
Le beau mensonge et la pieuse ruse!
Qui ne connaît, et qui ne les refuse,
Ce crâne vide et ce rire éternel!

Pères profonds, têtes inhabitées,
Qui sous le poids de tant de pelletées,
Etes la terre et confondez nos pas,
Le vrai rongeur, le ver irréfutable
N'est point pour vous qui dormez sous la table,
Il vit de vie, il ne me quitte pas!

Amour, peut-être, ou de moi-même haine?
Sa dent secrète est de moi si prochaine
Que tous les noms lui peuvent convenir!
Qu'importe! Il voit, il veut, il songe, il touche!
Ma chair lui plaît, et jusque sur ma couche,
A ce vivant je vis d'appartenir!

Zénon! Cruel Zénon! Zénon d'Elée!
M'as-tu percé de cette flèche ailée
Qui vibre, vole, et qui ne vole pas!
Le son m'enfante et la flèche me tue!
Ah! le soleil... Quelle ombre de tortue
Pour l'âme, Achille immobile à grands pas!

440

The shining blood where lips relent and blend,
The final gifts their fingers will defend,
All turns to dust and comes back into play.

Vast soul, and are you hoping for a dream
That will no longer flaunt the tints that seem,
Displayed by waves and gold to fool the eyes?
Will you still sing in such a misty chorus?
All things abscond! My presence will be porous;
Impatience too, however holy, dies!

Bleak immortality in black and gold,
Laurelled for cheer but fearsome to behold,
Making death out to be a mother's breast,
Ah! what a lovely lie and pious ruse!
Who does not know, and who does not refuse
That empty skull, that everlasting jest!

Fathers deep down there, heads without an inmate,
They've shovel'd on you such a mighty weight,
You mock our sober steps by being the dirt;
The actual, irrefutable worm
Is not for you who sleep beneath the loam;
He lives on life, it's me he won't desert!

Love, is he? Hate of self? His secret bite
Is with a tooth so close to me it might
Take any name that happens on the tongue.
He sees, wants, dreams; he touches till I'm led
To think he likes my flesh, and even in bed
For this live thing I live, to him belong.

Zeno of Elia! Zeno! Cruel Zeno!
With your winged arrow have you pierced me now,
That hums and flies and motionless abides?
The sound begets me and the arrow kills!
The sun!... Ah! what a tortoise-shadow stills
My soul and great Achilles in his stride!

Non, non!... Debout! Dans l'ère successive!
Brisez, mon corps, cette forme pensive!
Buvez, mon sein, la naissance du vent!
Une fraîcheur, de la mer exhalée,
Me rend mon âme... O puissance salée!
Courons à l'onde en rejaillir vivant!

Oui! Grande mer de délires douée,
Peau de panthère et chlamyde trouée
De mille et mille idoles du soleil,
Hydre absolue, ivre de ta chair bleue,
Qui te remords l'étincelante queue
Dans un tumulte au silence pareil,

Le vent se lève!... Il faut tenter de vivre!
L'air immense ouvre et referme mon livre,
La vague en poudre ose jaillir des rocs!
Envolez-vous, pages tout éblouies!
Rompez, vagues! Rompez d'eaux réjouies
Ce toit tranquille où picoraient des focs!

No, no!... Stand upright in the age to come!
And may my body smash this pensive form,
My breast drink in the wind that is awaking!
A coolness breathed upon me by the sea
Gives back, O salty might, my soul to me.
Let's dash in the waves and live to ride them breaking!

Vast ocean, yes! with fever fits possessed,
Chlamis and panther skin for ever pierced
With multiplying idols of the sun,
Absolute hydra, drunk with your own blue flesh,
Biting your glittering tail in a restless hush,
A still commotion with the sound of none,

The wind is rising!... We must try to live!
The immense air plucks my book, the dauntless wave
Leaps from the rocks in spray! Tear off, fly on,
My dazzled pages! Break, waves, break, subdue
With streams of joy this quiet roof where flew
The doves like white sails pecking there at noon!

Whither Poetry?

Le Soir Qui Tombe, by René Magritte

Whither Poetry?
Twentieth Century

"Home-keeping youths have ever homely wit," and "What do they know of England who only England know?" It would be perfectly possible to explore for the direction and treasure of great poetry through a re-examination of seven centuries of *English* poetry, probably the world's best, but by paradox relatively inaccessible for us, because, as with the Bible and wedlock, we are too enured to loaded presuppositions to make a completely open approach anything but painfully difficult. French poetry has to be for us so much more pristine, appears to have had so clear a rise, decline, fruition and frustration, that it can and does enable a widening reorientation; whilst translating it into English poetry, with all its pitfalls, is a crucial intercourse, defeat of delusions, and mother of lights, especially if we know we don't know enough about it.

It should be a matter of course that knowing about contemporary literature requires a well cleaned rear-view mirror. Today, and especially in America, we exhibit a parochialism in the way we take sides against the past. In some ways there is more to put us on our guard in translating moderns than ancients. If this is to be a book of classical French poetry, it must have some answer to the old question of what is a classic, and this in its turn of when a classic may safely be judged to have become one. It is only recently that the School of Language and Literature at Oxford closed its syllabus with works upwards of fifty years old, whereas about half the courses in English and American literature in American colleges commence, historically, near to where at Oxford they would end.

I would not wish to arbitrate between these two extremes, even if I could, except by way of pointing out what should be sufficiently obvious: that to resolve on the permanence of a work of art must necessarily become more arbitrary in proportion to that work's modernity. After all, the past shows no lack of nine-day wonders, totally forgotten in fifty years.[1]

Challenge to permanence is unlikely to arise very often for rhymed verse in modern French poetry, since there is so little of it, and any approved anthology of French moderns reveals a general lapse of both rhyme and rhythm in the translation, if not also in the original. Wallace Fowlie's useful collection, *Mid-Century French Poets* (Grove Press,

1955), contains very few poems either rhymed or cadenced, and those few prose in his translation. The same is true of Willis Barnstone's large volume, *Modern European Poetry* (Bantam Classics, 1966), with thirteen poets represented in the French delegation—if they may be "represented" without our being offered the original poems. Free verse may have its rewards for translators, as well as perils that stricter forms know not of. But at least the yield does not have to be a tasteless graft, like free verse translations of alexandrines.

One of the best translators of contemporary French *vers libre* is Kenneth Rexroth. His own occasional verse, especially in the more Attic spirit, or when he stays close to D.H. Lawrence and resists performing, consciously or not, Bohemian, solicits a separate study, for then he may stand at the top of the heap. As a translator, with all his quirks and swerves and cliquish loyalties, from which his *Classics Revisited* is blessedly exempt, he is at best, that is, when he listens seriously with his good ear, a valuable presiding guide; at worst, worth more vitally than versions more "right": guide, what's more, not only to French, but also to Chinese, Japanese, Spanish, Italian, Latin, and ancient Greek poetry. Rexroth is "something else." Yet with all his erudition and his more than Fittsian flavor and flair, Rexroth, too, can sometimes belong with those who leave us guessing whether the free-verse translations are matched by the original, or whether the latter, after we have looked them up, will turn out to have been in meter, and only Rexroth to be free.

Should not freedom be asked, "freedom from what?" Meanwhile, free form, not only in translation, but also when no poem in another language is posing for its form in our own, may still be in subjection to its own dream of freedom: an artifice of emancipation, which may result in an impression of anarchy, even when we are alone with the original, but an anarchy whose hazards will compound rapidly when we attempt to breathe a form of life, bereft of pulse, into a foreign poem originally pulsating in metrical form. It could be contended that the mortal lot is the task of discovering the utmost freedom within the restraints of necessity, and then to transmute that necessity into an authentic illusion of freedom. "It is the forged feature finds me," writes Hopkins in a line applicable enough to "Purcell's divine genius" and just as much to himself. Forge the lines right and "it strikes like lightning to hear them sing." If they are not forged, the liberty will soon fall lame. We are to flourish a ceaseless guard, since always, open or lurking, impend the usurpations by which the naked atavism of poetic inspiration undermines the necessity to bless that inspiration with enduring rituals of poetic form.

There are many moderns, of course, who do not invariably write in *vers libre* and whose names will be missed from this book—Paul Claudel, Oscar Milosz, Léon-Paul Fargue, Valéry Larbaud, Francis Ponge, Anne Hébert (French Canadian), Jacques Reda, Jacques Dupin, Robert Marteau, Nicole Houssa (Belgian), Pierre Oster, Jude Stefan. I cannot attempt to go through the list to the end, even of those I have tried my own hand at, or who were made available too late to be translated properly in *this* book, especially with anything best representative of either Claude Vigée (b. 1921) or Robert Sabatier (b. 1923). It's lucky that some of the latter's poems, especially, have been so well done by the poet, X.J. Kennedy, and Vigée's "Blues," at least, by Patricia Terry. The hope is that all the "moderns" here represented, in one way or another, reach strongly into both the past and the future, as the best poets have always done. At least half of these moderns have died. Many of those whose impact I would certainly regard as modern were born before the turn of the century—Jammes, Apollinaire, Valéry, Pozzi, Saint-Pol-Roux, Supervielle, Cendrars, Jacob, Jouve, Eluard, Aragon, Reverdy. . .I am sure I must be forgetting some that are here, besides those that are not. None of them are particularly "controversial," although there must be debatable inclusions. On contemporaries, there has always been "open season," not to mention the rule of the coterie and the eclipse by neglect.

If the reader cares to make a check against his own list, it may divert him to note that for this anthologist the main line goes about as follows: Saint-Pol-Roux to Apollinaire to Supervielle to Reverdy to Eluard to Desnos to Char to Emmanuel to Bonnefoy to (hopefully) Alyn, with La Tour du Pin standing rather alone—a throw-back, some might say, with ancient lineage in his style as well as name; if there were not too many difficulties about it, one might say a sort of French Keats.

But if we are leading up to the conclusion that the mass of modern French poetry is precautionary for translators of lyrics into lyrics, we had better take a hard look at some of that poetry in the light of what excellence we are trying to recover and preserve for the future. Total renunciation of past heritage should arouse suspicion of future stamina. There have been instances, in France also, of poets compiling, in deference to the market, traditional anthologies whose every underlying value flouts the poet's own practise of poetry. If that practise is pursued with altered rules, or no rules at all, it seems odd simultaneously to imply recognition of rules on which the "canon" they are now sponsoring depends. Or is it "stuffy" to hope that criteria for ancients and moderns should have *some* principle of continuity, however bold the changes rung on it?

I follow the anthropologist Joseph Campbell in the conviction that the structure and innovation jointly necessary to life are reflected, respectively, in ritual and experiment, and ideally neither without the other; that art is ritual, and that as experiment deprives ritual of form, the latter must fail to serve its own primordial function. Thus the shattering of form is the reflection in reverse of its freezing.

Investigation of contemporary French verse leads to the guarded conclusion that failures in English poetry belonging to the sleazy and slipshod or the wild and woolly tend to be accentuated in French poetry, of which the rooted, perhaps innate genius favors, now as always, a rage for order, a strict grace, such as persists in Saint-Pol-Roux's "Golgotha," La Tour du Pin's "Children of September," Emmanuel's "Erotic," Bonnefoy's "To the Trees," Herlin's "Blanche deroule sa spirale. . .," Jaccottet's "Be Calm," or the child Sicaud's dying poems. All these blossom from restrictions unrestricted by the tyranny of impulse and of disheveled habit. None are dadaists, concretists, spatialists, psychic automatists, or any other-*ists* that exalt or exploit the incoherence of free association or unfiltered dreams. All are subject to the vision of a unitary principle, without which "anything goes." Hence they are not in line for trophies assigned to the least anticipated exhibition, such as scrambling lines in a hat, drafting ouija-board transcriptions, punctuating with plus or minus signs, printing in different colored inks, with different odors, and even more surprising variants of the substitution of typography for poetry, the most popular (and least unrewarding) being to leave lines blank.

With surrealism that lives up to its name, things should be different, for it was in a "unitary principle" that it took its rise: namely, a fresh attack on Wordsworth's old adversary, Custom, "Heavy as frost and deep almost as life." If, for a while at least, it helped to shake the pillars of French metrics, this was a side effect, neither unanimous nor concerted, and almost certainly transient, as suggested by the reversion, among surrealists also, to such reluctantly retreating anachronisms as the sonnet and the alexandrine, which survive powerfully in the poets just named and others, some of them with surrealist affiliations. If it is asked, why, then, the popular association of surrealism with unmetrics, the answer is, in part, that André Breton, first among those to employ *vers libre* undistinguishable from prose if printed as such, exerted an authority almost unchallenged, whilst himself possessed of a very limited gift for verse.[2] It is said that Cézanne had no great facility as a draftsman, so he had to find shortcuts, which, *faute de mieux,* changed the course of art! If the analogy between drawing and writing verse should not be pushed

that far, there are the examples of Jean Jacques Rousseau, Chateau-
briand, and Lautréaumont, in each of whom, without themselves
writing verse, the uprush of a new sensibility helped to sow widespread
movements in poetry.

Never detract from the intrepid in the departures of an André Breton,
a Marcel Duchamp, a George Antheil, all those who, each in his own
domain, had the guts to carry things too far; nor ever question that by
their very wounds and bankruptcies, lo and behold, the immediate
checks to their triumph may for the future historian manifest, like
Genghis Khan or the electric drill, a zigzag of progress in disguise. Yet
the future is not obliged to exalt the means of anarchy for the hope of
glory, nor will historians be so apt to blur the perils of chaos out of infatuation with its alluring mist. Yet a Mondrian is hardly misty.
Moreover, the thickest mist surrounds the future development of
achievements that we least suspect of promise. It is only sad that so
much genuine promise is obliterated by successors who, in seeking to be
original, lose that essence which should be entering the life-blood of the
future. Meanwhile, our visual art seems to speak for us more clearly than
our poetry and music, and both of the latter tend to depict more vividly
than they sing. But no doubt in all our arts we shall have to wait at least
a hundred years before we can trace distinctly the requisite hereditary
descent of *l'esprit nouveau* from *l'ancien régime.*

What, then, did surrealism as a movement really stand for? Answers
might do a lot worse than start with Breton's manifesto: "I believe in
the future resolution of . . . dream and reality into a kind of absolute reality, a Surreality" — affirmation true enough to the feeling that at some
time comes over most of us that we have been hypnotized to mistake the
waking consciousness for the whole of reality; that, as Blake says, "The
world of dreams is better far,/Beyond the light of the morning star":
better, that is, less as means of ends of ecstacy than as clues to a more entire being.

Now this in itself should serve to show that, as symbolism was ex-
clusively a school of art and literature, surrealism was not. The intention
of symbolists like La Tailhède, Moréas, Henri de Régnier, Charles Van
Lerberghe, as best seen in a master, such as Mallarmé or Valéry, was still
to arrest the mind of the reader by a finished effect of rhythm and imagery that would perpetuate an aesthetic experience, undefinable in any
other way: that is to say, any other definition of that experience would
be thin gruel compared with the azure statement of the poem. Breton
and his cohorts admitted no necessity of going to all that trouble to

create a dazzling crystal, sufficient unto its own perfection, which thereafter would ensure a specific and enduring enfranchisement of the imagination. For them, the "beauty" effected by this enfranchisement was of little or no concern, compared with the liberation itself (by any means whatever) of the subconscious mind, enslaved by reason and habit. You might say that the difference lay between "mensonges," dream-lies (truths for Breton), and "gloire de mensonges," dreams winnowed and worked over for their "beauty." Hence the besetting pitfall for all but the greatest of the symbolists was a self-conscious aestheticism, the idolization of "pure poetry," in constant danger of the "precious"; whilst the fixed tendency of surrealism, not concealed but loudly celebrated, is the exaltation of the haphazard and infatuation with the absurd. The symbolists could water poetry down to insipidity; but the surrealists can lose track altogether of what poetry is about, sacrificing, one after the other, rhyme, rhythm, harmony, controlled intensity, everything, in fact, that has contributed to harmony and radiance in the poetry of the past. And all this is deemed to serve the more emancipated subconscious by which dreams live. It was felt so effortlessly transporting to confuse poetry with dreams ("my poems, my dreams"); but even poems like Coleridge's "Kubla Khan" or Reverdy's "Longue Portée" represent the harmonious marriage of dreamwork and brainwork.

What the surrealists have left is *surprise,* which is fine if, like Apollinaire, you can supply the real thing, and fuse it with poetry; but as surprise becomes incorporated in a school, and all is surprise, then nothing is any more surprising. One wonders if imaginative anarchy could have been so hypostatized in a culture that had not kept order too hard and too long. The shock value of the result may have been psychologically propitious, but the arts are concerned with their own end product, and not with the means of getting there, except in so far as that end shines brightly enough to arouse a fruitful curiosity about means.

We have had collections of anti-poetry, consisting entirely of such fortuitous poems that renounce all claim on the future. These poems may be assessed by a simple parlor game. Participants volunteer substitute lines. If fifty percent of these lines are acceptable to the other players, the original poem qualifies. It must be admitted that an inconsistency arises when the original poet, having asserted that his imagery is wholly fortuitous and that it stands above elucidation, devotes twenty pages to the explanation of it, as Breton does to his poem, "Tournesol." There is nothing shy about the way Breton addresses himself to these difficulties;

he makes a virtue of them, claiming for the mere juxtaposition of incongruities (vine leaves clinging to a vehicle, or crossed legs in silk stockings flaring from a clover leaf in a shop window) the shock value in which he maintains that beauty consists. No one will deny the influence of these expressions of surrealism on the decorative arts, especially, perhaps, on window-dressing; but in regard to the body of poetry, what is overlooked is the inevitability of its cumulative disrepair by the exaltation of the haphazard, and if nothing of that poetry remains to treasure, what could there be to look forward to but more of the same?

There is a paradox of some poignancy here. On the one hand, no reader not addicted to styles of writing grown old and cold and weary, or an attitude to life that "takes things for granted," will rest easily in satirical sallies at the expense of any sincere reaction from the moribund; whilst, on the other, no attempt to reduce poetry to anything less than the harmonious product of an enhanced way of knowing can penetrate far or endure long. And such an enhancement was what surrealism began by seeking.

The *fin de siècle* undoubtedly did bring with it, as well it might, a growing boredom with many household names of French poetry, especially with the tribe of Vigny, Lamartine, and Hugo. Furthermore, it is certain that neither the innovations (dubiously such) of the symbolists—Albert Samain, Georges Rodenbach, Maurice Maeterlinck, Henri de Régnier—nor the rhythmical variations of a Rémy de Gourmont or a Paul Claudel, were able to do more than scratch the surface of this disenchantment. Compared with such poems as theirs, those of Eluard and Reverdy created a new atmosphere and began to open up a new world.

I say "began"; but I sometimes think that this new atmosphere was felt at its purest when at its earliest and least conscious of itself as a movement. It was felt, for example, in Rimbaud's "Mémoire," examined in the previous section ("The Future Drags Its Feet") or in Apollinaire's "If I should die. . .," where the "deluge of blood" contributes mysteriously, but without a trace of obscurantism, to the "sun's ray"; or in Saint-Pol-Roux's "Golgotha," where the "herds" of clouds stooping down on the fatal hill, and the adder's tongue in the soldiers' lance, and the stars playing dead so as less to resemble the thirty pieces of silver, are not just similes, old-time exercises in pathetic fallacy, but *dramatis personae* in a cosmic event.

These progenitors reveal that surrealism at its best excels on the frontiers of thought, where thought debouches on something beyond or outside thought; but at its worst, like most revolutionary movements of the arts in their initial stages, it develops among its satellites a disdain for form itself in the painting and sculpture, the drama and poetry which it affects to render obsolete or to which it bows insincerely. But whilst you may jettison as many forms as you like in pursuit of your surrealist "expansion of consciousness," you can't get rid of *form* without a *reductio ad absurdum* of the arts.

If the word "surrealism" is to mean anything, it has to mean "super-realism," in which case, the one in whom surrealism comes home is, par excellence, that pride of profane visionaries, Pierre Reverdy, whom André Breton and company would have liked to recruit, but who managed to shun their advances. Reverdy's was primarily a contemplative plunge, launched and prolonged in solitude. For him modern life is incessantly teetering on the brink of a fearful dissolution. It may be asked how this pessimism differs from the prose poems of Fargue and the impending dismalness of their twilit city, with counterparts of that somber range of color familiarized in Eliot's "Preludes" and Prufrock's foghung London. It differs in this: Reverdy affects us as a stranger visiting from a foreign land or another planet, his eyes taking in what he sees with the preternatural clarity given by contrast with an apocalyptic landscape. It is as though he remembers this other landscape but only hints at its existence: landscape of a world where his spirit moves at ease ("son esprit meut avec aisance"), a world which provides him, in Anthony Hartley's choice phrase, with "lyrical equivalents" for this one.

At the same time, this super-real illuminate, so loth to be tagged, was a finished poet, a sure voice with the fitting incantation at his command. "Chauffage Central" ("Central Heating"), here finally dropped as defying a satisfactory translation, sustains a mystery plot in a city *mise en scène*, whilst conveying undertones of elusive erotic frustration. This *tableau vivant* is fraught with emblems which don't have to be *of* anything, for instead, they *suggest* the hidden connections, both psychological and supernatural. The much anthologized "Son de Cloche" ("Sound of Clock"), also suppressed here for the same reason as "Central Heating," does not, in the approved science fiction style, flirt with the end of the world: in twelve short lines, it precipitates it. In "Toujours Là" ("Always There"), the line, unpunctuated like the rest, which reads in translation, "I know all the world each step you take I know" is both a sentence of love and an unobtrusively exaggerated boast with a firm metaphysical "ground." Notice how the last line of the poem gathers reflexive force from its (again unobtrusive) reversal of the first. "Encore l'Amour" ("Love Still"), with its circles within circles, is a poem which, while remaining graphic, dense, and crystalline, is unmistakably mystical. The velvet shadows of its intensely colored manifold gain definition from those baffling "evening bowls," which enfold it and in turn give a luminous depth to the surrounding mystery.

If the critical procedure which annotates special effects and stunning "one-liners" ("note this. . .note that") did not make me nervous, we would in the same manner examine poems of Eluard and Desnos. Eluard's "Ready for Reviving Kisses" and Desnos' "Landscape," particularly, are fine surrealist poems, the former for its tough, pensive mystery, giving great intensity to recollections of a woman's sensuality; the latter, in the tightest of sonnets, substantiating the nameless streets, the knotless cord, and precipitating the unexpected conception, which only *resists* intelligence, that things give forth light as they "stiffen" with advancing age.

There is one other surrealist, absurdist, supreme translator of self, not included here: pure, austere, "master of despair," Samuel Beckett, who projects his pencil-thin dot-and-dash unerringly into the unloving dark. He is French? Of course he is. Find lyrics there naked, his ritual repetition of elipses chiming more hypnotic than rhyme. Is he "alone in the doorway"? Do we hope for anyone to come and stand beside him? ". . .only what was it it said come and gone was that it something like that come and gone come and gone no one come and gone in no time gone in no time".[3]

Let these few instances serve, however inadequately, to sketch the recondite world of surrealist imagery, without attempting to track it down in younger poets. As to its melody and harmony, heard again but little noticed in Beckett, my confessed dislike of singling images out for attention works as an *a fortiori* for cadences, whether or not anticipated. We are speaking of something which, just as for Beckett, was basic for Pope, according to his lights: " 'Tis not enough the words give no offence,/The sounds must seem an echo to the sense."

Nothing said, here or hereafter, complains or laments but only records the present state of poetry, capable of being just as marvelous as it was three thousand years ago, for Homer; but the composition of poetry is nowadays more arduous, and the recognition of it, let alone discriminating appreciation of it, especially in America, endangered to the verge of extinction. This is largely for the following reason: that whether or not our poetry is supported by a metaphysical vision (generally not), in either case, our phase of time is witnessing an uprising, supported by thought weak or strong, of the associational, the essentially accidental, a phase actually aspiring to expand consciousness through the unconscious, fleetingly, delusively, as by the agency of certain drugs. This widespread tendency may be seen as in sharp contrast to what was of old the instinctive preference for the controlled, the unified, and the harmonious: to what had once aspired to expose itself to the frontal light of consciousness and, in its triumphs, had the effect of expanding the consciousness forever, as do the ceiling of the Sistine Chapel, the B-Minor Mass, and *King Lear;* or, more modestly, "Le Voyage," "Les Premières Communions," and "Le Cimetière Marin." One might even say it is about time for some "golden years" to return, if not for the world's great age to begin anew.

1. We are surrendering for their essential irrelevance most of those "biographical studies" which substitute the political implications, sexual divagations, and other personal ramifications of poets for the serious evaluative experience of their poetry: another twentieth century epidemic.

2. We ought to look beyond France and the limitations of a single eminent spokesman like Breton to account for the immense, proliferating confusion that besets practitioners of free verse, alike in French and English, though it is instructive that it is in the French language from which the phrase *vers libre* is borrowed. Behind this confusion is an absence of "vision." In Reverdy, for example, we see something of what happens when the vision is steady. It might pay us now to take a closer look at a formative example of what happens when it is fitful; and the closer to home we find this example, the better.

It is fair to suspect that the rejection of rhyme and measure has implications which include and transcend problems of translation, for this rejection may belong to a temporary phase-out of poetry itself, or at least to the liquidation of its more powerful capabilities: rejection which brought at first elation by its ease, but, as time went on, the inevitable signs of failing confidence, preceded by ennui. It is always best to estimate a movement by its best and happiest hierophants. In America this could well be William Carlos Williams, who soon found himself writing: "And we thought to escape rime/by imitation of the senseless/unarrangement of wild things—the stupidest rime of all." Only by now he had already lost the ability to behave very differently, and so would have been impelled, in any case, to make a virtue of necessity. Besides, his experiments seemed to be working out for him. They bore a superficial resemblance to the ideogram, as it was to be espoused by Pound, and to the haiku, as not yet properly understood, either for the emancipating opportunity conferred by its formal rigor, or for the saturation with its oblique meaning, that echoed, but more softly, the koan's explosive resolution of the "ball of doubt": anyway, no relation of Williams. But *Poetry* (Chicago) has bought his poems, and already English departments were finding it unsafe not to have degrees conferred on him. He had honesty, kindliness, great personal charm; and of such is the kingdom of the literary career. Finally, he could scold the contrite Conrad Aiken for leaving him out of his anthology!

This early hero of the recusants, after confessing to his unsuccess in imitating Keats, worked up and worked on his consequent disenchantment with rhyme and meter. "The birds don't sing in pentameters," Williams said, though he truly loved birds and must have known that they don't sing anyway, but "sing," i.e., flute, chirp, twitter, twee-twee, jug-jug, etc., almost without fail duplicating their cadences in the birds' own version of rhyme. But it was against all such *shapes* of cadence and repetition, however ancient, that this poet's warm disposition turned cold, all poems in the sonnet form being especially distasteful to him. I trust it is not unduly cynical to entertain the suspicion that the discouragements aroused by attempting to write stanzas resembling in mastery those of "The Eve of Saint Agnes" or "Le Cimetière Marin," engender a special susceptibility to the *ease* of lines which may commence and terminate as absentmindedly as (to borrow Housman's figure for certain conjectural emendations) "leaning against a post and spitting." The ease belongs in large part to mistaking the randomness of line length (a favorite length is one word long) for spontaneous inevitability—until this randomness itself became so endemic, both here and in France, as to affect with the growing immunity to surprise the response to all poems in *vers libre:* a continent of monotonous incontinence, the prairie wind from whose grey land mass bears a peculiar neutral odor, in a general twilight, calculated to dim the response to the more highly wrought verse of such poets as Reverdy, Eluard, Bonnefoy, Henley, Hopkins, Berryman, selected Pound and Roethke. It is getting steadily harder for aspirants to publication in the Little Magazines to rate a serious second look without conforming to this non-conformity, whilst few "solid scholars" of the best modern poetry have a discriminating ear for the sound of it.

The aversion to form, however dressed up, was first consolidated in the heady twenties, which in America mistook for a revolt within the art of poetry what was actually a revolt against poetry itself. The apostasy took the form of infatuation with the idea, legitimatized by Picasso and Braque and misapplied by Gertrude Stein, heroine of Williams, that, as paint is paint and not the thing painted, so words are words and not the thing described, although, of course, form and inspiration should be the very two inseparables.

One would think that, if words as such were to be our whole concern, this might be expected to accentuate their melody and harmony, their intrinsic sound and rhythmic life. Instead, the new verse, having squeezed out the rhythm, proclaimed the whimsical coruscation of *things,* as such, things relieved of thought (for it was curiously insistent on this thought-starvation, having borrowed the idea without understanding it from André Breton and his followers in France): marsh-lights of objective objects winking on and off in an air darkened or twilit of any such thought or implicaton as is found supremely in the haiku, those three-line painterly miniatures, strict as any sonnet or dizain, saturated with implication, sometimes far beyond the ostensible scene. With their seventeen-syllable plop, they are like stones dropped in water on a still evening (or Basho's immortal frog!), with widening circles on the surface. But lacking the capacity for, or interest in, nuances of oblique meaning, these western poets and critics who have done without thought and music would feel a discomfort with such absence of superficiality as belongs to the haiku. To expect depth was pedantic and to require song, flapdoodle.

The rigorous form which has been so influential in the poetry of Japan is there scarcely in need of vindication, only of intuitive penetration; and it is likewise with the subtle metaphysical vision behind the contrived collision of widely disparate *things* in André Breton and those of his followers who were able to understand his intention and implement it in poems more successful than his own. This intention has an ancient heritage, best expressed for me by Shelley, in his "Defence of Poetry," when he says that "poetry binds under its light yoke all irreconcilable things," but again, more recently, by the surrealist, Max Ernst, who weakens the force of the idea by ascribing it to the *"fortuitous* meeting of distant realities,"* so that one has to prefer the humbler expression of poor Carl Sandburg (or "Sandbag," as Pound used to call him): "the synthesis of hyacinths and biscuits." It is surely in the "fortuitousness" that the weakness must lie; else there could be no grounds for any word or line, rather than any other. The fortuitousness is the depth of volcanic ash, not the transforming eruption itself.

"Poems are made of things," writes Williams. (This and other references and quotations from W.C. Williams are drawn from his *Autobiography*, Random House, 1948.) But surely this is wrong. Poems are made of sounds, images, and incandescent ideas in the form of speech made memorable. And how can one "ensure permanence," such as Williams wisely demands, unless there be some prospect of instant quotability? And if one is able to ensure this independently of the strategies and stratagems by which poetry has been driven and controlled, in every language, at least for the last four thousand years, then one could but respond with an unaffected "Lots of luck!" but would have to concede that it does not seem to have been happening much.

Actually, it is the thing-orientation of everyday time process that poetry dissolves by shifting focus from these obstructed things and the ordinary space and time that contain them, to reveal these objects, not as the content but the substance itself of plenary space-time. The elastic cadences of poetry are prime agents in this shift. Just as on the artist's canvas the space within and between objects animates dead models to make vision live, so the poem's rhythm, by unchanneling the opaque partitions of meter, and flooding moribund continuities, opens up the fixed focus at the mercy of which we compound to exist, and while discouraging sterile haphazard, gives a changing wonder to the predictable.

End of unrepentant excursus on the late, well-loved W.C. Williams, considered, not as, in warmth of heart, manifest intelligence, and powers of observation, the fine poet he undoubtedly was, but as executioner of verse form; and the excursus itself not a digression, because it bears directly on what is to be our interpretation of the word "lyrical" in the sub-title of this book, and because it is a book which concerns the state of poetry, ancient and modern, rhymed or unrhymed.

3. "Alone in the doorway" is Beckett's phrase in *Malloy*. The rest is the last half of the closing speech of *That Time*, his most recent play to date. Both are given in *I Can't Go On I'll Go On: A Selection from Samuel Beckett's Work*, Grove Press, 1976. The publisher kindly granted permission to quote them.

Guillaume Apollinaire

1880 - 1918

Automne

Dans le brouillard s'en vont un paysan cagneux
Et son bœuf lentement dans le brouillard d'automne
Qui cache les hameaux pauvres et vergogneux

Et s'en allant là-bas le paysan chantonne
Une chanson d'amour et d'infidélité
Qui parle d'une bague et d'un cœur que l'on brise

Oh! l'automne l'automne a fait mourir l'été
Dans le brouillard s'en vont deux silhouettes grises

Si je mourais là-bas...

Si je mourais là-bas sur le front de l'armée
Tu pleurerais un jour o Lou, ma bien-aimée
Et puis mon souvenir s'éteindrait comme meurt
Un obus éclatant sur le front de l'armée
Un bel obus semblable aux mimosas en fleurs

Et puis ce souvenir éclaté dans l'espace
Couvrirait de mon sang le monde tout entier
La mer les monts les vals et l'étoile qui passe
Comme font les fruits d'or autour de Baratier

Souvenir oublié vivant dans toutes choses
Je rougirais le bout de tes jolis seins roses
Je rougirais ta bouche et tes cheveux sanglants
Tu ne vieillirais point toutes ces belles choses
Rajeuniraient toujours pour leurs destins galants

Le fatal giclement de mon sang sur le monde
Donnerait au soleil plus de vive clarté

Guillaume Apollinaire

1880 - 1918

Autumn

THERE in the mist a limping peasant goes
Slowly with his ox in the mist of Autumn
That hides the wretched hamlet from its woes

And on his way he sings down there a random
Song of love and infidelity
That speaks about a ring and a broken heart

Oh Autumn Autumn has made Summer die
There in the mist two shapes of grey depart

If I should die

IF I should die down there on the battlefront,
O you would cry, Lou, for a day lament,
And then my memory fade away as fade
Shells bursting down there on the battlefront,
That like mimosas blossoming explode;

And then this memory, blossoming in space,
Would cover with my blood the whole wide world,
The sea, the mountains, valleys, stars that pass,
As do round Baratier those fruits of gold.

Forgotten memory, living in all things,
I would redden the tip where your rosy bosom springs,
I would redden your mouth and your blood-red hair;
You never could grow old, these beautiful things
Will stay young for your lovers evermore.

The fatal deluge of my blood on the world
Would give the sun a more illustrious ray;

461

Aux fleurs plus de couleur plus de vitesse à l'onde
Un amour inouï descendrait sur le monde
L'amant serait plus fort dans ton corps écarté

Lou si je meurs là-bas souvenir qu'on oublie
— Souviens-t-en quelquefois aux instants de folie
De jeunesse et d'amour et d'éclatante ardeur —
Mon sang c'est la fontaine ardente du bonheur
Et sois la plus heureuse étant la plus jolie
O mon unique amour et ma grande folie!

La jolie rousse

ME voici devant tous un homme plein de sens
Connaissant la vie et de la mort ce qu'un vivant peut connaître
Ayant éprouvé les douleurs et les joies de l'amour
Ayant su quelquefois imposer ses idées
Connaissant plusieurs langages
Ayant pas mal voyagé
Ayant vu la guerre dans l'Artillerie et l'Infanterie
Blessé à la tête trépané sous le chloroforme
Ayant perdu ses meilleurs amis dans l'effroyable lutte
Je sais d'ancien et de nouveau autant qu'un homme seul pour-
     rait des deux savoir
Et sans m'inquiéter aujourd'hui de cette guerre
Entre nous et pour nous mes amis
Je juge cette longue querelle de la tradition et de l'invention
          De l'Ordre et de l'Aventure

Vous dont la bouche est faite à l'image de celle de Dieu
Bouche qui est l'ordre même
Soyez indulgents quand vous nous comparez
A ceux qui furent la perfection de l'ordre
Nous qui quetons partout l'aventure

Flowers would bloom fairer, waves be fiercer hurled;
A love unknown would fall down on the world,
The lover be stronger in your spread limbs' play.

Lou, if I die down there, forgotten wholly,
—Think of it sometimes in the moments of folly,
Moments of youth and love and blossoming fire—
My blood's the burning fountain of desire;
And be you happiest because most lovely,
My only love and oh! my splendid folly!

The pretty redhead*

You see me here, a man of steady mind,
Who knows this life and what of death is known,
Has proved love's pains and pleasures, even imposed
A little something sometimes of his thought,
Known several languages,
Traveled here and there,
Took in the war, Infantry, Artillery,
Wounded in head, trepanned under chloroform,
And lost his best friends in that frightful fight.
I knew once, now see clear what the gods can teach
        one man.
And, though not grieving for this war today,
Between us, just for us, my friends,
I judge that long dispute of custom and essay,
        Old order and a new adventurous life.

You, whose lovely mouth is made in the image divine,
Mouth that is order itself for evermore,
Be merciful when you compare us men
Who seek adventure everywhere
With those who were perfection of an order.

*All the first part of this poem is unrhymed, but it drifts into rhyme as it proceeds—emphatically in the last 15 lines: itself an instructive compulsion. (This one it seemed more natural in English to punctuate.)

Nous ne sommes pas vos ennemis
Nous voulons vous donner de vastes et d'étranges domaines
Où le mystère en fleurs s'offre à qui veut le cueillir
Il y a là des feux nouveaux des couleurs jamais vues
Mille phantasmes impondérables
Auxquels il faut donner de la réalité
Nous voulons explorer la bonté contrée énorme où tout se tait
Il y a aussi le temps qu'on peut chasser ou faire revenir
Pitié pour nous qui combattons toujours aux frontières
De l'illimité et de l'avenir
Pitié pour nos erreurs pitié pour nos péchés

Voici que vient l'été la saison violente
Et ma jeunesse est morte ainsi que le printemps
O Soleil c'est le temps de la Raison ardente
   Et j'attends
Pour la suivre toujours la forme noble et douce
Qu'elle prend afin que je l'aime seulement
Elle vient et m'attire ainsi qu'un fer l'aimant
   Elle a l'aspect charmant
   D'une adorable rousse

Ses cheveux sont d'or on dirait
Un bel éclair qui durerait
Ou ces flammes qui se pavanent
Dans les roses-thé qui se fanent

Mais riez riez de moi
Hommes de partout surtout gens d'ici
Car il y a tant de choses que je n'ose vous dire
Tant de choses que vous ne me laisseriez pas dire
Ayez pitié de moi

We are not your enemies.
We would inherit regions vast and strange
Where mystery in full flower is given to those who pluck.
There burn the fires with colors never seen,
A thousand airy shapes to fashion real.
There's kindness to explore, that endless land where silence
There's time to chase away or else restore.   [rules,
Pity for us whose fate it is to fight
On frontiers beyond the finite now.
Pity for our blunders, pity for our sins.

Here comes the summer, season of violence,
And youth is just as dead for me as Spring.
O sun, it is the time when Reason burns
          I wait
To follow still the shape erect and sweet
She takes to have me love but her alone.
She comes and draws me like a load-stone.
          She has the charming air
              Of girls when they are lovely with red hair.

Her hair is red-gold; you might say
A flash of lightning here to stay,
Or else those flames that spread
Bright plumes among tea roses when they fade.

But laugh, yes, laugh at me,
You people everywhere, especially here;
There are so many things I dare not say,
So many things you would not let me say.
Take pity on me.

L'adieu du cavalier

Aн Dieu! que la guerre est jolie
Avec ses chants ses longs loisirs
Cette bague je l'ai polie
Le vent se mêle à vos soupirs

Adieu! voici le boute-selle
Il disparut dans un tournant
Et mourut là-bas tandis qu'elle
Riait au destin surprenant.

Cors de chasse

Notre histoire est noble et tragique
Comme le masque d'un tyran
Nul drame hasardeux ou magique
Aucun détail indifférent
Ne rend notre amour pathétique

Et Thomas de Quincey buvant
L'opium poison doux et chaste
A sa pauvre Anne allait rêvant
Passons passons puisque tout passe
Je me retournerai souvent

Les souvenirs sont cors de chasse
Dont meurt le bruit parmi le vent

Tristesse d'une étoile

Une belle Minerve est l'enfant de ma tête
Une étoile de sang me couronne à jamais
La raison est au fond et le ciel est au faîte
Du chef où dès longtemps Déesse tu t'armais

The horse-soldier's farewell

Ah God! What fun war is
A chance to be lazy and sing
The wind is mixed with your sighs
And I have polished this ring

Goodbye! Gitty-up! and see!
He vanished round the bend
And died over there, while she
Laughed at such a queer end.

Hunting horns

Our story is noble and tragic
Resembling a tyrant's mask
No casual plot or magic
Or detail luck could ask
To make our love pathetic

Thomas de Quincey burning
To drink sweet opium chaste
Still for his poor Anne yearning
Pass on pass on with all things past
I shall still be backward turning

Memories are horns that hunters wind
Whose echoes die along the wind

Sadness of a star

A beautiful Minerva is offspring of my head
A star of blood to crown me to the end
Reason's within and heaven to overspread
My skull where, Goddess, long since you were armed

C'est pourquoi de mes maux ce n'était pas le pire
Ce trou presque mortel et qui s'est étoilé
Mais le secret malheur qui nourrit mon délire
Est bien plus grand qu'aucune ame ait jamais celé

Et je porte avec moi cette ardente souffrance
Comme le ver luisant tient son corps enflammé
Comme au cœur du soldat il palpite la France
Et comme au cœur du lys le pollen parfumé

Hence of my ills this wound was not the worst
Though almost mortal and became a star
But the secret doom that my derangement nursed
Lies deeper than mind ever hid before

I bear with me this burning pestilence
As the glowworm keeps his body wrapped in flame
As the heart of a soldier palpitates with France
And the heart of lilies with pollen perfume

Max Jacob

1876 - 1944

Villanelle

Dis-moi quelle fut la chanson
Que chantaient les belles sirènes
Pour faire pencher des trirèmes
Les Grecs qui lâchaient l'aviron.

Achille qui prit Troie, dit-on,
Dans un cheval bourré de son
Achille fut grand capitaine
Or, il fut pris par des chansons
Que chantaient des vierges hellènes
Dis-moi, Vénus, je t'en supplie
Ce qu'était cette mélodie.

Un prisonnier dans sa prison
En fit une en Tripolitaine
Et si belle que sans rançon
On le rendit à sa marraine
Qui pleurait contre la cloison

Nausicaa à la fontaine
Pénélope en tissant la laine
Zeuxis peignant sur les maisons
Ont chanté la faridondaine!...
Et les chansons des échansons?

Max Jacob

1876 - 1944

Villanelle

TELL me what was the theme
Of the song the sirens sang
When the Greeks at their rowlocks sprang
Out of the long trireme?

Achilles, they say, took Troy
With a stuffed horse for decoy.
He was a captain tall,
But a song could make him fall
By the Greek virgins sung.
I pray thee, Venus, tell me
What was that melody?

A prisoner in his cell
Made a tune in Tripoli
So sweet it could compel
His guards to heed the cry
Of her outside the wall
And send her godson home
Without a ransom.

Nausicaa at the fountain
Penelope weaving her skein
Zeuxis painting a mansion
Have sung fa-la-la the refrain!…
And the songs their songsters* fashioned?

Echansons, of course, means butlers. There was a chance to keep one
side of the pun this time, though not both.

471

Echos d'échos des longues plaines
Et les chansons des émigrants!
Où sont les refrains d'autres temps
Que l'on a chanté tant et tant?
Où sont les filles aux belles dents
Qui l'amour par les chants retiennent?
Et mes chansons? qu'il m'en souvienne!

Lorsque l'empereur…

LORSQUE l'empereur qui devait renoncer à la souveraineté
Reçut le message, il prenait le thé
Dans la chambre des femmes, près de son marcassin.
Il porta la main gauche au-dessus de son sein
Et prononça tout bas, avec beaucoup de zèle,
Des paroles embarrassées et immortelles:
"J'ai mal écrit les lois, il faut les arranger,
Voici qu'il est trop tard pour les changer!"
Les flammes du foyer étaient comme des griffes,
Le papier dans le feu tordait des logogriphes,
Et le vieux roi prit le chemin du monastère.
Cette retraite stupéfia l'univers.

Echoes of echoes: wide plains
For the lonely traveler's song.
Where are the ballads gone
That were sung again and again?
And the smiling girls who bring
Love back in songs without number?
And my own songs? Let me remember!

When the emperor...

WHEN the emperor, who had to renounce his sovereignty
Received the message, he was having tea
In the ladies' chamber, close to his young wild boar.
He placed his left hand on his heart and swore,
In a very deep voice, with considerable zeal,
Certain words, embarrassed but immortal:
"I have made the laws wrong, this must be arranged,
Though now it is too late to have them changed."
The fire appended signatures in flames,
Twisting the paper into anagrams,
And the old king took to the cloister, a recourse
Which stupified the universe.

Saint-Pol-Roux

1861 - 1940

Golgotha

Le ciel enténébré de ses plus tristes hardes
S'accroupit sur le drame universel du pic.
Le violent triangle de l'arme des gardes
A l'air au bout du bois d'une langue d'aspic

Parmi des clous, entre deux loups à face humaine,
Pantelant ainsi qu'un quartier de venaison
Agonise l'Agneau déchiré par la haine,
Celui-là qui donnait son âme et sa maison.

Jésus bêle un pardon suprême en la tempête
Où ses os tracassés crissent comme un essieu,
Cependant que le sang qui pleure de sa tête
Emperle de corail sa souffrance de Dieu.

Dans le ravin, Judas, crapaud drapé de toiles,
Balance ses remords sous un arbre indulgent,
— Et l'on dit que là-haut sont mortes les étoiles
Pour ne plus ressembler à des pièces d'argent.

Frappez et l'on vous ouvrira

A François Coulon

J'allais, plein d'Elle.
Son nom?
Le sais-je!
L'inconnue.
Existait-elle seulement?
Elle, sans plus.
J'allais...

Saint-Pol-Roux

1861 - 1940

Golgotha

THE sky blacked out by its most dismal herd
Stoops on the cosmic drama of the hill.
The soldiers' weapon with the violent head
To tip the shaft thrusts with an adder's kill.

Nailed down between two wolves with faces human,
The anguished Lamb is rent with odium
And palpitates as if a slice of venison,
This one who'd given up his soul and home.

A crowning pardon Jesus bleats in the storm,
Bones grating like a crank with that grim load,
While the blood weeping from his head is warm
With pearls of coral for a suffering God.

In the dark ravine, Judas, a shrouded toad,
Swings from a tree indulgent to his sins,
—And high above, they say, the stars are dead
That they might less resemble silver coins.

Knock and it shall be opened unto you

To François Coulon

I WAS going along, full of Her.
Her name?
Do I know it!
The unknown.
Did only she exist?
She and no more.
I was going along...

475

Je m'arrêtai devant une porte, la porte d'une chambre, dans un logis, en une ville, que je ne saurais retrouver, ni la ville, ni le logis, ni la chambre, ni la porte.

— La chambre est vide et personne jamais n'y demeura. M'avait dit, à la première marche de l'escalier, un nain si parvule que j'étais comme aveugle le bref instant de sa phrase.

Je frappe
Toc...
Rien!
Toc toc...
Rien encore!
J'insiste.
Toujours le silence
Elle doit pourtant, protestai-je, être là,
puisque je suis venu.
Sinon serais-je venu, moi qui ne vais nulle part?
Je suis certain qu'elle est derrière cette porte.
Qui donc?
Elle, encore une fois!
Mon attente me paraît exorbitante à la fin.
Je m'acharne.
Toc toc toc...
Cela fait un vacarme à réveiller le néant.
Toc toc toc toc...

Impatient, je regarde par le nombril de fer de la porte.
Au milieu de la chambre, une petite fille...
Toute nue...
Lui fallut-il pas le temps de naître?
J'eus tort de m'irriter.
J'espionne derechef.
D'un regard à l'autre la voici demoiselle déjà.
Lui fallait-il pas le temps de grandir?
Toute nue toujours, et que jolie!
Si je n'appréhendais d'abuser, discrètement je frapperais.
Mais lui faut-il pas le temps de se vêtir?
Attendons encore l'espace d'un coup d'œil.

I stopped in front of a door, the door of a room, in a lodging, which I would not know how to find again, neither the town, nor the lodging, nor the room, nor the door.

—The room is empty and no one ever lived there. It's on the first floor, I was told, by a dwarf so small that it was as if I was blind for the brief moment of his phrase.

> I knock.
> Toc...
> Nothing!
> Toc toc...
> Still nothing!
> I insist.
> Always the silence.
> But she ought, I protested, to be there,

since I have come.
If not would I have come, I who go nowhere?
I am certain that she is behind that door.
Who's there?
Once more, she!
I can't stand it any longer.
I muster all my resolve.
Toc, toc, toc...
That's a racket to arouse the void.
Toc, toc, toc, toc...

In my impatience I peer through the door's iron key-hole.
In the middle of the room, a little girl...
Completely naked...
Didn't she need time to be born?
I was wrong to be annoyed.
I spy once more.
Between one look and the next, here she is already a young
Didn't she need time to grow up?   [woman.
Always completely naked, and how pretty!
If I were not afraid of offending, I would knock discreetly.
But doesn't she need time to dress?
Let's just wait for another glance

477

Une chemise, blanche comme un lange, à présent la couvre.
Risquons un appel timide.
Toc...
Eh laissons-lui le loisir de se blottir en la tulipe d'une robe.
Enfin!
Dieu, la belle Dame!
Le moment est propice.
Toc toc...
La porte s'ouvre.
J'entre.

Now a chemise covers her, white like a diaper.
Let's risk a timid knock.
Toc...
Well! let's leave her the choice of cowering in the tulip of a
Finally!   [dress!
God, the beautiful woman!
The moment is propitious.
Toc, toc...
The door opens.
I enter.

(1889!)

*What is "lyrical" about the poem? In appearance so disarmingly
random, it arranges and articulates speech patterns in a manner that
progresses like stanzas. Such a structure could be not so much eccentric
as conducive to rewarding imitation, as I am sure it has been.

Jules Supervielle
1884 - 1960

Dans la forêt sans heures...

Dans la forêt sans heures
On abat un grand arbre.
Un vide vertical
Tremble en forme de fût
Près du tronc étendu.

Cherchez, cherchez oiseaux,
La place de vos nids
Dans ce haut souvenir
Tant qu'il murmure encore.

Prophétie

Un jour la Terre ne sera
Qu'un aveugle espace qui tourne,
Confondant la nuit et le jour.
Sous le ciel immense des Andes
Elle n'aura plus de montagnes,
Même pas un petit ravin.

De toutes les maisons du monde
Ne durera plus qu'un balcon
Et de l'humaine mappemonde
Une tristesse sans plafond.

De feu l'Océan Atlantique
Un petit goût salé dans l'air,
Un poisson volant et magique
Qui ne saura rien de la mer.

Jules Supervielle

1884 - 1960

Low in the timeless forest...

Low in the timeless forest
They fell a lofty tree.
An upright void surviving
Shaped like a shaft still trembles
Near the prone trunk it resembles.

Seek, birds, seek again
The place you built your nests,
Still in the memory soaring,
The vanished leaves still murmuring.

Prophecy

One day the earth will be
Just a blind space that turns,
Confounding night and day.
Beneath the Andes' sky
The hills will be no more,
Not even one ravine.

From all the homes of men
One courtyard will remain,
From all the maps of men
One sad, unfathomed pain.

Where once the Atlantic washed
A faint salt taste will linger;
One magic flying fish,
That knows of sea no longer.

D'un coupé de mil-neuf-cent-cinq
(Les quatre roues et nul chemin!)
Trois jeunes filles de l'époque
Restées à l'état de vapeur
Regarderont par la portière
Pensant que Paris n'est pas loin
Et ne sentiront que l'odeur
Du ciel qui vous prend à la gorge.

A la place de la forêt
Un chant d'oiseau s'élèvera
Que nul ne pourra situer,
Ni préférer, ni même entendre,
Sauf Dieu qui, lui, l'écoutera
Disant: "C'est un chardonneret."

Le matin du monde

ALENTOUR naissaient mille bruits
Mais si pleins encor de silence
Que l'oreille croyait ouïr
Le chant de sa propre innocence.

Tout vivait en se regardant,
Miroir était le voisinage,
Où chaque chose allait rêvant
A l'éclosion de son âge.

Les palmiers trouvant une forme
Où balancer leur plaisir pur
Appelaient de loin les oiseaux
Pour leur montrer leurs dentelures.

Un cheval blanc découvrait l'homme
Qui s'avançait à petit bruit,
Avec la Terre autour de lui
Tournant pour son cœur astrologue.

In a carriage of 1905
(Four wheels and yet no road!)
Three bygone girls, alive
As vapor lives, will ride,
Will gaze through some remote
Window (is Paris near?)
And only catch that queer
Odor of sky in the throat.

A forest once grew where
The song of a bird will rise,
With no one left to care,
Or know it's even there,
But God, who'll hear and muse,
"That is a goldfinch there."

The morning of the world

A THOUSAND scattered sounds were born
But all so full as yet of silence
The listener heard, he could have sworn,
The song of his own innocence.

Everything lived in its own self-gaze,
The neighborhood was one vast mirror,
Where every object dreamed of ways
A later time would come to flower.

The palm-trees, chancing on a form
By which to shiver in delight,
Summoned the birds from far to swarm
And witness such a lacy sight.

A white horse first discovered man,
Advancing quietly apart,
While Earth revolved, as if by plan,
Around his star-divining heart.

Le cheval bougeait les naseaux
Puis hennissait comme en plein ciel,
Et tout entouré d'irréel
S'abandonnait à son galop.

Dans la rue, des enfants, des femmes,
A de beaux nuages pareils,
S'assemblaient pour chercher leur âme
Et passaient de l'ombre au soleil.

Mille coqs traçaient de leurs chants
Les frontières de la campagne
Mais les vagues de l'océan
Hésitaient entre vingt rivages.

L'heure était si riche en rameurs,
En nageuses phosphorescentes
Que les étoiles oublièrent
Leurs reflets dans les eaux parlantes.

The horse's nostrils pricked with glee,
He whinnied like one borne on wing,
And ringed with unreality,
Gave himself up to galloping.

Women and children on the roads
Were looking for a soul to own;
Assembled beautiful as clouds,
They passed from shadow into sun.

A thousand cocks traced with their cries
The frontiers of those early lands,
Although the ocean waves would rise
And hover between twenty strands.

Time was so rich in men who rowed
And phosphorescent girls who swam,
The stars forgot the lights they sowed
In water—for the water's psalm.

Blaise Cendrars

1887 - 1961

Tu es plus belle que le ciel et la mer

QUAND tu aimes il faut partir
Quitte ta femme quitte ton enfant
Quitte ton ami quitte ton amie
Quitte ton amante quitte ton amant
Quand tu aimes il faut partir

Le monde est plein de nègres et de négresses
Des femmes des hommes des hommes des femmes
Regarde les beaux magasins
Ce fiacre cet homme cette femme ce fiacre
Et toutes les belles marchandises

Il y a l'air il y a le vent
Les montagnes l'eau le ciel la terre
Les enfants les animaux
Les plantes et le charbon de terre

Apprends à vendre à acheter à revendre
Donne prends donne prends

Quand tu aimes il faut savoir
Chanter courir manger boire
Siffler
Et apprendre à travailler

Quand tu aimes il faut partir
Ne larmoie pas en souriant
Ne te niche pas entre deux seins
Respire marche pars va-t'en

Je prends mon bain et je regarde
Je vois la bouche que je connais
La main la jambe l'œil
Je prends mon bain et je regarde

486

Blaise Cendrars

1887 - 1961

You are more beautiful than the sky and the sea

WHEN you love you must clear out
Leave your wife and leave your brat
Boy friend girl friend leave them pat
She-love quit and he-love quit
When you love you just clear out

The world is full of black-skinned folk
Men and women women and men
Look at all the lovely shops
Buggy for woman buggy for man
All the lovely heaps of stock

There is the air there is the wind
Mountains water heaven and earth
All the children animals
Plants and pit-coal from the earth

Learn to sell buy sell again
Give and take give and take

When you love you must know the trick
To sing and run and eat and drink
To whistle
And to learn to work

When you love you must clear out
Never snivel while you smile
Nestle not between two breasts
Take a deep breath then walk out

I take my bath and look about
I see that mouth I know so well
And then the hand and thigh and eye
I take my bath and look about

Le monde entier est toujours là
La vie pleine de choses surprenantes
Je sors de la pharmacie
Je descends juste de la bascule
Je pèse mes 80 kilos
Je t'aime

Couchers de soleil

Tout le monde parle des couchers de soleil
Tous les voyageurs sont d'accord pour parler des couchers de
      soleil dans ces parages
Il y a plein de bouquins où l'on ne décrit que les couchers de
      soleil
Les couchers de soleil des tropiques
Oui c'est vrai c'est splendide
Mais je préfère de beaucoup les levers de soleil
L'aube
Je n'en rate pas une
Je suis toujours sur le pont
A poil
Et je suis toujours seul à les admirer
Mais je ne vais pas les décrire les aubes
Je vais les garder pour moi seul

The whole world's always there for me
Life has plenty to amaze
I walk out of the pharmacy
There I've just stepped off the scales
Weigh my 80 kilos still
Je t'aime

Sunsets

EVERYONE talks about sunsets
In these parts travelers all agree to talk about sunsets
There are plenty of books in which nothing is described but
     sunsets
Tropical sunsets
Well, they're fine it's true
But I greatly prefer sunrises
The dawn
I don't misfire on a single one
I am always on deck
Stripped to the pelt
And I am always alone to admire them
But I am not going to describe these dawns
I am going to keep them for myself

Pierre-Jean Jouve

1887 - 1900

Ville atroce

VILLE atroce ô capitale de mes journées
O ville infortunée, livrée aux âmes basses!

En toi quand j'arrivais sur l'avenue de flamme
Parmi juin miroitante des millions d'objets
En marche et d'espérance verte et d'oriflammes
De la dure Arche de Triomphe qui coulait

O ville célébrée! je voyais ta carcasse
De pierre rose et rêve immense et étagée
Le Louvre couché sous la zone du grand ciel
Lilas, et l'infini des tours accumulées
La vaste mer bâtie de la paix et la guerre
Entassement gloire sur gloire! et mes douleurs
Surprises par le temps pleines de rire et songes
Quand l'Obélisque monte à la place d'honneur.

Navire humain sous le plus vaste des étés
Lourd de détresse auquel j'avais rangé ma rame
Où tue était la mer dans les calculs infâmes
Du typhon préparé par tous les mariniers;
Sage et mauvais navire et la poupe encor reine
Trop de clarté méchante allongeait tes bas flancs
Trop d'assurance avait ton entrepont de haine
Trop de mensonge aux mâts bleus blancs rouges flottants,
Tout le monde était mort, et sans voir j'allais ivre.

490

Pierre-Jean Jouve

1887 -

Atrocious city

ATROCIOUS city, throning all my days,
Ill-fated city, ceded to base souls!

When first I viewed the avenue of flame
Millions of objects in mid-June ablaze
The marching green with hope when then I came
The penants from the Arch of Triumph streamed

I saw your stony carcase tinted rose
Immense and tapering as if I dreamed,
The Louvre asleep beneath the lilac sky
The towers heaped to infinity it seemed,
A mighty ocean raised in peace and war
Glory surmounting glory, and my care
Surprised by time replete with laughter asleep;
The Obelisk soared proudly in the air.

In that vast summer I laid aside my oar
Grown heavy with grieving in the human ship
The sea grown silent in the evil grip
Of the typhoon brewed by every seaman there;
O ship both wise and wicked and the poop still queen
Too much mean light exposed your underside
Too much aplomb and hate in decks between
And lies to crowd your masts white blue and red,
All dead, and I went reeling blind and drunk.

Pierre Reverdy

1889 - 1960

Encore l'amour

Je ne veux plus partir vers ces grands bols du soir
Serrer les mains glacées des ombres les plus proches
Je ne peux plus quitter ces airs de désespoir
Ni gagner les grands ronds qui m'attendent au large
C'est pourtant vers ces visages sans forme que je vais
Vers ces lignes mouvantes qui toujours m'emprisonnent
Ces lignes que mes yeux tracent dans l'incertain
Ces paysages confus ces jours mystérieux
Sous le couvert du temps grisé quand l'amour passe
Un amour sans objet qui brûle nuit et jour
Et qui use sa lampe ma poitrine si lasse
D'attacher les soupirs qui meurent dans leur tour
Les lointains bleus les pays chauds les sables blancs
La grève où roule l'or où germe la paresse
Le môle tiède où le marin s'endort
L'eau perfide qui vient flatter la pierre dure
Sous le soleil gourmand qui broute la verdure
La pensée assoupie lourde clignant des yeux
Les souvenirs légers en boucles sur le front
Les repos sans réveil dans un lit trop profond
La pente des efforts remis au lendemain
Le sourire du ciel qui glisse dans la main
Mais surtout les regrets de cette solitude
O cœur fermé ô cœur pesant ô cœur profond
Jamais de la douleur prendras-tu l'habitude

Pierre Reverdy

1889 - 1960

Love still

FOR those great evening bowls I would leave no more
To shake the frozen hands of the nearest shadows
I can no longer leave these airs of despair
Nor reach those larger circles waiting for me
Yet it is towards those formless faces that I go
Towards those moving lines that always close me in
Those lines my eyes can trace in what's unsure
Those landscapes blurred and those mysterious days
Beneath the cover of times greyed when love goes past
A love without an object burning night and day
And wearing out its lamp my weary breast
To claim the sighs which in their turn all die
Blue distances warm countries gleaming sands
The strands where waves roll gold and indolence grows
The drenched pier where the shore-leave sailors drowse
The treacherous water come to caress hard stone
Beneath the gluttonous sun browsing on the grass
Thought drowsing heavy under the half-closed eyes
Ephemeral memories curling on the brow
Rest without waking in a bed too deep
Steep slope of effort postponed till tomorrow
The smile of heaven slipping through the hand
But most the sorrows of this being alone
O closed heart heavy heart O heart too deep
You never will learn to get used to pain

Toujours là

J'ai besoin de ne plus me voir et d'oublier
De parler à des gens que je ne connais pas
De crier sans être entendu
Pour rien tout seul
Je connais tout le monde et chacun de vos pas
Je voudrais raconter et personne n'écoute
Les têtes et les yeux se détournent de moi
Vers la nuit
Ma tête est une boule pleine et lourde
Qui roule sur la terre avec un peu de bruit

Loin
Rien derrière moi et rien devant
Dans le vide où je descends
Quelques vifs courants d'air
Vont autour de moi
Cruels et froids
Ce sont des portes mal fermées
Sur des souvenirs encore inoubliés
Le monde comme une pendule s'est arrêté
Les gens sont suspendus pour l'éternité

Un aviateur descend par un fil comme une araignée
Tout le monde danse allégé
Entre ciel et terre
Mais un rayon de lumière est venu
De la lampe que tu as oublié d'éteindre
Sur le palier
Ah ce n'est pas fini
L'oubli n'est pas complet
Et j'ai encore besoin d'apprendre à me connaître

Always there

I NEED to see myself no more and to forget
To speak to those I do not know
To cry without being heard
For nothing all alone
I know everyone each of your steps I know
I want to tell my tale and no one listens
Their heads their eyes all turn away from me
Towards the night
My head is a ball full and heavy
Which rolls on the earth with a little noise

Afar
Nothing behind me and nothing before
In the void where I sink lower
Some lively currents of air
Blow to enfold me
Cruel and cold
They are from doors half shut
On memories still not forgot
The world like a pendulum is stopped
The people are eternally afloat

A flier by a spider web is landing
Everyone is feeling lighter dancing
Between sky and earth
But a ray of light came down
From the light you forgot to put out
On the landing
Ah! it is not finished
Forgetting not complete
And I still have this need to know myself

Longue portée

Poissons dorés surpris dans les mailles du vent
Catapultes de la lumière
Regains de soif lancés dans tous les coins
Détentes révolues des appétits déteints
Tout se mêle dans les remous des ondes prisonnières
La poitrine résonne comme un sol creux
Il y a des ombres sur le buvard de tes joues
Et des claquements de porcelaine bleue
Par-dessus tous les toits aux lames de violettes
Un rouge de valeur plus dense sans écho
Un sang plus étendu au flanc de la colline
Des oiseaux migrateurs sans orientation
Et tous ces hommes morts sans rime ni raison
Tant de cœurs desséchés
Sans plomb
Comme des feuilles

Pour vivre ici

Je fis un feu, l'azur m'ayant abandonné,
Un feu pour être son ami,
Un feu pour m'introduire dans la nuit d'hiver,
Un feu pour vivre mieux.

Je lui donnai ce que le jour m'avait donné:
Les forêts, les buissons, les champs de blé, les vignes,
Les nids et leurs oiseaux, les maisons et leurs clés,
Les insectes, les fleurs, les fourrures, les fêtes.

Je vécus au seul bruit des flammes crépitantes,
Au seul parfum de leur chaleur;
J'étais comme un bateau coulant dans l'eau fermée,
Comme un mort je n'avais qu'un unique élément.

Long range

GOLDEN fish surprised in the meshes of the wind
Catapults of light
Revivals of thirst in every corner found
Restraints that reached their end in failing appetites
All mingle in the eddy of imprisoned waves
The chest reverberating like a hollow ground
There are shadows on the firm down of your cheeks
And clatter of blue porcelain falling down
While over the roofs with their edges of violet
A scarlet more intense without an echo
A blood more widely spread on the slope of the hill
The migratory birds not knowing where to go
And all these men dead without rhyme or reason
So many dried out hearts
Weightless
Like leaves

To live here

I MADE a fire, the blue sky having left me,
A fire to be its friend,
A fire so I could enter the night of winter,
A fire to live better.

I gave it what the day had given me:
The forests, hedges, fields of wheat, the vines,
Nests and their birds, the houses and their keys,
The insects, flowers, and furs, the festivals.

I lived with only the sound of crackling flames,
And only with the perfume of their heat;
I was like a ship going down in closed straights,
Like a dead man I had no element but one.

Jean Cocteau
1889 - 1963

Plain-Chant (No. 1)

J'AI, pour tromper du temps la mal-sonnante horloge,
 Chanté de vingt façons.
Ainsi de l'habitude évitai-je l'éloge,
 Et les nobles glaçons.

C'est peu que l'habitude une gloire couronne
 Lorsqu'elle a vieux le chef;
Il faut qu'un long amour souvent le cœur étonne
 A force d'être bref.

Alors, jeune toujours, libre de récompenses,
 Et son livre à la main,
On devine les jeux, les manœuvres, les danses,
 Qui formeront demain.

Voilà pourquoi la mort également m'effraye,
 Et me fait les yeux doux;
C'est qu'une grande voix murmure à mon oreille:
 Pense à mon rendez-vous;

Laisse partir des gens, laisse fermer la porte,
 Laisse perdre le vin,
Laisse mettre au sépulcre une dépouille morte;
 Je suis ton nom divin.

Jean Cocteau

1889 - 1963

Plain Song (No. 1)

I SANG to fool the evil-sounding clock
    In twenty different ways
And so I have avoided all the stock
    Renown and rigid praise.

Who cares if stock tricks win a handsome crown
    For heads grown old and deaf?
Long lasting love will frequently astound
    The heart by being brief.

Then, young for ever, free of all rewards,
    You venture, book in hand,
Guessing the games, drills, dances, accolades
    Tomorrow will demand.

That is why death creeps up so on my fear
    And makes his glances sweet,
With such a great voice murmuring in my ear:
    Think now of when we meet;

Let people all go home and shut the door,
    Let perish the turned wine,
Let keep a carcass from the tomb no more;
    I am your name divine.

Paul Eluard
1895 - 1952

Prête aux baisers résurrecteurs

PAUVRE je ne peux pas vivre dans l'ignorance
Il me faut voir entendre et abuser
T'entendre nue et te voir nue
Pour abuser de tes caresses

Par bonheur ou par malheur
Je connais ton secret par cœur
Toutes les portes de ton empire
Celle des yeux celle des mains
Des seins et de ta bouche où chaque langue fond

Et la porte du temps ouverte entre tes jambes
La fleur des nuits d'été aux lèvres de la foudre
Au seuil du paysage où la fleur rit et pleure
Tout en gardant cette pâleur de perle morte
Tout en donnant ton cœur tout en ouvrant tes jambes.

Tu es comme la mer tu berces les étoiles
Tu es le champ d'amour tu lies et tu sépares
Les amants et les fous
Tu es la faim le pain la soif l'ivresse haute

Et le dernier mariage entre rêve et vertu.

La courbe de tes yeux…

LA courbe de tes yeux fait le tour de mon cœur,
Un rond de danse et de douceur,
Auréole du temps, berceau nocturne et sûr,
Et si je ne sais plus tout ce que j'ai vécu
C'est que tes yeux ne m'ont pas toujours vu.

Paul Eluard

1895 - 1952

Ready for reviving kisses

I MAY be poor but cannot live in ignorance
I have to see to hear and to abuse
Hear you nude and see you nude
Only to abuse your caresses

In happiness or hurt
I know your secret by heart
All the entries of your empire
Door of your eyes door of your hands
Of your breasts and mouth where each tongue melts

And the door of time opened between your legs
Flower of summer nights with the lips of lightning
At the threshold of the country where the flower laughs and
Even in guarding that pallor of dead pearl   [weeps
Even in giving your heart even in opening your legs

You are like the sea you cradle the stars
You are the field of love you bind and cleave
The lovers and the mad
You are hunger and bread thirst and high drunkenness

And the last marriage between virtue and dream.

The curve of your eyes...

THE curve of your eyes makes the tour of my heart,
A round of dance and of sweetness afoot,
Halo of time, night cradle past doubt,
If I know no more of all I have been
It's because by your eyes not always seen.

Feuilles de jour et mousse de rosée,
Roseaux du vent, sourires parfumés,
Ailes couvrant le monde de lumière,
Bateaux chargés du ciel et de la mer,
Chasseurs des bruits et sources des couleurs,

Parfums éclos d'une couvée d'aurores
Qui gît toujours sur la paille des astres,
Comme le jour dépend de l'innocence
Le monde entier dépend de tes yeux purs
Et tout mon sang coule dans leurs regards.

Mauvaise nuit bon jour

JE rêve j'obéis aux ordres de la nuit
Je change le duvet de ma naissance en plomb
Je fais d'un pur cristal un sourd dans les ténèbres

Le silence s'accroît au long des branches mortes
En rêve la blancheur de ta chair me calcine.

*

Le soleil entre au cœur de la chambre tremblante
Voici double au grand jour notre amour qui s'embrasse
Et sa longue caresse nous fait tout comprendre

Le feu frais de l'aurore est comblé d'un seul corps
Le tien je suis assez ébloui pour y croire.

Leaves of the day and moss drenched with dew,
Reeds moved by the wind, smiles smelling of you,
Wings that cover the world with light,
Ships with the sky and the sea for freight,
Hunters of sound and sources of hue,

Perfumes hatched from a nest of dawns
Which always sleep on the straw bed of stars,
As the day depends on innocence
The whole world depends on your pure eyes
And all my blood streams in their glance.

Bad night good day

I DREAM I obey the commands of night
I change the pillow of my birth to lead
I make of pure crystal one deaf in the dark

The silence grows along branches dead
Your white flesh burns me to ash in dream.

*

Sun enters the heart of the trembling room
The clasp of our double love here in broad day
And its long caress makes us understand all

The fresh fire of dawn is heaped in one form
Your body I'm dazzled enough to believe.

Critique de la poésie

C'est entendu je hais le règne des bourgeois
Le règne des flics et des prêtres
Mais je hais plus encore l'homme qui ne la hait pas
Comme moi
De toutes ses forces.

Je crache à la face de l'homme plus petit que nature
Qui à tous mes poèmes ne préfère pas cette *Critique
de la poésie.*

Criticism of poetry *

I HATE, of course, the reign of the bourgeois
The reign of cops and priests
But I hate still more the man who does not hate it
Like me
With all his strength.

I spit in the face of that sub-natural man
Who of all my poems does not like best this *Criticism
of Poetry.*

*It might gratify the poet to learn that I have thrown out fifty much
better poems of his translated by me, in deference to this preference,
which is more a spasm than a poem and is, of course, among all those
which present no challenge to a translator. It should invite comparison
also with the poems included in Eluard's own admirable *Première
Anthologie Vivante de la poésie du passé,* which is considerably more
conservative than mine. At least the present poem could be said to
conform with one interpretation of the requirement, valid when understood, that a poem be *about* nothing but itself!

Jacques Prévert

1900 - 1900

Paris at night

Trois allumettes une à une allumées dans la nuit
La première pour voir ton visage tout entier
La seconde pour voir tes yeux
La dernière pour voir ta bouche
Et l'obscurité tout entière pour me rappeler tout cela
En te serrant dans mes bras.

Pour toi mon amour

Je suis allé au marché aux oiseaux
Et j'ai acheté des oiseaux
Pour toi
mon amour
Je suis allé au marché aux fleurs
Et j'ai acheté des fleurs
Pour toi
mon amour
Je suis allé au marché à la ferraille
Et j'ai acheté des chaînes
De lourdes chaînes
Pour toi
mon amour
Et puis je suis allé au marché aux esclaves
Et je t'ai cherchée
Mais je ne t'ai pas trouvée
mon amour

Jacques Prévert

1900 -

Paris at night

THREE matches one by one struck in the night
The first to see your face there all complete
The second to see your eyes
The last to see your mouth
And endless blackness to bring back these forms·
And hold you in my arms.

For you my love

I WENT to the bird market
And I bought some birds
For you
my love
I went to the flower market
And I bought some flowers
For you
my love
I went to the scrap iron market
And I bought some chains
Heavy chains
For you
my love
And then I went to the slave market
And I looked for you
But I did not find you
my love

Robert Desnos

1900 - 1945

Le paysage

J'avais rêvé d'aimer. J'aime encor mais l'amour
Ce n'est plus ce bouquet de lilas et de roses
Chargeant de leur parfums la forêt où repose
Une flamme à l'issue de sentiers sans détours.
     J'avais rêvé d'aimer. J'aime encor mais l'amour
Ce n'est plus cet orage où l'éclair superpose
Ses bûchers aux châteaux, déroute, décompose,
Illumine en fuyant l'adieu du carrefour.
     C'est le silex en feu sous mon pas dans la nuit,
Le mot qu'aucun lexique au monde n'a traduit,
L'écume sur la mer, dans le ciel ce nuage.
     A vieillir tout devient rigide et lumineux,
Des boulevards sans noms et des cordes sans nœuds.
Je me sens me roidir avec le paysage.

Le coteau

Derrière ce coteau la vallée est dans l'ombre,
L'odeur du bois qui flambe et de l'herbe parvient
Jusqu'au désert présent, lueurs et rocs sans nombre,
Avec des cris d'enfants et des abois de chien.

Les cris sont déchirants de l'enfant qu'on égorge.
Le chien appelle en vain. Un sort est sur ces lieux.
Rien n'est réel ici que cette odeur de forge
Qui nous berce et nous saoûle et nous rougit les yeux.

L'aube peut revenir et le soleil nous prendre.
En vain: les aboiements et les cris perceront
L'épaisseur de la nuit, l'épaisseur de la cendre
Qui remplissent nos cœurs, qui brûlent sous nos fronts.

508

Robert Desnos

1900 - 1945

The landscape

I HAVE dreamed of loving. I still do, but love
No longer is the bunch of lilac and roses
Disturbing with perfume the forest which discloses
The path without turnings and the flame thereof.

    I have dreamed of loving, but the love I have
No longer is that lightning which imposes
Its pyres on castles, waylays, discomposes,
Illumines in the square the farewell wave.

    It's the flint on fire beneath my feet in the night,
The word no lexicon in the world got right,
The foam on the sea, the cloud against the sky.

    In aging all things stiffen and give forth light,
Streets lose their names, string comes without a knot.
I feel myself grow stiff with the scenery.

The hill

BEHIND this hill the valley lies in shadow;
The burning of the grass and timber smells
As far as this desert, countless rocks aglow;
There are cries of children and a dog that howls.

The cries of the slaughtered child are rending the air.
The dog calls in vain. A fate is on places like these.
Nothing is real here but the smell of the fire
Which lulls and gluts us while it reddens our eyes.

The dawn can come again and the sun find us.
In vain: the howls, the cries will pierce and raze
The thickness of night, the thickness of the cinders
That choke our hearts and burn beneath our brows.

Raymond Queneau

1903 - 1976

Je crains pas ça tellment…

JE crains pas ça tellment la mort de mes entrailles
et la mort de mon nez et celle de mes os
Je crains pas ça tellment moi cette moustiquaille
qu'on baptisa Raymond d'un père dit Queneau

Je crains pas ça tellment où va la bouquinaille
les quais les cabinets la poussière et l'ennui
Je crains pas ça tellment moi qui tant écrivaille
et distille la mort en quelques poésies

Je crains pas ça tellment La nuit se coule douce
entre les bords teigneux des paupières des morts
Elle est douce la nuit caresse d'une rousse
le miel des méridiens des pôles sud et nord

Je crains pas cette nuit Je crains pas le sommeil
absolu Ça doit être aussi lourd que le plomb
aussi sec que la lave aussi noir que le ciel
aussi sourd qu'un mendiant bêlant au coin d'un pont

Je crains bien le malheur le deuil et la souffrance
et l'angoisse et la guigne et l'excès de l'absence
Je crains l'abîme obèse où gît la maladie
et le temps et l'espace et les torts de l'esprit

Mais je crains pas tellment ce lugubre imbécile
qui viendra me cueillir au bout de son curdent
lorsque vaincu j'aurai d'un œil vague et placide
cédé tout mon courage aux rongeurs du present

Un jour je chanterai Ulysse ou bien Achille
Enée ou bien Didon Quichotte ou bien Pansa
Un jour je chanterai le bonheur des tranquilles
les plaisirs de la pêche ou la paix des villas

Raymond Queneau

1903 - 1976

I'm not so scared of that…

I DO not fear the death of visceral me
death of my bones and death of my poor nose
I'm not so scared to end mosquito me
baptised Raymond Queneau as a father chose

I'm not so scared where stacks of books may go
secondhand dealers rest-rooms dust and boredom
I'm not so scared I too who scribble so
distilling death into my verse at random

I'm not so scared of that The night will flow
between the scurvy eyelids of the dead
honeyed meridian of the polar snow
as gentle as a readhead's touch in bed

I don't fear night I don't fear absolute sleep
It must be heavy as lead and lava-dry
dark as the sky and deaf as beggars who keep
bellowing at bridge corners where they ply

My real fear is mischance bereavement pain
anguish bad luck and being away too long
I fear the fat abyss where ailments reign
and time and space and all the spirit's wrongs

but not so much that mournful imbecile
who'll come to gather me on his toothpick
when I am sunk and with a vague calm smile
yield to the rats of the present all my luck

One day I'll sing Ulysses even Achilles
Quixote and Panza   Dido and her Aeneas
One day I'll sing of tranquil women's bliss
the joys of fishing and the peace of villas

Aujourd'hui bien lassé par l'heure qui s'enroule
tournant comme un bourrin tout autour du cadran
permettez mille excuz à ce crâne — une boule —
de susurrer plaintif la chanson du néant

Today I'm sick of time that is self-wound
Circling like some old nag the same old dial
pardon a thousand times this numbskull round
for whispering the song of nothing without a smile

Pierre Seghers

1906 - 1900

Racines

QUEL est cet homme universel qui se cache dans les racines
Quel est ce si profond secret vivant au cœur de ces Dieux
    morts
Et qui, dans le silence des nuits anciennes d'avant l'homme
Appelle et reconstruit le monde par le miracle de la voix?

Forêts, forêts crépues, hautes cascades du déluge
Chairs molles mêlées d'eaux qui deviendrez des continents
Iles, qui dérivez sur des fleuves énormes,
Caillots de boues et d'arbres verts au fil des veines couleur
    d'argent,

Quelles forces vous ont fixées et quelles forces vous arrachent,
Qui vous construit et vous divise, quel architecte fou d'oiseaux
Délire et crée, avec de la vase et des germes,
Un univers où les forêts par pans entiers tombent dans l'eau?

Racines, vous réconciliez la mort fugitive et les marées
Et vos monstres occasionnels n'expriment rien que l'accident,
Il y a mieux en vous que des masques et des parures
L'histoire de la mer, de la terre et du temps.

Pierre Seghers

1906 -

Roots

WHAT is that universal man who hides in the roots
What is that secret so deep in the heart of those dead Gods
And who, in the silence of ancient nights before man,
Calls and rebuilds the world by the miracle of the voice?

Forest on flocculent forest, deluging cascades,
Soft flesh stirred by waters to be continental plains,
Islands tossed into being on the crest of gigantic streams,
Mud clots, green trees with their current of silver veins,

What forces fixed you and what forces snatched you away,
Who builds you and plans you, what mad designer of birds
Raves on and fashions, with the slime and germs,
A universe where hummocks of jungle collapse in the floods?

Roots, while you reconcile fugitive death and tides
And your random monsters signify nothing but whim,
There's something better in you than pageant and mask:
The history of the sea, of the earth, and of time.

Réné Char

1907 - 1900

Les inventeurs

Ils sont venus, les forestiers de l'autre versant, les inconnus de
    nous, les rebelles à nos usages.
Ils sont venus nombreux.
Leur troupe est apparue à la ligne de partage des cèdres
Et du champ de la vieille moisson désormais irrigué et vert.
La longue marche les avait échauffés.
Leur casquette cassait sur leurs yeux et leur pied fourbu se
    posait dans le vague.
Ils nous ont aperçus et se sont arrêtés.
Visiblement ils ne présumaient pas nous trouver là,
Sur des terres faciles et des sillons bien clos,
Tout à fait insouciants d'une audience.
Nous avons levé le front et les avons encouragés.

Le plus disert s'est approché, puis un second tout aussi
    déraciné et lent.
Nous sommes venus, dirent-ils, vous prévenir de l'arrivée
    prochaine de l'ouragan, de votre implacable adversaire.
Pas plus que vous, nous ne le connaissons
Autrement que par des relations et des confidences
    d'ancêtres.
Mais pourquoi sommes-nous heureux incompréhensiblement
    devant vous et soudain pareils à des enfants?

Nous avons dit merci et les avons congédiés.
Mais auparavant ils ont bu, et leurs mains tremblaient, et leurs
    yeux riaient sur les bords.
Hommes d'arbres et de cognée, capables de tenir tête à
    quelque terreur mais inaptes à conduire l'eau, à aligner
    des bâtisses, à les enduire de couleurs plaisantes,
Ils ignoreraient le jardin d'hiver et l'économie de la joie.

Réné Char

1907 -

*The discoverers**

THEY have come, the rangers from the opposite slope, people
    unknown to us, rebels against our ways,
They have come in numbers.
Their company appeared at the line between the cedars
And the field of the old harvest, nowadays watered and green.
Their long trek had made them hot.
Their caps came over their eyes and their tired feet fell at
    odds.
They saw us and they stopped.
Clearly they did not expect to find us there,
On easy lands and tidy well-ploughed furrows,
Not caring who might talk to us.
We raised our heads and said hello.

Their spokesman came towards us, then another just as
    rootless and slow.
We have come, they said, to warn you that the hurricane
    approaches, that remorseless enemy.
We know no more than you about it,
Except by what they say and what our fathers said.
But why are we so strangely happy with you and suddenly
    like children?

We spoke our thanks and let them go away.
But first they drank, and their hands trembled, and their eyes
    smiled over the cups.
Men of the tree and the axe, able to keep their heads in a
    terror, but no good at piping water, lining up bricks and
    mortar, or plastering them with pleasant colors,
They would not know the winter garden and the economy of
    joy.

*This influential poem comes closer to unmeasured measures than any
other in the book. At the end, like "La Jolie Rousse" (see p. 462), it
more than hankers after rhyme, of which Char is a master (see next
poem).

Certes, nous aurions pu les convaincre et les conquérir,
Car l'angoisse de l'ouragan est émouvante.
Oui, l'ouragan allait bientôt venir;
Mais cela valait-il la peine que l'on en parlât et qu'on
    dérangeât l'avenir?
Là où nous sommes, il n'y a pas de crainte urgente.

Complainte du lézard amoureux

N'EGRAINE pas le tournesol,
Tes cyprès auraient de la peine,
Chardonneret, reprends ton vol
Et reviens à ton nid de laine.

Tu n'es pas un caillou du ciel
Pour que le vent te tienne quitte,
Oiseau rural; l'arc-en-ciel
S'unifie dans la marguerite.

L'homme fusille, cache-toi;
Le tournesol est son complice.
Seules les herbes sont pour toi,
Les herbes des champs qui se plissent.

Le serpent ne te connaît pas,
Et la sauterelle est bougonne;
La taupe, elle, n'y voit pas;
Le papillon ne hait personne.

Il est midi, chardonneret.
Le séneçon est là qui brille.
Attarde-toi, va, sans danger:
L'homme est rentré dans sa famille!

L'écho de ce pays est sûr.
J'observe, je suis bon prophète;

Doubtless they could have been convinced and overcome,
For it's a terrible thing, this hurricane scare.
Yes, it was coming soon, the mighty storm;
But was it worth the pain of all this talk and troubling the
    days to come?
There where we are, there is no urgent fear.

Complaint of the lovesick lizard

NEVER pluck the sunflower,
This will give your cypress pain,
Goldfinch, fly about once more,
To your nest of wool return.

Country bird, no pebble you
In the sky, for wind to treat
Like a pebble; rainbow hue
Blends the sky and marguerite.

Hide now, man's for shooting you;
Sunflower his accomplice.
Only grass is safe for you,
Fields to fold you deep in grass.

Serpent doesn't notice you,
Grasshopper can only scold;
Mole is blind, can't look at you;
Butterfly loves all the world.

Goldfinch, it's the height of noon.
See, the ragwort is in bloom.
There's no danger; linger on;
Man is now returning home!

Echo in this land tells all,
I'm a seer with second sight;

Je vois tout de mon petit mur,
Même tituber la chouette.

Qui, mieux qu'un lézard amoureux,
Peut dire les secrets terrestres?
O léger gentil roi des cieux,
Que n'as-tu ton nid dans ma pierre!

Pyrénées

MONTAGNE des grands abusés,
Au sommet de vos tours fièvreuses
Faiblit la dernière clarté.

Rien que le vide et l'avalanche,
La détresse et le regret!

Tous ces troubadours mal-aimés
Ont vu blanchir dans un été
Leur doux royaume pessimiste.

Ah! la neige est inexorable
Qui aime qu'on souffre à ses pieds,
Qui veut que l'on meure glacé
Quand on a vécu dans les sables.

A ☆☆☆

TU es mon amour depuis tant d'années,
Mon vertige devant tant d'attente,
Que rien ne peut vieillir, froidir;
Même ce qui attendait notre mort,
Ou lentement sut nous combattre,
Même ce qui nous est étranger,
Et mes éclipses et mes retours.

I see all things from my wall,
Even the lurching owl in flight.

Who like lovesick lizard's given
To construe earth's secret work?
Airy, gentle king of heaven,
Would you nested in my rock!

Pyrenees

MOUNTAINS of the wronged, once great,
Crowning your perfervid towers
Dies away the failing light.

Only void and avalanche,
Tribulation and regret!

All those lovelorn troubadours
Watched their sad sweet realm turn white
In a single summer's course.

Ah! the inexorable snow
Craves we suffer at its feet,
Wills we die on frozen heights
Who have lived in sands below.

A☆☆☆

You'VE been my love so many years,
My turbulence through so much waiting,
That nothing can grow old or cold;
Not even what waited for our death,
Or slowly knew the way to fight us,
Not even what is strange to us,
And my eclipses and returns.

André Frénaud

1907 -

Je ne t'ai jamais oubliée

SANS nom maintenant sans visage
sans plus rien de tes yeux ni de ta pâleur

Dénoué de l'assaut de mon désir dans ton égarante image
dénué par les faux aveux du temps
par les fausses pièces de l'amour racheté
par tous ces gains perdu
libéré de toi maintenant
libre comme un mort
vivant de seule vie moite
enjoué avec les pierres et les feuillages

Quand je glisse entre les seins des douces mal aimées
je gis encore sur ton absence
sur la vivante morte que tu fais
par ton pouvoir ordonné à me perdre
jusqu'au bout de mon silence.

André Frénaud

1907 -

I have never forgotten you

NAMELESS and faceless now you are
Gone your eyes your face so pale

Untangled from the assault of my desire in your mocking form
Denuded by the false avowals of time
Ransomed by the false coinage of love
By all these gains destroyed
Set free now from your name
Free like one who's dead
Or lives with a damp life alone
Enjoying leaf and stone

Slipping between the breasts of those sweet ones unloved
I lie down still on your absence
On you who being dead are proved
Alive by power to take my life
Even to the end of my silence.

Guillevic

1907 -

L'école publique

A SAINT-JEAN-BREVELAY notre école publique
Etait petite et très, très pauvre: des carreaux
Manquaient et pour finir c'est qu'il en manquait trop
Pour qu'on mette partout du carton par applique,
    Car il faut voir bien clair lorsque le maître explique.
Alors le vent soufflait par tous ces soupiraux
Et nous avons eu froid souvent sous nos sarraux.
Par surcroît le plancher était épisodique
    Et l'on sait qu'avec l'eau du toit la terre fait
Des espèces de lacs boueux d'un bel effet.
— Pourtant j'ai bien appris dans cette pauvre école:
    Orthographe, calcul, histoire des Français,
Le quatorze juillet, Valmy, la Carmagnole,
Le progrès, ses reculs, et, toujours, son succès.

Au pays natal

LES bois à Colpo, la mer à Carnac, la lande
A Saint-Jean-Brévelay, j'ai bien vu moi qu'ils ont
Une égale colère et crient sur l'horizon
Par le terrible gris, guéri de la légende,
    Qu'ils crient par tous les vents, par les corbeaux en bandes,
Par les couleurs de leurs arbres, de leurs maisons,
Crient contre les maudits et leurs combinaisons
De remettre debout une armée allemande,
    Pour nous tenir et s'il faut pour nous tuer
Et voir leur règne encore un peu continuer —
Alors que nous voulons vivre en paix et en joie
    Sur la terre autour de nous, belle comme elle est.
La mer à Carnac, les bois à Colpo, qu'ils soient
Entendus, et la lande à Saint-Jean-Brévelay.

Guillevic

1907 -

The public school

At Saint-Jean-Brevelay our public school
Was small and very poor; few panes of glass
Remained and soon too many gaps, alas!
For us to stuff old cartons in them all,
    And when the master expounds, light should not fail.
But then through all those vents the wind would pass,
Till in our overalls we felt like ice.
Besides, the episodic floor would fill
    With water dripping from the roof, to make,
You know, a lovely sort of muddy lake.
And yet I learned a lot in that poor school:
    Spelling, arithmetic, French history,
July the fourteenth, Valmy, the Carmagnole,
Progress, decline, and always every victory.

In native land

The woods at Colpo, sea at Carnac, land
Of Saint-Jean-Brévelay, in each I've seen
An equal anger, on the horizon known
Them cry in terrible gray, relieved of legend:
    Cry out in flocks of rooks, in every wind,
In colors of trees, colors of homes between,
The cry against the damned who still combine
To bring a German army back to stand
    And hold us down again, if need be kill,
Only to see them rule again a while,
Just when we wish to live in peace and joy
    Upon this earth surrounding us so beautifully.
Hear, then, the sea at Carnac, woods at Carpo
Cry with the land of Saint-Jean-Brévelay.

527

Georges Schéhade
1910 -

Dans le sommeil quelquefois…

Dans le sommeil quelquefois
Des graines éveillent des ombres
Il vient des enfants avec leurs mondes
Légers comme des ossements de fleurs
Alors dans un pays lointain si proche par le chagrin de l'âme
Pour rejoindre le pavot des paupières innocentes
Les corps de la nuit deviennent la mer

Il y a des jardins…

Il y a des jardins qui n'ont plus de pays
Et qui sont seuls avec l'eau
Des colombes les traversent bleues et sans nids
Mais la lune est un cristal de bonheur
Et l'enfant se souvient d'un grand désordre clair.

Si tu es belle comme les Mages…

Si tu es belle comme les Mages de mon pays
O mon amour tu n'iras pas pleurer
Les soldats tués et leur ombre qui fuit la mort
— Pour nous la mort est une fleur de la pensée

Il faut rêver aux oiseaux qui voyagent
Entre le jour et la nuit comme une trace
Lorsque le soleil s'éloigne dans les arbres
Et fait de leurs feuillages une autre prairie

Georges Schéhade

1910 -

In sleep sometimes…

In sleep sometimes
Seeds awaken shadows
Children come with their worlds
Light as the bones of flowers
Then in a land brought near by the soul's sorrow
To join again the poppy of innocent sleep
The bodies of the night become the sea

There are gardens…

There are gardens that no longer have a country
And that are alone with the water
Doves fly across them blue and having no nests
But the moon is a crystal of happiness
And the child remembers a wide shining disorder.

If you are lovely like the Magi…

If you are lovely like the Magi of my land
O my love you are not going to weep
For the soldiers slain and their shade which fled from death,
Death is for us a flower of thought

We have to think of those migrating birds
Who trace a path between the day and night
At the hour when the sun recedes among the trees
Making their foliage another field

O mon amour
Nous avons les yeux bleus des prisonniers
Mais notre corps est adoré par les songes
Allongés nous sommes deux ciels dans l'eau
Et la parole est notre seule absence

My love we have the blue eyes of prisoners
But our body is adored by dreams
Lying full length we are two heavens in the water
And then our only absence is the word

Patrice de la Tour du Pin

1911 -

Les enfants de Septembre

Les bois étaient tout recouverts de brumes basses,
Déserts, gonflés de pluie et silencieux;
Longtemps avait soufflé ce vent du Nord où passent
Les Enfants Sauvages, fuyant vers d'autres cieux,
Par grands voiliers, le soir, et très haut dans l'espace.

J'avais senti siffler leurs ailes dans la nuit,
Lorsqu'ils avaient baissé pour chercher les ravines
Où tout le jour, peut-être ils resteront enfouis;
Et cet appel inconsolé de sauvagine
Triste, sur les marais que les oiseaux ont fuis.

Après avoir surpris le dégel de ma chambre,
A l'aube, je gagnai la lisière des bois;
Par une bonne lune de brouillard et d'ambre,
Je relevai la trace incertaine parfois,
Sur le bord d'un layon, d'un enfant de Septembre.

Les pas étaient légers et tendres, mais brouillés,
Ils se croisaient d'abord au milieu des ornières
Où dans l'ombre, tranquille, il avait essayé
De boire, pour reprendre ses jeux solitaires
Très tard, après le long crépuscule mouillé.

Et puis, ils se perdaient plus loin parmi les hêtres
Où son pied ne marquait qu'à peine sur le sol;
Je me suis dit: il va s'en retourner peut-être
A l'aube, pour chercher ses compagnons de vol,
En tremblant de la peur qu'ils aient pu disparaître.

Il va certainement venir dans ces parages
A la demi-clarté qui monte à l'orient,
Avec les grandes bandes d'oiseaux de passage,

Patrice de la Tour du Pin

1911 -

The children of September

THE woods were covered with a clinging mist,
Deserted, big with silence and with rain;
For long had blown this wind from the north where passed
The Wild Children, sailing once again
To other skies in the evening, high and fast.

I had been aware of wings whistling at night
When they came down to look for a ravine,
To rest, perhaps, below in the hours of light,
And that the desolate call of waterfowl had been
Belling in the marshes where the birds check flight.

I rose, surprised the dawn thawing my room,
And soon attained the outskirts of the wood;
By a full moon of misty amber form,
I traced the scattered footprints in the mud
Of one September child—those that were firm.

The steps were delicate, not all distinct,
At first criss-crossing an old wagon way,
Where tranquil in the dark he hoped to drink,
Before resuming late his lonely play,
After the dew fell and the sun would sink.

And then beyond the beech trees they were gone,
Where in the soil the marks dwindled from sight;
I told myself, perhaps he will return
At dawn, to seek his comrades on the flight,
Trembling with fear that they'd already flown.

Surely to these still waters he will come
By the half-light now mantling in the east,
With the great flocks of birds migrating home,

Et les cerfs inquiets qui cherchent dans le vent
L'heure d'abandonner le calme des gagnages.

Le jour glacial s'était levé sur les marais;
Je restais accroupi dans l'attente illusoire
Regardant défiler la faune qui rentrait
Dans l'ombre, les chevreuils peureux qui venaient boire
Et les corbeaux criards aux cimes des forêts.

Et je me dis: Je suis un enfant de Septembre,
Moi-même, par le cœur, la fièvre et l'esprit,
Et la brûlante volupté de tous mes membres,
Et le désir que j'ai de courir dans la nuit
Sauvage, ayant quitté l'étouffement des chambres.

Il va certainement me traiter comme un frère,
Peut-être me donner un nom parmi les siens;
Mes yeux le combleraient d'amicales lumières
S'il ne prenait pas peur, en me voyant soudain
Les bras ouverts, courir vers lui dans la clairière.

Farouche, il s'enfuira comme un oiseau blessé,
Je le suivrai jusqu'à ce qu'il demande grâce.
Jusqu'à ce qu'il s'arrête en plein ciel, épuisé,
Traqué jusqu'à la mort, vaincu, les ailes basses,
Et les yeux résignés à mourir, abaissés.

Alors je le prendrai dans mes bras, endormi,
Je le caresserai sur la pente des ailes,
Et je ramènerai son petit corps parmi
Les roseaux, rêvant à des choses irréelles
Réchauffé tout le temps par mon sourire ami...

Mais les bois étaient recouverts de brumes basses
Et le vent commençait à remonter au Nord,
Abandonnant tous ceux dont les ailes sont lasses,
Tous ceux qui sont perdus et tous ceux qui sont morts,
Qui vont par d'autres voies en de mêmes espaces!

And nervous deer sniffing the wind, to test
When they should leave the meadows where they roam.

The frigid day had risen in the marsh;
I crouched there, waiting with a dreamy hope,
Watching the fawns file back into the lush
Shadows, the timid does that pause and stoop
To drink, the rooks on tree-tops cawing harsh.

And I said: September child I also am,
Yes, by the hunger in my heart and mind,
The burning fever in my every limb
To run wild in the night and leave behind
The walled-in suffocation of a room.

He'll treat me surely as a brother sprite,
Give me, perhaps, a name among his own;
My eyes would smother him with friendly light,
Unless to run to him with arms out-thrown
Abruptly in a glade should cause him fright.

He'll fly away appalled, like a bird hurt,
I'll follow him until he pleads for grace,
Until he halts in the open sky, inert,
Tracked down by death, defeated, wings effaced,
His eyes resigned to dying, dark and shut.

Then I will take him in my arms, even while
Asleep, and I will smooth his sloping wings;
I'll carry back his little frame, so frail,
Among the reeds to dream of unreal things,
Reviving slowly by my loving smile.

But once again the woods are swathed in mist;
The wind begins to rise again in the north,
Forsaking those whose wings tire easiest,
All those that are lost and those fallen to earth,
By different ways in the same wilderness.

Et je me dis: Ce n'est pas dans ces pauvres landes
Que les Enfants de Septembre vont s'arrêter;
Un seul qui se serait écarté de sa bande
Aurait-il, en un soir, compris l'atrocité
De ces marais déserts et privés de légendes?

And I said to myself: not here in this drear land
The children of September shall abide;
Will some lone one, dissevered from his band,
Perceive one evening the atrocious side
Of these waste fens where legend reached an end?

Catherine Fauln

1912 - 1951

Le lien d'orties

L'ANGE évadé des processions
Mourait au fond d'un tabernacle.
Les astres, las de nos saisons,
Bouleversèrent les oracles
Et sortirent de leurs maisons.

Ils confondirent nos deux vies.
Ainsi l'hiver avec l'été
Et le soleil avec la pluie.
Et pour mieux nous apparenter,
Ils ont lié nos mains d'orties.

Nous errions parmi les bouleaux
Qui semblent blanches jeunes filles
Ou pâles et fins damoiseaux.
Mêlé au mien, ton nom scintille
Sur chaque arbre des boqueteaux.

Je savais d'étranges histoires
De sorciers et d'enchantements.
Hautaine enfance, ma mémoire
Les effaça de ses tourments
Et n'osa plus jamais y croire.

L'oiseau d'avril est au soldat.
Je t'écris où le canon gronde.
Les militaires sont au roi,
Mais le ciel est à tout le monde
Et mon cœur ne bat que pour toi.

J'ai pleuré sur des personnages
Gonflés de mystère et d'amour.
O douceur, douceur des images,
Dans les lignes et les contours,
Je n'ai cherché que ton visage.

Catherine Fauln

1912 - 1951

The bond of nettles

THE angel that eludes processions
Died deep inside a tabernacle.
The stars, grown weary of the seasons,
Invalidated every oracle
And made a sortie from their mansions,

They twined our lives that once were twain.
So summer is conjoined to winter
Or sunlight mingles with the rain.
And then to unify us better,
Our hands with nettles they constrained.

We wandered in the birchwood glen,
White girls those silver trees resembling,
Or pale important gentlemen,
Your lucent name, with mine commingling,
To blaze against oblivion.

I once knew many an allegory
Of sorcery and strange enchantment.
Imperious childhood ruled my memory
To expurgate its tales of torment,
Afraid to credit them as history.

The April bird's for soldiers too.
I wrote to you where cannon growled.
The king commands that retinue,
And yet the sky commands the world
And my heart only beats for you.

I've wept for persons of high place
That love and mystery fatten on.
But O such gentle gentleness,
In whatsoever shape or line,
I only looked for in your face.

Sabine Sicaud

1913 - 1928

Le chemin de l'amour

AMOUR, mon cher Amour, je te sais près de moi
Avec ton beau visage.
Si tu changes de nom, d'accent, de cœur et d'âge,
Ton visage du moins ne me trompera pas.
Les yeux de ton visage, Amour, ont près de moi
La clarté patiente des étoiles.
De la nuit, de la mer, des îles sans escales,
Je ne crains rien si tu m'as reconnue.
Mon Amour, de bien loin, pour toi, je suis venue
Peut-être. Et nous irons Dieu sait où maintenant?
Depuis quand cherchais-tu mon ombre évanouie?
Quand t'avais-je perdu? Dans quelle vie?
Et qu'oserait le ciel contre nous maintenant?

Ah! Laissez-moi crier

AH! laissez-moi crier, crier, crier...
Crier à m'arracher la gorge!
Crier comme une bête qu'on égorge,
Comme le fer martyrisé dans une forge,
Comme l'arbre mordu par les dents de la scie,
Comme un carreau sous le ciseau du vitrier...
Grincer, hurler, râler! Peu me soucie
Que des gens s'en effarent. J'ai besoin
De crier jusqu'au bout de ce qu'on peut crier.
Les gens? Vous ne savez donc pas comme ils sont loin,
Comme ils existent peu, lorsque vous supplicie
Cette douleur qui vous fait seul au monde?
Avec elle on est seul, seul dans sa geôle.
Répondre? Non. Je n'attends pas qu'on me réponde.
Je ne sais même pas si j'appelle au secours,
Si même j'ai crié, crié comme une folle,

Sabine Sicaud

1913 - 1928

The road of love

LOVE, my dear Love, I know you're near to me
With your beautiful face,
If you can change your name, your age, heart, voice,
At least your face won't tell me what's untrue.
Your eyes, Love, when they're near to me,
Will have the patient radiance of a star.
The night, the sea, the isles where no ports are,
Nothing I'd fear if you found me again.
My Love, from very far for you I came,
Perhaps. And God knows where we shall go now?
How long have you been looking for my shade?
In what life was my loss of you decreed?
What would the sky dare do against us now?

Ah! Let me cry

AH! let me cry and cry and cry...
Cry till I tear my very throat out!
Cry like a beast whose throat is cut,
Like the iron the furnace twists white-hot,
Like trees the saw's teeth rend and tear,
Like sheets of glass the glaziers split...
Lash, gnash, thrash! Little I care
If people are scared. I have to scream
Until one can't scream any more.
People? You don't know how far they seem,
How little do they live when this pain's there,
This pain that leaves you all alone in the land,
All alone with the pain, alone in its jail.
Respond? No, I don't hope they will respond.
I don't know even if it's for help I pray
Or even if I did cry, cry like a fool,

Comme un damné, toute la nuit et tout le jour.
Cette chose inouïe, atroce, qui vous tue,
Croyez-vous qu'elle soit
Une chose possible à quoi l'on s'habitue?
Cette douleur, mon Dieu, cette douleur qui tue...
Avec quel art cruel de supplice chinois
Elle montait, montait, à petits pas sournois,
Et nul ne la voyait monter, pas même toi,
Confiante santé, ma santé méconnue!
C'est vers toi que je crie, ah! c'est vers toi, vers toi!
Pourquoi, si tu m'entends, n'être pas revenue?
Pourquoi me laisser tant souffrir, dis-moi pourquoi
Ou si c'est ta revanche et parce qu'autrefois
Jamais, simple santé, je ne pensais à toi.

Vous parler?

Vous parler? Non. Je ne peux pas.
Je préfère souffrir comme une plante,
Comme l'oiseau qui ne dit rien sur le tilleul.
Ils attendent. C'est bien. Puisqu'ils ne sont pas las
D'attendre, j'attendrai, de cette même attente.

Ils souffrent seuls. On doit apprendre à souffrir seul.
Je ne veux pas d'indifférents prêts à sourire
Ni d'amis gémissants. Que nul ne vienne.
La plante ne dit rien. L'oiseau se tait. Que dire?
Cette douleur est seule au monde, quoi qu'on veuille.
Elle n'est pas celle des autres, c'est la mienne.
Une feuille a son mal qu'ignore l'autre feuille.
Et le mal de l'oiseau, l'autre oiseau n'en sait rien.

Like a damned soul all the night and all the day.
About this vile, unheard-of thing, that kills,
Do you believe your informant
That one can grow accustomed to these ills?
This pain, my God, this pain that kills...
With what fine art of cruel Chinese torment
It climbed and climbed with short steps sly and dormant;
Not even you have seen what these steps meant,
Dear sanguine health, my health to me unknown:
To you it is I cry, to you, to you!
Why, if you hear me, leave me so alone?
Why let me hurt so, tell me why you do,
Or, if it is your revenge, that long ago,
Dear simple health, I never thought of you.

Speak to you?

SPEAK to you? No. I'd rather not.
I'd rather suffer like a plant,
Like the bird in the lime tree, silent, still,
They wait. That's good. And since they weary not
Of waiting, I'll wait too, the same long wait.

They suffer alone. We must learn to suffer alone.
I want no callous ones prepared to smile
Nor friends that groan. Let no one come.
The plant, the bird tell nothing. What's to tell?
This pain's alone in the world, like it or not.
It's no one else's pain, only my own.
The leaves ignore the leaf that is beset.
This bird's pain to another bird is not known.

On ne sait pas. On ne sait pas. Qui se ressemble?
Et se ressemblât-on, qu'importe. Il me convient
De n'entendre ce soir nulle parole vaine.
J'attends — comme le font derrière la fenêtre
Le vieil arbre sans geste et le pinson muet...
Une goutte d'eau pure, un peu de vent, qui sait?
Qu'attendent-ils? Nous l'attendrons ensemble.
Le soleil leur a dit qu'il reviendrait, peut-être...

Not known. Not known. Whose pain can be another's?
And if it could, what then? It suits me well
Tonight no idle word to hear them tell.
I wait—like them outside the window pane,
The silent finch, the old tree that gives no sign...
Who knows, a breath of wind, pure water drops?
What do they wait for? We shall wait together.
The sun has told them he'd return, perhaps.*

*Sabine Sicaud's strange dates again (see Biographical Notes) were 1913–1928. Her poems achieve, or approach, surprising technical maturity, although the mysterious sickness of which she died left her little leisure between when the frightful pain invaded her. Poems like "When the doctors came" and the one last translated ("Ah! let me cry..."), where the cries, as Hopkins says, "heave herd-long," are well able to defeat any translator, for the shrieks are mimicked by the diction whilst the verse remains, as always, in stern control. The great quietness of this one depends in part on the carefully paced pauses and subtly spaced rhymes, for which to find identical incidence would threaten to shatter the fragile spontaneity. So I resorted to approximate spacing and half-rhymes, without hoping to do half as well. The last line seems to contain something of the same sort of semi-conscious *double entendre* as the famous closing half-line of Wilfred Owen's ostensibly unfinished "Strange Meeting"—the unfinish being the perfect close. "Perhaps" then she could die.

René Guy Cadou

1920 - 1951

Celui qui entre par hasard

CELUI qui entre par hasard dans la demeure d'un poète
Ne sait pas que les meubles ont pouvoir sur lui
Que chaque nœud du bois renferme davantage
De cris d'oiseaux que tout le cœur de la forêt
Il suffit qu'une lampe pose son cou de femme
A la tombée du soir contre un angle verni
Pour délivrer soudain mille peuples d'abeilles
Et l'odeur de pain frais des cerisiers fleuris
Car tel est le bonheur de cette solitude
Qu'une caresse toute plate de la main
Redonne à ces grands meubles noirs et taciturnes
La légèreté d'un arbre dans le matin.

René Guy Cadou

1920 - 1951

Whoever chances to enter

WHOEVER chances to enter a poet's place
Won't know the furniture has power upon him
That every knot of wood encloses more
Of birdsong than the whole heart of the forest
A lamp neck only has to look like a girl's
At nightfall in the room's lighted corner
To loose of a sudden a thousand tribes of bees
And the fresh-bread smell of cherry trees in bloom
Because so happy is this solitude
That one caress bestowed by the palm of the hand
Gives back to the dark still things in the room
The lightness of a tree in the early morning.

Pierre Emmanuel
1916 -

De *Chansons du dé à coudre*

III

FAIRE de chaque mot
Une nichée de colombes folles
Qui toutes ensemble s'envolent
Aux quatre vents des eaux

Le sens unique et pur
Est-il pas l'ironie innombrable
Vertige d'ailes impalpables
Autour du réel dur

Erotique

DERRIÈRE la cloison elle est nue elle chante
Son linge à terre épand sa gerbe déliée.
Hirondelle au miroir le geste d'essuyer
Ses flancs, rompt d'un envol de caresses l'attente
Dans la chambre qu'un lit juge sévère enchante
L'homme est assis les yeux au sol tout habillé.
La bête qui lui disjoint l'âme le bélier
Est-ce désir battant ou peur impatiente?
Parais, hiératique idole sur fond rouge!
Seule une torche d'or entre les cuisses bouge
Et polit de ses feux l'armure des seins nus
Elle, humble chair dont la nudité est l'hommage
Innocente se fige et se trouble au visage
De la honte qui vêt ce coupable inconnu.

548

Pierre Emmanuel

1916 -

From *Thimble songs*

III

To make of every phrase
A flock of crazy doves
Which all together roves
The four winds of the seas

The sense unique and pure
Bids countless mocking things
Whirl insubstantial wings
About the hard and sure

Erotic

BEHIND the screen she is naked and she sings,
Her garments spread, an untied sheaf on the floor;
She wipes her sides, a swallow caught in the mirror,
Breaking suspense with a swift touch of the wing.
    In the room the bed is a stern judge and a thing
Of sorcery, the man sitting dressed with his eyes lowered:
The ram, the beast, soul sundered in its power,
Does it quake with restless fear, or only long?
    Hierarchic idol on a red ground, rise!
Only a golden torch between her thighs
Moves, glancing fire on the armor of her bare breasts.
    She, humble flesh, is troubled without blame;
Being naked is her homage, chilled by the shame
In which this unknown guilty man is dressed.

De *Hymne de la liberté*

. . . O MES frères dans les prisons vous êtes libres
Libres les yeux brûlés les membres enchaînés
Le visage troué les lèvres mutilées
Vous êtes ces arbres violents et torturés
Qui croissent plus puissants parce qu'on les émonde
Et sur tout le pays d'humaine destinée
Votre regard d'hommes vrais est sans limites
Votre silence est la paix terrible de l'éther.

Par-dessus les tyrans enroués de mutisme
Il y a la nef silencieuse de vos mains
Par-dessus l'ordre dérisoire des tyrans
Il y a l'ordre des nuées et des cieux vastes
Il y a la respiration des monts très bleus
Il y a les libres lointains de la prière
Il y a les larges fronts qui ne se courbent pas
Il y a les astres dans la liberté de leur essence
Il y a les immenses moissons du devenir
Il y a dans des tyrans une angoisse fatale
Qui est la liberté effroyable de Dieu.

From *Hymn of liberty* *

. . . My brothers, in your jails you still are free,
Free still the burning eyes, the limbs in chains,
The face deformed with scars, lips mutilated.
You are the boisterous and tortured trees
Which flourish more the more we cut them back,
Especially in the land of human fate;
Your men of truth have the untrammelled look,
Your silence is the terrible peace of space.

Above the tyrants mutiny makes hoarse
There is the vaulted silence of your hands;
Above the sneering order of the tyrants,
The order of the clouds and spacious skies,
The breathing of the mountains very blue,
The unobstructed distances of prayer,
There are the lofty brows that will not bend;
There are the stars in the freedom of their sway;
There are the boundless harvests yet to be;
There is the fatal anguish of the tyrants,
Which is the fearsome liberty of God.

* For the fourth and last time in this book we transgress about cutting.
Of course, I have translated all seventy-three lines of this exalted hymn,
which injects an alien passion essentially political, in this book, but it's
a poem we could not quite afford to forget. Its subject has the same
contemporaneity as Chénier's *Iambes* and Wordsworth's *Toussaint
l'Overture,* but recent poems, except for the Pisan Cantos, have mostly
managed to avoid this comfortless area.

Dieu parle

Je n'écris que pour Toi Seigneur
Pour T'irriter, pour Te séduire
Pour Te présenter ma douleur
Puis de ce tribut Te maudire

Pour Ton courroux pour Ta pitié
Pour m'accuser et pour me plaindre
Pour m'échapper pour me lier
Pour Te fuir et pour T'atteindre

Pour être devant Toi toujours
Pour me terrer sous mes paroles
Pour Te vouer mon seul amour
Pour Te narguer devant l'idole

Pour en Ton Nom m'anéantir
Pour faire de Ton Nom ma chose
Pour me briser de repentir
Pour Te moudre au poids de mes fautes

Combien m'ennuie ce triste jeu
Tu le sais, ah! qu'il cesse vite
Fais-moi connaître enfin mon Dieu
Cette grâce que nul n'évite

Quand las de ruser Tu le veux.

Let God speak

ONLY for You, O Lord, I write
To irritate You and seduce
To pour my griefs out in Your sight
Then with this tribute aim my curse

For all Your pity for Your wrath
Accuse myself present my plea
Absolve my blame and plight my faith
Flee You and bring You close to me

To stay with You and never move
To hide beneath what I entreat
To promise You my single love
And scorn You at the idol's feet

To be as nothing in Your Name
Make of Your Name my constant sign
Break myself sorrowing in shame
And grind You by my weight of sin

How much this sad game makes me ill
You know, ah! that it soon may cease
Make me at last, my God, fulfill
Your own inexorable grace

When tired of play it is Your will.

Yves Bonnefoy

1923 -

Aube, fille des larmes…

AUBE, fille des larmes, rétablis
La chambre dans sa paix de chose grise
Et le cœur dans son ordre. Tant de nuit
Demandait à ce feu qu'il décline et s'achève,
Il nous faut bien veiller près du visage mort.
A peine a-t-il changé… Le navire des lampes
Entrera-t-il au port qu'il avait demandé,
Sur les tables d'ici la flamme faite cendre
Grandira-t-elle ailleurs dans une autre clarté?
Aube, soulève, prends le visage sans ombre,
Colore peu à peu le temps recommencé.

Aux arbres

VOUS qui vous êtes effacés sur son passage,
Qui avez refermé sur elle vos chemins,
Impassibles garants que Douve même morte
Sera lumière encore n'étant rien.

Vous fibreuse matière et densité,
Arbres, proches de moi quand elle s'est jetée
Dans la barque des morts et la bouche serrée
Sur l'obole de faim, de froid et de silence.

J'entends à travers vous quel dialogue elle tente
Avec les chiens, avec l'informe nautonier,
Et je vous appartiens par son cheminement
A travers tant de nuit et malgré tout ce fleuve.

Le tonnerre profond qui roule sur vos branches,
Les fêtes qu'il enflamme au sommet de l'été
Signifient qu'elle lie sa fortune à la mienne
Dans la médiation de votre austérité.

Yves Bonnefoy

1923 -

Dawn, daughter of tears...

DAWN, daughter of tears, once more create
The room in its calm of something gray
And the heart in its order. So much of the night
Implored that fire to fade and burn out.
We must keep steady watch by that dead face.
It has hardly changed... Will the lamp-lit ship
Heave to and enter the port it wanted?
Will the flame on the tables here burned to ash
Wax brighter elsewhere in another radiance?
Dawn, lift up, receive the shadowless face,
Color little by little the time recommenced.

To the trees

You who have moved aside to let her pass,
Who closed your path around her once again,
Impassive proofs that although Douve is dead
She will be brightness still now she is gone.

You fibrous matter, density itself,
Trees that were near me when she threw herself
Into the bark of the dead and closed her mouth
Upon the coin of hunger, silence, and cold.

Through you I hear the language she essays
With that misshapen boatman and the dogs,
And by her trudging on through so much night
In spite of all this river I am yours.

The deep thunder rolling in your branches,
The revels in high summer set afire
Mean that she binds her fate to mine, for such is
The mediation of your force austere.

Toute la nuit

Toute la nuit la bête a bougé dans la salle,
Qu'est-ce que ce chemin qui ne veut pas finir,
Toute la nuit la barque a cherché le rivage,
Qu'est-ce que ces absents qui veulent revenir,
Toute la nuit l'épée a connu la blessure,
Qu'est-ce que ce tourment qui ne sait rien saisir,
Toute la nuit la bête a gémi dans la salle,
Ensanglanté, nié la lumière des salles,
Qu'est-ce que cette mort qui ne va rien guérir?

Le jour franchit le soir...

Le jour franchit le soir, il gagnera
Sur la nuit quotidienne.
O notre force et notre gloire, pourrez-vous
Trouer la muraille des morts?

La lumière, changée

Nous ne nous voyons plus dans la même lumière,
Nous n'avons plus les mêmes yeux, les mêmes mains.
L'arbre est plus proche et la voix des sources plus vive,
Nos pas sont plus profonds, parmi les morts.

Dieu qui n'es pas, pose ta main sur notre épaule,
Ebauche notre corps du poids de ton retour,
Achève de mêler à nos âmes ces astres,
Ces bois, ces cris d'oiseaux, ces ombres et ces jours.

Renonce-toi en nous comme un fruit se déchire,
Efface-nous en toi. Découvre-nous
Le sens mystérieux de ce qui n'est que simple
Et fût tombé sans feu dans des mots sans amour.

All the night

ALL night long the beast has stirred in the room,
What is this path that never wants to end,
All night long the bark has searched for the shore,
What are these absent ones who would sail home,
All night long the sword has probed the wound,
What is this pain that can grasp nothing at all,
All night long the beast has groaned in the room,
Drenched in blood, denied the light of the rooms,
What is this death that will make no illness well?

Day leaps the evening...

DAY leaps the evening, it will gain
Its daily victory over night.
Our strength and glory, will you then
Transpierce the ramparts of the dead?

The light, changed

WE see ourselves no more in the same light,
We have no more the same eyes, the same hands.
The tree is nearer now, the voice of streams more live,
Our footsteps traverse deeper, among the dead.

Thou God who art not, put thy hand on our shoulder,
Rough-hew our body with weight of thy return,
Make mingle with our souls the stars' illumination,
These woods, these cries of birds, these shadows and these
[days.
Renounce thyself in us as fruit is torn away.
Annul us in thyself. Enable us to find
The meaning fraught with mystery of what is only simple
And fell down without fire in words without love.

Bonnefoy

A la voix de Kathleen Ferrier

TOUTE douceur toute ironie se rassemblaient
Pour un adieu de cristal et de brume,
Les coups profonds du fer faisaient presque silence,
La lumière du glaive s'était voilée.

Je célèbre la voix mêlée de couleur grise
Qui hésite aux lointains du chant qui s'est perdu
Comme si au delà de toute forme pure
Tremblât un autre chant et le seul absolu.

O lumière et néant de la lumière, ō larmes
Souriantes plus haut que l'angoisse ou l'espoir,
O cygne, lieu réel dans l'irréelle eau sombre,
O source, quand ce fut profondément le soir!

Il semble que tu connaisses les deux rives,
L'extrême joie et l'extrême douleur.
Là-bas, parmi ces roseaux gris dans la lumière,
Il semble que tu puises de l'éternel.

To the voice of Kathleen Ferrier

ALL sweetness gathered here, all irony,*
For this farewell of crystal and of mist;
The deep and gonglike strokes were almost silence;
Swords flashed behind a veil of secrecy.

I pledge the voice softly mingled with grey
That hesitates far off with a missing song,
As if beyond all purity of form
Trembled another, the absolute song.

O light and birth of light, O tears
Smiling from heights above anguish and hope,
O swan, real place in this dim unreal water,
The source of light when evening gathers deep!

It seems that you must know both river banks,
The farthest gladness and the farthest pain.
Down here, among grey reeds, in light that wanes,
It seems you borrow light from the eternal.

*This almost too devotional oblation does not lend itself easily to
translation, but then neither does the heroic voice of the greatest
contralto of our time, a Lancashire mill hand, who continued to
concertize during the blitz, whilst enduring terminal cancer of the
throat: an exceptionally beautiful young woman, as the album covers
show, who fancied herself incapable of being loved, knowledge of
which may have contributed to Bonnefoy's choice of the word "irony".

Philippe Jaccottet
1925 -

De *Le livre de morts*

I

Celui qui est entré dans les propriétés de l'âge,
il n'en cherchera plus les pavillons ni les jardins,
ni les livres, ni les canaux, ni les feuillages,
ni la trace, aux miroirs, d'une plus brève et tendre main:
l'œil de l'homme, en ce lieu de sa vie, est voilé,
son bras trop faible pour saisir, pour conquérir,
je le regarde qui regarde s'éloigner
tout ce qui fut un jour son seul travail, son doux désir...

Force cachée, s'il en est une, je te prie,
qu'il ne s'enfonce pas dans l'épouvante de ses fautes,
qu'il ne rabâche pas de paroles d'amour factices,
que sa puissance usée une dernière fois sursaute,
se ramasse, et qu'une autre ivresse l'envahisse!

Ses combats les plus durs furent légers éclairs d'oiseaux,
ses plus graves hasards à peine une invasion de pluie;
ses amours n'ont jamais fait se briser que des roseaux,
sa gloire inscrire au mur bientôt ruiné un nom de suie...

*

Qu'il entre maintenant vêtu de sa seule impatience
dans cet espace enfin à la mesure de son cœur;
qu'il entre, avec sa seule adoration pour toute science,
dans l'énigme qui fut la sombre source de ses pleurs.

Nulle promesse ne lui a été donnée;
nulle assurance ne lui sera plus laissée;
nulle réponse ne peut plus lui parvenir;
nulle lampe, à la main d'une femme jadis connue,
éclairer ni le lit ni l'interminable avenue:

Philippe Jaccottet

1925 -

From *The book of the dead*

I

HE who inherits the estates of age
no longer looks for gardens or pavilions,
or books, or aqueducts, or pasturage,
or the trace, in mirrors, of a dear hand gone.
Placed here in this his life, man's eye is clouded,
his arm too weak to seize or overpower;
I watch him watching how all that receded
which one day was his single task, his fond desire...

I pray you, hidden power, if such there be,
let him not sink subjected by old shame,
or dwell on words of love beguiling hope;
let his exhausted strength rise one last time,
intoxicated by a different cup.

His toughest fights were mild lightnings of birds,
his gravest hazards hardly raids of rain;
his loves have never broken anything but reeds,
his fame to write his name in soot on walls too soon torn down.

*

Dressed in his sole unrest, now let him go
at last into that region where his heart is king,
and, with his adoration all there is to know,
let him enter the enigma of his tears' dark spring.

No promise has been given him for sure;
nought certain will be left him any more;
for him no more can answer penetrate;
no lamp, in the hand of a woman he once knew,
to light the bed or endless avenue:

qu'il veuille donc attendre et seulement se réjouir,
comme le bois n'apprend qu'en la défaite à éblouir.

Sois tranquille, cela viendra...

Sois tranquille, cela viendra! Tu te rapproches,
tu brules! Car le mot qui sera à la fin
du poème, plus que le premier sera proche
de ta mort, qui ne s'arrête pas en chemin.
Ne crois pas qu'elle aille s'endormir sous des branches
ou reprendre souffle pendant que tu écris.
Même quand tu bois à la bouche qui étanche
la pire soif, la douce bouche avec ses cris
    doux, même quand tu serres avec force le nœud
de vos quatre bras pour être bien immobiles
dans la brûlante obscurité de vos cheveux,
    elle vient, Dieu sait par quels détours, vers vous deux,
de très loin ou déjà tout près, mais sois tranquille,
elle vient: d'un à l'autre mot tu es plus vieux.

Lune à l'aube d'été

Dans l'air de plus en plus clair
scintille encore cette larme
ou faible flamme dans du verre
quand du sommeil des montagnes
monte une vapeur dorée

Demeure ainsi suspendue
sur la balance de l'aube
entre la braise promise
et cette perle perdue

let him consent, then, to rejoice and wait,
as the wood learns to dazzle only in defeat.

Be calm, for it will come...

BE calm, for it will come! You're closing fast,
you're burning! For the word which you will say
last in the poem is nearer than the first
to death, which never pauses on its way.
    Don't think it flies to sleep beneath the branches
or gathers breath a moment while you write.
Even as you drink from the sweet mouth that quenches
the worst thirst with the cries belonging sweet,
    even as you tighten with force the knot to hold
you in four arms and linger perfectly still
in the burning dark of your hair against the cold,
    it will come, God knows by what detours, to fold
you both, from near or far; be calm, it will:
from one word to the next you're growing old.

Moon of summer dawn

IN the air more and more clear
glitters still that tear
or faint flame in glass
where from the sleeping mountains
rises a golden mist

Dwells thus suspended
on the balance of dawn
between the promised blaze
and that lost pearl

Louise Herlin

1925 -

Blanche, déroule sa spirale…

BLANCHE, déroule sa spirale
la route vide qui charpente
et sape tour à tour l'attente.

Tantôt bordée de forêts,
sûre de l'enjeu, elle serpente
changeant les hêtres en platanes,
les peupliers en sapins,

tantôt parmi la campagne
elle élargit ses desseins
comparant l'or des avoines
et le genêt des ravins,

tantôt pure obstination,
passé l'essaim des villages,
passé bosquets et prairies,
champs, taillis et garrigues,
désertique et cahotante,
elle se mesure au ciel nu
aveugle et persévérante.

564

Louise Herlin

1925 -

White unwinds the empty road...

WHITE unwinds the empty road
saps and chops the expectation
every spiraling direction.

Soon it borders on a wood,
sure of winning combinations,
changing beeches into planes,
poplars into sapling pines,

soon in country more remote
striding with enlarged designs,
paralleling gold of oats
with the furze in the ravines,

till pure fixedness prevails,
past the villages in swarms,
past the meadows and the groves,
fields and thickets gone to waste,
jolting over desert land,
while it spans the naked sky,
persevering still though blind.

Robert Benayoun

1926 -

Perception de la ligne droite

QUAND l'auto sera réparée je réglerai toutes mes dettes,
Je tuerai mon voisin et je peindrai ma salle de bains en jaune
    canari.
J'aurai un défaut de langue, et une garde-robe sans défaut,
Quand l'auto sera réparée.
J'aurai des silences recherchés.
Un air tranquille qui se monnaie fort sur les rives du Tchad.
Quand l'auto sera réparée, je serai beau.
Je serai bleu, avec une grande barbe rose et des oiseaux dans
    les cheveux.
J'achèterai le Taj Mahal,
J'y mettrai le chauffage central.
J'aurai la fortune, les femmes, la richesse, les femmes,
    l'argent, les femmes, un compte en banque, les femmes, de
    l'oiselle, des femmes.
J'aurai des milliers et des milliers de femmes.
J'aurai aussi des femmes millionaires.
Je serai prodigue, pensez, quand l'auto sera réparée.

Quand l'auto sera réparée (Qui donc a dit que l'auto serait
    réparée?)
Quand elle sera réparée, il fera beau.
Les poissons se prendront la main deux par deux, pour y
    glisser un anneau d'or.
Les lavandières se parfumeront à la lavande.
On verra des narines d'hippopotame sur tous les trottoirs,
Et les églises s'écrouleront dans un grand bruit de mastication.
Une abeille aura le fou-rire.
Nous ne jetterons plus un seul regard vers le passé.
Nous serrerons les dents,
Nouerons un mouchoir noir autour de notre front baigné de
    camphre,

Robert Benayoun

1926 -

Perception of the straight line

WHEN the car is repaired I shall pay all my debts,
I shall kill my neighbor and paint my bathroom canary
    yellow.
I shall have a speech fault and a faultless wardrobe,
When the car is repaired.
I shall go into studied silences.
A tranquil air which pays well on the banks of the Tchad.
When the car is repaired, I shall be handsome.
I shall be blue, with a large red beard and birds in my
    hair.
I shall buy the Taj Mahal,
I shall put central heating in there.
I shall have a fortune, women, wealth, women, money,
    women, a bank account, women, a chick, women
I shall have millions and millions of women.
I shall also have women millionaires.
Think how lavish I'll be when the car is repaired.

When the car is repaired (But who has said that the car would
    be repaired?)
When it is repaired, the weather will be fine.
Fish will come to hand two by two, to glisten as a gold ring.
Laundresses will smell of lavender.*
Hippopotemus nostrils will emerge from all the side-walks,
And the churches will crumble with a loud sound of
    mastication.
A bee will get the giggles.
We shall no longer cast a look at the past.
We shall clench our teeth,
Bind a black handkerchief soaked in camphor around our
    forehead,

*The pun, "les lavandières se parfumeront à la lavande" is irrecoverable.

567

Nous dirons un dernier bonsoir au caprice des alcazars,
Nous piétinerons notre feu de camp,
Sans une seule rapsodie hongroise,
Et les yeux une bonne fois clos, nous partirons.

Bid a last goodnight to the craze for alcazars,
Stamp out the camp fire
Without a single Hungarian rhapsody,
Once for all close our eyes, and leave.

Pierre Garnier

1928 -

Jeanne d'Arc en Picardie

Ici
elle traversa son miroir
et retourna à la lumière.

Jeanne d'Arc au bûcher

le feu
rejoint
le feu

la lumière
la lumière

la nuit
la nuit

Pierre Garnier

1928 -

Joan of Arc in Picardy

HERE
she crossed her mirror
and returned to the light

Joan of Arc on the stake

fire
rejoins
fire

light
light

night
night

Joyce Mansour

1928 -

Les machinations aveugles de tes mains...

Les machinations aveugles de tes mains
Sur mes seins frissonnants
Les mouvements lents de ta langue paralysée
Dans mes oreilles pathétiques
Toute ma beauté noyée dans tes yeux sans prunelles
La mort dans ton ventre qui mange ma cervelle
Tout ceci fait de moi une étrange demoiselle

Pericoloso Sporghesi

Nue
Je flotte entre les épaves aux moustaches d'acier
Rouillées de rêves interrompus
Par le doux hululement de la mer
Nue
Je poursuis les vagues de lumière
Qui courent sur le sable parsemé de crânes blancs
Muette je plane sur l'abîme
La gelée lourde qu'est la mer
Pèse sur mon corps
Des monstres légendaires aux bouches de pianos
Se prélassent dans les gouffres à l'ombre
Nue je dors

Joyce Mansour

1928 -

The machinations blind beneath your hands...

THE machinations blind beneath your hands
Upon my quivering breasts,
The stealthy movements of your palsied tongue
In my imploring ears;
My beauty drowned in your eyes, the pupils drained,
Death in your belly that devours my brain,
All this does make of me a girl most strange.

Pericoloso Sporghesi

NUDE
I float among wrecks with moustaches of steel
Rusted with dreams interrupted
By the soft howling of the sea
Nude
I pursue the waves of light
Which run on the sand strewn with white skulls
Mute I glide on the deep
The heavy frost which is the sea
Weighs on my body
Legendary monsters with piano mouths
Strut in the shadow of caves
Nude I sleep

Jacques Roubaud

1932 -

Sept 0

le temps fuit le temps, le temps est comme larve
le temps est l'inconscient de la terre étale
le temps est regard le temps est transparence
aux morts à la passion aux fausses épreuves
durée d'homme seul durée de femme seule
lumières de la lumière de l'absence
l'alliance n'est que toute petite écume
véloce ensuite les vagues se séparent
le temps est rougeoiement le temps est de l'ombre
le temps est cette écriture qui s'allume
sur les pages sur les langues de hasard
le temps le temps est fourmi le temps est nombre
rapproche les reflets les bouge les mêle
efface l'homme et la femme, les enfances

Jacques Roubaud

1932 -

Seven 0

time flees from time, time is a larval form
time is of stable earth the unconscious one
time is long look time is transparence
to the dead to passion to the proofs that are sham
the span of man alone of woman alone
lights of the light of absence
the coming together is but a fleck of foam
as rapid as the waves to draw apart
time is slow reddening time is of the somber
time is this writing which becomes warm
on the pages on the tongues of chance retort
time time is termite time is number
brings reflections together shifts them blends them
cancels man and woman, effaces nascence

Marc Alyn

1937 -

C'est un visage

Au fond du temps, ce temps qui n'a plus rien à dire,
J'écoute le silence d'un merveilleux visage.
Il est de feuille verte, il est de feuille morte,
C'est un rien qui soupire en frappant à la porte
De mon cœur dépouillé de serrures, de chaînes;

C'est un visage blanc, sans ombre, aux cheveux blonds,
Si frais que le mystère en dérange les boucles;
Des grilles m'en séparent, ce sont des cils, des rides,
Un masque de métal ouvragé sur mes joues.

Au fond du temps tué, je marche si souvent
Que je ne suis plus seul avec ma solitude;
Je me fais des amis dans le passé d'autrui,
J'ai mes saules, mes rues, mes hautes croix martyres
Dans ce que vous jetez de vos lourds souvenirs.

Mais ce visage-là m'appartient comme un râle,
Comme la folle pluie lorsqu'elle déshabille
Les arbres de leurs chants, comme l'eau des étoiles
Quand la soif a fermé ses volets pour dormir;

C'est un visage sans histoire, un astre tendre
Qui veille sur mon âme et la tient par la main
Pour la garder du froid, des failles et des hommes.

Marc Alyn

1937 -

It is a face

At the end of time, which has no more to say,
I listen to the silence of a marvelous face,
Of leaf still green and leaf alive no more;
It is a void that sighs knocking at the door
Of my heart untrammeled of its bolts and chains:

A white face, shadowless, with flaxen hair,
So fresh the mystery disturbs its curls;
Bars fence me from it, eyelashes, old wrinkles,
A metal mask engraved upon my cheeks.

At the end of time that's slain, I walk so often
That I'm no more alone with my aloneness;
I make friends in the past of fellow creatures,
I have my willows, streets, high anguished crosses
Projected by your heavy memories.

And yet that face is mine like the last throes,
Like the fond rain when it would strip the trees
Of their songs, or like the water of the stars
When thirst has closed its shutters down for sleep:

Face without history, a tender star
That watches by my soul and holds my hand
To guard it from the cold, the flaws, and men.

*This is rather a special poet. To provide other poems by him might
blunt the impact of this one, with its Buddhist overtones, seldom at
home in poetry. Perhaps one should say seldom to the present. There
is no telling what transmogrified *haiku* and *waka*, with western music,
may develop in the future.

J. Ph. Salabreuil

1940 - 1970

Je t'apprends à mourir

Non pas en face jamais ainsi
Une épaule d'abord et puis l'autre
Tête légère et basse et presque assise
A petits cris doucement tu entres
Et voici l'ombre t'a saisie
Te souvenant que tu n'existes pas
Qu'il n'y a plus les eaux qu'il n'y a pas
Encore un feu qui ont chanté qui chantent
Et chanteront tout au long de l'oubli
Peut-être avec l'érable aux lentes branches
Et plein d'oiseaux pour te remplir
Mais nul regret surtout nul repentir
Qu'importe à présent si je t'aime qu'importe
Les paroles jetées perdues car tu n'emportes
Avec toi qu'un peu de cendres pour là-bas
Qu'un peu de larmes sans détresse
Il te suffit de ces deux doigts dans les deux doigts
De celle qui t'apprête qui te presse
Et mort ou volupté n'a pas choisi son nom
Il te suffit d'aller sans souci corps et âme
Au-delà de ce temps de vivre et d'être femme
Avec légèreté maintenant transparence en dehors
De tout regard ici ou là pour être nue
Puisque déjà le jour ne te distingue plus
Puisque la nuit devant ne t'attend pas encore.

J. Ph. Salabreuil

1940 - 1970

I teach you to die

Nor head-on it was never so
One shoulder first and then the other
Light-headed crestfallen crouching low
Softly with small cries you enter
And here the shade has seized on you
Reminding you that you exist no more
That there is no more water and no more
Fire which sang and sings and still will sing
Along with all that is forgotten
With maybe the maple tree its lazy branches
Alive with birds to give replenishment
But no regret above all never repent
What does it matter now if I love you
What words were tossed away and lost if you
Keep only a little dust with you down there
Only a few tears without distress
Two fingers in two fingers are for her
Enough to rouse you if she only press
Nor death nor bliss has chosen names to bear
Enough that body and soul need feel no care
To live a woman beyond this time of fear
With lightness now transparent to forget
Disquiet here or there for being nude
Since day no longer marks you as it would
And the night ahead does not expect you yet.

579

Envoy

Charles Baudelaire

1821 - 1867

Le guignon

Pour soulever un poids si lourd,
Sisyphe, il faudrait ton courage!
Bien qu'on ait du cœur à l'ouvrage,
L'Art est long et le Temps est court.
     Loin des sépultures célèbres,
Vers un cimetière isolé,
Mon cœur, comme un tambour voilé,
Va battant des marches funèbres.
     — Maint joyau dort enseveli
Dans les ténèbres et l'oubli,
Bien loin des pioches et des sondes;
     Mainte fleur épanche à regret
Son parfum doux comme un secret
Dans les solitudes profondes.

Charles Baudelaire

1821 - 1867

The jinx

To lift so great a load were wrong
If blessed with more of heart than luck.
We laud in Sisyphus his pluck,
But time is short, this art is long.

    Far from each celebrated grave
I seek alone my private tomb;
My heart beats like a muffled drum
For all the luck I did not have.

    So many jewels buried deep,
Forgotten in the darkness, sleep
Far from all spade and sounding line.

    So many flowers, so little skill
Their secret perfume to distill
And save for solitudes like mine.

Permissions

Grateful acknowledgement is due the following authors and publishers for permission to quote selections from their works.

Editions Denoël: For "Tu es plus belle que le ciel et la mer" and "Couchers du soleil" by Blaise Cendrars, from *Poésies Completes,* ed. by J.H. Lévesque, copyright 1944, by Editions Denoël.

The following poems are used by permission of **Editions Gallimard:** "Plain-chant (No. 1)" by Jean Cocteau, from *Morceaux Choisis,* copyright 1923.

Patrice de la Tour du Pin's "Les enfants de Septembre" is from *La Contemplation Errante,* copyright, 1948.

Two selections by Robert Desnos, "Le paysage" and 'Le coteau" from *Fortunes,* copyright, 1942, and *Contrées,* copyright, 1944, included in *Choix de Poèmes,* copyright, 1946.

All the selections by Paul Eluard are from *Œuvres Complètes,* © 1968.

"Je ne t'ai jamais oubliée" by André Frénaud, reprinted by permission of Gallimard.

"L'école publique" and "Au pays natale" by Guillevic, from *Terraque,* copyright, 1942.

"Jeanne d'Arc en Picardie" and "Jeanne d'Arc au bûcher" by Pierre Garnier, from *Perpetuum Mobile,* © 1968.

"Blanche déroule sa spirale" by Louise Herlin, from *Commune Mesure,* © 1971.

From "Le livre de morts" and "Lune à l'aube" from *Poésies,* 1946-67, by Philippe Jaccottet; and "Sois tranquille" from *L'Effraie et Autres Poésies,* copyright, 1953.

"Lorsque l'empereur" and "Villanelle" by Max Jacob, from *Morceaux Choisis,* copyright, 1923.

"Pour toi, mon amour" and "Paris at night", by Jacques Prévert, from *Paroles,* copyright, 1946, and *Spectacles,* by Jacques Prévert, copyright, 1951.

"Je crains pas ça tellment" by Raymond Queneau, from *Si Tu T'Imagine,* copyright, 1952.

"Sept O" by Jacques Roubaud, from Σ, © 1967.

Three poems by Georges Schéhade are from *Poésies II and Poésies III,* and here published by permission of Gallimard.

"Je t'apprends à mourir" by J. Ph. Salabreuil, from *La Liberté des Feuilles,* © 1964.

Mercure de France: The poems of Yves Bonnefoy, from *Du Mouvement et de l'Immobilité de Douvre;* copyright, 1953; and *Hier Régnant Désert,* copyright, 1958.

The poems of Francis Jammes, from *Choix de Poèmes,* copyright, 1922.

"Ville atroce" from *La Vierge de Paris,* copyright, 1945, by Pierre Jean Jouve.

The poems of Pierre Reverdy, from *Main-d'oeuvre,* copyright, 1949.

Les Editions de Seuil: "Chansons du dé à coudre" (III) and "Dieu parle" from *"Chansons du Dé à Coudre";* "Erotique" from *Sophia,* and a passage from "Hymne de la liberté" by Pierre Emmanuel, are reprinted with the kind permission of the poet, his publisher, Editions du Seuil, and their U.S. representative, Georges Borchardt, Inc.

Editions Seghers: "C'est un visage" by Marc Alyn, from *Brûler le Feu,* © 1959;

Biographical Notes

The main object of this book is optimum transposition of authentic lyrical essence—object far removed from either the establishment of maximum authenticity of every textual source, or revelation of previously unsuspected biographical material. When one seeks to exact the flavor of a lyric in another language, one does not always go to the most comprehensive library, there to ferret out the incunabula most unassailable as such. Mostly, one avails oneself of what is to hand, while the thought is still warm. Thus, the following notes for the reader's information and convenience will be more costive than exhaustive.

Most anthologists consult other anthologies—at least, they should. Hence, there follow here, first, a shortened list of the most useful anthologies, as known to me; and then, at the end of each biographical note (held strictly to less than a hundred words each), the most recent reliable source which, if available, was the one directly used, and if not, indirectly, as used by others. If, as sometimes happened, the text used was one accompanied by a translation, mention is made of it, although one tried not to be distracted by literal "blow-by-blows," such as occur as footnotes in the Penguin collections, or in *French Poetry from Baudelaire to the Present* (see following list). These may be serviceable for rare moments of obscurity—without being to the present purpose—whilst attempts to make free verse poems in English out of poems not written in free verse, even when these versions have interest in themselves, are capable of being quite misleading as regards the lyrical effect.

All French publications are from Paris, unless otherwise signified, and all works with titles in English contain poems in the original French.

Allem, P.E., ed. *Anthologie Poétique Française: XVIIIe Siècle*. Garnier-Flammarion, 1966.

Appelbaum, Stanley, ed. *French Poetry: A Selection from Charles d'Orleans to Yves Bonnefoy*. Dover Publications, 1969.

Aspel, Alexander, and Donald Justice, eds. *Contemporary French Poetry*. Univ. of Michigan Press, 1965.

Boase, Alan M. *The Poetry of France*. London, Methuen & Co. Ltd., 1973 (3 vols.).

Boisdeffre, Pierre de, ed. *Une Anthologie Vivante de la Littérature d'Aujourd'hui: Le Poésie Française de Baudelaire à Nos Jours*. Librairie Académique Perrin, 1966.

Canfield, Arthur G., and Warner F. Patterson, eds. *French Poems*. Holt, 1941.

Flores, Angel, ed. *An Anthology of French Poetry from Nerval to Valéry in English Translation*. Doubleday Anchor, 1958.

Fouchet, Max-Pol, ed. *La Poésie Française: Anthologie Thématique*. Club des Libraires de France, Editions Seghers, 1958.

Gachot, François, and Pierre Chapelot, eds. *Les Chefs-d'œuvre du Rêve*. Editions Planète, 1969.

Gavronsky, Serge, ed. *Poems & Texts: Translations and Interviews*. October House Inc., N.Y., 1969.

Gide, André, ed. *Anthologie de la Poésie Française*. Librairie Gallimard, pour Pantheon Books, N.Y., 1949.

Hackett, C.A., ed *Anthology of Modern French Poetry*. Macmillan, N.Y., 1952.

Hackett, C.A., ed. *New French Poetry*. Basil Blackwell, Oxford, 1973.

Hubert, Renée, and Judd Hubert, eds. *Anthologie de la Poésie Française du XXe Siècle*. Appleton-Century-Crofts, Meredith Corp., 1971.

Biographical

Lagarde, A., and L. Michard, eds. (avec la collaboration de Audibert, Lemaitre, et Van der Elst). *XXe Siècle.* Bordas, 1962.

Lucas, St. John, and P.M. Jones, eds. *The Oxford Book of French Verse: XIIIth-XXth Century.* 1957-68.

Marks, Elaine, ed. *French Poetry from Baudelaire to the Present.* Dell Publishing Co., 1962.

Matthews, J.H., ed. *An Anthology of French Surrealist Poetry.* Univ. of London Press, 1964; Univ. of Minnesota Press, 1966.

Maulnier, T., ed. *Poésie du XVIIe Siècle.* 1943.

Moulin, Jeanine, ed. *Poésies Feminine: Epoch Moderne.* Editons Seghers.

Pauphilet, A., ed. *Poètes et Romanciers du Moyen Age.* Bibl. de la Pléiade, 1952.

Schmidt, Albert-Marie, ed. *Poètes du XVIe Siècle.* Bibl. de la Pléiade, 1953.

Terry, Patricia, and Gavronsky, eds. and trans. by, *Modern French Poetry: A Bilingual Anthology.* Columbia University Press, 1975.

Woledge, Brian, et al, eds. *The Penguin Book of French Verse,* 4 vols., 1958-64. (Also the later single, comprehensive volume, both condensed and expanded.)

SOME ABBREVIATIONS

CFMA = Classiques Français du Moyen Age
Pleiade = Bibliotheque de la Pléiade
MF = Mercure de France
NRF = Nouvelle Revue Française (Librairie Gallimard)
SATF = Société des Anciens Textes Français

Alyn, Marc (1937-   ). Born in Rheims, recently published a novel, *Le Displacement,* and earlier a study of François Mauriac. His verse has been prolific, from *Le Chemin de la Parole* (1953) to *Brûler le Feu* (1959), both Editions Seghers. The present poem is included in *Une Anthologie Vivante de la Litterature d'Aujourd'hui,* edited by Pierre de Boisdeffre, who says of him, "There is a fire in his universe, in his memory, and in his verse."

Apollinaire, Guillaume (1880-1918). Born in Rome, his real name Kostrowitzsky. Schooled in France, he settled in Paris, where he became as central to the group of new poets as Picasso to the painters. He was wounded in the war of 1914-18, married his nurse in 1918, and died of his wounds the same year. He has been a formative force of modern poetry. *(Œuvres Poétiques,* ed. by M. Adema and M. Decaudin, Pleiade, 1956; consult *Guillaume Apollinaire* by Roy C. Breunig, Columbia University Press, 1969)

Baudelaire, Charles (1821-67). Born in Paris, first aspired to be principally a "dandy," before becoming a poet. This was also the period when he loved to go on sea voyages. He later became a penetrating critic and psychologist, as well as the redoutable author of *Les Fleurs du Mal,* the collection of poems which at first provoked a court case for obscenity. Yet he had a lofty spirit and, at this remove, towers over his time as one of those few who set a style of living and loving, as well as of writing. He may have been France's greatest lyrical poet since Ronsard. *(Œuvres Complètes,* ed. by Y.-G. Le Dantec, Pleiade, 1954; consult also Enid Starkie's *Baudelaire,* 1934)

Benayoun, Robert (1926-   ). Born in Morocco and joined the Surrealists in 1948. His chief interest seems to have been in the cinema. He helped to found *L'Age du Cinéma,* as well as having had a hand in most of the Surrealist reviews. He said that he liked to surprise himself; hence it is not surprising that the rapid humor of his verse should surprise. *(Anthologie du Nonsense,* Pauvert, 1957; this poem used also by J.H. Matthews in *An Anthology of French Surrealist Poetry,* Minnesota, 1966)

Béranger, Pierre-Jean de (1780-1857). Notably famous in his own time, especially between 1815 and 1830. His political songs, for which he also provided the melodies, became weapons against the restoration and circulated as freely as the mediaeval *chanson.* His fortunes flagged, however, in a double sense, for not only was he imprisoned as a hazard to the state, but his poetry came to stand for much against which Baudelaire and his followers were in revolt. *(Textes Choisis et Commentes,* ed. by Stephane Strowski, 1913)

Bonnefoy, Yves (1923-   ). On the basis of the two volumes of verse published in 1954 and 1958, he is a poet already of considerable accomplishment, though sometimes difficult. His obscurity is not, however, of the rootless sort, for his verse strategies are grounded in tradition, especially in the volume called *Du Mouvement et de l'Immobilité de Douve,* MF, 1953. (See also *Hier Regnant Désert,* MF, 1958. "To the Voice of Catherine Ferrier" appears in Boisdeffre.)

Cadou, René Guy (1920-51). Born in Brittany, completed his secondary education at Nantes but failed his baccalaureate. Like his father, he became an elementary school teacher. He joined a group of poets and critics who met at the Ecole de Rochefort. In his own poems he followed the example of Apollinaire, Jacob, and Reverdy. He published quite widely in literary journals. His early death forestalled the full traditional development in him of the lyrical warmth which, like Francis Jammes, he sought to restore. *(Hélène ou le Règne Vegital,* Pierre Seghers, 1952; *Poésie la Vie Entière, tome I: 1937-1942.* Fay-aux-Loges, Loiret: coll. Les Amis de Rochefort, Cahiers de Rochefort, Bonhier, 1961)

Cendrars, Blaise (1887-1961). Born in Paris and lived and adventured everywhere. He lost an arm in World War I but did not allow this to impede him from plunging into an extraordinarily full life: fiction, cinema, Negro art, jewel traffic, travel, and more travel. Poetry was for him another expression of intensified living: conscious composition as boring as "sunsets"; and dawn, something not to be written about but stripped naked in. *(Poésies Complètes,* ed. by J.H. Lévesque, Editions Denoël, 1944)

Char, René (1907-   ). Spent most of his distinctly retired life in his native Provence. He was not retiring as a freedom fighter, however, having been a leader of the maquis. His first volume of verse, *Arsenal,* appeared in 1929; since then he has published at least seven others, in a deepening affirmation, seldom easy of penetration. (Especially, *Fureur et Mystère,* 1948; *Les Matineaux,* 1950,—both Gallimard—which last contains "Les Inventeurs," translated also by Charles Guenther in *Poetry,* March 1957)

Chénier, André (1762-1814). Born in Constantinople of a French father and Greek mother. A diplomat and a journalist as well as a poet, he was guillotined in the Revolution. He was not published till 1819. Alas! few of the poems he lived to write translate interestingly enough, but in French we feel the ardor which made him acceptable to the Romantics, and undoubtedly he would have been an even more important transitional figure if he had lived. (Best and most available of later editions is: *Poems of André Chénier,* ed. by F. Scarfe, Oxford, 1965)

Cocteau, Jean (1889-1963). Born near Paris but moved away and lived by choice on the Côte d'Azur. His whole life displayed an extraordinary versatility. He was not only a poet but an essayist, critic, dramatist, novelist, cinematographer, choreographer, stage designer, balletomane, avid sports fan, etc., but self-declared first a poet. He was deeply influenced by Eric Satie, Raymond Radiguet, and always Picasso. The Surrealists repudiated him, partly, no doubt, because his own poetry turned from them to restore more traditional forms. *(Poésies* and *Morceaux Choisis* ["Plain-Chant," 1923]: Gallimard)

Coignard, Gabrielle de (?-1594). Lived at Toulouse, farming the land, and clearly "close to the earth." We know very little about her, aside from what is said by her poems. She sounds deeply religious, was married to a judge, but lived in the country. It was her children, after her death, who published her *Œuvres Chrétiennes.* (This selection appears in *The Penguin Book of French Verse, Vol. II,* with literal translation by Geoffrey Brereton)

Corbière, Tristan (1845-75). Born the son of a Breton sea-captain, who also wrote novels. The coasts of Brittany gave more impulse to his poetry than the salons of Paris. It was from Verlaine that his ironical verse first gained recognition, since when it has set the tone for much that is characteristic of modern poetry. *(Les Amours Jaunes,* ed. by Y.-G. Dantec, Gallimard, 1953; consult I. Angelot, *La Poétique de Corbière,* 1951)

Cros, Charles (1842-88). Less of an inventor as a poet than as an engineer. He associated with the group which patronized (and antagonized) the boy Rimbaud on his arrival in Paris. Most of his poems, sometimes of much charm, if not depth, are to be found in the posthumous *Le Collier de Griffes* (1908). *(Œuvres Complètes,* 1964; also the edition of J. Brenner and I. Lockerbie, *C. Cros,* 1955)

Desbordes-Valmore, Marceline (1786-1859). An actress, whose works, in three volumes, include stories, as well as poems. She belongs perhaps more to the 18th than the 19th century. Her most persistent theme is disappointed love, but she wrote poems also of passionate religious fervor. *(Poésies Complètes,* ed. by B. Guégan, Edition du Trianon, 1932)

Desnos, Robert (1900-45). At first a journalist, with a literary column in *Paris-Soir.* He did his military service in Morocco. Shortly thereafter, he met Breton and Aragon and joined the Surrealist movement. During the occupation, he was arrested as an activist of the Resistance, was sent to a concentration camp in Germany and, soon after having been freed by the liberation armies, died of malnutrition and typhus, incurred while he was interned. To a greater degree than with the other Surrealists, his love poems are affected by lyrical romanticism. (Gallimard published *Fortunes* in 1942; *Choix de Poèmes,* 1946. "Le Coteau" appeared in *Coutrée,* 1944)

Du Bellay, Joachim (1522-60). Liked to proclaim his birthplace, at Liré, in Anjou. His cousin was a cardinal and a diplomat stationed in Rome, whom he accompanied, none too happily, on that prelate's assignment. He grew homesick for his own Angevin country, and perhaps also for his fellow poets of the Pléiade, for whom he wrote a well-known manifesto. *(Œuvres Poétiques,* ed. by H. Chamard, Collection de la Pléiade Française, 1931)

Du Guillet, Pernette (1520-1545). In her brief life, wrote numerous *Rimes,* somewhat under the influence of Maurice Scève, and largely in response to his passion, with quite as much grace and a good deal more humor. *(Poètes du XVIe Siècle,* ed. by Albert-Marie Schmidt, Pleiade, 1953)

Eluard, Paul (1895-1952). Pseudonym for Eugène Grindel, at first a Surrealist, then a Communist, and, during the war, a freedom fighter. He also wrote chiseled love poetry, of as much interest, at least, as his politically inspired verse; for it proclaims an exaltation of women in poems than which few, if any, in the 20th century have been written in a style more devout or alluring. *(Œuvres Complètes,* Gallimard 1968)

Emmanuel, Pierre (1916-   ). Born in the Pyrenees and spent his early years in the U.S.A. Thereafter he was educated as an engineer at Lyons, before defecting to poetry and fiction, the former often deeply religious in inspiration. He is a member of the *Académie Française. (Chansons du Dé à Coudre; Poèmes Inédits* from *Poètes d'Aujourd'hui,* ed. by Alain Bosquet. "Hymn to Liberty" appears in Boisdeffre.)

Fauln, Catherine (1912-51). Born Raymonde Thora Jensen, in Belgium. She lived in the outskirts of the forest of Soignes, from which her poetry derived something of its dreamlike quality. Like Jouve, she was devoted to Mozart and closer to his spirit. Her poems were privately printed and scarcely at all known at the time of her early death in Mexico. *(Fenêtre sur le Paradis,* 1946, and *Chants pour la Statue,* 1948, were both published by the author. The poem used here was found in *Poésies Feminine,* ed. by Jeanine Moulin, Seghers, 1963)

Fort, Paul (1872-1960). Known for his Ballades Françaises, a multi-volume work whose title might be misleading, for they are not ballads in any ordinary sense, but rather regular and even rhymed poems, printed as prose. This is not to question his love for the popular ballad, but his chief love is for nature, which gives depth of color to his word landscapes. *(Ballades Françaises,* Flammarion, 1923. This is in 38 volumes! But there is *Anthologie des Ballades Françaises,* 1925)

Frénaud, André (1907-   ). a Burgundian by birth and speech, he served as a private in the last war, was taken prisoner, and, after his release, returned to Paris, working as a civil servant in the Ministry of Public Works. His poems have considerable and still somewhat widening range and, when concentrated in memorable speech, they can become real lyrics. His books of verse to be noted here are *Femme de Ma Vie,* 1947; *Source Entière,* 1953; and, for our purposes, *Les Roismages,* 1943, publ. by Seghers.

Garnier, Pierre (1928-   ). Published his first book of poetry when he was 26 and *La Nuit est Prisonnière des Etoiles* four years later, but it was in his third volume, *Second Géographie,* that he first came forward as a "spatialist" and exponent of "poésie concrète." The two minute poems on Joan of Arc, which may subserve the purpose of this volume, appear in his fourth book, *Perpetuum Mobile.* Garnier teaches German at Amiens and has published studies of Goethe, Novalis, and Nietzsche, *(Perpetuum Mobile,* Editions Gallimard, 1968)

Gautier, Théophile (1811-72). May have been, next to his friend Hugo, the most influential literary figure of his time. His critical views, so often since proclaimed as "art for art's sake," reach forward to Walter Pater and Ezra Pound. Like Hugo, he wrote voluminously—novels and travelogues, as well as volumes of verse, of which the best is to be found in *Emaux et Camées.* After a somewhat flamboyant youth, he settled into a life of retirement in the company of his sister. *(Poésies Complètes,* ed. by R. Jasinski, 1932; see also Crit. Ed. of *Emaux et Camées* by J. Pommier and G. Matoré, 1947)

Guillevic, Eugène (1907-   ). Prefers to be known as just "Guillevic." He was born at Carnac in Brittany, the scene of some of the best of his poems. Later, his Communist ideology began to supersede the poetry of his poetry and turn the short lyrics of personal feeling into prolix manifestoes of inter-class struggle. His first volume, *Terraqué* (1942), was admired by fellow poets, particularly Max Jacob. By now he had become a member of the Comité National des Ecrivains, as which, during the occupation, he published under the pseudonym "Serpières." It is from this first volume that the present selections are taken, leaving the later *Exécutoire* (1947) and *Gagner* (1949), NRF.

Guyon, Madame (Jean Buvier de la Motte, 1648-1717). Born at Montargis and married a wealthy invalid in 1664. Twelve years later, she was widowed with three children. After meeting *le père* Lacombe, she became deeply involved in Quietism, thereafter embarking on missionary work with all her charismatic ardor. She wrote extensively on prayer and contemplation. When Lacombe was imprisoned, she also was confined in the Visitandine convent. Her close friendship with Fénelon led to her release, till her enemy Bossuet had her immured again till 1703. In her final years at Blois, she outlived Bossuet, Fénelon, and the king. "Foi sans assurance" was written to an air by Lully. *(Poésies et Cantiques, 1790)*

Herédia, José-Maria de (1842-1905). Born in Cuba and educated in Havana. Subsequently he moved to Paris and became interested in archeology. There he was influenced by Leconte de Lisle and became his principal successor as a "Parnassian." *(Les Trophées, Lemerre, 1931. This was his only book of verse, first published in 1893)*

Herlin, Louise (1925-   ). Born in Cairo but not, like Joyce Mansour, Egyptian, for Mlle Herlin's parents were Italian. She graduated from the University of Florence and lived for a while both in England and the United States, before settling in Paris and marrying the author George Auclair. She is currently translating Yeats. She is a conscientious theorist of poetry, searching, in her prose as well as verse, for the best way to bring words and reality together. *(Le Versant Contraire, 1967; Commune Mesure, 1971: both Editions Gallimard)*

Hopil, Claude (c. 1585-after 1633). Of this poet little is known, except that he was Parisian. He dedicated his early *Œuvres Chrétiennes* to his brother, who was Fermier Général des Cabelles du Lyonnais. The mystical poem here is from the volume, *Les Doux Vols de l'Ame Amoureuse de Jésus,* but it would present no problem to a Sufi or Vaisnavist mystic. One can think of Hopil as a French Crashaw, less dependent on the sectarian idiom. *(Œuvres,* ed. by Tenant de Latour, 1857. "Du Cachot Divin" is in A. Boase's *The Poetry of France,* Vol. II)

Hugo, Victor (1802-85). Decidedly prolific, having written novels, plays, and political tracts, in addition to his immense poetic output. When Napoleon II came to power, he was exiled to the Channel Islands, whence it was unsafe for him to return to France until that monarch's fall in 1870. Thereafter, and until our own times, Hugo was established as a national figurehead, literary and otherwise. Now there are doubts concerning the full height of this acclaimed stature as a writer; but the pendulum may swing back for world appraisal, if not for this anthologist's. *(La Légende des Siècles,* etc., 1 vol., Pleiade, 1950)

Jaccottet, Philippe (1925-   ). Born in Switzerland and came to Paris when he was 21, working for a publisher, whilst at the same time being poetry editor for *Nouvelle Revue Française.* He stands with Bonnefoy as a twin bulwark of restoration for the great tradition of French verse. *(Poésies 1946-67,* Editions Gallimard; "Sois tranquille. . ." is from the volume, *L'Effraie et Autres Poésies,* 1953)

Jacob, Max (1876-1944). Born of Breton and Jewish parentage and schooled in Paris—a typical boulevardier, till he became a Catholic and joined a presbytery. The Germans interned him in 1944, and he died ten days after his arrest. He would write, about equally, of city and country, with humor and tenderness, *(Morceaux Choisis,* NRF, 1917)

Jammes, Francis (1868-1938). Born in the Pyrenees, He is one of those poets whose popularity has detracted from their more lasting fame. His novels too were successful. He would probably have said that the chief event in his life was his conversion to

Roman Catholicism under the influence of Claudel, although neither this influence nor the conversion is much reflected in his nostalgic pastorals. *(Choix de Poèmes, MF,* 1922; consult references in Gide's *Journal,* 1939)

Jouve, Pierre-Jean (1887-1976). His early passion for music remained. His ruling ideas, however, changed decisively. He broke with Romain Roland and his group of "poets of the Abbey," and in 1924 renounced all his earlier work, becoming a convert to Catholicism. During the second World War he took refuge in Switzerland. In 1962 he was awarded Le Grand Prix National des Lettres, and in 1965 Le Grand Prix de Poésie de l'Académie Française. He has written novels and essays—on Mozart, on Baudelaire—as well as fourteen volumes of verse. *(Œuvres Poétiques I, 1925-1938 et II, 1939-1947; Inventions, MF,* 1958)

Labé, Louise (1524-66). Belonged to the group of poets at Lyons which succeeded Scève (q.v.). She wrote especially fervid love poems, but she was also a combat soldier, believed to have fought at the siege of Perpignan. *(Œuvres Complètes,* ed. by P.C. Boutens, Maestricht, 1928

La Fontaine, Jean de (1621-95). Made his way in the court of Louis XIV through the good offices of Fouquet, the minister of Finance. His poetical works were more versatile than he is given credit for, but it will always be for his six books of fables that he will keep his reputation as France's purest "Classical" poet, who moralizes in better taste than any of the rest. It's a matter less of lyricism than of perfect manners, but there is music in his "conversational note." *(Œuvres Diverses,* P. Clarac, 1942)

Laforgue, Jules (1860-87). Born in Montevideo and educated in France, he died even younger than Corbière, with whom he has been compared. He is, however, freer in form than Corbière, his irony sharper, more flavored with bitterness, and his style even more imitated abroad and up to our own time, especially by the tribe of Eliot. *(Poésies Complètes,* ed. by M.G. Jean-Aubry, MF 1922-62; consult W. Ramsey, *J.L. and the Ironic Inheritance,* 1953)

Lamartine, Alphonse de (1790-1869). A highly regarded diplomat, belonging to the personal bodyguard of Louis XVIII. His "Le Lac" is the standard poem of French Romanticism—scenic, nostalgic, and moralistic, the last quality being as well represented by the six lines here included as by anything else, whilst the first two qualities are exhibited more successfully by Hugo. Being ostensibly an impromptu, these lines manage to elude the labored effect. *(Œuvres Poétiques Complètes,* ed. by M.F. Guyard, 1963)

La Tailhède, Raymond de (1867-1938). Became one of those who attached themselves to the poet whose pseudonym was Jean Moréas and who came from Greece, although to judge by the poems in his volume entitled *De la Métamorphose des Fontaines* (1805), the disciple commanded a wider range than the master. (This poem, "Ombres," was selected also by *The Penguin Book of French Verse, Vol. IV*)

La Tour du Pin, Patrice de (1911-1975). Of noble birth on both his father's and his mother's side. He was educated as a Catholic. His high talent was encouraged by Supervielle. He lost some time when taken prisoner by the Germans, after which he set to work on his ambitious *Somme de Poésie,* a sort of massive epic on the scale of Dante and Blake and, like the latter, very uneven as such, but rising on occasion to heights of lyrical grace and even splendor. *(La Contemplation Errante,* 1948, contains all his poems previous to that date, including "Les Enfants de Septembre")

Lescurel, Jehannot de (1290?-1350?). About all that we know of this poet is that his ballades and rondeaux are the best of those written by poets preceding Guillaume de Machaut, who died in 1377. *(Anciennes Textes,* Firmin-Didot, 1908-21)

Levet, Henry J.-M. (1874-1906). Born at Montbrise, on the Loire. He published some stories in his twenties, before leaving France to travel in the Indies and Indo-China, where he wrote most of the piquant poems of the collection, *Cartes Postales*. He was appointed to the post of "chancelier" at Manila. There he remained till 1906, when he returned to France to die. His *Poèmes* were collected by Valéry Larbaud in 1921.

Lisle, Leconte de (1818-94). Born in the West Indies and came to Paris in 1846, at first studying law. He translated Greek plays, and it was towards a Grecian ideal that he became the chief of the "Parnassian" school of poets, which exalted stylistic perfection and, within the limits they set for themselves, achieved it. *(Poésies Complètes, Lemerre, 1932)*

Mallarmé, Stephane (1842-98). Worked all his life as a schoolmaster, a teacher of English—always decidedly hard up. He was the chief source of poetic authority in his "Tuesday salon," which became the nucleus for many of the most brilliant rising writers and artists of the period. He was an infinite perfectionist and could take a year to write one of his sonnets—and worth it. *(Œuvres Complètes, ed. by H. Mondor and G. Jean-Aubry, Pléiade, 1945; later edition, 1970; consult Mallarmé et le drame solaire by Gardner Davies, J. Corti, 1959)*

Mansour, Joyce (1928-). Born in England of Egyptian parents and lives in Paris. She is a dedicated Surrealist, who has inscribed books of her verse to André Breton and joined his crusade against God, war, logic, etc. She advances her eroticism as a path of "spiritual dilation." Some few of her poems in the volume entitled *Cris*, would resemble the ones here included, in conforming to the endeavor of this book. *(Rapaces, Editions Seghers, 1960)*

Marguerite de Navarre (1492-1549). Born Marguerite de Valois at Angoulême, sister of Francis I, and married the King of Navarre. Her spirit and talent range wide, for they are manifested, not only in the bold stories of the *Heptaméron*, which rival Boccaccio's, but in a wealth of poems of profound devotion, of which the "Epître," here included, may serve as a fair example. *(Dernières Poésies de Marguerite de Navarre, ed. by A. Lefranc, 1896)*

Marot, Clément (1497-1544). The son of the poet Jean Marot (1463-1523). He gave up the law to follow the life of a poet in the court of Marguerite of Navarre (q.v.). The heresies with which he was charged, because of his sympathy with the Reformation, caused him to flee to Italy; but his poetry is more courtly than religious. His influence counted subsequently with the Pléiade poets, than whom he took himself a good deal less seriously. *(Œuvres, ed. by Guiffrey, Yves-Plessis and Plattard, 1931)*

Molière (Jean-Baptiste Pocquelin, 1622-73). Born to a well-to-do family, which provided for him the best humanistic education in the Jesuit college of Clermont. They disapproved when he joined the theatrical profession, spending thirteen years as an actor in the provinces and returning to Paris in 1659. There he wrote, produced, and played in his numerous masterpieces of wit, satire, and luminous laughter, couched in faultless verse. In life, owing to the unfailing patronage of Louis XIV, the church remained powerless against him, contriving only, loved though he was, that his grave, like Mozart's, remained unmarked. *(Œuvres Complètes, Pleiade, 1965)*

Moréas, Jean (1856-1910). Pseudonym of Yannis Papadiamentopolis, born at Athens and settled in Paris when he was 24, becoming a leading, not to say flamboyant, figure among the French symbolists of the time. Most of his work, though not the poem here represented, appears in the *Stances* (1899-1920), which develops a neoclassical style of grave if circumscribed beauty. *(Choix de Poèmes, MF, 1932; consult R. Niklaus, Jean Moréas, Poète Lyrique, 1936)*

Musset, Alfred de (1810-57). Better known, unfortunately, for his disastrous affair with George Sand than for his fine plays, or his poems, whose quality faded after his twenties. In his *Confessions,* he appears very much as the self who has taught us to think of him as an exaggerated romantic: a sort of early "hippy," perhaps. He both gained and lost by his commitment to the idea that verse must be written red-hot, under the instant impulse. *(Poésies Complètes,* Pleiade, 1933; consult also *Les Nuits de Musset,* Jean Cassou, 1930)

Nerval, Gérard de (1808-55). His real name was Labrunie. For long he was best known for his short stories, especially "Sylvie," and for the vivid accounts of his wide travels. But back in Paris, he fell on hard times, twice lost his reason, and finally hanged himself from a lamp post. Probably his best work is in the sonnets from *Les Chimères,* whose magnificent deployment of proper names unfortunately makes them almost inaccessible to natural verse translation. *((Œuvres,* ed. by A. Béguin and Jean Richer, Pleiade, 1952)

Noailles, Anna-Elizabeth de (1876-1933). The Comtesse Mathieu de Noailles, born Princess de Brancovan, of a Greek mother and a Romanian father. Her poems are intensely personal, imbued with an ardent pantheism, the emotion held in leash by severe ideals of poetic form. She was wealthy, beautiful, versatile (drew and painted, especially herself), a friend of Proust, and elected to l'Académie Royal de Belgique (but not to l'Académie Française). *(Œuvres,* Grasser, 1927-33)

Orléans, Charles d' (1394-1465). The father of Louis XII of France. He was taken prisoner in 1415 at Agincourt, and it was during his 25 years of captivity in England that he took to poetry. After his return to France in 1440, he spent the last years of his life at Blois, where he gathered around him a group of poets, few of whom could write a ballade or a rondeau with his mastery. *(Poésies,* ed. by P. Champion, CFMA, 1923-27)

Parny, Evariste-Désiré de Forges, vicomte de (1753-1814). Born of minor aristocracy on the island of Réunion, or l'Isle de Bourbon, as it was then called, he was sent to school in France and joined the army. Returning home in 1773, he had a child by a Mlle Troussais, whom his family refused to accept, so although he wrote his poems to her as "Eléonore," she married another. He was elected to the Academy in 1804. The pagan songs which he questionably advanced as adaptations of Madagascan *chansons* are more striking as romantic anticipations than as poetic achievement. Some of these were set to music later by Ravel. *(Œuvres Complètes,* 1808)

Pellisson-Fontanier, Paul (1624-93). Born at Castres, of a Protestant family and became, like his father, a *conseille.* After he contracted smallpox he gave up practising law and went to Paris. In 1653 appeared his Histoire de l'Académie Française. He became attached to the circle of Fouquet and, like him, was imprisoned in the Bastille. After his release, he was converted to Catholicism in 1670 and (post hoc ergo propter hoc?) was appointed Historiographer Royal. Famous in his later life was his friendship with Mme de Scudéry. (See the *Recueil de Pièces Galantes en Prose et en Vers,* c. 1660, containing compositions by Pellisson, as well as by the Comtesse de la Suze and others)

Pisan, Christine de (1365-1431?). Partly Italian but raised in the French court, where her father practiced medicine. She had three children. Partly, perhaps, because she was widowed in 1390, she had time to cultivate literature and became an exceptionally prolific author in prose, as well as verse. As a poet, she can get a ballade air-borne as gracefully as Villon or Marot, despite the thickets of rhyme with which it was surrounded and which inhibit translation of all these early poets. *(Œuvres Poétiques,* ed. by M. Roy, SATF, 1886-96)

Pozzi, Catherine (1882-1934). First published posthumously in 1935. Her poems have
become scarce, which is a shame, for they achieve a pure note of passion, together
with a distinctly mystical strain, both pulsating with the movement of the verse.
Alas! her work is most difficult to find, as confessed by other anthologists. (Originally
publ. by Editions de Mesures, a house apparently no longer in existence)

Prévert, Jacques (1900-1977). Like all songwriters who can compose acceptably for the
"pop" circuit, he can be popularly sentimental, but then again he has written verse
to make the snobs apologize. *(Paroles,* 1946; *Spectacles,* 1951. Editions de la NRF)

Prudhomme, René-François Sully (1839-1907). Real name: René-Françoise-Armand. A
philosopher-poet, much involved with science. If "the style is the man," he was an
unusually intellectual individual. The conflict between faith and doubt in him had
certain Tennysonian overtones, although he may not measure up to Tennyson as a
lyrical poet. *(Œuvres,* Lemerre, 1883-97)

Queneau, Raymond (1903-76). Had a strongly humorous, self-mocking vein in both his
novels and his poems. The latter were drawn together in the volume called *Si Tu
T'Imagine.* They may rise to no great heights but accomplish for poetry something
comparable to the late Poet Laureate, John Betjeman. *(Bucoliques,* 1947; *L'Instant
Fatal,* 1948; *Petite Cosmogonie Portative,* 1950; poems collected in *Si Tu T'Imagine,*
1952)

Racine, Jean (1639-99). France's great tragic dramatist was born to an upper bourgeois
family, orphaned early, and sent by his grandparents to the college at Port Royal. His
earlier life was far from the austerity of his later years. His dramatic triumphs, some
of them played by Molière's company, began with *Andromarque* in 1667, pro-
ceeding to *Phèdre, Atalie, Iphigénie,* etc. He fought at the siege of Ypres in 1678. In
later life he abandoned the stage as unworthy of his religious commitment. He
became, with his friend Boileau, historiographer to the king, and died "in the odor
of sanctity." *(Œuvres Complètes,* Pleiade, 1969)

Reverdy, Pierre (1889-1960). A poet whom the Surrealists would have liked to claim, he
declined to join them; yet as early as the 1914 war he formed, together with
Apollinaire and Max Jacob, the review *Nord-Sud,* which during its brief life became a
nucleus for Cubists and other avant-gardists of the time. His own verse is condensed,
subtle, and, for the ear that is attuned, decidedly lyrical. But it was only after his
retirement to Solesmes, in 1930, that he drew on the cloak and sandal of great
poetry. *(Main-d'œuvre,* MF, 1949)

Rimbaud, Arthur (1854-91). Or one might say, "1854-73," for it was at the age of 19
that, to the world's bewilderment ever since, he put an abrupt stop to his extraordinary poetic career and, after wanderings far from completely traced, became a
trader and almost certainly a gun-runner, in Abyssinia, till he got cancer in the leg
and limped home to have it amputated, then almost at once to die. Having given no
encouragement to his own vogue during his life, it is a question what he would do
about his unequaled fame now. *(Œuvres Complètes,* ed. by Antoine Adam, Pleiade,
1977; consult Wallace Fowlie's *Rimbaud,* Univ. of Chicago, 1965)

Ronsard, Pierre de (1524-85). The chief poet of the French Renaissance and the founder
of the original Pléiade of France, under Henry III, which, together with him, was
composed of Du Bellay, Remi Belleau, Jodelle, Dorat, Baïf, and Pontus de Thïard.
(There was a later group so named under Louis XIII, of whom the least un-
distinguished was Rapin.) Ronsard's purview signified wide learning, which he carried lightly, but with which he still renewed the poetry of his age. His own works
traversed an immense range, philosophical, political, and religious, as well as what

belongs to one of the world's supreme love poets. *(Œuvres Complètes,* ed. by G. Cohen, Pleiade)

Roubaud, Jacques (1932-   ). A mathematician and lecturer on mathematics at the University of Paris. His first volume, *Poésies Juveniles,* was published when he was twelve. He first became well-known for his volume with the title of the mathematical symbol Σ. This was awarded the Prix Fénelon in 1968. Since then, and in collaboration with poets English and Italian, he has become increasingly drawn to Japanese literature and culture. The volume *Renga,* which employs irregular sonnets like linked haiku, is well described by C.A. Hackett as "enriched by four cultures." (Σ, Editons Gallimard, 1967; *Renga* [in collaboration with Octavio Paz, Eduardo Sanguineti, and Charles Tomlinson], Gallimard, 1971)

Saint-Pol-Roux (1861-1940). Born Paul Roux, a native of Marseilles, but settled in a chateau of Brittany, living a strange secluded life and dying while fighting off the Nazi murderers of his servant and attackers of his adored daughter. He had gone to Paris in 1882, to study law, but was, among his actual contemporaries, as much a misfit as was Rimbaud and is almost as much exalted by the Surrealists a generation later. In fact, it was André Breton who said of him at the end of his life, "Among the living, he is the only authentic precursor of the modern movement." (see *Les Réposoirs de la Procession, 1893-1907,* MF)

Salabreuil, Jean-Philippe (1940-70). Seemed to be the poet with a good chance of getting French poetry back on the track when he died. He went to law school but had already published his first volume of verse in 1964, where the preoccupation with death would appear to have been prophetic of his own. *(La Liberté des Feuilles,* Editoins Gallimard, 1964)

Scève, Maurice (1505?-c. 1563). The most learned of the group of poets who flourished at Lyons (where he was born), previous to the rise of the Pléiade (see under Ronsard). He wrote 450 "dizains," condensed testimonies of love, many of them personally inspired by Pernette du Guillet (q.v.) *(Œuvres Poétiques Complètes,* ed. by B. Guégan, 1927)

Schéhade, Georges (1910-   ). Born in Egypt and felt deep affinities with the Near East. He has made more impression as a playwright than as a poet and has written about the experimental theatre in France. This does not detract from the truth of the tribute by his fellow poet and Surrealist, André Pieyre de Mandiargues, who compared his poetry to "a rare and marvelous crystal." *(Poésies II,* Gallimard; *Poésies III,* Gallimard. For two of these poems I am indebted to the selections of J.H. Matthews in *An Anthology of French Surrealist Poetry,* University of Minnesota Press, 1966. A third is in the collection of Boisdeffre)

Seghers, Pierre (1906-   ). Born in Paris and went south, to Villeneuve-lès-Avignon, there to publish annually the review, *Poésie* (1940-48), "where," as he himself said, "hope could express itself." He had been known as a freedom fighter, but though his own verse, especially in *Jeune Fille* (1948), can rank close to the best, it was henceforward as a great and forward-looking publisher that he was to be best known. Important too is his critical work, *Le Résistance et Ses Poètes* (1974).

Sicaud, Sabine (1913-28). There is no error in these dates. She died of a mysterious and agonizing disease (see footnote, p. 545), without having been informed of the only volume of her poems to be published before her death, that presented by Madame la Comtesse de Noailles, entitled *Poèmes d'Enfant.* After this the public knew nothing more of the work of this genius until 1958, when there appeared *Les Poèmes de Sabine Sicaud,* ed. by Stock.

Signoret, Emmanuel (1872-1900). Of more promise than fulfillment, he had some of the lavishness which in England we associate with the "Nineties," although in the volume *La Souffrance des Eaux* (1899), from which the *élégie* here is selected, there is the redeeming color of *le Sud*. His poems may have too much extravagance, like Swinburne's (and early Keats), but as such, they occupy a place in the declining splendors of nineteenth century French poetry. (Discovered in André Gide's *Anthologie de la Poésie Française*, 1949)

Sponde, Jean de (1557-95). Served in the court of Henry IV of France, though much disillusioned by its pretensions, especially after he became a devout Catholic. His religious verse appeared as *Essai de Quelques Poèmes Chrétiens. (Poésies*, ed. by F. Rouchon and A.M. Boase, Geneva, 1949)

Supervielle, Jules (1884-1960). Born in Montevideo, like Laforgue, and brought up in Uruguay till he was eleven. He returned at intervals to South America, from which his poetry never for long remained distant in color. It is poetry fraught with a mystic's disquiet but was embraced by the Resistance movement. (Principal works: *Gravitation*, 1925; *Choix de Poèmes*, 1947; *Oublieuse Mémoire*, 1949. Publ. by NRF)

Thomas, Antoine-Léonard (1732-85). Mostly an essayist, but his "Ode sur le temps" redeems the lyrical aridity of the period and will always be the work by which he is remembered. (I found "Ode sur le temps" in *Anthologie Poétique Française: XVIIIe Siècle*, ed. by P.M. Allem, Garnier Frères, 1966. I am indebted to Geoffrey Brereton for the idea of cutting it where I did.)

Toulet, Paul-Jean (1867-1920). Born and lived in the southwest of France, although so many of the condensed poems written in his favorite "contrerimes" have a sophisticated air, which, together with his uninhibited style of life, suggest the reverse of provincialism. *(Contrerimes*, 1921; *Vers Inédits*, 1936. I am indebted to Mr. Hartley's selections in *The Penguin Book of French Verse*, which included these three.)

Valéry, Paul (1871-1945). By birth half Italian. His meeting with Mallarmé when he was twenty turned him seriously towards poetry, which in 1896, however. he vowed to stop writing and kept this vow till he published *La Jeune Parque* in 1917! He was as much philosopher and critic as poet but this did not take from the intensity of his poetry, written with a detached perfectionism, as exorbitant as Mallarmé's. He said, "The completed work of art I consider as without interest. The only thing which arouses my curiosity is its actual creation." *(Poésies*, Gallimard, 1942)

Verhaeren, Emile (1855-1916). A Belgian, a Christian, and a socialist, much of whose poetry has a Whitmanesque *élan* but wrestles powerfully with the uglier encroachments of industrialism. *(Choix de Poèmes*, MF, 1914; consult P. Mansell Jones, *Emile Verhaeren*, 1957)

Verlaine, Paul (1844-96). Born at Metz, educated in Paris, and married when he was 27, he deserted his wife for a life of vagabondage in company with Rimbaud, whom he wounded with a pistol in a quarrel and was jailed for it. Thereafter he wavered between spells of intense religiosity and debauchery, although neither, it could be said, at the expense of his lyrical gift, which was more graceful than profound. *(Œuvres Poétiques Complètes*, ed. by Y.-G. Dantec, Pleiade, 1949; consult O. Nadal, *Paul Verlaine*, 1961)

Viau, Théophile de (1590-1626). Born a Huguenot and while absent on a mission to London, condemned to the stake for being a free thinker; but, previous to this, he was stigmatized as a libertine in other respects. While his friends were appealing the sentence, he languished in jail, from the effects of which he died a year after his release. Some of his lines reveal rather startling anticipations of a species of Surrealism. *(Œuvres Poétiques,* ed. by Jeanne Streicher, Geneva and Paris, 1951 and 1958)

Villon, François (1431-65?). This extraordinary genius, a Master of Arts of the University of Paris, wrote some of his finest poems in jail and was twice condemned to be hanged. It is not known for what crimes: he probably disliked being hungry, and poetry was not a profitable profession. The sentence was commuted to ten years banishment from Paris—almost as bad for him. His poetry is hot, rapid, and intensely personal, having little in common with the conventional verse of the period. Unfortunately, it fiercely resists translation—into English, at least. *(Œuvres Complètes,* rev. by L. Foulet, CFMA, 4th ed., 1932)

Voltaire (François Arouet, 1694-1778). Born in Paris, his education was derived mostly from the library bequeathed him by Ninon de Lenclos. His long life alternated between fame (successful production of his numerous plays, such as *Edipe, l'Henriade,* and *Marianne;* the patronage of Frederick of Prussia, as well as of Louis XVI) and political disgrace (twice imprisoned in the Bastille and exiled to England, where he met Pope and Bolingbroke). He finally settled at Ferney in Switzerland, living there in state till the end, fighting for humanitarian causes, and visiting Paris for a final triumph shortly before his death. *(Œuvres Complètes,* ed. by Moland, 1885)

INDEX